Principles of
Laboratory Animal Science

*A contribution to the humane use and care of animals
and to the quality of experimental results*

Principles of Laboratory Animal Science

A contribution to the humane use and care of animals and to the quality of experimental results

Edited by

L.F.M. van Zutphen
V. Baumans
A.C. Beynen

1993

ELSEVIER

AMSTERDAM • LONDON • NEW YORK • TOKYO

ELSEVIER SCIENCE PUBLISHERS B.V.
P.O. Box 211, 1000 AE Amsterdam, The Netherlands.

Library of Congress Cataloging-in-Publication Data

Laboratory animal science : handbook on the humane use and care of
  animals in research / edited by L.F.M. van Zutphen, V. Baumans, A.C.
  Beynen.
      p.   cm.
  Includes bibliographical references and index.
  ISBN 0-444-81270-9. -- ISBN 0-444-81487-6 (pbk.)
    1. Laboratory animals. 2. Animal experimentation. 3. Animal
  welfare.   I. Zutphen, L. F. M. van. II. Baumans, Vera, 1946-   .
  III. Beynen, Anton C., 1953-   .
  QL55.L272 1993
  591'.0724--dc20   93-7467
                                                              CIP

ISBN: 0-444-81270-9 (hardback)
       0-444-81487-6 (paperback)

This book is printed on acid-free paper.

Printed in the Netherlands.

Preface

It is now widely recognized that education and training in laboratory animal science are essential for the humane use of animals for scientific purposes and for the quality of results.

Scientists who are responsible for the design and conduct of animal experiments must not only be educated in one of the biomedical sciences (biology, medicine, veterinary medicine, pharmacy, etc.), but should also have taken an introductory course in laboratory animal science, encompassing welfare issues and ethical aspects. Indeed, in some countries these requirements on competence have been made compulsory by law.

This book contains basic facts and principles covering the main theoretical aspects of such a course. More than 50 authors, all experts in their fields, have contributed relevant topics for the graduate student or young scientist who wishes to become a "competent" researcher. After a general introduction (chapter 1) and a glimpse into legislation (chapter 2), information is presented on the biology and husbandry of the most frequently used animal species (chapter 3) and on the relationship between behaviour, stress and well-being (chapter 4). Standardization can contribute to a reduction of animal use and several aspects are covered in chapters 5–8. Chapter 9 deals with diseases of laboratory animals and the consequences brought about by impaired health on both the welfare of the animals and the results of the experiments. Chapters 10–13 outline several factors which should be taken into account when designing and conducting animal experiments. Persons involved in animal experimentation must be able to recognize signals of pain and distress (chapter 14). The researcher must also have some basic knowledge of anaesthesia (chapter 15), particularly when invasive techniques are part of the experiment (chapter 16). The book concludes by outlining the possibilities and limitations of the use of alternatives (chapter 17), together with a chapter on the ethical aspects of animal experimentation (chapter 18). For further reading, a list of recommended literature is given at the end of each chapter.

It should be emphasized that the completion of a biomedical training programme that includes a course in laboratory animal science, may provide a basis for a humane and responsible use of animals, but does certainly not provide full competence. The great diversity of biomedical disciplines and the wide range of animal experiments performed by scientists, working in the field of biomedical science, implies that a standard training programme in which every requirement for the various kinds of animal experiments is fully met, is not feasible. There is no substitute for learning in the field, and a close cooperation with conscientious and experienced investigators, animal caretakers and animal technicians remains essential in order to fill any gaps in skill and knowledge.

We would like to thank all those people who have contributed to the realization of this book. We are particularly grateful to Ineke Zaalmink and Tillie In der Maur for their accurate secretarial support and Muriel Eversden for editorial assistance. We also would like to thank the European Commission (DG XI) for financial support.

The text of this book is, to a large extent, based upon the book "Proefdieren en dierproeven" (L.F.M. van Zutphen, V. Baumans and A.C. Beynen, eds.) as published by Bunge Scientific Publishers, Utrecht, The Netherlands. We would like to thank dr. M.H. Bunge for his cooperation and for providing the originals of illustrations.

The editors

Contributors

Prof. dr. M. Balls
European Centre for the Validation of Alternative Methods (ECVAM), Joint Research Centre of the EC, Ispra, Italy

Dr. V. Baumans
Department of Laboratory Animal Science, Utrecht University, P.O. Box 80.166, 3508 TD Utrecht, The Netherlands

Dr. R.G.M. ten Berg
The Netherlands Cancer Institute, Plesmanlaan 121, 1066 CX Amsterdam, The Netherlands

Dr. A.P.M.G. Bertens
Department of Laboratory Animal Science, Utrecht University, P.O. Box 80.166, 3508 TD Utrecht, The Netherlands

Prof. dr. ir. A.C. Beynen
Department of Laboratory Animal Science, Utrecht University, P.O. Box 80.166, 3508 TD Utrecht, The Netherlands

Dr. H.J.M. Blom
Department of Laboratory Animal Science, Utrecht University, P.O. Box 80.166, 3508 TD Utrecht, The Netherlands

Prof. dr. L.H.D.J. Booij
Institute for Anesthesiology, University of Nijmegen, P.O. Box 9101, 6500 HB Nijmegen, The Netherlands

Drs. R. Boot
National Institute of Public Health and Environmental Protection, P.O. Box 1, 3720 BA Bilthoven, The Netherlands

Dr. M.C. Bosland
Institute of Environmental Medicine, New York University Medical Center, Long Meadow Road, Tuxedo, NY 10987, U.S.A.

Prof. dr. P.F. Brain
  *School of Biological Sciences, University of Wales, Singleton Park, Swansea
  SA2 8PP, Wales, United Kingdom*

Dr. M. Coates
  *School of Biological Sciences, University of Surrey, Guildford, Surrey GU2
  5XH, United Kingdom*

Prof. dr. Tj. de Cock Buning
  *Department "Dierproefvraagstukken", Faculty of Medicine, University of
  Leiden, P.O. Box 9606, 2300 RA Leiden, The Netherlands*

Dr. M.F.W. Festing
  *M.R.C. Exp. Embryology & Teratology Unit, Woodmansterne Road, Carshal-
  ton, Surrey SM5 4EF, United Kingdom*

Dr. P.A. Flecknell
  *Comparative Biology Centre, Medical School, University of Newcastle upon
  Tyne, Framlington Place, Newcastle upon Tyne NE2 4HH, United Kingdom*

Dr. R.T. Fosse
  *Laboratory Animal Veterinary Services, Haukeland Hospital, University of
  Bergen, N-5022 Bergen, Norway*

Prof. dr. K. Gärtner
  *Institut für Versuchstierkunde, Constanty-Gutschow-Straße 9, D-3000 Han-
  nover 61, Germany*

Drs. P.C.M. de Greeve
  *Department of Animal Experimentation, Veterinary Public Health Inspec-
  torate, P.O. Box 5406, 2280 HK Rijswijk, The Netherlands*

Prof.dr. W.J.I. van der Gulden
  *Central Animal Laboratory, University of Nijmegen, P.O. Box 9101, 6500 HB
  Nijmegen, The Netherlands*

Prof. dr. H.J. Hackbarth
  *Institut für Versuchstierkunde, Ruprecht-Karls Universität Heidelberg, Im
  Neuenheimer Feld 347, D-6900 Heidelberg, Germany*

Dr. J. Hampson
  *Earth Wave, St. John's Priory Park, Faringdon Road, Lechlade, Glos GL7
  3EZ, United Kingdom*

Prof. dr. J. Hau
  *Department of Veterinary Pathology, The Royal Veterinary College, Royal
  College Street, London NW1 0TU, United Kingdom*

Dr. R. Havenaar
TNO Nutrition and Food Research, P.O. Box 360, 3700 AJ Zeist, The Netherlands

Prof. dr. H.J. Hedrich
Zentralinstitut für Versuchstierzucht, Hermann-Ehlers Allee 57, D-3000 Hannover 91, Germany

Prof. dr. F.R. Heeger
Utrecht University, Heidelberglaan 2, 3584 CS Utrecht, The Netherlands

Dr. C.F.M. Hendriksen
National Institute of Public Health and Environmental Protection, P.O. Box 1, 3720 BA Bilthoven, The Netherlands

Drs. H. van Herck
Central Laboratory Animal Institute (GDL), Utrecht University, P.O. Box 80.166, 3508 TD Utrecht, The Netherlands

Drs. P.G.C. Hermans
Central Animal Facility, Utrecht University, P.O. Box 80.190, 3508 TD Utrecht, The Netherlands

Prof. dr. D. von Holst
Department of Animal Physiology, University of Bayreuth, P.O. Box 101251, 8580 Bayreuth, Germany

Prof. dr. J.A.R.A.M. van Hooff
Ethology and Socio-ecology, Utrecht University, Padualaan 8, 3584 CH Utrecht, The Netherlands

Prof. dr. J.M. Koolhaas
Department of Animal Physiology, P.O. Box 14, 9750 AA Haren, The Netherlands

Dr. J.P. Koopman
Central Animal Laboratory, University of Nijmegen, P.O. Box 9101, 6500 HB Nijmegen, The Netherlands

Drs. B.C. Kruijt
National Institute of Public Health and Environmental Protection, P.O. Box 1, 3720 BA Bilthoven, The Netherlands

Prof. dr. I. Kunstýř
Institut für Versuchstierkunde, Postfach 610180, D-3000 Hannover, Germany

Prof. dr. E. Lagerweij
Department of Veterinary Anaesthesiology, Utrecht University, P.O. Box 80.153, 3508 TD Utrecht, The Netherlands

Dr. ir. G.W. Meijer
Laboratory of Toxicology, National Institute of Public Health and Environ-
mental Protection, P.O. Box 1, 3720 BA Bilthoven, The Netherlands

Dr. J.C. Meijer
Trouw International B.V., Research and Development, P.O. Box 50, 3880 AB
Putten, The Netherlands

Dr. ir. M.A.J. van Montfort
Department of Mathematics, Wageningen Agricultural University, Dreijenlaan
4, 6703 HA Wageningen, The Netherlands

Prof. dr. D.B. Morton
Department of Biomedical Science and Biomedical Ethics, University of
Birmingham, The Medical School, Birmingham B15 2TT, United Kingdom

Dr. J.W.M.A. Mullink
Organisation for Applied Research TNO, P.O. Box 360, 3700 AJ Zeist, The
Netherlands

Drs. J. Nab
Department of Laboratory Animal Science, Utrecht University, P.O. Box
80.166, 3508 TD Utrecht, The Netherlands

Prof. dr. K.J. Öbrink
Institut für Fysiologi, Biomedisinsk Centrum, P.O. Box 572, S-75123 Uppsala,
Sweden

Dr. G.A. van Oortmerssen
Department of Animal Physiology, P.O. Box 14, 9750 AA Haren, The Nether-
lands

Dr. ir. J.B. Prins
John Radcliffe Hospital, Nuffield Department of Surgery, Headington, Ox-
ford, OX3 9DU, United Kingdom

Dr. J. Ritskes-Hoitinga
Diet & Health Research, Unilever Research Laboratory, P.O. Box 114, 3130
AC Vlaardingen, The Netherlands

Dr. J.T.W.A. Strik
National Institute of Public Health and Environmental Protection, P.O. Box
1, 3720 BA Bilthoven, The Netherlands

Mr. A. Timmerman
National Institute of Public Health and Environmental Protection, P.O. Box
1, 3720 BA Bilthoven, The Netherlands

Dr. P.J.A. Timmermans

Psychological Laboratory, Department of Comparative and Physiological Psychology, University of Nijmegen, P.O. Box 9104, 6500 HE Nijmegen, The Netherlands

Dr. H. Verhoog

Institute for Theoretical Biology, University of Leiden, P.O. Box 9516, 2300 RA Leiden, The Netherlands

Prof. dr. P.R. Wiepkema

Agricultural University, P.O. Box 338, 6700 AH Wageningen, The Netherlands

Prof. dr. L.F.M. van Zutphen

Department of Laboratory Animal Science, Utrecht University, P.O. Box 80.166, 3508 TD Utrecht, The Netherlands

Prof. dr. P. Zwart

Department of Veterinary Pathology, Utrecht University, P.O. Box 80.158, 3508 TD Utrecht, The Netherlands

Contents

Preface V

Contributors VII

1   Introduction 1
     L.F.M. van Zutphen, B.C. Kruijt, K.J. Öbrink

2   Legislation and animal experimentation 9
     P.C.M. de Greeve, J. Hampson, L.F.M. van Zutphen

3   Biology and husbandry of laboratory animals 17
     R. Havenaar, J.C. Meijer, D.B. Morton, J. Ritskes-Hoitinga,
     P. Zwart

4   Behaviour, stress and well-being 75
     J.M. Koolhaas, V. Baumans, H.J.M. Blom, D. von Holst,
     P.J.A. Timmermans, P.R. Wiepkema

5   Standardization of animal experimentation 101
     A.C. Beynen, K. Gärtner, L.F.M. van Zutphen

6   Nutrition and experimental results 109
     A.C. Beynen, M.E. Coates, G.W. Meijer

7   Genetic standardization 127
     L.F.M. van Zutphen, H.J. Hedrich, G.A. van Oortmerssen,
     J.B. Prins

8   Microbiological standardization 143
     R. Boot, J.P Koopman, I. Kunstýř

9   Diseases in laboratory animals 167
     H. van Herck, J.W.M.A. Mullink, M.C. Bosland

10   Animal models 189
     W.J.I. van der Gulden, A.C. Beynen, J. Hau

11   Phases in an animal experiment 197
     A.C. Beynen, M.F.W. Festing

12   Design of animal experiments 209
        A.C. Beynen, M.F.W. Festing, M.A.J. van Montfort

13   Organization and management of animal experiments 241
        P.G.C. Hermans, R.T. Fosse, W.J.I. van der Gulden, J.T.W.A. Strik

14   Recognition of pain and distress 255
        J.A.R.A.M. van Hooff, V. Baumans, P.F. Brain

15   Anaesthesia, analgesia and euthanasia 267
        A.P.M.G. Bertens, L.H.D.J. Booij, P.A. Flecknell, E. Lagerweij

16   Experimental procedures 299
        *V. Baumans, R.G.M. ten Berg, A.P.M.G. Bertens, H.J. Hackbarth,
        A. Timmerman*

17   Alternatives to animal experimentation 319
        J. Nab, M. Balls, C.F.M. Hendriksen

18   Ethical aspects of animal experimentation 335
        Tj. de Cock Buning, F.R. Heeger, H. Verhoog

Annex   Council Directive of 24 November 1986 on the approximation of
        laws, regulations and administrative provisions of the Member
        States regarding the protection of animals used for experimental
        and other scientific purposes 353

Index 363

1   Introduction

Laboratory animal science

Laboratory animal science can be defined as a multi-disciplinary branch of science, contributing to the humane use of animals in biomedical research and to the collection of informative, unbiased and reproducible data. Laboratory animal science encompasses the study of the biology of laboratory animals, their husbandry and environmental requirements, genetic and microbiological standardization procedures, the prevention and treatment of diseases, the optimization of experimental techniques, and the improvement of anaesthesia, analgesia and euthanasia. Ethical aspects of animal experimentation, together with the search for alternatives, also fall within the domain of laboratory animal science.

The primary objectives of laboratory animal science are to contribute to the quality of animal experimentation and to the welfare of the animals.

The term *"animal experiment"* can be applied to any scientific procedure involving animals, irrespective of whether the animal used is vertebrate or invertebrate. In most, if not all legislative regulations on the protection of experimental animals, the term is restricted to experiments with vertebrates. In this book the description, "animal experiment" will be applicable to both vertebrates and invertebrates.

Most animal experiments are performed in the fields of medical, biological, veterinary and agricultural science.

In biology, veterinary science or agricultural science, experiments are frequently designed to collect information that is relevant to, or meaningful for, the animal or animal species in which the experiment has been performed. The vast majority of animals, however, is used for medical research and safety testing. Here the animal is almost exclusively used as a substitute or model for man.

History of animal use

The development of the use of animals as a model for man runs, to a great extent, parallel to the development of medical science. The basis of Western medicine stems from Greece, where philosophers were amongst the first to practise vivisection (literally: cutting into living organisms) for scientific purposes. Several examples of animal use are described in the first medical handbook, the *Corpus Hippocraticum* (about 400 B.C.). In this period medical science was mainly descriptive, with an emphasis on anatomy, whereas later physiological experiments were also performed. Galen (130–201 A.D.), who worked in Rome, was a physician and medical physiologist, and his experiments with pigs, monkeys and dogs have provided a basis for medical practices not only during that period but for many centuries thereafter.

With Galen the first era of medical research ended. Roman culture did not provide a good environment for the further development of medicine and biology. After the emergence of Christianity, experimental science ceased almost completely. Empirical studies were banned for more than a millennium, and no animal experiments worth mentioning were carried out. This situation lasted until the fifteenth century, the beginning of the Renaissance period. The revival of experimental medicine and biology, was part of the total revival of learning. The empirical approach rapidly gained ground. Initially, the emphasis which prevailed in medicine and biology was mainly on the anatomy (Vesalius, *De Humani Corporis Fabrica*, 1543) but, from the seventeenth century, physiological processes (Harvey, *Anatomica de Motu Cordis et Sanguinis in Animalibus,* Exercitatio, 1628) were also subjects of study.

At this time animals were not regarded as sentient creatures. This view was nourished by the publications of the French philosopher René Descartes (1596–1650) who proposed that living systems could be understood on purely mechanical principles. The main difference between man and animals was believed to be the fact that animals have no soul and therefore no consciousness. Man is able to feel and think but the animal acts as an insensate machine.

From the eighteenth century onwards, it was gradually accepted that the results of experimental medicine contributed to man's welfare and living conditions. It also became evident that the further development of medicine was dependent upon the results of animal experiments.

In the nineteenth century, a major movement began against animal experimentation, first in Victorian England, but later also in France, where physiologists such as Francois Magendie and Claude Bernard were targets of criticism for the anti-vivisectionists. The first anti-vivisection organisation, "The Victoria Street Society", was established in 1875 in England. It was also in England that the first law on the protection of experimental animals (*Cruelty to animals Act*, 1876) was introduced. A major contribution to the debate on animal experimentation was presented by Jeremy Bentham in his *Introduction to the Principles of Morals and Legislation, 1789* ("The question is not, can they reason? nor, can they talk? but, can they suffer?").

The viewpoint of some extremists, demanding the total abolition of animal experiments, was not generally supported in society. On the contrary, from the end of the nineteenth century animal experimentation increased rapidly.

There are several points to be considered, as contributory factors to this increase:

– The discovery of anaesthetics in the first half of the nineteenth century enabled scientists to anaesthetize animals before exposure to painful experiments.

– In 1859 Charles Darwin published *"The origin of species"*, in which he gave a scientific basis for the concept of evolution. The evidence that the similarity between man and animals is based on homology, provided a rational basis for the use of animals as a model for man.

– In 1865 Claude Bernard's *"Introduction à l'étude de la médecine expérimentale"* was published. In this book Bernard introduced methodology as a tool for the design of physiological experiments. He strongly emphasized the need of animal usage for furthering the development of experimental medicine.

– Developments in the field of microbiology also greatly influenced the increase of animal use. In 1884, Koch's *"Postulates"* were published, wherein it states that, amongst other things, the evidence for the pathogenicity of a micro-organism can be obtained, after successfully infecting healthy susceptible animals. Thus, the experimental animal became an indispensable substitute for man in microbiology. The need for experimental animals in microbiology was further increased when the production of antisera and vaccines began, and their potency and safety was tested in animals.

– The development of several biomedical disciplines (pharmacology, toxicology, virology, immunology, etc.), and in particular the development of the pharmaceutical industry, caused a rapid increase in animal usage. This increase provided new impulse to the debate on the moral justification of animal experiments. Animal experimentation became a major political issue. In several Western countries legislative regulations on the protection of experimental animals have been proposed and have taken effect during the last decades (see chapter 2).

Not only has the total number of animals used increased, but also the number of different animal species. Until the end of the last century mainly domestic animals were used, but from the beginning of this century researchers have taken advantage of the availability of inbred strains of mice and rats. More recently several other mammalian species are being used, as are also birds, reptiles, amphibians and fish species.

   In 1940 about 1 million laboratory animals were used in the UK, in 1960 3.5 million and in 1970 5.5 million. More than 90% of these animals were rodents. No reliable figures on animal use in other countries are available for that period. According to a rough estimate, in 1960 worldwide about 30 million vertebrates were used, and in 1970 between 100 and 200 million. In the 70's several countries outside the UK also started to collect data on animal experimentation and to register the number of animals. Animal use seemed to stabilize during the late 70's and has started to decrease from the early 80's: e.g. in the UK from 5.5 million in 1980 to 3.0 million in 1990, and in the Netherlands from 1.5 million in 1978 to less than 1.0 million in 1990.

Animal use: species and purposes

The registration of animal experiments also provides insight into the variability of species and into the purpose of animal usage.
   Figures 1.1 and 1.2 illustrate the distribution of animal species used in 1990 in the UK and in the Netherlands, respectively. It can be seen that this distribution is rather similar. In both countries more than 75% of all animals used are either mice or rats.
   Animals are used for a wide range of purposes. Major areas are drug research (20–25%), vaccine testings (15–20%), toxicity testings (15–20%), and

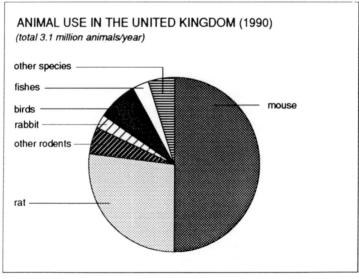

Fig. 1.1. Distribution of animal species (vertebrates) used for research and education in the United Kingdom (1990).

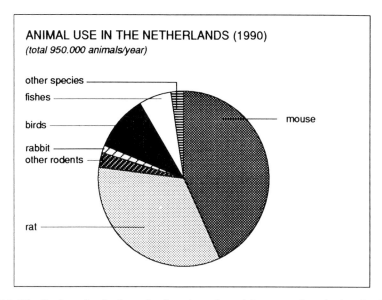

Fig. 1.2. Distribution of animal species (vertebrates) used for research and education in the
Netherlands (1990).

cancer research (10–15%). Approximately 30% of the animals are used for
other purposes, e.g. for basic biomedical research, genetic studies, diagnosis,
experimental surgery, education etc.

The number of animals used for the various purposes may vary between
countries, depending upon the degree of development of biomedical research.

Laboratory animal science associations

In many countries, scientific associations in the field of laboratory animal
science have been founded. In the USA, the American Association for
Laboratory Animal Science (AALAS) is most prominent whereas in Europe
several national associations have established the Federation of European
Laboratory Animal Science Associations (FELASA).

A worldwide organization in the field of laboratory animal science is
ICLAS (International Council for Laboratory Animal Science), with national
members from about 40 different countries. The aim of ICLAS is to promote
international collaboration in the field of laboratory animal science and, in
particular, to support developing countries in achieving the standard required
for both high quality research and humane use of animals.

Russell and Burch: The three R's

Legislative regulations, recently introduced by several countries, have a large influence on the development of laboratory animal science. The approach of Russell and Burch as elaborated in the late fifties in their book, *"The principles of humane experimental technique"*, has become a central theme in laboratory animal science. This book deals with the question of how the inhumane aspects of animal experimentation can be diminished or removed. The authors have introduced the "Three R concept" (Replacement, Reduction, Refinement) as a main guideline for the responsible use of animals in experiments.

Replacement refers to the substitution of living animals by *in vitro* techniques, computerized models, videos, film, etc. The experiment is replaced by an alternative procedure which yields the same result without the use of live animals.

Reduction refers to a decrease in the number of animals required for a given experiment. This can be achieved by choosing suitable experimental procedures, by controlling environmental factors and by standardizing the animal population. The introduction of standardization reduces the variation in the results. Chapter 12 explains in detail how the reduction of variation will lead to a decrease in the number of experimental animals required. During recent decades significant developments in the field of health monitoring and standardization of genotype and environmental conditions, including nutrition, have contributed to a further reduction of variance. In particular, the improved organization within and between animal research institutes has contributed to the reduction of animal use.

Refinement refers to any decrease in the incidence or severity of painful or distressing procedures applied to animals. Refinement can be realized prior to experimentation on the animal e.g. by a better "reading" of the biological needs of the animal and translating them into adequate husbandry and environmental conditions. Adjustment of the environment to suit the behavioural and physiological needs of the animal, is a prerequisite for the animal's homeostasis, whereas prolonged deviation from homeostasis may result in abnormal behaviour and disease. Refinement can also be realized during the course of the experiment, e.g. by improving experimental procedures or methods of anaesthesia, which may reduce distress.

The researcher should be aware of the fact that refinement not only contributes to the welfare of animals but also to the quality of the animal experiment.

Education and training

Competence, originating from adequate education and training, is a main condition for the quality of research and for a careful and responsible use of animals. The *Council of Europe Convention for the protection of vertebrate animals used for experimental and other scientific purposes (1985)*, and the *EC Council Directive on the protection of vertebrate animals used for experimental and other scientific purposes (1986)* both state that "persons who carry out experiments or take part in them or take care of animals used for experiments, including supervision, shall have the appropriate education and training" (see chapter 2). Also, according to the US Animal Welfare Act (1986), persons involved in the use and care of animals in research must be trained properly.

Several categories of people are involved in animal experimentation e.g. the animal caretaker; the animal technician; the laboratory animal specialist/ animal welfare officer; and the scientist.

In several countries training courses are being organised for the *animal caretaker and animal technician*. This type of training may take 2–3 years and most of these courses have a major practical component.

Usually the *laboratory animal specialist/animal welfare officer* is a veterinarian who has specialized in one of the areas of laboratory animal science, and who may be the authorized person for supervising the welfare of the laboratory animals at institutional level. Some countries are organising a post-graduate course in laboratory animal science for this group. This course may take 6 months–4 years, depending upon the graduate training programme and previous experience of the trainee.

The *scientist,* as the designer of the animal experiment, has the ultimate responsibility for the humane treatment of the animals. The welfare of the animals and the quality of animal research depends upon an understanding of animals. And, as stated by Sir Peter Medawar in *The hope of progress (1979),* "one does not come by this understanding intuitively; it must be learned".

Education in the field of laboratory animal science is a *conditio sine qua non* for the researcher. This has been neglected for a long period of time. Only recently in some countries has education in this field been made mandatory for "new" scientists. FELASA has addressed the question of how the competence of the scientist must be defined. According to FELASA a scientist may be considered competent for the design or performance of animal experiments after having completed a graduate training in one of the biomedical disciplines (e.g. biology, medicine, veterinary medicine) and, in addition, having taken a course in laboratory animal science. The minimum duration for such a course being not less than 80 hours. Besides scientific and technical information necessary for the proper design of an animal experiment, the course should also deal with welfare issues and ethical aspects of animal experimentation. It must provide the tools for improving the quality of research, as well as for the careful and responsible use of animals. Replacement, reduction and refinement should be the guiding principles for the course.

This handbook has been compiled with the objective of covering the theoretical components of such a course.

Education and training, though essential, do not provide a free permit for animal experimentation. It should be noted that the performance of an animal experiment is acceptable and justified only if:

– the experiment is necessary (no alternatives available)

– the benefit outweighs the animal's suffering (according to the judgement of an ethics committee)

– the experiment is carefully designed and performed with maximum attention for the welfare of the animals.

Literature

Bentham J. An introduction to the principles of morals and legislation. 1789. In: Bowring J, ed. The works of Jeremy Bentham. New York: Russel and Russel, 1962.

Garrison F H. History of medicine. London: Saunders, 1961.

Heinecke H, ed. Angewandte Versuchstierkunde. Jena: Fischer, 1989.

Medawar P B. The hope of progress. London: Methuen, 1972.

National Research Council. Education and training in the care and use of laboratory animals. Washington, DC: National Academy Press, 1991.

Paton W. Man and mouse. Animals in medical research. Oxford: Oxford University Press, 1984.

Rollin B E, Kesel M L, eds. The experimental animal in biomedical research. Vol. I. A survey of scientific and ethical issues for investigators. Boca Raton, Fl.: CRC Press, 1990.

Rowan A N. Of mice, models and men: a critical evaluation of animal research. Albany: State University of New York, 1984.

Rüpke N A. Vivisection in historical perspective. London: Croom Helm, 1987.

Russell W M S, Burch R L. The principles of humane experimental technique. London: Methuen, 1959.

Svendsen P, Hau J. Forsøgsdyr og dyreforsog. Odense: Odense Universiteitsvorlag, 1982.

Tuffery A A, ed. Laboratory animals: an introduction for new experimenters. London: Wiley, 1987.

2   Legislation and animal experimentation

Introduction

As already indicated in chapter 1, the first legislation concerning animal experimentation was enacted in the United Kingdom in 1876 in the form of the *Cruelty to Animals Act*. This statute emerged as a result of a long debate between scientists and animal protectionists.

The UK was thus the first and, for many years, the only country with legislation protecting animals used for scientific purposes. However, concern for laboratory animals has now grown and become a focus of major political interest in many countries.

In the USA, the principle federal law concerning the protection of laboratory animals, the *Animal Welfare Act*, was amended significantly in 1985 through the *Improved Standard for the Laboratory Animals Act*. Originally the law focused on preventing illegal transfer of pet animals to research institutions and on the humane care and treatment of non-human primates, dogs, cats, rabbits, guinea pigs and hamsters used in research, for exhibition, or as pets. The amendments include provisions for the use of anaesthetics and analgesics, and environmental enrichment for dogs and non-human primates. Subsequent amendments have been adopted, encompassing requirements for the review of animal facilities and protocols of animal studies by *Institutional Animal Committees* and for veterinary care and personnel qualifications. It is a responsibility of the Committees to assure that the institution is providing training on relevant aspects of laboratory animal science to investigators and other personnel involved in the care and treatment of animals. The *Animal Welfare Act* was extended in 1990 to horses and farm animals and is likely to include rats, mice and birds in the near future. In addition to these *Animal Welfare Act* regulations, the *Health Research Extension Act* was introduced in 1985. As a result of the latter, institutions receiving grants from the Public Health Service (PHS) are required to comply with the PHS policy on the

9

humane care and use of laboratory animals. Principle features of the PHS policy are adoption of the guidelines set out in the *Guide for the Care and Use of Laboratory Animals* and requiring the establishment of an *Institutional Animal Care and Use Committee*. The composition and responsibilities of this Committee are consonant with those defined for *Institutional Animal Committees* in the *Animal Welfare Act*. All vertebrate animals are covered under the PHS policy.

Two important documents controlling the use of animals in experiments have also been issued recently in Europe.

The first was initiated by the Council of Europe in Strasbourg. In 1985, after several years of discussion, the 26 countries of the Council of Europe reached an agreement on the *Convention for the Protection of Vertebrate Animals used for Experimental and other Scientific Purposes (ETS 123)*. This Convention, however, is not a binding document and has no legislative force. It contains the provision that parties should hold multilateral consultations to examine the progress of the implementation of the Convention, and the need for the revision or the extension of any of its provisions on the basis of new facts or developments.

The second European document is the *Directive for the Protection of Vertebrate Animals used for Experimental and other Scientific Purposes (86/ 609/EEC)* adopted in 1986 by the Council of the European Communities (EC Directive, see Annex, page 353). This document was based upon the Convention although its text is more concise, and its requirements are more stringent.

All EC Member States are compelled to implement the provisions of the EC Directive *via* their national laws. These provisions must be seen however, as minimum requirements. Member States are free to regulate specific issues more strictly if they wish to.

All such legislation is based on the premise that, under certain conditions, it is morally acceptable to use animals for experimental and other scientific purposes. Most laws, however, contain provisions ensuring that the number of animals used is kept to a minimum. In addition, most regulatory systems have the following general objectives:

 – to define legitimate purposes for which laboratory animals may be used;
 – to ensure competence for all persons involved in animal experimentation;
 – to limit animal use where alternatives are practicably available;
 – to prevent unnecessary pain or distress to animals;
 – to provide for the inspection of facilities and procedures;
 – to ensure public accountability.

Scientists using animals for research will be increasingly subjected to legislative regulations. In this chapter the EC Directive of 1986 is used as an example to illustrate the main elements and implications of legislation.

The EC Directive

Scope

The provisions of the Directive apply to vertebrate animals which are used in experiments likely to cause pain, suffering, distress or lasting harm. The development of genetically modified animals likely to suffer pain and distress is also covered by the Directive. The killing of, or the marking of, an animal using the least painful method is not considered to be an experiment.

The Directive is restricted in its application to experiments undertaken for the development and safety testings of drugs and other products, together with the protection of the natural environment (article 3). However, in 1987, the European Parliament passed a resolution stating that its provisions should also apply, through national legislation, to all animal experiments, including those undertaken for fundamental or basic research and for educational purposes.

Most national laws are put into operation by a government-controlled "authority", as described by the Directive. The mechanism of control may rest with the authority itself, through a central licensing system such as operated in the UK, or may be (partially) deployed at an institutional level, i.e. through institutional (ethics) committees.

Accommodation and animal care

Article 5 of the Directive contains provisions to ensure that animals are treated humanely not only prior to, but also during and after, any procedure. Detailed guidelines for the implementations of these provisions are set out in Annex II of the Directive. These guidelines are based mainly upon common laboratory practice. They can be amended as new scientific or other evidence emerges with improved methods for the housing and care of animals. Article 5 states that the well-being and state of health of the animals must be observed by a competent person. In article 19 it is indicated that a veterinarian or other competent person should be charged with advisory duties in relation to the well-being of the animals.

Competence

The provisions on competence warrant special attention. Laws and regulations are poor tools if not based upon the understanding of the need for both the humane and responsible use of animals. Education and training provide the opportunity for obtaining the correct attitude and for the evaluation of the ethical aspects of animal experimentation.

Article 7 of the Directive states that animal experiments should be performed solely by a person who is considered to be competent or under the direct responsibility of such a person. This provision is amplified by article 14 which states that persons who carry out experiments, take part in procedures, or take care of animals (including supervision) should have appropriate education and training. It is essential that the people involved in the designing or the conducting of experiments should have received an education in a scientific discipline relevant to the experimental work. They also need to be capable of handling and taking care of laboratory animals.

Each Member State must specify how the provision of competence is to be implemented within national legislation. A proposal concerning the educational requirements for the scientist has been prepared by FELASA (see chapter 1). Some countries have already introduced strict legislative regulations regarding competence.

Alternatives to animal experiments

The concept of possible alternatives to experiments involving the use of animals is briefly described in chapter 1 and will be discussed further in chapter 17. Article 7 of the Directive not only deals with competence but also with alternatives. Performance of an experiment is not permissible if the result can be reasonably and practically obtained without the use of animals. If there is no alternative to animal use then one must select the animals with the lowest degree of neurophysiological sensitivity, or those with the least capacity for suffering, whilst still being able to achieve satisfactory results.

Animals taken from the wild may not be used unless other animals would not fulfil the aims of the experiment.

All experiments must be designed to avoid distress and suffering as far as possible. Article 23 of the Directive states that the Commission of the EC and the Member States should encourage research into the development and validation of alternatives.

Anaesthesia

All experiments must be carried out under general or local anaesthesia (article 8), unless anaesthesia is judged to be more traumatic than the experiment itself, or is incompatible with the aims of the experiment. If anaesthesia is not possible, then pain, distress or suffering must be limited and analgesics or other appropriate methods should be used. No animal should be subjected to severe pain, distress or suffering.

Euthanasia

At the end of the experiment, a veterinarian or other competent person must decide whether the animal should be kept alive or humanely killed. No animal is to be kept alive if it is likely to remain in permanent pain or distress, or if its well-being is otherwise jeopardized (article 9). It is not permissible to use animals more than once in experiments entailing severe pain, distress or equivalent suffering (article 10).

Registration

There is an obligation to notify the (governmental) authority in advance about the proposed experiments and who will be conducting them. If an animal is expected to experience severe pain which is likely to be prolonged, the experiment must be specifically declared and justified to, or specifically authorized by, the authority. Such an experiment is only permitted if it is of sufficient importance in meeting the essential needs of man or animal (article 12). Information on the total number of animals used and more detailed information on the number of animals for specific purposes must be collected by the authority. As far as possible this must be made available to the public in the form of published statistics.

Supply of animals

Breeding or supplying animals for experiments is only allowed by an establishment that is approved by the authority in each Member State. The establishment must keep records of the number and species of animals sold or supplied, and the names and addresses of the recipients. Dogs, cats, and non-human primates must be supplied with an individual identification mark (article 18).

Animal facilities

Establishments for animal use must be registered with or approved by the authority. Each user establishment must have sufficient numbers of trained staff and provisions for adequate veterinary support. Only animals bred within the animal facility or from authorized breeding or supplying establishments may be used. The use of stray animals is not allowed. Records must be kept of all animals which are used.

Inspectorate

In most countries, the authority for supervising the observance of the regulations is a governmental inspectorate. The inspectors are mainly veterinarians or biologists, with experience in research and training in laboratory animal science.

Ethics committee

In several countries there are institutional committees in operation that are specifically dedicated to review the ethical aspects of animal experimentation. There is, however, no specific provision in the Directive demanding the establishment of such committees. As in the USA, in some European countries the review of protocols by a committee, prior to the commencement of an animal experiment, has been made compulsory by a provision in the national legislation.

Ethical aspects of animal experimentation are considered in more detail in chapter 18.

Impact and limitations of legislation

The central purpose of laws introduced to control animal experiments was set out by a UK Royal Commission in 1875: "to reconcile the needs of science with the just claims of humanity". This principle was enshrined in the *Cruelty to Animals Act* and is implicit in all laws, Conventions and Directives which have been passed since.

The extent to which these systems are effective in their stated aims of controlling animal research will depend not only on the implementation machinery, such as effective inspection or an in-house institutional monitoring system, but also on the attitudes and sensitivities of those conducting the research and caring for the animals. Thus, good education and training, not only including the acquisition of relevant practical skills but also a background in alternative methodologies and the ethical issues surrounding animal use, are an essential component of the control system.

No enforcement system could be effective if it were forced upon an insensitive research community which was hostile to the provisions of the law. In fact, what we have seen developing over the last decade as controls have been debated, is an increasing awareness in the scientific community both of practical and ethical issues, and the increasing involvement of the researcher in the devising and implementation of these controlling systems.

The law can set up the rules but rules cannot be effective if the institutional monitoring and implementation is inadequate. Legislation is only as effective as the strategy of measures to implement it on a day to day basis. Adequate daily care and proper conduct of experiments must be effected within the institution itself.

What centralized control does do, however, is ensure that research work is not authorized unless it is shown to be valuable and necessary and carried out by fully competent persons in institutions where adequate facilities exist for the care of the animals. In going through the authorization procedure, applying for a licence and discussing it with a government inspector, or explaining a research proposal to an institutional ethics committee, the mind of the researcher should be focused on the need to keep the use of animals to the minimum, to think about alternatives and to think of ways of minimizing the pain or distress both during and after the experiment. Legislation has opened up a whole new debate on these topics, between researchers, veterinarians, animals technicians and government inspectors. In this sense, new legislation brings about improvements of animal welfare not immediately apparent in the content of the law itself.

These improvements can be seen in anaesthetic technique, better employment of analgesics or refinements of experimental procedure, all of which might result from discussions about authorization of a research project, or at symposia discussing implementation of the law.

It is at the authorization level that the question of the purpose of the experiment might also be addressed, either by a governmental authority, or by an institutional committee appointed under the control system. In some national laws the provision is made stating that the licensing authority or the institutional committee should weigh up the proposed benefits likely to flow from the research (such as new medical or scientific knowledge) against the likely degree of suffering to which the animals will be subjected. Thus there may be cases where a proposed experiment is disallowed on the grounds that its scientific merit is particularly poor or because the proposed suffering is in excess of what is legitimized by the law or which can be justified by the scientific importance.

This, however, does not imply that the use of animals for research purposes is fundamentally being questioned by these laws. Critics of animal experiments see that as a major failing of all legislation and argue that, as the law stands at present, the central question of whether certain types of experiment should be done at all, such as the testing of novel but non-essential consumer products, is not even addressed.

It is arguable that if this issue of the legitimacy of the research is not debated at some level, then the performance of any kind of cost/benefit analysis will be placed under severe limitations. Such limitations may be one of the reasons why legislation has, to date, not succeeded in fully satisfying

Legislation and animal experimentation

public demand for greater accountability of what research is allowed to be performed on animals in the name of public interest. It seems reasonable to assume that institutional ethic committees are in the best position to debate such matters, and that when these committees incorporate lay people from the local community among their membership, they do go some way towards satisfying the demand for public accountability.

Public perception of the use of animals in research will continue to change as the moral consensus in society as a whole, over such issues, evolves. This is merely a part of a developing societal consciousness relating to the wider issues of medical ethics. Although strict laws now control the use of animals, and the conditions of their use and care continue to improve, these deeper questions still remain to be addressed.

Literature

Committee on Care and Use of Laboratory Animals of the Institute of Laboratory Animal Resources, Guide for the care and use of laboratory animals. US Department of Health and Human Services, Public Health Service, National Institute of Health, Bethesda: NIH Publication No. 85–23, 1985.

Hampson J. Legislation and changing consensus. In: G. Langley, ed. Animal experimentation: The consensus changes. Basingstoke, Hampshire: McMillan, 1989, pp. 219–251.

Newcomer C E. Laws, regulations and policies pertaining to the welfare of laboratory animals. In: BE Rollin, ML Kesel eds. The experimental animal in biomedical research. Vol. I. A survey of scientific and ethical issues for investigators. Boca Raton, Fl.: CRC Press, 1990, pp. 37–47.

Ritskes-Hoitinga J, Bosland M C, De Greeve P, Van Zutphen L F M. Legislation and animal experimentation: is there a difference in approach between the USA and the Netherlands? Lab Animal 1992; 21: 28–37.

Van Emden M H, De Cock Buning T J, Lopes da Silva F H, eds. Competence of biologists for experiments on animals. Report Workshop of the EC Biologists Association, Amsterdam, the Netherlands, March 7–9, 1988. Amsterdam: ECBA Publications, 1989.

Van Zutphen L F M, Rozemond H, Beynen A C, eds. Animal experimentation: Legislation and education. Proceedings EC Workshop, Bilthoven, the Netherlands, May 22–24, 1989. Utrecht: Dept. Lab. Animal Science, Rijswijk: Veterinary Public Health Inspectorate, 1989.

3   Biology and husbandry of laboratory animals

Introduction

One of the prerequisites for the responsible use of animals in biomedical research is a thorough knowledge of the biological characteristics and husbandry requirements of the species to be used. The choice of animal species and the particular strain largely depends on whether their anatomical, physiological and behavioural characteristics are suited to the research demands. Housing, feeding and care must be appropriate to the requirements of the animal species that has been selected. In this chapter some biological and zootechnical aspects of the most widely used vertebrates will be discussed.

Mammals

Of all laboratory animals, rodents are the most frequently used, accounting for approximately 80% of all vertebrate laboratory animals. This category boasts the largest order among mammals, and consists of approximately 1800 species. In general they are nocturnal animals, rather unspecialized and can adapt readily to their environment. Due to their extensive use within biomedical research, a great deal of biological data concerning them is currently available. The table which follows shows the most important suborders of rodents used in biomedical research.

Together with rodents, the rabbit is also frequently used in biomedical research. The rabbit is classified with the hare within the order Lagomorpha. They can be distinguished from rodents by, amongst other things, the presence of a pair of small incisors placed just behind the larger upper incisors.

Other mammals, for example non-human primates, dogs, cats, pigs, sheep and goats are less frequently used.

Order	Suborder	Family	Genus	Species
Rodentia	Myomorpha	Muridae	Mus	M. musculus (house mouse)
			Rattus	R. norvegicus (Norwegian rat)
		Critcetidae	Mesocricetus	M. auratus (Syrian hamster)
			Meriones	M. unguiculatus (gerbil)
	Histricomorpha	Caviidae	Cavia	C. porcellus (guinea pig)

Mice

Use. In biomedical research the house mouse (*Mus musculus*) is the most widely used vertebrate species, with more than 1000 genetically defined inbred strains (see chapter 7). Considerable differences in both anatomical and physiological characteristics exist amongst the inbred strains of mice. Due to the presence of these distinctive characteristics some strains are used as a specific animal model, e.g. the athymic nude mouse. Mice are mainly used for cancer and drug research, vaccine and monoclonal antibody preparation, and toxicity research.

Physiology and anatomy. Taking the small size of the mouse into account a number of physiological parameters such as heart and respiratory frequency, are relatively fast (table 3.1), but these can vary considerably depending on strain, age, environmental conditions and microbial status.

Like most other rodents, the mouse has a nocturnal rhythm with peaks of activity occurring during the dark period. These activity patterns can be strain specific.

The dental formula for the mouse is 2(1003/1003), which means that each half of the jaw contains one incisor and three molars. Canine teeth and premolars are absent, resulting in an open space, the diastema. The incisors grow continuously whilst the animal lives, and are kept short by chewing. The labial surface of the incisors is covered with a thick layer of enamel. The mouse is omnivorous and possesses grinding molars.

The sex of the animal can be determined by comparing the anogenital distance (fig. 3.1), which is larger in males than in females. In females this area is also hairless. The urethra enters the floor of the vagina shortly before the external opening. Testicles can be present in the scrotum, but they can also be retracted through the inguinal canal into the abdomen.

Table 3.1

Environmental requirements and physiological parameters of mice, rats and golden hamsters

	Mice	Rats	Golden hamsters
Environmental requirements			
Temperature (°C)	20–24	20–24	20–24
Relative humidity (%)	50–60	60	50–60
Ventilation (changes/hour)	15	10–15	10–15
Light/dark (hours)	14/10	12–14/12–10	12–14/12–10
Minimum cage floor size			
One individually housed adult (cm^2)	180	350	180
Breeding animal with pups (cm^2)	200	800	650
Group (cm^2/adult)	80	250	n/a
Minimum cage height (cm)	12	14	12
General physiological parameters			
Adult weight (g)			
Male	20–40	300–500	120–140
Female	25–40	250–300	140–160
Life span (years)	1–2	2–3	2–3
Heart rate (/min.)	300–800	300–500	250–500
Respiration rate (/min.)	100–200	70–110	40–120
Body temperature (°C)	36.5–38.0	37.5–38.5	37–38
Number of chromosomes (2n)	40	42	44
Body surface (cm^2)	20 g: 36	50 g: 130 130 g: 250 200 g: 325	125 g: 260
Water intake (ml/100g/day)	15	10–12	8–10
Puberty (weeks)			
Female	5	6–8	4–6
Male	–	–	7–9
Breeding age (weeks)			
Female	8–10	12–16	6–8
Male	8–10	12–16	10–12
Oestrous cycle (days)	4 (2–9)	4–5	4
Duration of oestrus (hours)	14	14	2–24
Duration of pregnancy (days)	19 (18–21)	21–23	15–17
Nest size	6–12	6–12	6–8
Weight at birth (g)	0.5–1.5	5	2–3
Weight at weaning (g)	10	40–50	30–40
Weaning age (days)	21–28	21	20–22
Blood parameters			
Blood volume (ml/kg)	76–80	60	80
Haemoglobin (g/100 ml)	10–17	14–20	10–18
Haematocrit (vol. %)	39–49	36–48	36–60
Leucocytes ($\times$ 1000/mm^3)	5–12	6–17	3–11
Glucose (mg/100 ml) [1]	124–262	134–219	60–150

[1] under stress conditions this value may rise up to 2$\times$ normal.

n/a = not applicable.

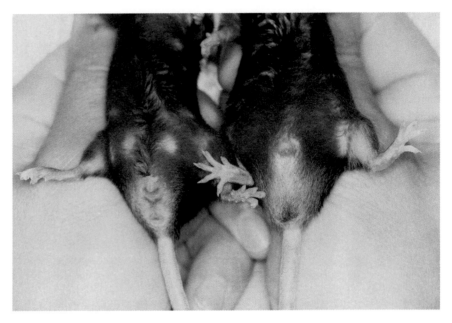

Fig. 3.1. The distance between anus and genital opening is larger in a male than in a female mouse.

Housing. Wild mice live in groups with an evident social hierarchy. The behaviour of the laboratory mouse has partially adapted to life in captivity, but there are still some similarities with its wild counterpart. In the design of caging systems considerable attention has been paid to economic and hygienic aspects but the animals' requirement to carry out natural behaviours has hardly been taken into account. Mice can be housed in transparent macrolon cages with a tightly fitting lid. The maximum number of mice that may be housed in type 1 cage (200 cm^2) is one female with pups or one breeding pair. Larger numbers can be housed in cages types 2 (450 cm^2) and 3 (900 cm^2). In 1986, guidelines for minimum cage sizes per animal were issued by the EC (table 3.1).

When males are housed together, aggressive behaviour may occur. This depends upon the strain, the space available for each animal and the "furniture" within the cage. Individually housed mice exhibit more aggression when re-housed in groups, than animals permanently housed in groups. In the case of group housing, no more than 30 animals should be put together in one cage, as overcrowding may lead to the death of individual animals.

Sawdust is commonly used as bedding material and it should be free of fine dust and microbial and chemical contaminants. Shredded paper or cotton wool can be used as nesting material. Sometimes mice are housed on wire mesh floors, for example in toxicological studies. This is to facilitate cleaning and prevents animals from being in contact with the bedding material, but this type of housing should be used only when strictly necessary for the experiment. Breeding animals with neonate pups should not be housed on wire mesh as thermoregulation in neonates would be disturbed due to the absence of nest material. In metabolism cages, animals are housed individually in order accurately to regulate individual feed and water intake, and in order to collect and quantify urine and faeces production separately.

The optimal values for the environmental conditions in the animal room (macroclimate) are set out in table 3.1. Large fluctuations in temperature and draught must be avoided, as these can increase susceptibility towards air-borne infections, especially if levels of relative humidity are high. The microclimate (inside the cage) will depend upon for example, the cage type, the location of the cage in the animal room, the ventilation system, the number of animals in the cage, the use of a filter top, and the frequency of cage cleaning. A regular day/night cycle is essential for establishing normal behaviour patterns, and for the normal expression of many physiological processes, such as reproduction. Light intensity and noise can have a distinct influence on breeding and on the results of experiments.

Food and drink.   Usually the same type of diet is fed to all mice, irrespective of age, pregnancy or lactation. It is usually administered *ad libitum* in the form of pellets. On average, depending upon the energy content of the diet, approximately 3–4 g is eaten per mouse per day. The food rack must be properly filled as it is difficult for the animals to gnaw the food when there are only a few pellets in the food-hopper. Microbial digestion and the subsequent consumption of faeces (coprophagy) make certain nutrients available to the animal in an indirect manner (see rabbit).

Fresh drinking water must be available at all times. Water requirements will largely depend on the water content of the diet and environmental circumstances. It can be made available via bottles or an automatic watering system. If drugs have to be supplied in the drinking water, bottles have to be used. Acidification or chlorination of the drinking water inhibits microbial contamination. To prevent the risk of drowning caused by leakage into the solid bottomed cage, the drinking nipple of an automatic watering system should be situated just outside the cage and the nipple checked regularly for any obstruction.

Reproduction.   Sexual maturity in mice occurs very early. Females are poly-oestrous. When an animal is individually housed, its cycle is more regular than when group housed. When females are housed in groups without males, there

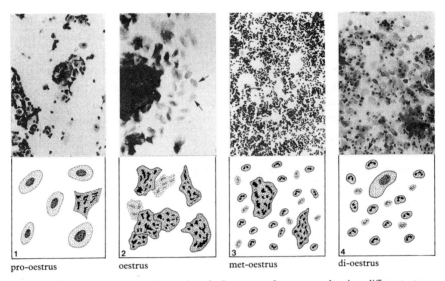

1 pro-oestrus   2 oestrus   3 met-oestrus   4 di-oestrus

Fig. 3.2. Microscopical preparations of vaginal smears of a mouse showing different stages of the oestrous cycle. 1. pro-oestrus: many nucleated and few keratinized epithelial cells; 2. oestrus: many keratinized epithelial cells; 3. met-oestrus: a few keratinized cells and leukocytes; 4. di-oestrus: mainly leukocytes are present.

is a tendency for them to be anoestrus. The introduction of a male into such a colony will lead to synchronization of their oestrous cycles (Whitten-effect). The different stages of the oestrous cycle can be identified by means of a May-Grünwald Giemsa staining of vaginal swabs (fig. 3.2). If the female is housed with a second male within 24 hours after a successful mating, implantation of fertile egg cells will not take place, and therefore no pregnancy will occur (Bruce-effect). The Bruce and Whitten effects are induced by pheromones present in the urine of male mice. For 24 hours after mating, a coagulation plug (secretion of the accessory glands in the male genital tract) can be detected in the vagina. This is a simple, though not very reliable, way to detect that mating has taken place. Another way is by determining the presence of spermatozoa microscopically in fluid which has been used to flush the vagina.

Pups are born both blind and naked after an average pregnancy period of 19 days. Passive immunity is passed via the placenta (placenta haemochorialis) and the colostrum to the pups. Pups are weaned 3 weeks after birth. If mating takes place during a postpartum oestrus, lactation and pregnancy may occur simultaneously. Lactation may delay implantation, and prolong the gestation period from 3 to 5 days.

Different mating systems can be used. In the case of monogamous pairs (one male with one female) and with "trios" (one male with two females), the male remains constantly with the female(s), so that postpartum matings can take place. Pups must be weaned prior to the next nest being born. In the case of polygamous breeding ("harem-system"), 3–6 females are housed with one male. With this system it is common to house the females separately a few days prior to the partition. When animals are housed together continuously, breeding may be less successful due to a higher level of disturbance and, furthermore, it is difficult to maintain proper records as females may foster oneanother's pups.

Handling and simple techniques.   The best way to lift a mouse up is to hold it firmly at the base of the tail. If the animal needs to be restrained, it should be placed on a rough surface (e.g. the cage lid). Then the skin of the neck is taken between the thumb and index finger of the other hand. The mouse should then be lifted and the tail held between the ring finger and the palm of the hand (fig. 3.3a, b). For determining sex, the hind part of the mouse can be lifted slightly by the tail (fig. 3.3c).

Mice can be marked for identification by means of punching small holes in the ear(s) or by toe amputation. The latter method is not recommended and, if inevitable, should be carried out before the animal is three days old in order to minimize trauma. The combination of ear marking with toe amputation results in a possible numeration scale from 0 to 12,999. The application of coloured marks on the fur or on the tail(base) provides a means of identification within small groups on a temporary basis (fig. 3.3d). Tattooing of ears and tails, and the subcutaneous implantation of microchips are other possibilities for identification.

Transport.   When transporting mice, solid boxes must be used, and good ventilation must be ensured even when the boxes are stacked (fig. 3.4). For SPF animals (see chapter 8) infection should be prevented by HEPA filters in the ventilation openings. Wire netting should be fixed to the inside of the boxes, so that the mice cannot gnaw holes and escape. Bedding material must also be provided. For long periods of transportation food and water must be supplied in the form of wet cotton wool, agar gel or vegetables for example potatoes, which contain water.

Transport always causes considerable stress to animals and may result in loss of weight. The animals may need a week or more in order to acclimatize to their new surroundings.

Detailed guidelines on transportation of laboratory animals can be expected to be issued by the EC in the near future.

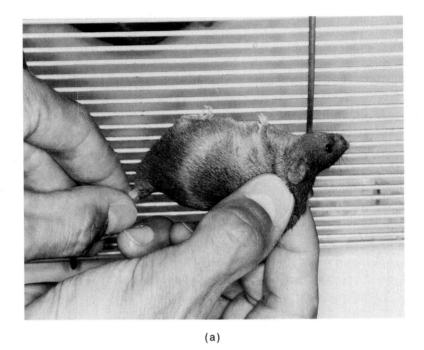

(a)

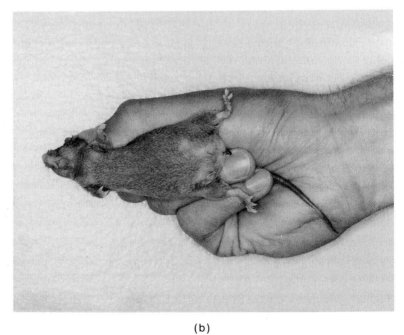

(b)

Fig. 3.3. Lifting (a) and restraining (b) of a mouse.

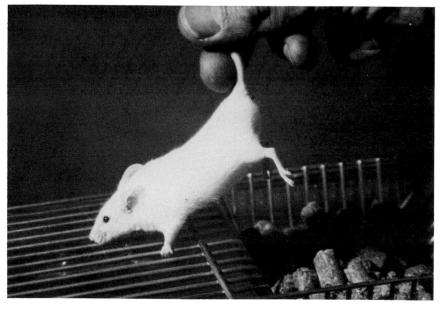

(c)

(d)

Fig. 3.3 (continued). (c) Handling to determine the sex. (d) Identification by staining the tail.

Fig. 3.4. Example of a transport-box for rodents.

Rats

Use. The laboratory rat has descended from the brown rat (*Rattus norvegicus*). The name "brown rat" is misleading, as the colour may vary. The first rat strains for biomedical research were developed at the Wistar Institute in Philadelphia. Many of the inbred strains which are used at present are descendants of these Wistar albino rat strains.

The rat is the most commonly used vertebrate after the mouse, and is used mainly in medicine, food, behavioural and toxicity research. Currently there are more than 400 genetically defined inbred strains and about 50 outbred strains on record.

Physiology and anatomy. The physiology and anatomy of the rat resemble those of the mouse (table 3.1).

The nephrons in the kidney cortex are quite near the surface, and therefore reasonably accessible. The adrenal glands are located away from the major blood vessels, which makes adrenalectomy in the rat less risky than for example, in the rabbit.

Within the eye-socket lies the Harderian gland which produces a brown-red secretion which contains porphyrins. This secretion is removed by grooming

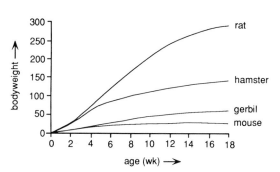

Fig. 3.5. The average body-weight of the mouse, rat, (Syrian) hamster and gerbil at different ages.

and the presence of reddish secretion around the eyes and nose indicates a diminished well-being (less grooming or excess of secretion due to an infection of the upper respiration tract). Between the eye and the base of the ear an extra-orbital lacrimal gland is located. In contrast to mice, rats have no gall bladder.

The body-weight of the adult rat is about 10–15 times the body-weight of the adult mouse (see fig. 3.5).

Housing. There are many similarities between the housing of mice and rats. Rats are usually housed in macrolon cages or stainless steel cages with wiremesh bases. In these latter cages there is a lack of environmental stimuli and therefore this type of housing cannot generally be recommended.

Rats are less aggressive than mice and usually male rats can be housed in groups without any problems, depending on the strain. Different groups of adults, however, should not be housed together in one cage, as this will lead to aggressive behaviour.

Group housed rats have significantly higher plasma corticosteroid concentrations than their individually housed counterparts. The behaviour of the grouped animals in this social structure changes when a solitary housed rat is introduced into the group. This may influence the level of some of their reference values.

Cage temperature must be monitored closely in the case of group housing, as it can quickly become too high. Heat loss occurs, just as with the mouse, through sweat glands in the foot pads along with the dilatation of blood vessels in the tail. After weaning, the number of animals per cage should not be too high, as excessive heat production along with the reduced facility for heat loss may cause death as a result of hyperthermia. In the case of high environmental temperature or overcrowding, rats cover their body with saliva.

When relative humidity remains lower than 45% for a long period of time, "ringtail" (localized constrictions of the tail) can develop, especially in young animals.

Rats are sensitive to infectious diseases of the respiratory tract, and therefore ventilation has to be well controlled, avoiding draughts and high cage levels of ammonia.

Rats and mice are sensitive to ultrasonic sounds, whereas sudden noise may evoke audiogenic seizures in some strains. Light is an important factor in the regulation of physiological activities. A high intensity may cause retinal atrophy in albino animals.

Food and drinking water.   The supply of food and drinking water is on the whole comparable with the mouse. Under *ad libitum* conditions, the feed intake of rats, in contrast to mice, occurs mainly during the dark period.

Reproduction.   The breeding of the rat is, to a large extent, comparable with that of the mouse. However, the Bruce-effect does not occur, and oestrous cycle synchronization due to male pheromones is not as apparent. Synchronization of oestrus and pregnancy can by achieved by administering progesterone for a period of 4 days (induces anoestrus), followed by an injection of PMSG (pregnant mare serum gonadotrophin). The oestrous cycle responds to variation in the length of the light cycle. A period of 12–16 hours of light per day results in the best breeding performance. Exposure to continuous light seriously disturbs fertility, even after only 3 days.

After mating has taken place a vaginal plug is usually present during the following 12–24 hours. The breeding systems for rats are similar to those for mice. When the female is mated during postpartum oestrus, the period before implantation, and therefore the length of pregnancy, will be extended by a few days.

Handling and simple techniques.   Most strains of rats are domesticated and easy to handle. The rat should be lifted by placing a hand around the chest with the thumb placed under the chin and the index finger around the neck. In this way the head is secured firmly. Another way of lifting a rat is by taking it around the shoulders and supporting it in the full hand (fig. 3.6a, b). The other hand should be used to support the hind part of the body in the event of the animal being large or pregnant. A less preferable way is to pick it up by the base of the tail and place it on a solid surface. For oral administration of fluids or for injections the rat can also be restrained by grasping the loose skin at the base of the neck.

(a)

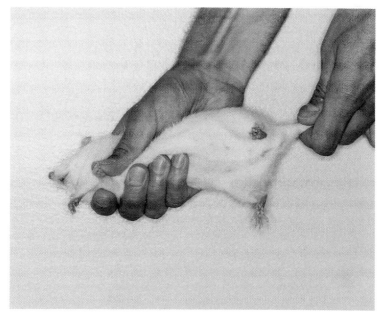

(b)

Fig. 3.6. Handling (a) and restraining (b) of a rat.

When housed on wire mesh bases, rats should not be picked up quickly or unexpectedly by their tails, as they will try to hold on to the wire mesh and their nails could be torn off.

Plastic cylinders may be useful for restraining the rat during a short period of time. For identification and transport: see the mouse.

Syrian hamsters

Origin and use.   The Syrian or golden hamster (*Mesocricetus auratus*) and the Chinese hamster (*Crisetulus* griseus) are the most widely used hamster species (fig. 3.7). The natural habitat of the Syrian hamster is Southeast Europe and the Middle East. All of the domesticated Syrian hamsters have probably originated from one male and two females which were captured in the neighbourhood of Allepo in Syria, in 1930. The wild Chinese hamster lives in the area between the Caspian Sea and the east coast of China. The number of hamsters used in biomedical research is relatively small (less than 1%). The Syrian hamster is mainly used for reproduction and teratogenicity studies, as well as for tumour and blood circulation research. Due to its hibernating habit, the hamster is also used to study effects of hypothermia. Hamsters are not very susceptible to common spontaneous infections, but are rather sensitive to experimentally-induced infectious diseases such as leptospirosis, influenza, and dog distemper.

Fig. 3.7. Syrian hamster (upper) and Chinese hamster (below).

The Chinese hamster is used for karyotype research and as a model for diabetes mellitus in humans.

Physiology and anatomy.   The Syrian hamster hibernates when the environmental temperature reaches below 5–6°C and when the light period is less than 8 hours per day. During hibernation its body temperature, heart and respiration rate decrease considerably. Hamsters which are in hibernation can be awakened by stimuli such as touch. During hibernation, hamsters sleep for periods of approximately 2–3 days, and are awake for periods of 12 hours or less. During these "awake periods", physiological parameters reach normal levels. This implies that food and water must be available during the hibernating period.

On both flanks of the animals there is a dark coloured spot with sturdy hair, containing sebaceous glands. These hip glands, which are well developed in sexually mature males, secrete pheromones, and one of its functions is to mark out territory. The cheek pouches are extensible and stretch from the cheeks to the shoulder blades. They are used for the transport of food and sometimes of pups as well. The fundus of the stomach is rather large and has a thin wall. It is connected to the rest of the stomach by a very narrow passage. Adrenal glands are larger in males than in females. The urine has a pH of 8 and often has a turbid, milky appearance.

Compared with most other rodent species, hamsters are less sensitive to morphine, and they have a greater tolerance to pentobarbitone. Histamine attracts a reduced response and they do not readily develop anaphylactic shock. However, they are more sensitive to corticosteroids. Some antibiotics such as penicillin, erythromycin and tetracyclines are indirectly toxic, because they may cause lethal endotoxaemia due to dysbacteriosis in the intestinal tract (decrease of Gram-positive and an increase of Gram-negative gut bacteria). Other antibiotics can lead to an excessive growth of *Clostridium difficile* which can cause serious inflammation of the intestinal wall, toxaemia and death.

Housing.   Hamsters are solitary, nocturnal animals. In general they are housed individually, but nest mates can be housed together for long periods. Females are more aggressive than males and sometimes it may be necessary to house females individually from the onset of puberty (around 40 days). Hamsters are housed preferably in cages with solid floors, bedding material (sawdust) and a lid that can be closed tightly. The types of cages used for rats and mice are also suitable for hamsters. Coprophagy will take place even when the hamsters are housed on wire mesh, which is also the case for rats and mice. When hamsters are disturbed during the daytime i.e. their resting period, they may become aggressive and try to bite. By reversing the day/night cycle, hamsters will become active during the day-time and will react less aggressively when handled.

Solid food intake commences at the age of 7–10 days. Pellets must be deposited near the nest inside the cage, so that the pups can reach the food. When they start eating solid food, they must be able to drink water as well, otherwise disturbances of the intestinal tract may develop. To allow for this, the drinking nipple should be of a sufficient length so as to be accessible to the young animals. It therefore has to be checked regularly for obstruction.

Food and drink. The hamster is omnivorous, just like the rat and the mouse. It is common practice to give mouse and rat pellets to hamsters and care has to be take to ensure that the hamster can actually reach the food, as they have a flatter face than mice and rats. It is advisable to put some pellets on the cage floor, so that they can practise their natural behaviour of hoarding. The drinking nipple should not be made of glass, as it can be easily broken by biting.

Reproduction. The oestrous cycle is very regular in hamsters and lasts exactly 4 days. The morning after ovulation, a vaginal excretion can be seen. This excretion has a milky appearance with a high viscosity and a distinctive smell. On observing this excretion, mating can be successfully achieved in the evening three days later. When a female in oestrus is placed into a cage with a male, she will respond to the sniffing of the male by lordosis. Copulation will be repeated several times within a 20–60 minute period. After mating has taken place the female must be removed, otherwise she will attack the male. If 5 or 9 days after the mating a vaginal excretion is observed, then the female is not pregnant. Compared with the Chinese hamster, with a pregnancy period of 21 days, the Syrian hamster has a relatively short duration of pregnancy (table 3.1). The hamster has a postpartum oestrus just like the mouse and the rat; the difference being that in the hamster it is not fertile.

For reproduction, both monogamous and polygamous mating systems can be used. After weaning it is possible to form monogamous pairs which can stay together for the entire reproductive phase. However, it is usually the case that the animals are housed individually due to the risk of aggressive behaviour. In the case of "hand mating", the female is placed into the cage of the male just after dark. If applying the harem system then 1–4 males are housed with 5–15 females. Pregnant females are housed separately until after weaning. When these female hamsters are returned into the colony, fighting will often occur, therefore polygamous systems are best be avoided.

Cannibalism, carried out by the mother on the pups, occurs primarily in primiparous animals during the first postpartum week. Possible causes are thought to be lack of experience, too much excitement, disturbance and/or insufficient lactation. The pups should not be touched during the first week, especially when the female is primiparous. In contrast to rats and mice, the fostering of newborns is hardly ever successful.

Handling and simple techniques. Hamsters should not be picked up until you are sure that they are awake. The easiest way is to grasp the animal around the head and thorax. It is also possible to pick up a hamster by placing the hand over the animal with the thumb near the head and then grasping the loose skin of the neck and back region firmly. Another possibility is to place the thumb on the inside of the femur with the index and middle fingers around the rear, securely holding the head and front legs with the remaining free fingers.

Hamsters can be marked by ear clips, by subcutaneously implanted microchips, and by tattooing the shaved skin, for example on the hind leg.

Transport. If hamsters are very aggressive, they can be caught and transported from one cage to another using a tin. The tin should be placed into the cage and, as a rule, the animals will crawl into the tin. (For more details: see mouse).

Gerbils

Origin and use. The gerbil (*Meriones unguiculatus*) is indigenous to the deserts of Mongolia and northern China. In captivity the gerbil will reproduce well and is relatively free of the normal "spontaneous" diseases. These factors have favoured the use of the gerbil in biomedical research. Epilepsy in gerbils has a genetic background and it is used in neurological research as a model for human idiopathic epilepsy. Gerbils develop high serum and liver cholesterol concentrations, even when on a diet with relatively low amounts of fat. They are therefore used for studying cholesterol metabolism and experimental atherosclerosis. Some other research areas in which gerbils are used are obesity, filariasis and brain infarcts.

Physiology and anatomy. In the wild, gerbils live as monogamous pairs in a self-built system of tunnels. Periods of activity alternate with resting periods both during the day as well as the night. However, the highest activity takes place during the night. The gerbil usually excretes only a few drops of urine per day as their nephrons have adapted to desert life. The gerbil is capable of compensating for the lack of drinking water for several weeks. They possess a considerable adaptability to fluctuations in environmental temperature and few signs of discomfort are seen between 0 and 35°C. When the relative humidity exceeds 50%, the fur may then have a rough and greasy appearance.

Table 3.2

Environmental requirements and physiological parameters of gerbils, guinea-pigs and rabbits

	Gerbils	Guinea pigs	Rabbits
Environmental requirements			
Temperature (°C)	20–24	20–24	15–21
Relative humidity (%)	35–45	50	50–60
Ventilation (changes/hour)	15–20	10–15	5–15
Light/dark (hours)	12/12	14/10	12/12
Minimum cage floor size			
One individually housed adult (cm^2)	230	600	1 kg: 1400 2 kg: 2000 3 kg: 2500 4 kg: 3000 5 kg: 3600
One breeder with nest (cm^2)	1300 (couple)	1200	1 kg: 3000 3 kg: 4000 5 kg: 5000
Group (cm^2/adult)		1000	
Minimum cage height (cm)	15	18	1–2 kg: 30 3 kg: 35 4–5 kg: 40
General physiological parameters			
Adult weight (g)			
Male	80–110	900–1000	2–5 (kg)
Female	70–100	700–900	2–6 (kg)
Life span (years)	3–4	5–6	5–6
Heart rate (/min.)	360	230–380	130–325
Respiration rate (/min.)	90	42–104	30–60
Body temperature (°C)	38.1–38.4	38–40	38.5–39.5
Number of chromosomes (2n)	44	64	44
Body surface (cm^2)	190 g: 205	400 g: 565 800 g: 720	2–5 kg: 1270 4–8 kg: 3040
Water intake (ml/100 g/day)	4–7	10	6
Puberty (weeks)			
Female	9–12	4–5	16
Male	9–12	8–10	20
Breeding age (weeks)			
Female	9–12	9–10	20–36[1]
Male	9–12	9–10	24–40[1]
Oestrous cycle (days)	4–6	14–18	n/a
Duration oestrus (hours)	–	1–18	n/a
Duration pregnancy (days)	25–26	68 (59–72)	30 (28–35)
Nest size	4–6	1–6	4–10[1]
Birth weight (g)	2.5–3.0	70–100	30–100[1]
Weight at weaning (g)	–	180–240	–
Weaning age (days)	20–30	15–28	35–56

Table 3.2 (continued)

	Gerbils	Guinea pigs	Rabbits[2]
Blood parameters			
Blood volume (ml/kg)	66–78	69–75	60
Haemoglobin (g/100 ml)	13–16	12–15	10–16
Haematocrit (vol. %)	44–47	38–48	36–48
Leucocytes ($\times$ 1000/mm^3)	7–12	7–13	5–11
Glucose (mg/100 ml)	50–135	60–125	78–155

[1] Dependent upon the strain: small breeds reach breeding age at an earlier age and have a smaller nest size than larger breeds.
[2] Blood values apply to young adult New Zealand White rabbits.

The fur of the gerbil is tight, short-haired and agouti-coloured. In contrast to most other rodents, the ears and footpads are covered with hair. The skin of the tail is loose and can be easily stripped if the animal is not handled properly. A well-developed sebaceous gland is present around the umbilicus.

Housing. The use of solid bottomed cages is preferable for the housing of gerbils. Their general condition improves when they are housed on solid floors with a thick layer of bedding rather than when they are housed on wire mesh floors. Reproduction is also more successful when a shelter is offered in the cage. The height of the cage must be at least 15 cm to allow the gerbil to stand upright on its hind legs. Bedding usually remains dry and odourless for long periods of time and will need to be cleaned once every two weeks, depending on the stocking density.

When introducing animals into an unfamiliar environment epileptiform attacks may occur. Overpopulation, or the housing together of unfamiliar individuals, can lead to serious fighting, but this will not usually be a problem when gerbils are housed together from weaning age.

Food and drink. It is common practice to feed gerbils *ad libitum* with rat and mice pellets. It is not advisable to feed the animals a diet with a high fat content, as they may develop obesity or atherosclerosis. In females, fat will accumulate around the ovaries, which will have a negative influence on fertility. Young gerbils, between 2 and 5 weeks old, may sometimes have problems in eating pellets which are too hard.

Gerbils drink approximately 4–5 ml of water per day per 100 g of body weight, when fed a diet of pellets. However, they are able to maintain their body weight when they drink only 2 ml per day. In the wild, gerbils can survive on seeds and roots, but when fed dry pellets in the laboratory, water must be offered *ad libitum*, taking care to ensure that young animals are able to reach the drinking nipple.

Reproduction.   The gerbil shows monogamous sexual behaviour. An adult gerbil will usually accept only its own partner. Gerbils are polyoestrus. If the lighting regime is kept constant with 12 hours light, they can breed all the year round. Since breeding couples are usually permanently kept together, oestrus detection is not necessary. Vaginal swabs are not reliable for oestrus detection and behaviour patterns of the two sexes are a better indicator. Mating usually takes place in the late evening. A copulation plug is generally not noticeable, as it is small and retained deep inside the vagina. When the female is mated whilst suckling a large number of pups, the time for implantation and the duration of the pregnancy will be lengthened by more than 2 weeks.

Monogamous pairing is the most successful way and breeding pairs can be formed preferably around puberty (8 weeks). If the male and female start to fight, it is better to find another partner for both of them. Pairing new partners in a neutral, clean cage will decrease aggressive behaviour. The male remains in the cage when the pups are born and helps take care of the young. In the event of a fight occurring, for example when the male rejects the pups or even attacks them, the breeding pair must be separated temporarily. Removing the male from the cage during the 2 weeks post partum, in order to prevent mating and disturbing the nest, may also be done as a matter of routine. This period should not last longer than 2 weeks, as otherwise the two partners may start fighting again when reunited.

If the polygamous breeding system (trio) is to be used it is necessary to house the gerbils together before puberty.

Cannibalism of pups seldom occurs. Young can be fostered when the age of the pups in the two litters does not differ by more than a couple of days.

Handling and simple techniques.   The best way to lift a gerbil is by raising it in one hand. Less preferable is grasping it by the base of its tail. Grasping the distal part of the tail must be prevented, as the skin can easily be torn off. To restrain the animal, it is necessary to hold it by the base of the tail and the other hand should hold the skin of the neck or its back. It is not advisable to turn a gerbil on its back.

Guinea pigs

Origin and use.   The guinea pig or cavy (*Cavia porcellus*) originates from the Andes in South America. The wild type (*Cavia cutleri*) has been domesticated by the Indians for meat production. The Spaniards probably introduced the guinea pig into Europe in the 16th century.

Of the three hair-types (short-haired or English guinea pig, rough-haired or Abyssinian and long-haired or Peruvian) the short-haired variety is used almost exclusively in biomedical research, accounting for approximately 2–3% of all registered laboratory animals. The main purpose for using guinea pigs is for the production and control of sera, vaccines and other biological products. The guinea pig can be sensitised easily. This is achieved by repeated injections resulting in a hyper-sensitivity reaction. Due to its high susceptibility to infectious diseases, such as tuberculosis, diphtheria, leptospirosis and brucellosis, the guinea pig is, or was, important for diagnostic reasons. The guinea pig is a useful animal model for immunological research as for example its plasma-complement has a high activity level, for otology experiments due to the favourable anatomy of its middle ear, and for nutritional studies into vitamin C, folic acid, thiamine, arginine and calcium.

There are a limited number of inbred strains available. Most work is carried out using out-bred strains; many of them originating since 1926 from the Dunkin-Hartley line.

Physiology and behaviour. The guinea pig is strictly herbivorous, has transversely inclined molars, and the jaw movements are made from front to back. Both incisors and molars grow continually. The animals are active for roughly 20 hours a day. There is no clear circadian rhythm; periods of activity alternate with short sleeping periods which last for about 10 minutes. Guinea pigs eat their own faeces (coprophagy) directly from the anus. Obese and pregnant animals eat their droppings from the floor, because they can not reach the anal opening. Newborn animals eat their mother's droppings, from which they obtain the same intestinal microflora as their parent animals.

The skin around the anus is naked and invaginated (fossa perinealis) and has many sebaceous glands. Just above the rudimentary tail there are some large sebaceous glands (coccigeal glands). Males (boars) as well as females (sows) have one pair of nipples in the inguinal region. Males can be distinguished by extruding the penis using gentle pressure on the abdomen just cranial to the genital opening. The vagina of a female which is not in oestrus and not delivering, is closed by a membrane. The caecum is large with a crenated edge and fills a significant part of the abdomen. There are many mono-nuclear leucocytes carrying an oval inclusion body in the blood of guinea pigs, known as Kurloff's-bodies. They are present especially during pregnancy. These leucocytes probably protect the foetus against immunocompetent cells of the mother, because they are present in high concentrations within the placenta.

Guinea pigs are very sensitive to antibiotics, even more so than hamsters. In particular, antibiotics against Gram-negative bacteria such as penicillin, erythromycin and chlortetracycline can be fatal. The animals are relatively unaffected by corticosteroids. On the other hand, histamine can lead to lethal contractions of the smooth muscular tissue of the bronchioles.

Housing.　Guinea pigs are social animals and therefore should preferably be housed in groups. They are hardly ever aggressive towards each other, and only when unfamiliar male adult animals are put together does fighting take place. A solid bottomed cage with bedding material is better than a cage with a wire bottom, as the animals lose hair and body weight on wire and there is also a risk of bone fracture and footpad inflammation. Guinea pigs usually do not climb and, if the cage sides are higher than 20–25 cm, they can be housed without a lid. Cages with a lid must have a minimum height of 18 cm. Care must be taken with bedding material as sawdust, for example, can pile up in the preputium of the males and obstruct the erection of the penis, or can cause vaginitis in females.

A high environmental temperature (above 28°C) in combination with high relative humidity (above 70%) is not well-tolerated by guinea pigs. In pregnant animals this can result in abortion. The guinea pig is very sensitive to temperature fluctuations and draught. Sudden changes in environmental conditions, such as during transportation, can lead to dramatic weight loss.

Guinea pigs are nervous and easily liable to panic, for example, if subjected to sudden strange noises. They will emit loud squeals and possibly run in circles. Over-population, boredom and stress can induce behaviour disorders, notably hair-biting.

Food and drink.　Guinea pigs have a good appetite and eat regularly during the day as well as the night. Within a few days after birth they should be introduced to solid food. In general guinea pig refuse bitter, salty or sweet-tasting food and synthetic diets. Restricting the intake of food and drinking water can be harmful. Vitamin C cannot be synthesized by guinea pigs and is therefore, in most cases, added to commercial guinea pig feed. However, the shelf-life of feed containing vitamin C is less than 3 months, and it has to be stored in a cool and dark place. Vitamin C can also be given via the drinking water (220 mg/litre); the water should be free from chlorine, otherwise the vitamin will be inactive. The supplementation of good quality hay to the diet provides a good source of crude fibre, and provides the animals with a distraction which also helps to prevent hair-biting.

Guinea pigs do not lick the drinking nipple but gnaw on it. That is why the nipple must be made of stainless steel. In a breeding colony the nipple must be long enough to allow the newborns to reach it as well. During drinking, guinea pigs blow mouth-fluid and food particles back into the bottle and therefore the water becomes polluted very quickly. The water must be frequently changed and the bottle must be cleaned and disinfected regularly.

Reproduction. The guinea pig is poly-oestrous. The oestrous period is recognizable because at this time the vaginal membrane is open. There are also typical behavioural patterns exhibited by the sow; for example the sow will attempt to mount cage mates just like a boar. When a sow on heat is approached by a male, she will show lordosis (hollow back) and will "shoot" small quantities of urine in the direction of the male. The act of mating shortens the oestrous period and can be recognized afterwards by the presence of a copulation plug in the vagina. The average length of pregnancy of the guinea pig is 68 days, which is significantly longer than that of other rodent species. Just prior to delivery the pelvic bones on the ventral side (sacro-iliac symphisis) separate, providing a spacious birth canal. During oestrus and parturition the vaginal membrane is open.

Guinea pigs are well developed at birth: they possess a complete coat of hair, their eyes and ears are open, and they can walk almost immediately. Within a few hours after birth, the young guinea pigs can eat solid food. Fostering by other females can also be successful. The sow should have her first litter before she herself is fully grown, thereby preventing the firm fusion of the sacro-iliac joint, which results in dystocia. Older animals develop obesity and ovarian cysts which can lead to diminished fertility and a greater risk of the young being stillborn.

Both monogamous and polygamous breeding systems are used. Monogamous pairs stay together during the reproductive period. Postpartum mating is common and can result in approximately five litters per sow per year. In polygamous groups one male is housed with 8–10 females. In this situation it is usual for pregnant females to be housed separately until some weeks after delivery.

Handling and simple techniques. Guinea pigs should be lifted by grasping them gently but firmly around the shoulders and thorax, whilst at the same time supporting the back and hind legs with the other hand (fig. 3.8). If the animal is gripped too tightly around the trunk and belly, this can cause shock or possibly lead to liver and lung injuries.

The identification of multi-coloured guinea pigs using sketch cards can be useful. However as the majority of laboratory guinea pigs are white the best method for long-term marking is the tattooing of the ear(s) or the naked skin behind the ear. Ear clipping, punching or tagging should not be applied, as they can be easily torn out. Temporary marking can be achieved by the staining of the coat with dyes such as fuchsin, acriflavine or gentian violet.

Fig. 3.8. Handling of a guinea-pig.

Rabbits

Origin and use. The origins of the European wild rabbit (*Oryctolagus cuniculus*) are thought to begin on the Iberian Peninsula, from whence it spread to the Mediterranean area. There are many different breeds, which are selected by coat type and colour. As a laboratory animal, the most widely used are the Dutch breed which weigh less than 2 kg, and the New Zealand White which weigh 2–5 kg. There are a limited number of inbred strains. Compared with the numbers of mice and rats used in biomedical research, the number of rabbits used is rather low, being approximately 2% of all registered laboratory animals. The areas of research where they are used are toxicity (teratogens) and pyrogenicity tests, the production of antiserum, the calibration of biologically active products, eye and skin irritation tests and studies on atherosclerosis.

Physiology, anatomy and behaviour. Rabbits are classified according to their body weight i.e. large breeds weigh more than 5 kg, medium breeds (2–5 kg) and small breeds less than 2 kg. Small breeds are sometimes sub-divided to cover dwarf breeds of less than 1 kg. The rabbit is omnivorous and produces two types of faeces: the soft "night" faeces and the hard, dry "day" faeces. During the second half of the night and early morning, the content of the caecum is transported virtually unaltered to the colon and rectum in small spherical particles surrounded by a mucous layer. These soft droppings, which have a relatively low fibre content but contain high levels of proteins and vitamins B and K, are eaten by the rabbit directly from the anus (coprophagy or caecotrophy).

The rabbit's urine may vary in colour from turbid yellow to reddish brown, depending upon the composition of the feed. The sebaceous glands under the skin of the chin and around the anus (fossa perinealis) secrete odorous products (pheromones) used by the rabbit when marking out its territory. Hares and rabbits which belong to the order Lagomorpha, have one pair of small incisors just behind the large incisors of the upper jaw. At the outlet of the ileum into the caecum there is a dilation known as sacculus rotundus, the walls of which contain lymphatic tissue (tonsilla ileocaecalis). The large caecum is coiled up like a spiral, the blind end of which also contains a large amount of lymphoid tissue (appendix caeci). The female rabbit (doe) has a double cervix. The male rabbit (buck) can be distinguished from the female by protruding the penis. When determining the sex of young animals experience is needed.

When a rabbit is resting it breathes from the abdomen.

The neutrophilic leucocytes contain many eosinophilic granules in the cytoplasm (pseudo-eosinophilic leucocytes).

Approximately 30% of rabbits do not react to atropine, because this drug is inactivated by atropine-esterase in the blood.

Housing. Stainless steel cages with a wire floor were commonly used for housing laboratory rabbits, but now plastic cages are used more frequently, or animals are kept in groups in pens (fig. 3.9). Cages should be constructed in such a way that young animals do not get their legs trapped in the wire floor, and the adult animals do not suffer from wounds or inflammation of their foot pads. The toe nails must be clipped at regular intervals. The cage must be of a sufficient size that an adult rabbit can stretch to its full length and can sit upright on its hind legs. The minimum requirements for cage dimensions for rabbits are set out in the European guidelines and are related to body weight but do not seem to meet their behavioural requirements. In these guidelines no attention is paid to measurements on environmental enrichment.

Male rabbits can be housed individually immediately after weaning, and female rabbits at the age of 12 weeks. Group housing in relatively small pens is preferable, if the experimental protocol permits it. However, group housing of sexually mature animals can be problematic, as the animals will defend their own territory.

Due to the high concentration of crystals present in the urine of rabbits which stick to the floor of the cage, the cleaning of the cages is made rather difficult. They should therefore be treated periodically with detergents.

Fig. 3.9. Group housing of rabbits.

The optimal temperature for rabbits is between 15 and 19°C. In contrast to low temperatures, heat and draught are not well tolerated. Temperatures above 30°C in combination with high relative humidity leads to a risk of heat stress, which can cause infertility and mortality.

Food and drink. Rabbits are fed on pellets of a diameter of approximately 3 mm. Young animals and does with a litter are fed *ad libitum*, whilst other animals should be rationed in order to prevent obesity. The crude fibre content of the diet must not be lower than 10%; therefore, it is advisable to supplement the feed with hay as this prevents intestinal disturbances and obstructions caused by hairballs, and also enriches their environment. Any changes to the composition of the feed, such as after weaning, should always be performed gradually, at least over a period of 4–5 days, in order to give the intestinal microflora the opportunity to adapt to the new conditions. Fresh drinking water must be available *ad libitum*.

Reproduction. Although a true oestrous cycle with spontaneous ovulation does not occur in does, there are certain periods during which she will not accept the buck. Ovulation takes place 10 hours after mating (post-copulatory ovulation). As result of mating the pituitary gland secretes luteinising hormone (LH) which induces ovulation. This also means that ovulation can be induced by injecting LH, which has applications in the case of artificial insemination and for research in the field of reproduction such as studies on maturation of germ-cells, fertilization, cleavage and implantation. When the induction of ovulation is not followed by fertilization, pseudopregnancy occurs which lasts 16–18 days. If the animals are not subjected to artificial lighting, then the activity of the ovaries will be lower during the autumn and the winter, due to the shorter periods of light. Some days prior to parturition, the doe gathers hair from her abdominal region. This exposes her nipples (4 pairs) and provides material for the nest. The newborn are naked and remain in the nest for approximately 3 weeks. If a pup accidentally falls out of the nest, it will not be retrieved by the mother. The young pups are only suckled once or twice a day for a period of 4–5 minutes. This is sufficient, however, because doe milk is extremely concentrated, containing 13% fat and 10% protein. After the suckling period is over, the nest is closed.

The optimal breeding age is between 5 months and 3 years. One buck is sufficient for 10–20 does, providing the buck is only used for mating no more than 5 times a week. When mating is to take place, the doe is brought to the buck for 15–20 minutes. If the female will not mate or the animals start fighting, it is possible to try another buck or to reintroduce the same buck 1–2 days later. Ten to 14 days after mating, pregnancy can be confirmed by abdominal palpation. A nesting box and nesting materials should be provided during the last week of pregnancy. Newborns do not need to receive colostrum, due to the passage of immunoglobulins across the placenta. Newborns can only be fostered if they are not older than 2 weeks, and if the adopting litter is younger than 3 days. The smell of the nest should be masked by sprinkling the young pups and the nose of the foster mother with perfume. The mortality of fostered pups is, however, high.

Does can be mated again after weaning (after 4–5 weeks), although mating immediately after parturition is also possible.

Handling and simple techniques. Lifting rabbits out of their cage can be done by grasping the skin of the neck and the back firmly with one hand, while supporting the belly and the hind legs with the other (fig. 3.10). When carrying the rabbit, the head of the animal is firmly held between the arm and the body of the handler. The rabbit should now be lying quietly on the handler's arm. Struggling animals risk breaking their backs. Should this occur then euthanasia should be carried out immediately. For long-term restraint, a rabbit can be placed in a restraining box. This should be done with care because when struggling fatal back damage can occur. For the permanent identification of a rabbit, microchips or ear tattoos are recommended. Ear tags are not suitable. Short-term marking can be done using dyes such as fuchsin, acriflavine, or gentian violet.

Fig. 3.10. Handling of a rabbit.

Transportation.   Rabbits should not be transported without adequate ventilation as they cannot tolerate heat. The transportation boxes must have sufficient room, with a minimum specifications $40 \times 25 \times 35$ cm ($l \times b \times h$) and good ventilation openings. It is recommended that animals fast for 12 hours prior to transportation, in order to prevent the risk of stomach ruptures.

Monkeys

Origin and use.   The origin of the monkey (non-human primate) depends upon the species. The lower monkeys (Prosimiae) are found on the Indonesian islands and in Madagascar. The true monkeys (Simiae) are found in Central and South America, such as the squirrel monkey (Saimiri) and marmoset (Callithrix); in Africa, such as the chimpanzee (*Pan troglodytes*), and in South and East Asia, where the rhesus monkey (*Macaca mulatta*) and the cynomolgus monkey (*Macaca fascicularis*) are found. Years ago, it was common practice to use wild monkeys for research. Nowadays, most of the monkeys used are bred and reared under laboratory conditions. The number of monkeys used as experimental animals is declining. Most monkeys are used for the testing of vaccines and medicines, but they are also used for a variety of scientific investigations, such as behavioural research and specific studies into (infectious) diseases which occur in man.

Table 3.3

Environmental requirements and physiological parameters of marmosets, cynomolgus, rhesus monkeys and chimpanzees

	Marmo-sets	Cynomol-gus	Rhesus monkey	Chimpan-zees
Environmental requirements				
Temperature (°C)	22–28	20–24	20–24	20–24
Relative humidity (%)	40–60	50–70	50–70	50–70
Ventilation (changes/hour)	–	9–12	9–12	9–12
Light/dark (hours)	13/11	13/11	13/11	13/11
Minimum cage floor size				
One individually housed adult (m^2)	0.25	0.7–0.9	0.9–1.1	2.5
Breeding animal with young (m^2)	0.25	0.9	1.1	–
Group (m^2/adult)	0.25	0.7	0.9.	–
Minimum cage height (cm)	60	90	90–120	200
General physiological parameters				
Adult weight (kg)				
Male	0.4–0.6	2.5–6	4–9	35–45
Female	0.4–0.5	4–8	6–11	45–60
Life span (years)	10–16	15–25	20–30	40–50
Heart rate (/min.)	–	100–150	100–150	85–90
Respiration rate (/min.)	–	40–65	40–65	30–60
Body temperature (°C)	–	37–40	36–40	36–39
Number of chromosomes (2n)	–	–	42	48
Body surface (cm^2)	–	–	–	–
Water intake (ml/100 g/day)	–	–	–	–
Puberty (years)				
Female	0.8–1	3–4	3–4	6–8
Male	0.8–1	3–4	3–4	8–10
Breeding age (years)				
Female	1.5–2	4–5	3–4	9–11
Male	1.5–2	4–5	4–5	10–12
Oestrous cycle (days)	27–29	31	29	32–38
Duration of menstruation (days)	none	4	3	–
Duration of pregnancy (days)	142–146	161	155–170	210–250
Nest size	2–3	1	1	1
Weight at birth (g)	25–35	300–400	450–500	1500
Weight at weaning (g)	80–120	800–1200	1000–1500	–
Weaning age (months)	2–3	4–6	4–6	6–9
Blood parameters				
Blood volume (ml/kg)	70	–	50–90	62–65
Haemoglobin (g/100 ml)	–	–	11–12.5	10–14
Haematocrit (vol. %)	–	–	39–43	38–43
Leucocytes ($\times$ 1000/mm^3)	–	–	7–13	10–14
Glucose (mg/100 ml)	–	–	60–160	80–95

Physiology, anatomy and behaviour. Besides possessing the general characteristics of primates, each species has its own physiological and anatomical peculiarities. This is also the case for nutritional requirements and behavioural patterns. To illustrate this point, lower monkeys are active during the dark period, have large eyes and ear shells. Most of them are insectivores or omnivores, the most primitive amongst them being the tupaias (e.g. *Tupaia glis*). The true monkeys are more highly developed and some, notably the Homidae, bear a strong resemblance to man.

Detailed biological knowledge and practical experience in relation to the particular species of monkey used for research is crucial when using them as laboratory animals. The section which follows gives only some general information in terms of housing conditions, nutrition and handling of the frequently used species.

Housing. Many primate species, such as the macaques and the chimpanzees, live in groups which have a very distinct social order. These animals should preferably be housed, therefore, in large rooms or pens. When forming these groups the species, age, sex, etc. of the monkeys must be taken into account. The behaviour within the group should be under continuous observation, so that the handler can intervene in the case of extreme aggression.

The minimum dimensions regarding floor area and cage height vary according to the species and the size of the animals. The European guidelines divide monkeys into seven groups according to body weight. The height of the cage must at the minimum give the monkeys the possibility of standing upright. For spider monkeys there must be sufficient room for them to hang freely from the ceiling extended to their full length. Apart from actual floor area and height, the shape of the cage is also important. Whenever possible there should be small shelves in the cage so that the animals can sit and rest near the top of the cage. It is sometimes necessary to house monkeys individually on a temporary basis, for example during quarantine or whilst carrying out experimental procedure or during recovery after anaesthesia. The cages should then be arranged in such a way that the animals can still see each other. Long-term solitary confinement may lead to abnormal behaviour. However, some primates, such as the male orang-utan live alone, and marmosets live as monogamous couples.

The optimal environmental temperature for most of the monkey species is 20–24°C, although marmosets prefer a somewhat higher temperature of between 22 and 28°C.

Nutrition. Monkeys can be fed commercially produced monkey food. However, the exact composition must be adapted to the specific requirements of any given species. For example South American monkeys, such as marmosets, cannot absorb vitamin D2, whereas macaques can use both vitamin D2 and D3 as a source of vitamin D. All primates need vitamin C (1–5 mg/kg b.w./day). Food is primarily a source of nutrients, but is also a means of keeping the animal occupied. The composition of the menu greatly influences the amount of time the animals spend on both the collection and eating of food.

Reproduction. The breeding of monkeys should be carried out in specialized centres, as it requires not only optimal housing but also specific knowledge and training.

The reproductive cycle of marmosets is of a shorter duration than that of macaques and chimpanzees. Macaques have external bleeding (menstruation) and ovulation occurs during oestrus in the middle of the menstrual cycle. During oestrus, hyperaemia of the peri-vaginal skin occurs.In order to ascertain whether mating has taken place or not, the vagina is checked for the presence of a coagulation plug or spermatozoa. After approximately four weeks of gestation, pregnancy can be diagnosed by rectal palpation of the uterus. Towards the end of pregnancy the position of the foetus should be checked regularly as in the event of an abnormal position natural delivery may not take place. In some situations it is necessary to perform a Caesarean section. Most monkey species produce only one offspring at a time, twins are exceptional. After approximately 3–6 months the young can be weaned.

Handling. Appropriate handling is very important and must be taught by a competent supervisor. This is especially true in the case of the larger monkey species, as these animals are strong, fast and occasionally aggressive. The long, sharp canine teeth which they possess can be dangerous, and, in some cases, it may be necessary to tranquillize the animal, for example with a ketamine injection, before handling it. Whilst administering such an injection the animal can be restrained against the front of the cage by means of a movable cage wall (squeeze back). A monkey which is housed within a pen can be captured using a net. Whilst the animal is captive in the net, the arms should be secured behind its back. During such handling and securing it is advisable to wear thick gloves. A variety of harnesses and chairs are available for restraint.

Dogs

Origin and use. The dog (*Canis familiaris*) has a long history of domestication and is a probable descendent of the wolf (*Canis lupus*). Nowadays there are approximately 300 breeds, ranging from the very small (±18 cm high and 1–2 kg) to very large and heavy varieties (±80 cm high, ±90 kg body weight). Next to cross-breds, beagles (10–12 kg body weight) are the most frequently used as laboratory animals. Beagles are particularly suitable, because they are rather docile and can be kept both in groups or individually. The number of dogs used in experiments has been steadily decreasing over the last 10 years. Dogs are mainly used for the testing of vaccines and medicines, for developing surgical techniques and for research into cardiovascular disease.

Physiology and behaviour. Many physiological parameters of the dog are well known; a number of them are shown in table 3.4. Given the extreme variation between breeds, it goes without saying that the biological differences will also be considerable.

When using dogs as experimental animals, detailed knowledge of their behaviour is required. The dog is a social animal. There is a complicated social ranking which exists within the group, the hierarchy of which is dependent largely upon the sex of the animal. In general male dogs are more aggressive than females (bitches), especially towards other males and unfamiliar adult dogs. As a rule beagles tend to be more tolerant and do not show many signs of aggression. Male dogs mark out their territorial boundary by regularly spraying urine on different places. Working in a uniform and consistent way in close and regular contact with the animals, especially during the socialization period between the age of 4–8 weeks, is extremely important for good adaptation to both humans and other dogs and to prevent nervous behaviour of the dogs. When in contact with dogs, the handler must always be the dominant party. When reintroducing an animal that has been temporarily away from the group, extra care must be taken to ensure that the animal is not rejected. Experimental handling must never be carried out within the animal's territory.

Housing. Dogs can be housed indoors as well as outdoors and should preferably housed in small groups with an indoor sleeping area and an outdoor run. The indoor pens should have a metal grid floor or preferably a tender-foot floor and must be kept warm with no draughts. There should also be a dry insulated sleeping area possibly with under-floor heating. The floor of the outside run should have a suitable slope (approximately 5%) to ensure adequate drainage. If an animal has to be housed temporarily on its own, then cages can be used. According to the European guidelines the minimum dimensions of the cage are relative to the size of the dog. For example, a beagle needs a minimum floor area of 1 m² and a height of 80 cm for a short stay. When grouped together beagles require an indoor area of 1.2 m² with a run of at least 1.6 m² per animal. The environmental temperature for a group of dogs could be lower than that for dogs housed individually. Newborn pups depend upon external heat for regulating their body temperature. In order to achieve the ambient temperature of between 26 and 29°C for the first 5–10 days, a heating lamp should be placed at a height of at least 1 metre.

Table 3.4

Environmental requirements and physiological parameters of dogs, cats, pigs, sheep and goats

	Dogs	Cats	Pigs	Sheep/goats
Environmental factors				
Temperature (°C)	15–21	15–21	17–24	10–24
Relative humidity (%)	40–60	40–60	40–60	40–60
Ventilation (m^3/h/animal)	20–80	20–50	100–180	100–150
Light/dark (hours)	–	–	–	–
Minimum cage floor size [1]				
One individually housed adult (m^2)	0.75–1.75	0.2–0.6	0.35–0.8	1.4/1.6
Breeding animal with young (m^2)	–	2	–	–
Group (m^2/adult)	1–4	0.2–0.6	0.2–2.5	0.7/0.8
Minimum cage height (cm) [1]	60–180	50	50–80	1200/2000
General physiological parameters				
Adult weight (kg)				
Male	10–80	3–7	200–300	50–70
Female	10–60	3–4	150–220	50–60
Duration of life (years)	10–15	10–17	14–18	10–15
Heart rate (/min.)	80–150	100–120	60–90	70–80
Respiration rate (/min.)	20–30	20–40	8–18	12–25
Body temperature (°C)	38–39	38–39.5	38–40	38.5–40
Number of chromosomes (2n)	78	38	38	–
Water intake (ml/100 g/day)	–	0.03–0.25	2–6	–
Puberty (months)				
Female	8–14	6–8	5–7	6–10
Male	7–8	6.5–7	5–7	6–10
Breeding age (months)				
Female	>12	10–12	>7	>10
Male	9–14	>12	>7	>10
Oestrous cycle (days)	4–8 months	15–18	18–24	14–20/15–24
Duration of pregnancy (days)	63–67	60–65	110–118	144–155
Litter size	3–6	3–5	11–16	1–2
Weight at birth (g)	200–500	90–130	900–1600	–
Weight at weaning (g)	1.5–4	0.6–0.8	6–8	–
Weaning age (months)	6–7	7	4–7	4–8
Blood parameters				
Blood volume (ml/kg)	72–74	65–75	74	80/60–70
Haemoglobin (g/100 ml)	12–17	11–14	11–13	11–13/8–12
Haematocrit (vol. %)	37–55	24–55	41	32/34
Leucocytes ($\times$ 1000/mm^3)	7–17	9–20	8–16	15–20/8–12
Glucose (mg/100 ml)	60–80	75–110	60–90	30–60

[1] Dependent upon body weight and/or height.

Food and drink. Adult dogs should be fed once a day with commercial dog chow, either in a dry or wet form. Variation in the type of food in the diet is advised. This food should be given in durable and easy-to-clean pans. For dogs housed in groups, it is essential to check that all the animals get sufficient food. Water should be provided *ad libitum*, either in a drinking dish or by means of an automatic watering system.

Reproduction. In general, the breeding of dogs does not take place in a research institute, as it is very time consuming. The physiological data related to reproduction in dogs are shown in table 3.4. The (pro-)oestrus of the bitch can be detected by the swelling of the vulva, followed by a haemorrhagic discharge lasting 6–10 days. The best time for mating to occur is around the 10th to 12th day after the start of vulval bleeding. Pregnancy can be confirmed by palpation between day 21 and 28 after mating or by echoscopy after about 14 days. After the 25th day diagnosis by palpation becomes more difficult. In the last week prior to parturition, the bitch should be provided with a special box to make a nest. The interval between the delivery of the pups is usually not much longer than 1 hour. After the birth of each pup, the umbilical cord is bitten through and the placenta is eaten by the bitch.

During the first week of life, the pups will be suckled every 2 hours, after which the frequency will diminish. The eyes and ears of the pups open between the 10th and 14th day and the pups can walk and start eating puppy feed after the 20th day. The use of artificial milk is possible, but one must take into account that dog milk has a higher percentage of fat, protein, calcium and phosphorus than cow milk. There are high quality milk substitutes available for dogs.

Handling and simple techniques. A dog should always be approached quietly from the front, whilst talking to it. The animal can be lifted up with one hand supporting the belly with the other hand holding the skin of the neck. The most successful way to hold a dog securely is to put it on its side, whilst firmly fixing its underlying legs, and using the arms of the handler to push down the neck and the pelvis of the dog. Animals which have a nervous and aggressive disposition, which is often induced by fear, should be calmed down. As a last resort one can use a sedative or apply a bandage (> 7 cm) around the nose and jaws of the dog knotted once under the lower jaw with a second knot tied firmly at the back of the neck. Dogs can be marked for identification by tattooing the ear (mandatory in several countries). Temporary identifications can best be done by the use of numbered or named collars.

To prevent infectious diseases, dogs are vaccinated according to a vaccination schedule. Regular treatment must be given to prevent ecto- and endoparasites. Scale on teeth should be removed regularly. In order to prevent oestrus, bitches can be injected with hormones every 5–6 months. These treatments may influence the results of experiments, depending upon the type of study being undertaken.

Cats

Origin and use. The European domestic cat (*Felis catus*) has been domesticated for a long time. It has probably developed as a result of cross breeding between two wild cats, *Felis silvestris* and *Felis lybica*. At the moment there are more than 100 breeds in existence. A variety of differently coloured European short-haired cats are used as laboratory animals. The number of cats used in experiments has strongly declined during the last decade. Cats are still used for the development of medicines, mainly short-term experiments under general anaesthesia, neurological investigations and research into cardiovascular diseases.

Physiology and behaviour. Cats are solitary hunting animals with good eyesight and acute hearing. They communicate with each other, with other animals and with man, by producing different sounds, such as miaowing and purring, by facial expressions using their ears and teeth and by body positioning i.e. hairs on end and an arched back). Generally speaking female animals (queens) and castrated males will behave in a friendly way towards each other. Male cats (toms) are more aggressive, especially towards unfamiliar males. Both queen and tom cats are strong territorial predators. The territory is marked by an excretion from their circum-anal glands and by their urine.

Housing. Female cats can be housed in groups of up to 20 animals. Group housing for tom cats is much more difficult. From the age of 4–6 months onwards, tom cats have to be separated, unless they are nest mates. It is impossible to introduce new tom cats in an existing group. Castrated toms can be treated as females, providing it is carried out before sexual maturity.

Cats can be housed in an indoor pen, preferably with an outdoor run. The indoor area for a group of 10–20 cats should have a minimum floor size of 12–25 m^2 with a height of 2–3 m. The floor must have a slope of 3–5% for drainage purposes. The pen must be provided with scratching and climbing facilities, places for sleeping other than on the ground, a number of dirt-trays with cat litter and with a double door to prevent escape. It should be possible to see inside the cat area to observe their behaviour. An outdoor run, accessible via two or more doors, is advisable. If there are only a few cats located in one large area, it is possible that two sub-groups will be formed, each with its own territory, which can result in fighting.

It is possible to house cats individually on a temporary basis in cages with a minimum floor area of 0.4 to 0.6 m^2 for animals of 3–4 and 4–5 kg body weight, respectively, and with a height of at least 50 cm. There should be a shelf installed above the ground for the cat to sleep upon, a litter tray and both scratching and climbing facilities following the European guidelines.

Other recommendations (UK Home Office) require a minimum floor area of 0.75 m^2 and a height of 80 cm for cats with a body weight of 3 kg and more. Cats that are housed on their own are generally more nervous and less easy to handle, and their reintroduction into a group can cause serious problems.

Food and drink. Adult cats can be fed once a day with a variety of commercial cat food. Kittens up to 2 months old must be fed at least three times a day, and kittens up to six months old, twice a day. When cats are housed in groups it is necessary to check that each animal gets sufficient food. Cats are rather choosy, and additions to the feed can easily lead to them refusing it. The cat has a relatively high requirement for protein, vitamin B5 (nicotinic acid), vitamin A, arachidonic acid and taurine. The drinking water can be chlorinated (0.2–1.0 ml free chlorine per litre), but should not be acidified. The intake of drinking water will vary according to the water content of the food.

Reproduction. The queen cat is seasonally polyoestrous and this usually occurs from February to October. The duration of the cycle is approximately 14 days with an inter-oestrous period of between 3 and 6 days. Oestrus is generally obvious due to the behaviour of the female cat: the tail will be held erect, the body stretched and the back sunken. In order to guarantee pregnancy, mating should take place 2–3 times, mainly as ovulation is induced by copulation (post copulatory ovulation). To avoid territorially defensive behaviour, it is better to bring the female to the male for mating rather than the other way around. Queen cats who are in a late stage of pregnancy should be removed from the group, and housed in, for example, a breeding cage. Approximately 10 days prior to delivery, the cage must be provided with a kittening box. Kittens are born at close intervals, normally about 30 minutes apart. When the queen cat does not produce sufficient milk, kittens can be fostered by another queen. Bottle feeding is possible and must be given 4 times per day, but the high protein content of the mother's milk must be taken into account. After 3–4 weeks, the kittens can start to eat solid food. During parturition, and the first weeks of rearing, the ambient temperature should be higher than normal (23 ± 2°C).

Handling and simple techniques. The handling and caring of cats should ideally be carried out by one person. The approach of, and handling by, unfamiliar people can have an influence on the results of experiments. The cat can be taken out of its cage by firmly holding the skin of the neck, resulting in the occurrence of a rigidifying reflex. The animal can now be supported under the arm of the technician using the hand to support the chest and the fingers to fix the forelegs of the cat. A cat can be most easily restrained on a table lying on its side. The fore and hind legs should be held firmly between the fingers, and the head is pushed onto the table by the wrist of the handler. Intractable cats can be contained in a cloth. Wild cats should be dealt with using protective gloves and given a tranquillizer.

To prevent infectious diseases, cats can be vaccinated and, if necessary, treated against ecto- and endoparasites at regular intervals. In order to prevent oestrus, queens can be treated with hormones. However, these treatments may influence experimental results.

Pigs

Origin and use. The European wild swine (*Sus scrofa*) probably originated from the Asian swine (*Sus vitatus*). Many varieties and breeds have been developed from the European swine. In biomedical research there are many commercial breeds in use, such as the Large White Landrace and Yorkshire pig, along with the miniature Göttingen pig from Germany, and Pittmoore, Minnesota and Yucatan varieties from the USA. Even smaller pigs (micropigs), are becoming commercially available. The number of pigs which are used in research, e.g. for vaccine development and food research, is limited in comparison with the total numbers of laboratory animals used (less than 1%). The pig is used as an animal model for man as it has many similarities to humans in areas such as the skin, skeleton, gastro-intestinal tract, pancreas, kidneys and cardiovascular system.

Physiology and behaviour. Physiological data related to pigs are shown in table 3.4. Miniature pigs will, in some instances, show different values for some of the parameters. Pigs live in social groups and in the wild there is a distinct hierarchical ranking. Adult male pigs (boars) either live a solitary existence or are the leader of a group.

When it is necessary to use groups of piglets for a biomedical study, these must be formed at a very early age, i.e. immediately after weaning. When older piglets are placed into a group, fighting will occur which can last 1–2 days.

Young piglets are by nature very active and enjoy to play. If bored they will exhibit abnormal behaviour in the form of tail and ear biting, or the sucking of the umbilicus, the vulva or preputium. Although piglets have the tendency to get excited, to struggle, to resist and to scream, they become tractable and docile with time (with the exception of the Vietnamese mini pig).

Housing. Young pigs can be housed in groups in indoor pens on a metal grid or wooden statted floor without litter, or better still on a concrete floor with straw or sawdust. Straw provides the animals with an opportunity to play, which keeps them distracted, and they will also eat it. According to the European guidelines the minimum floor area must be 0.3–0.8 m² per animal of 50 to 100 kg bodyweight, respectively. The best way to establish new groups of piglets is to bring the animals together simultaneously into a clean pen just prior to feeding or the dark period. The bodily smells can be camouflaged by eau de Cologne. If problems remain, then tranquillizers will have to be used. If it is necessary, then pigs of up to 40 kg can be housed individually in cages with a floor area of at least 0.35, 0.55, or 0.8 m² and a height of at least 50, 60, or 80 cm, depending upon the body weight of the animals. Here the figures apply to pigs of up to 15, 25, or 40 kg, respectively.

The recommended environmental temperature for adult pigs is between 17 and 24°C, with a relative humidity of 40–60%. Newborn piglets need an ambient temperature of 30–32°C. This can be achieved by positioning a heating lamp in one corner of the pen. The temperature can then be gradually reduced to 22°C over a 3 week period. Good ventilation is also necessary. The velocity of the air stream has to remain low; for adult animals lower than 0.3 m/sec., for newborn piglets lower than 0.1 m/sec.

Food and drink.   Piglets, as well as adult pigs, can be fed with commercially available food, which can be adapted to suit the requirements of different ages. The feed can be supplied as pellets, meal or swill. There must be sufficient feeding places per cage or pen, which, according to the European Guidelines, must be at least 20–30 cm per animal between 10 and 100 kg body weight. Feeding troughs must be constructed in such a way that they can be fixed to the wall or the door, ensuring that no feed is wasted. Drinking water is provided *ad libitum* by means of automatic drinking nipples or troughs. Young animals frequently waste a good deal of water through playing with the nipple.

Reproduction.   The physiological data concerning reproduction are shown in table 3.4. The first signs of a pig being on heat are seen on the 2nd and 3rd days of pro-oestrus and are characterized by restlessness, diminished food intake and by reddening and swelling of the vulva. A sow in oestrus reacts to pressure on the back or to the smell of a boar (for example from a spray) by showing the so called standing-reflex. At this point the sow will allow natural mating. However, it is more often the case that artificial insemination will be used. In general, the piglets will be delivered every 10–30 minutes. The placentae either come out during the delivery of the piglets, or 2-3 hours after the last piglet is born. Drinking of colostrum should begin within 45 minutes of birth and, after that, the newborns should drink every hour. A high environmental temperature is essential during the first days postpartum (see housing). Piglets can be fostered very easily during the first week of life.

This may be necessary in order to equalize the number or to share out the maternal effects amongst the experimental groups. Between the 2nd and 5th day after birth, the piglets are injected with iron (150–200 mg/piglet, i.m.); this is to counteract an iron deficiency which may otherwise develop due to the low concentration of iron in the sow's milk and the high growth rate of the piglets. After the 3rd week, piglets will start to eat pig meal or baby pellets, and can be weaned after the 4th week.

Handling and simple techniques. The method for handling pigs depends upon the age of the animals. Young piglets of up to 5 kg, can be caught by a hind leg and then carried in both arms. Heavier animals need to be supported with one arm beneath the trunk and the belly, thus directing the head backwards and fixing it by the elbow against the body of the handler. Pigs can scream loudly and at a high frequency, and it is therefore recommended to use ear defenders. Adult animals, in particular unfamiliar boars or sows with piglets, have to be treated with caution, as they can react aggressively. Pigs can be marked for identification with ear tags or by ear tattooing.

To prevent infectious diseases, pigs can be vaccinated, for example against Aujeszky's disease, Swine Erysipelas, and Atrophic Rhinitis, and if necessary they can be treated against ecto- and endoparasites.

Transport. Pigs are very sensitive to stress which can even be fatal during transportation. To help overcome this, gentle handling and a ventilated transport vehicle with a rough floor is recommended. If thought necessary the food can be withdrawn for a period of 12–24 hours prior to transportation. Very sensitive animals, such as the Pietrain breed, can be tranquillized using a beta-blocker.

Sheep and goats

Origin and use. The number of sheep (*Ovis aries*) and goats (*Capra hircus*) used in biomedical research is limited (less than 0.2% of the total number of vertebrates) These animals are used for a variety of purposes, such as blood donors for microbiological culture media, for the induction of antibodies, for obtaining surgical experience, and for various scientific research topics. Pregnant sheep are used for perinatal research.

Physiology and behaviour. Sheep and goats are ruminants; in addition to a true stomach (abomasum) they have 3 pro-ventriculi: the rumen, the reticulum and the omasum. The microbial fermentation of vegetable material takes place in the rumen. This process begins as soon as the animal changes from a milk diet to solid feed rich in fibre. The content of the rumen consist of three layers: a fluid mass fills the base above which is a structured porous layer consisting of just eaten or ruminated food, above which is a layer of gas (methane). Regular contractions of the rumen cause some mixing of the liquid and the structured layers. By a process of microbial fermentation, the crude cell materials are broken down; proteins are transformed into other proteins and certain vitamins are synthesised (mainly of the B-complex). Every 24 hours, approximately 15 ruminating periods will take place, which vary drastically in length from 1 to 120 minutes. Altogether approximately 8–10 hours per day are spent in rumination. Sheep belong in herds, whereas goats are more "loners". Although these animals are rather timid whilst in the field, they do get used to people who take regular care of them.

Housing. Sheep and goats can be housed outdoors as well as indoors. The choice made will depend upon the facilities available and the purpose for which they are to be used. For individual housing in pens, which should not be encouraged, the European guidelines prescribe the following minimum dimensions of a pen for sheep or goats: 1.4 m^2 or 1.6 m^2, respectively with a minimum length of 1.8 m for one of the sides. These dimensions are smaller than those suggested by the UK Home Office, which are 2.0 (< 35 kg) or 2.8 m^2 (> 35 kg). When animals have to be housed individually, they should be able to have contact with each other. For group housing (6–12 animals) the guidelines require 0.7 or 0.8 m^2 per sheep or goat, respectively (fig. 3.11). Special attention must be paid to (in)tolerance between the animals of a group and to the behaviour of horned animals. When planning the floor area it must always be taken into account that the animals should be able to lay down easily. The floor can be covered with straw or sawdust, which should be replaced every other day. The animals can also be housed on a metal grid floor or a tender-foot floor with no ground cover, which makes the labour required less intensive.

The recommended environmental temperature for sheep and goats is between 10 and 24°C with a relative humidity of 55% ± 10%. The ventilation capacity should be around 3 m^3/hour/kg body weight, in order to prevent the accumulation of rumen gas (methane) and ammonia.

Food and drink. Sheep and goats should be fed with a good quality hay, provided in a rack fixed to the wall or the front grill, with sheep pellets given as supplementary feed. Drinking water should be provided *ad libitum* from automatic drinking trays.

Reproduction. Sheep and goats are seasonally polyoestrous, with active oestrous cycles from September to December, with the lambs being born between February and June. Oestrus synchronization can be induced by

Fig. 3.11. Group housing of goats.

administering two injections of synthetic prostaglandin with an interval of 10 days in between. Outside the breeding season, oestrus can be induced and synchronized using progesterone, followed by an injection of PMSG (pregnant mare serum gonadotrophin). Depending upon the breed, 1–2 offspring are born per litter, and breech presentations are quite frequent. Immediately after birth, the umbilical cord should be treated to prevent infection. Newborns can walk unaided within one hour of being born and start looking immediately for the nipple, in order to drink colostrum. Only weak animals will need external heat after birth. The fostering of lambs is not always successful. Ewes recognize their own lambs by smell, therefore it sometimes helps to transfer the smell of the new ewe or her own lambs onto the lamb to be fostered. Bottle feeding is possible, but it must be taken into account that sheep milk contains 1.5 times more dry matter than cow's milk (220–250 g milk powder for calves per litre water at 40°C). After 2.5–3 weeks the lambs can start to eat solid food.

Handling and simple techniques. Sheep and goats which are being used in biomedical research must come into direct contact with people from early on. When sheep and goats are to be housed under experimental conditions, they will need a period of at least 3 weeks to adapt. Young lambs can be caught by their hind legs and carried in the arms of the handler. In order to secure an adult sheep firmly it should be put in a sitting posture or laid on its back. This can be achieved by bending the head sidewards and then by pushing them in the side. Due to the production of gas in the rumen they should only be held in this position for a few minutes. The male sheep or goats must be treated carefully.

The tails of lambs are often docked and male lambs are generally castrated. The animals can be marked by tattooing the ears, or by fixing an ear tag soon after birth.

To prevent infectious diseases the animals can be vaccinated (for example against *Clostridium* infection, foot-rot and treated against ecto- and endoparasites, such as gastro-intestinal helminths and lungworms. In the case of the hooves becoming too long, or horn-edges curled or crumbly, these should be clipped. Sheep housed outdoors need to be shorn once a year, whilst those housed indoors should be shorn more often.

Birds

Introduction

Approximately 8–10% of the vertebrates used annually, are birds. The chicken (*Gallus domesticus*) is the most widely used whereas the pigeon (*Columba livia*), the dove (*Streptopelia risoria*) and Japanese quail (*Coturnix coturnix japonica*) are also commonly used.

Physiology and anatomy. Birds have specific physiological and anatomical characteristics when compared with mammals. For example, their skin is devoid of sweat and sebaceous glands. In order to facilitate preening, birds possess either powdery, downy feathers and/or two preening glands. Birds have no diaphragm; the lungs are connected to the rib cage and they possess a system of air sacs which are an essential structure in the process of respiration.

The abdominal cavity is rather small and includes the caudal part of the gizzard, and the intestine, the spleen, and either the ovaries with the oviduct, or the testicles with the ductus deferentes. Birds have no urinary bladder; urine is transported via the ureters, which empty into the cloaca.

Erythrocytes of birds are oval and nucleated. Platelets are absent and "replaced" by nucleated thrombocytes. In birds the female is heterogametic (2 different sex chromosomes), whereas the male is the homogametic sex.

Compared with mammals, birds have a high metabolic rate. This means that a continuous intake of food of a high quality must be guaranteed in order for their energetic and nutritional requirements to be met. The absorption, metabolism and elimination of nutritional elements and waste is performed at a high rate. These aspects need to be considered when using birds as experimental animals.

The chicken, the pigeon and the Japanese quail are herbivorous (granivorous). Food is mixed with the saliva in the mouth, which contains amylase, and then it is passed down to the crop where it is predigested. Further digestion takes place in the proventriculus, where it is worked upon by stomach juices, which contains pepsin and hydrochloric acid. Grinding of seeds and food takes place in the gizzard. Nutrients are subsequently mainly digested and absorbed in the small intestine, and a certain amount of cellulose will be fermented in the two caeca.

Chickens

Origin and use. The various breeds of the chickens now in existence stem from the red jungle-chicken (*Gallus gallus*), which was domesticated in Burma many centuries before Christ. Centuries of careful selection has led to two basic types of chickens: the light breeds which are used for egg production (the layers) and the heavy breeds which are used for meat (the broilers).

Of particular use in laboratory experiments are the embryos which are used in areas such as virology, embryology and toxicology. When conducting a series of experiments it is important to use eggs which have the same origin, preferably from SPF stock. This is to avoid variations in response caused by the different strains or infections. Chickens are mainly used for research into feeding, vaccination/immunology and toxicology.

Housing. Chicken are frequently kept in wire cages, usually stacked in two or more levels. This, however, must be considered as a poor housing system in which the behavioural needs cannot be exercised. It is possible to house them individually, but also in pairs or groups. Chickens, when grouped together, are probably better able to meet their behavioural needs but may show a marked social hierarchy (pecking order), which can lead to the violent plucking of each others feathers, and may even lead to cannibalism. There are minimum measurements for cages which are laid down as European guidelines. There are 5 variations, depending upon the weight of the animals and the number of animals per cage (3–5). The wire mesh floors should have a maximum mesh width of 10 mm when they are to be used for chicks and 25 mm width when constructed for young and adult animals. The thickness of the wire must be at least 2 mm in every case. The floors must be well supported and should be strengthened by 6 mm rods. Laying hens should be provided with a tilted wire mesh floor with maximum 14% tilt. When carrying out experiments of a relatively long duration involving young chicks, the fast rate of growth of the animals must be taken into account. This is necessary to

Table 3.5

Environmental requirements and physiological parameters of chickens, pigeons and quail

	Chickens	Pigeons	Quail
Environmental requirements			
Temperature (°C)	15–21	18–20	18–23
Relative humidity (%)	40–60	60–80	40–60
Ventilation (m^3/hour)	7/kg	–	34/animal
Maximum air velocity (m/s)	20–40	–	–
Light/dark (hours)	14/10	14/10	14/10
Minimum cage floor size			
One individually housed adult (cm^2)	25–1400 [1]	1600	350
Group (cm^2/adult)	150–650 [2]	–	200
Minimum cage height (cm)	25–40 [2]	40	15
General physiological parameters			
Adult weight (g)			
Male	2500–5000	–	100–130
Female	1500–3000	250–600	120–160
Life span (years)	6–12	15–20	1–2
Heart rate (/min.)	350–470	150–250	450–600
Respiration rate (/min.)	20–40	20–40	–
Body temperature (°C)	40–43	40–43	40–42
Number of chromosomes (2n)	–	–	–
Body surface (cm^2)	–	–	–
Water intake (ml/100 g/day)	–	–	–
Puberty (weeks)			
Female	5–6	6	40 days
Male	5	6	40 days
Breeding age (weeks)			
Female	6–8	6	50 days
Male	6–8	6	60 days
Weight of the egg (g)	50–60	–	9–10
Incubation period (days)	20–22	16–18	16
Weight at birth (g)	30–45	20	6–8
Blood parameters			
Blood volume (ml/kg)	78–92	78–92	78–92
Haemoglobin (g/100 ml)	8–12	11–15	–
Haematocrit (vol. %)	40	58	–
Leucocytes ($\times$ 1000/mm^3)	18–40	16–30	–
Glucose (mg/100 ml)	–	13–21	–

[1] Dependent upon the body weight (0.1–2.4 kg).
[2] Cocks: floor area 1800 cm^2; height 60 cm.

minimize or exclude reallocation and regrouping of the animals during the experiment.

The amount of ventilation which is required depends upon the number of animals, their size and the environmental temperature. The standard is

7 m³ of fresh air/hour/kg bodyweight, which needs to be of a low velocity. The optimum temperature for chicks which are between 1 and 3 days old is 35°C which should be provided by one or more heating lamps. After this age temperatures should be lowered gradually over the next 4 days at a rate of 0.5°C per day, and thereafter at 1°C per day, until the lower temperature of 18–21°C is reached.

Food and drink.   Food must be available immediately as the chicks hatch out, and needs to be supplied on flat dishes. The older animals can have their food in feeding troughs rationed according to the size of the chicks. Generally commercial feed is given, and the presence of grit is also essential in order to optimize the grinding of the food in the gizzard. Drinking water is usually provided via an automatic system with nipples, which require frequent checking.

Reproduction.   After copulation, several egg follicles will be fertilized, therefore there is no need for copulation to occur daily. The eggs are collected 2–4 times a day and, after disinfection, are incubated at 37°C with a relative humidity of 60%. During the first 18 days the eggs should be turned 3–5 times per day.

Handling and techniques.   Young chicks should be picked up in one hand with the thumb and index finger placed gently around the neck. When removing a fully grown hen from its cage, both hands will be necessary, with the fingers spread widely and the thumbs placed dorsally over the wings. These need to be positioned around the body of the hen in such a way that the bird's head is facing the handler. The hen can then be held under the handler's arm, facing backwards, whilst the handler fixes the legs with one hand. Fixation is possible by taking the wings together on its back. Thereafter the hen can be placed on its side.

Determining the sex of chicks is the work of a specialist. When they reach the age of 4–6 weeks hens and cocks can be differentiated by their external features. The cocks develop a prominent comb, their legs are thicker and they possess spurs. Hens can be marked for identification with (multicolored) rings on their legs or with numbers clipped to their wings.

Pigeons and doves

Origin and use.   There are approximately 650 species of pigeons. Over the centuries more than 800 breeds have developed. Pigeons (*Columba livia*) and doves (*Streptopelia risoria*) account for less than 0.1% of the total of experimental animals. They are used for research in the field of physiology, behaviour, pharmacokinetics and toxicology. The White Carneau, which is mainly used for its meat, is also used for research into atherosclerosis.

Housing.   Pigeons are best kept in large flocks. Given sufficient space and sufficient nest boxes or sitting places, rivalry will hardly ever occur in the indoor enclosures, even when one sex may predominate. This can, however, not be applied across the board for pigeons and doves, for example with turtle doves persistent quarrels will occur when the number of males exceeds that of females. Doves which are to be used as experimental animals can be accommodated individually in cages which are 40 × 40 × 40 cm, the front being made from metal bars, with provisions made for containers for feed and water. The floor can be made from metal bars which need to be 3 mm in thickness and 2 cm apart to permit faeces to pass through onto sand or paper. The racing pigeon can survive extremely low temperatures, but housing should provide an adequate shelter against rain and wind.

Food and drink.   Food for pigeons is commercially available as is food for turtle doves, although they require specialized feed. Drinking water is provided *ad libitum*. The containers for feed and water should preferably be situated outside the cages with access from the inside, in order to prevent contamination by faeces. Containers for water should be cleaned on a daily basis. Pigeons whose regime is undisturbed by human activity and kept under a light/dark schedule of 14:10 hours, have their maximum intake of food between 17.00 and 20.00 hours. The effect on blood values of substances administered via the food or the drinking water are markedly influenced by this physiological aspect.

Reproduction.   The breeding of pigeons is not difficult. Pigeons will breed all year round when kept indoors under appropriate light conditions. The females are monogamous as a rule and only break this if their own partner is unavailable. Egg production is initiated by copulation. In a normal and complete reproductive cycle, the female produces clutches of 2 eggs every 34–40 days. Veins from tobacco leaves are used as nesting material which helps to reduce feather lice and may be available from pet shops. Both parents are active in caring for and raising the squabs. They both produce crop milk which is the only food given to the young during the first 5–7 days of life. Young squabs grow very quickly and within 48 hours their birth weight has doubled, and by the 28th day the squabs are virtually fully grown. Artificial incubation of eggs is possible, but there are still problems encountered when trying to hand-rear the squabs. They must be kept at a temperature of about 32°C and frequently fed with a high protein and fat diet.

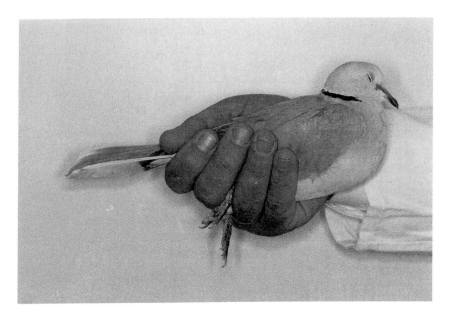

Fig. 3.12. Handling and restraining of a pigeon: the legs are fixed between the middle and ring finger, the tail and the tips of the wings are held by the thumb.

Handling and simple techniques.   The daily handling of pigeons and doves should be performed in a peaceful way. In the dark they can easily be picked up when dazzled with a light beam. Pigeons can either be held in one or both hands. When held in one hand, they should be placed in the palm of the hand, with their feet held between the middle and 4th finger, the thumb being free to hold the tail and the tips of the wings (fig. 3.12).

There is no sexual dimorphism in pigeons. Determining the sex of doves and pigeons requires a great deal of experience. In the male squab the eyes are generally further apart than in the female, and the head is flatter. Adult male pigeons have in general a heavier build than the females and the head is larger. If there is an element of doubt, then endoscopy should be performed to determine the sexual anatomy. Marking pigeons for identification can be done by fixing a ring permanently around the leg. This ring should be put on when the pigeons are only a few days old, and the size is determined by the species. Temporary marking is possible using rings which are simply bent around one of the legs (fig. 3.13).

Quail

Origin and use.   Approximately 600 years ago the quail (*Coturnix coturnix*) was domesticated in Japan. Since about 1950, the quail has been in use as

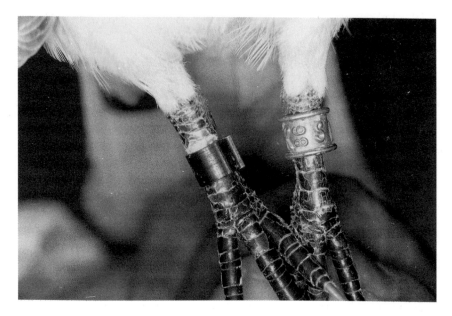

Fig. 3.13. Marking of birds for identification with a temporary (left) or a permanent (right)
ring around one of the legs.

an experimental animal, mainly due to its rapid reproduction of up to five
generations per year, and its high output of eggs which can number 80–90 in
100 days. Quails are used in embryological, pharmacological and toxicological
research.

Housing.   Quail can be housed in large groups, in cages with sawdust. A
disadvantage with these circumstances is that quail will not make a nest and
as a result the eggs will be spaced throughout the cage. It is better, therefore,
to house quails in small groups in separate cages. According to the European
guidelines, adult quail should have a minimum area of 200 cm^2 per animal,
if they are kept in groups of three or more. In small breeding groups, for
instance one male and 4 females, the females may be aggressive towards the
male. Individual housing is possible in small closed cages or wire mesh cages
with a minimum floor measurement of 350 cm^2 and a minimum height of
15 cm, but this type of housing is poor and does not meet their behavioural
needs.

The minimum environmental temperature depends upon the age of the
animals. Day-old chicks should be kept at 35–37°C, with localised heating
provided by an electric heating bulb. During the next few weeks, the temperature should be lowered gradually by 4–5°C per week, until a temperature

of 19–23°C is reached. A good ventilation system is necessary, both for the handlers and for the animals, as quails produce a penetrating smell. A prescribed velocity of 1.7 m³/hour/animal in growing animals is recommended and 30–35 m³ /hour/animal in the case of adult quails. The relative humidity does not appear greatly to influence quail. The day/night rhythm is important within breeding units, the norm being 14 hours of light and 10 hours of darkness.

Food and drink.   Due to the high growth rate and their egg production, quail require a food rich in protein and energy; e.g. turkey starter-crumbs have a crude protein content of 25–28% and 2 kcal/per g. Food and water can be provided in containers used for chicks.

Reproduction.   Egg production starts at an age of 40–45 days. This diminishes after the quail reach 26 weeks. In total they may lay up to 300 eggs per year. Eggs are primarily laid during the last 6 hours of the light period. In order to guarantee that the eggs are fertilized, 20 males and 40–50 females should be grouped and permanently housed together. For effective fertilization one male is necessary for every 2–3 females. Under these circumstances a fertilization rate of 80–90% can be expected. The best results are obtained using animals between 8 and 20 weeks old. The eggs will hatch after an (artificial) incubation period of 16 days.

Handling and simple techniques.   Quail tend to be nervous and need therefore to be approached quietly. The young chicks are very tiny and should be caught between the thumb and index finger. Fully grown quail need to be taken in one hand with the thumb on the breast, the index and middle finger over the wings, and the legs held between the ring and the little finger.

Sexing of young quail on the basis of anatomical differences in the cloaca requires a great deal of experience. Between the ages of 2–3 weeks, animals can be sexed by the colour of the breast feathers: in males these feathers are brown, whilst in the female they are grey with black spots.

Eggs and young quail are very vulnerable and should not be handled or transported if possible. If transportation is necessary then it should preferably be done when the quail is at least 4 weeks old. They are transported in cardboard boxes with a layer of sawdust.

Poikilothermic vertebrates

Reptiles

Use.   The use of reptiles, such as chelonians (turtles), snakes and lizards, in research is very limited. Main areas of research for which they are used are in zoology, immunology and endocrinology. Only some general features of reptiles will be discussed here.

Anatomy and physiology.   Reptiles are unable to regulate their body temperature by endothermic processes. The body temperature and related physiological processes depend on the environmental temperature and the presence of heating devices. The skin is thick and cornified and, in many reptiles (the squamata), provided with scales. The horny layer prevents dehydration to a large extent. The skin is, with a few exceptions, devoid of glands, which further minimizes evaporation and the loss of body fluids.

Housing and feeding.   Their anatomical and physiological characteristics imply that the reptiles' environment must be constructed in such a way that they can maintain their normal physiology. In their vivarium, reptiles must be given the opportunity of varying their distance from the heating device, thereby maintaining their own physiologically preferred body temperature.

Male lizards should be housed outside visual contact of each other, otherwise their instinct to defend their territory will keep them under constant stress. This also leads to disregulation of body temperature and a loss of appetite.

Many reptiles catch their prey and are very selective and specialized for this task. Some snakes will only eat (living) vertebrates and can be fed with freshly killed mice and/or rats; other species will only eat birds, whilst others still will eat insects, snails or fish. For omnivorous and insectivorous reptiles it is essential to add a multivitamin and mineral mixture to the fruit, vegetables or insects. For meat-eating reptiles, such as terrapins, the meat should have added calcium and vitamin A. Young animals should be provided with plenty of food.

Reproduction.   Reptiles kept in captivity may breed if exposed to seasonal fluctuations, with regard to day-length either by natural or artificial means. The majority of reptiles are oviparous. Under laboratory conditions the eggs are incubated artificially. A few species are ovoviviparous and in these species the young develop and hatch within the female's oviducts.

Handling and simple techniques. Restraining of snakes should be done with both hands: one directly after the head, the other around the second part of the body (fig. 3.14).

Sexing of reptiles requires experience. Chelonian males have a relatively large tail, both with regard to width and length. The opening of the cloaca is situated near the tip of the tail. With male lizards and snakes, if two hemipenises are retracted it is possible to see a pouch in the base of the tail. This can be examined by inserting a probe.

Marking of chelonians for identification purposes can be achieved by painting, or by putting a tab through a hole in the carapace or by making cuts in the non-living edge of the carapace. Snakes and lizards can be marked by branding them with an appropriately shaped piece of metal, cooled down in liquid nitrogen.

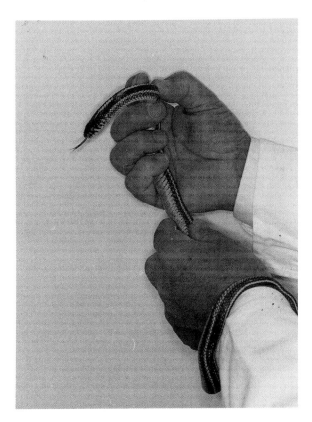

Fig. 3.14. Handling and restraining of a snake.

Amphibians

Use.   The African clawed toad (*Xenopus laevis*) and the axolotl or Mexican salamander (*Ambystoma mexicanum*) are the most generally used amphibians for experimental purposes. Both species lay fairly large fertilized eggs into water, which makes them of particular use in research concerning organogenesis.

Physiology.   Amphibians are not able to maintain an elevated body temperature via the endogenic production of energy. The skin is moist and contains many secretion glands. Amphibians have no firm cornified epidermis, and are therefore even more dependent upon and sensitive to environmental factors than are reptiles. Water can pass through the skin in both directions. The aquatic species, such as the clawed toad and the axolotl are particularly susceptible to dehydration. Respiration in amphibians is either via (external) gills at the larval stage or via lungs at the adult stage after metamorphosis has taken place. In both cases intake of oxygen across the skin is an additional route. In the axolotl, which is kept in vivaria in its larval stage, the external gills are a permanent feature. Larvae of the clawed toad metamorphosize at the age of 4 months. From that time onwards they depend upon the lungs for the exchange of gas. When metamorphosized a clawed toad will drown if respiration is blocked, because the intake of oxygen via the skin will be insufficient.

Axolotls are fully grown at around 18 months, and they may live to reach an age of 15 years. There are three known varieties according to colour: the colour which occurs in the wild which is browny-blackish, the white coloured form which has black eyes, and the albino variety which is yellowish with red eyes.

The clawed toad is fully grown at 12 months and they may live to reach a maximum age of 25 years. There are two known colour varieties: the colour which occurs in the wild which is browny-grey with black areas, and the albino which is white with red eyes, which also has three black claws on its hind legs. The lateral line system of clawed toads is visible with the naked eye and is seen as a symmetrical pattern of elongated greyish dots, each 2–3 mm in length. In both these species di-, tri- and tetraploid animals are in existence.

Housing and feeding.   Both of the species which have been discussed are strictly aquatic. They need to be kept in clean water, free from chlorine and copper, preferably in containers attached to running tap water to prevent the accumulation of waste products. Water depth should be approximately 30 cm, the pH value between 7.5 and 8.5, and the water temperature between 18 and 20°C. Variations in the ambient temperature in excess of 5°C may harm the animals. Exposure of the animals to direct sunlight should be avoided. Some shelter should be provided in the form of *Elodea canadensis* or a flower pot. When using an artificial source of light for a ratio of day to night of 12:12 hours, fluorescent tubes colour 33 (Philips), 40 W are appropriate.

Animals should be fed *ad libitum*, 3 times per week, with slices of meat into which a multivitamin and mineral mixture should have been intensively rubbed; it is not sufficient to merely powder the mixture over the meat. It is essential to leave the food in the container for one and a half hours, in order to ensure that each animal has had sufficient time to eat; any remnants remaining should be removed. Animals which are housed individually can be fed using a blunt pair of forceps. Over feeding will lead to vomiting.

Reproduction. For reproduction purposes animals aged between 2 and 5 years are used. The reproduction period of the axolotl is restricted to between December and July. One week prior to mating the water temperature should be kept at 22°C. The female will produce pheromones which stimulates the male into depositing spermatophores. The female positions herself over the cone-shaped spermatophores and takes them into her cloaca. When this has taken place the water temperature should be lowered to 12°C and oviposition will take place within 12 hours. If plastic threads are put into water the eggs will deposited on them, or otherwise the eggs are deposited on the floor of the vivarium. Eggs should be kept isolated in subdued lighting in order to create a restful environment. Females can be used every three months for reproduction.

Female clawed toads are about twice the size of the males. Males can be identified by the copulatory pads on their thumbs, which are a blackish colour, and are found on the inner side of the fore feet.

To induce oviposition, the males are injected with gonadotrophin; 24 hours later the females are given the same injection. The temperature of the water at that time should be 10°C. Eight hours after the hormonal treatment of the females, the water temperature should be gradually increased over an 8 hour period to 23°C. Prior to mating, the lips of the female's cloaca will become noticeable swollen. Amplexus then occurs, during which the male embraces the female around the loins with his forelegs. The female will then deposit eggs which can then be (artificially) fertilized.

Handling and identification. Axolotls and clawed toads should be lifted out of the water by hand, as the use of a net can damage them, in particular the axolotls. To hold the clawed toad securely it should be grasped around the hind legs. The handler's fingers should be placed at the top of the legs, near the body, while the body section should rest in the palm of the hand (fig. 3.15). Axolotls should be approached from the front with the thumb and

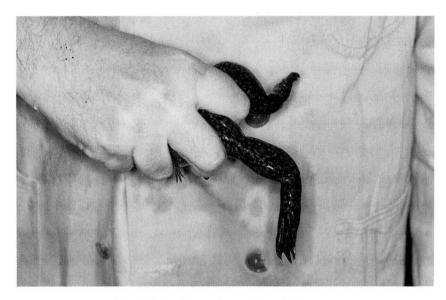

Fig. 3.15. Handling and restraining of a *Xenopus*.

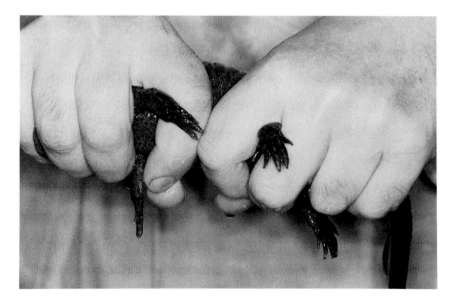

Fig. 3.16. Handling and restraining of an axolotl.

index finger of one hand placed around the body, just behind the gills, being careful not to damage them. The thumb and index finger of the second hand should be positioned just cranially to the hind legs with the tail in the palm of the second hand (fig. 3.16).

Fig. 3.17. Marking an amphibian for identification by means of auto-transplantation of a darker coloured piece of skin into the lighter coloured skin of the abdomen.

Marking of clawed toads for identification purposes can be performed by means of an autotransplant (under MS 222 anaesthesia), in which a piece of the lighter coloured abdominal wall is implanted into the animals back, or a piece of the darker coloured skin is implanted onto the abdomen (fig. 3.17).

Fish

Use.   Approximately 6–8% of experimental vertebrates are fish (cf. fig. 1.1). They have particular use in (environmental) toxicological research such as drinking water control. The main species which are used are the guppy (*Poecilia reticulata*), the zebra fish (*Brachydanio rerio*), the trout (*Salmo trutta*), and members of the carp family.

Physiology.   Fish are poikilotherms. This means that the body temperature and all physiological functions depend upon the temperature of the water. For example, both the body temperature and the oxygen consumption will diminish directly in relation to a lowering of the water temperature. Temperature stress, induced by rapid changes in the water temperature, will result in a rise of oxygen consumption. When the water temperature stabilizes after such a change, the fish will need approximately one week to adjust their oxygen consumption to the normal level for that specific temperature. Lifting a fish out of the water or transporting the fish will result in stress, which may lead to behavioural disturbances. The time required for restoration of normal behaviour will vary, depending upon the severity of the stress. Recovery from severe stress, such as being imported from tropical areas, may require an 8–12 week recovery period. Extreme temperatures may also lead to stress which will lower the animal's resistance to infection.

The skin of fish is covered with a mucous layer. Damage to this layer, by dehydration, through rough handling, or by placing the fish on a dry piece of cloth or paper tissue, will destroy its first defensive barrier and may facilitate local or even systemic infections.

The growth and life span of a fish depends on the species, but is also related to the circumstances under which the animals are kept. The goldfish (*Carassius auratus*) can reach 8 cm in length within 9 months, given a water temperature of 22°C. There can, however, be marked variations in growth within one clutch of eggs of externally identical parents. In outdoor ponds, a length of 8 cm can be reached after the fishes' second summer, at an age of 12–15 months. The goldfish has a maximum life span of 15 years; by contrast the zebrafish has a life span of approximately 4 years.

Housing. For most freshwater fish originating from moderate climatic zones, optimal temperatures range from 8 to 16°C. Variations in temperature should not exceed 5°C at a speed of more than 1°C per hour. The pH of the water should be between 6.5 and 8.5. When tap water is used, it should be free from chlorine and copper. In general, the best way to keep fish is in a system with flowing water. The temperature-controlled water should be put into the tank in the form of a shower, with a flow length of 20–30 cm. This is to ensure that there is an exchange of gasses which were under pressure in the pipeline system, and to ensure a minimum O_2 content of 7–10 ppm. The outlet should be situated at water level. A separator, usually made of perforated aluminum, will prevent the escape of fish via the drain. Both the aquarium and the filtering system, should be installed at least 2 weeks prior to the actual start of the experiment. This is particularly important with biological filtering systems, to ensure an optimal detoxification and denitrification of the tank water. The number of fish kept per volume of water will vary according to the species. In a closed system, with a biological filter the general rule is 1 gram of fish per litre of water. In general, 12–16 hours of daylight and/or artificial illumination should be given.

Food. Commercial fish food is available for carp, trout, catfish, and eel. Such food can also be used for related fish species. In general, fish should be fed once a day, but the amount of food has to be adapted according to the circumstances. A general rule is to provide the amount of food which can be eaten within 15 minutes. An excess of unused food will lead to putrefaction, to the production of toxic substances such as ammonia and nitrite, to a shortage in oxygen, and to changes in the pH of the water. Such changes may lead to the death of the fish. Consequently any remnants of food together with faeces should be removed.

Reproduction. There are wide variations in the reproductive system of fish; the majority are oviparous, some, such as the guppy, are ovoviviparous. The methods of depositing and fertilizating the eggs are species specific. Some species, such as the eel cannot be bred in captivity, whereas the guppy (*P. reticulata*) is bred with relative ease. Female guppies are placed in a "birth receptacle", which should be at least 40 cm in length. This birth receptacle is constructed in such a way that the young can escape and will not therefore be eaten by the mother. An optimal temperature for young guppies is between 25 and 28°C, at a pH of 7. The largest females produce the largest number of offspring. The average period between births is approximately 31 days.

Handling and identification. For movement of a single fish to another aquarium, the fish should be lifted carefully out of the water by hand or caught with a net. When fish are taken out of the water, they should be placed on a moist surface, in order to prevent damage to the mucous layer covering the skin.

Determination of sex can be very difficult depending on species. In the case of the guppy, however, males are smaller than females, their dorsal fin is elongated caudally and their abdominal fin is almost as long as the copulatory organ (gonopodium). The female has a rounded or an only slightly elongated dorsal fin.

For the temporary identification of fish a small piece of a fin can be clipped away.

Literature

Baker H J, Lindsey R J, Weisbroth S H, eds. The laboratory rat. Vol. 1–2. New York: Academic Press Inc., 1979.

Cook M J. The anatomy of the laboratory mouse. New York: Academic Press Inc., 1965.

Cooper G, Schiller A. Anatomy of the guinea pig. Cambridge, Mass.: Harvard University Press, 1975.

Foster H L, Small J D, Fox J G, eds. The mouse in biomedical research. Vol. 1–4, Academic Press Inc., N.Y., 1981.

Guide to the care and use of experimental animals. Vol. 1 and 2. Ottawa: Canadian Counsel on Animal Care, 1980.

Harkness J E, Wagner J E. The biology and medicine of rabbits and rodents. Philadelphia: Lea & Febiger, 1983.

Hebel R, Stromberg M W. Anatomy and embryology of the laboratory rat. Baltimore: Williams & Wilkins, 1988.

Popesko P, Rajtová V, Horák J. A colour atlas of the anatomy of small laboratory animals. Vol. 1 and 2. London: Wolfe Publishing Ltd., 1992.

Sanderson J H, Philips C E. An atlas of laboratory animal haematology. Oxford: Clarendon Press, 1981.

Siegel HI, ed. The hamster. Reproduction and behavior. New York: Plenum Press, 1985.

UFAW Handbook on the care and management of laboratory animals. Harlow: Longman Scientific & Technical, 1987.

Wagner J E, Manning P J, eds. The biology of the guinea pig. New York: Academic Press Inc., 1976.

Weissbroth S H, Flatt R E, Krans A L, eds. The biology of the laboratory rabbit. New York: Academic Press Inc., 1974.

Williams W. Anatomy of the mongolian gerbil (Meriones unguiculatus). West Brookfield, Mass.: Tumblebook Farm Inc., 1974.

4　Behaviour, stress, and well-being

Introduction

During the 20th century, the nature of the relationship between human beings and animals has changed considerably. In mankind's early history, cattle were used to provide food, clothes and labour. By a process of gradual domestication, wild animals have been turned into domestic animals and later into pet animals as well. This process has taken many centuries to develop. The first animals used for experimental purposes were, as a rule, from the domesticated groups i.e. pigs, dogs, cats, chickens, rabbits, etc. Industrialization in the second half of the 19th century caused an important change in the traditional relationship between animals and man. With the commencement of intensive livestock farming and the breeding of animals specifically for experimental purposes, both housing conditions and care for the animals changed rapidly. In particular during recent decades, changes in size, structure and the interior of housing systems along with density and group composition are such that animals frequently have problems to adapt to these conditions. Modern housing systems for farm and experimental animals often give rise to abnormalities in behaviour and physiology, mainly due to the fact that these conditions do not appear to fulfil the minimum environmental requirements.

It is man's moral obligation to keep animals in a state of optimal well-being. Also, from a practical standpoint, it is essential to avoid causing serious suffering to animals during experimentation, as this may give rise to deviations in experimental results.

With this in mind, the EC has formulated the "Directive for the protection of vertebrate animals used for experimental and other scientific purposes" (see chapter 2). One of the fundamental paragraphs within the Directive states that all experimental animals must be provided with suitable housing, environment, adequate freedom of movement, food, water and care appropriate to their health and well-being. Any constraints on the physiological needs of the animal or ethological needs should be kept to the absolute minimum (art. 5). This paragraph has wide consequences on a practical level, and demands a detailed and thorough knowledge of the biology of the various animal species being used. As seen in chapter 3, many uncertainties along with a lack of sufficient knowledge, do still exist.

What then are the environmental desiderata, which of them are essential, and to what extent are behaviour, physiology, and well-being affected when animals are deprived of some of their needs? This chapter will discuss in general terms the behavioural and physiological mechanisms which allow mammals to adapt to environmental challenges. Attention will also be given to the constraints within these adaptation mechanisms, to the development of stress-pathology, and to the consequences for the animals' well-being.

Basic mechanisms

Homeostasis

A useful concept when discussing stress, adaptation and well-being in animals is "homeostasis". This implies that aspects of both the internal milieu (such as body temperature, blood glucose, water content of the body, etc.) and those of the environment (such as positioning within a social group etc.) will be kept at a constant or at least a predictable level for a certain period of time. An animal can only maintain homeostasis when it can compare its actual situation with the norm for certain internal or external factors, and when it has the behavioural and physiological means to realize the norm. Figure 4.1 depicts the most basic form of such a homeostatic regulatory mechanism.

Environmental factors may challenge the biological balance. So long as the animal is able to adapt to these changes without any problems, it is said to be

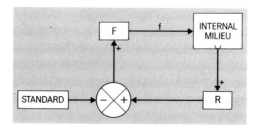

Fig. 4.1. Principle of a homeostatic mechanism. The actual state of the internal milieu is detected by a receptor mechanism (R) and compared with an internal standard. A difference between the observed situation and the expectation will activate mechanisms (F) which will normalize the situation.

in homeostasis or in harmony. However, when an animal is unable to maintain homeostasis, stress will develop in the course of time. This can manifest itself as abnormal behaviour or disease. Clearly, in such a situation the animal will suffer or its well-being will be reduced. Accordingly, the lawyer Albert Lorz in his comments to the German Tierschutzgesetz (Animal Protection Act) defined well-being as "living in physical and psychological harmony with the environment" a definition which is not far from a state of homeostasis. Later in this chapter we will discuss the issue of animal well-being in greater detail.

Two quite distinctive mechanisms are involved when considering the capacity of animals to adapt to the environmental challenges in every-day life within a natural habitat. Firstly, in the course of evolution the animals have been selected from amongst a population of genetically different organisms, because they can cope the best with the environmental demands morphologically, physiologically, and behaviourally. This type of selection forms the basis of speciation (phylogeny). The second mechanism is selection by the individual itself, i.e. the selection from a variety of potential behavioural solutions to the demands of the environment. This mechanism (which is learning) is especially important during the development of the individual (ontogeny) but also in the adult. These two selection mechanisms lead to behaviour in animals which is adapted to the environment.

Phylogeny

Many studies have shown that behaviour has a firm genetic basis. This is due to the fact that, in the course of evolution, the more poorly genetically adapted individuals have been eliminated. This form of selection is the basis of species-specific behaviour, as well as the species-specific morphology and physiology of animals, including that of present day experimental animals. In their original, natural habitat, animals are characterized according to the adequacy of their morphology, behaviour, and physiology. The regulatory range of homeostatic mechanisms is therefore geared up to and restricted to the environmental variation which the animal might meet in its everyday life. Therefore, the adequacy of homeostatic mechanisms may fail, should changes in the environment suddenly require completely different characteristics of these mechanisms. For example, when a wild animal is kept in a cage which radically differs from its natural habitat, it may repeatedly exhibit maladaptive behaviour. By so doing it will be indicating the feelings of constraint due to obstruction of the inherited adaptive capacity.

During the process of domestication, experimental animals have acquired new specific characteristics. This does not mean, however, that species-specific behaviour has disappeared; generally speaking only minor aspects will change. Behaviour which is essential for survival (i.e. feeding, nest building and social

Fig. 4.2. Species-specific behaviour: even after many generations of domestication, a pregnant
female rat will try to build a nest even though the type of bedding is not suitable.

behaviour such as offensive, defensive, sexual, and parental behaviour) is
strongly genetically determined. This will be present in the offspring even
when selection is not in their favour. These species-specific behaviours cannot,
or at least not without great difficulty, be changed by experience, and they will
be performed even though the environment does not allow for full expression
of these behaviours (fig. 4.2).

Selection by the environment is an important factor in the phylogeny of
adaptive behaviour. Animals are, however, not fully dependent upon genetically programmed behaviour. Individual animals can, within their genetic
limits change their behavioural repertoire by learning during both ontogeny
and adulthood.

Learning

The phenotype of an individual is the result of a complex interaction between
genotype and a specific environmental problem. One important, and therefore
an intensively studied aspect of the phenotype, is the ability of learning

based upon genotype and specific experiences. Learning is a mechanism which allows both flexible and rapid behavioural adaptation to short-term changes in the environment. There are, however, considerable species-specific constraints with regard to learning abilities. One of these constraints involves the stimuli which any given animal is able to perceive. Behavioural studies have shown that certain stimuli will elicit species-specific behaviour even in the absence of any previous experience. These stimuli, known as sign stimuli, represent environmental aspects which have species-specific significance to the animal. Given certain internal conditions, this significance will not change and will have a fixed relationship to certain behaviours. A classic example is the red belly of a male stickleback during the reproductive season. This red belly acts as a sign stimulus in eliciting aggressive behaviour from other male sticklebacks.

The remaining stimuli can be associated with behaviour via learning processes, and as such may gain certain significance or may change in significance (Pavlovian stimulus conditioning). The first response of an animal to an unknown stimulus (for example a noise of certain intensity) is arousal and — in many cases — an orientation response. If the stimulus has no consequences (either positive or negative) to the individual, after repeated presentations it will no longer respond. This process of habituation thus prevents the organism from reacting to irrelevant stimuli. If, however, the stimulus is associated with positive or negative consequences, learning takes place, in this case stimulus conditioning. Both habituation and conditioning, however, may disappear. When a stimulus to which the animal has become habituated is absent for a period of time, then the original orientation response will emerge again. Similarly, when a conditioned stimulus frequently occurs in the absence of the associated unconditioned stimulus, the reaction to this stimulus will also disappear. The organism will have learned that the stimulus is of no further significance. Sign stimuli will, however, neither totally habituate nor wholly disappear, if either does occur, it will only be for a very short period of time.

An organism can also learn that behaviour has pleasant or unpleasant consequences. This conditioning of behaviour or operant conditioning can lead to an increase or decrease in frequency of performance when considering certain behaviours under specific environmental conditions. For example, rats generally prefer the dark. When put into the illuminated side of a two-chambered box, they will usually move to the dark side immediately. If this response is followed by a punishment however (e.g. a weak electric shock), then the next time they are placed into the light side, they will stay there, i.e. they have learned to avoid the "unpleasant" situation.

The same mechanisms which are involved in stimulus conditioning are also involved in the conditioning of behaviour. These learning processes can be thought of as mechanisms involved in the capacity of animals to distinguish causal relationships within their environment, i.e. to distinguish information from noise.

Usually both stimulus and operant conditioning will occur simultaneously, and will take place with respect to both pleasant and aversive situations.

There are large variations between species with regard to learning processes, not only in the degree to which learning is important in behavioural adaptation, but also to the types of behaviour that can be changed through learning. It is not possible to associate every stimulus with all subsequent events in the same way that not every type of behaviour can be used to obtain the desired effect. With rats, for example, it is almost impossible to associate light or sound stimuli with a subsequent illness induced by poisoned water, but an association can very easily be made between the taste of the water and the illness. It is virtually impossible to teach hamsters to obtain food by using grooming behaviour, whereas this can easily be taught using other operants such as digging or exploring. When certain housing systems require a learning process, for example to obtain food or water, it has to be realized that the particular combination of stimulus and operant is one that can easily be learned by the animals. Many chickens kept in battery cages have died due to their inability to learn that to obtain water they had to peck at the water nipple.

Knowledge of the environment, in combination with the available behavioural and physiological tools, allows the animal to maintain homeostasis. While this knowledge is based upon learning processes, there are considerable constraints in learning. Species have specific programmes when obtaining food and water, but also with regard to reproduction and social contacts etc. Many of these programmes have within them a certain degree of rigidity and cannot be changed through learning, i.e., certain components cannot be omitted without there being consequences for the animal. For example, in young mammals, food has to be obtained by sucking. Similarly, feeding has to be accompanied by rooting in pigs, or by digging and scratching in chickens or by gnawing in rodents. When these behaviours become redundant due to the supply, for example, of ready made food, they may be redirected to other objects or individuals, manifesting itself in feather pecking in chickens, or mutual sucking in calves. A good housing system should therefore suit the species-specific behaviour programmes of the animals.

Ontogeny

Ontogeny makes a large contribution with regard to adaptation capacities of the organism during adulthood, within its genetic limits of course. Both prenatal and postnatal factors have considerable influence on both the behavioural and the physiological characteristics of the adult offspring. In mammals the internal milieu of the mother will affect the development of the offspring from the moment of conception. For example, offspring from mothers which experienced stress during pregnancy or nursing will show different social behaviour in adulthood. Not only is the relationship with the mother important, but also experiences with conspecific animals will be important in the development of adult social behaviour. The complexity and variability of the environment will also largely affect the development of exploratory behaviour and learning capacity. There are two important aspects of behaviour that determine the adult capacity to adapt to environmental challenges.

The periods in ontogeny during which certain behaviour can be affected by environmental factors are more or less limited. A clear example of the significance of such sensitive periods in life is imprinting. This is the learning and long-term consolidation of the significance of stimuli (conspecific animals, food), and the orientation of behaviour towards the stimulus. Imprinting is an important phenomenon in many birds and mammals in which the young are fully developed after hatching or birth and can follow their mother from the beginning. In such precocial or nidifugous species, the young are imprinted to the mother. In many precocial species of mammals, the mother becomes attached to her young during a very short sensitive period immediately after giving birth. Pet animals which have contacts both with conspecific animals as well as with human beings during a critical period of life, may develop a double bond to their own species as well as to human beings.

The period during which behaviour patterns develop is generally limited. Modulating behaviour beyond the sensitive period is difficult and sometimes even impossible. For example, male rhesus monkeys which had no playful mounting experiences with conspecifics in their first year of life will have serious difficulties in performing normal sexual behaviour in adult life. The species-specific performance of agonistic behaviour also appears to depend upon the playful, non-violent type of aggression, performed in the early years. Deprivation of conspecifics, or insufficient space for normal social relationships, may result in abnormal behaviour patterns which may seriously disrupt social groups.

An important question for animal research is how to house experimental animals, taking not only the requirements of the experiment into account, but also of the environmental conditions which are necessary for the animal itself with regard to its species and specifically individual habits. Experiments on deprivation show that animals raised under conditions which lacking stimuli, will have serious problems when coping with more complex (social) stimuli as an adult. It seems that conditions of rearing must fulfil certain species and strain-specific conditions. Only under these conditions will animals develop the full capacity to cope with environmental challenges.

Interaction between the animal and its environment

The relationship of animals with regard to aspects of their environment is such that certain behaviour is strongly linked to certain specific locations. For example, Calhoun in a study of wild rats describes that the incidence of aggression is largely area-specific. He observed a male rat transporting a piece of cake it had found outside its territory. During this process the animal dropped some cake, which meant it had to run back and forth several times. At a given moment, the animal noticed that an unfamiliar male had intruded into its territory. Immediately an aggressive interaction followed and the intruder was chased away from the territory. However, only a few minutes later the same male which intruded was eating the pieces of cake which were dropped outside the territory and the territorial animal peacefully joined the meal. Such examples demonstrate that within a certain area intruders are not acceptable, whereas outside this area a certain degree of tolerance exists.

An animal will familiarize itself with its environment by means of exploratory behaviour before it will start feeding in, or defending the area. In fact, an unfamiliar environment will elicit physiological (endocrine) responses which cannot be distinguished from other arousing or even painful stimuli such as weak electric shocks. By exploring its environment, the animal develops a kind of neural map. This can be illustrated by a classical experiment using a maze in which there were three routes leading from the starting point to the finish, where there was some food. The three routes differed in length: a short, a medium, and a long route. Hungry rats were placed inside the maze. After a period of exploration all the rats used the short route to the reward. As part of the experiment, the short route was barred using a sliding door (see fig. 4.3). Having discovered the blockade, most rats used the longest route instead of first trying the medium one. It seems as if they chose the secure side of the design.

The concept of cognitive maps was introduced to explain this phenomenon, indicating that the behaviour of animals in their home territory is not only guided by simple reflexes and habits, but also by knowledge of the environment. Subsequent experiments confirmed these ideas which were at first disputed. Now it is widely recognized that animals develop a detailed knowledge of the spatial structure of their environment. In vertebrates, the main central nervous structure involved in this cognitive mapping is the hippocampus. In this structure of the brain, neurons respond in relation to the location of the animal in its environment, irrespective of its behaviour at that location. Other neurons are active when the animal is at another location.

This knowledge of the environment depends, of course, on the sensory capacities of the animal. In this respect there are large differences across the species. Consider, for example, the ability of rodents or bats when detecting

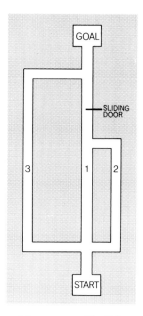

Fig. 4.3. Schematic representation of the maze used by Tolman. 1. short route, 2 medium route, 3 long route.

ultrasonic sounds, the ability of mammals detecting minimal amounts of specific odours, or the sensitivity of pigeons and chickens to the flicker-frequency of ordinary fluorescent light. It is very important then to realize that each animal species (or individuals, depending on experience, sex, and age) has its own way of life. Von Uexküll called all the aspects of the environment which can be perceived (Merkwelt) and those which can be influenced (Wirkwelt) by an individual, the Umwelt of the organism (fig. 4.4).

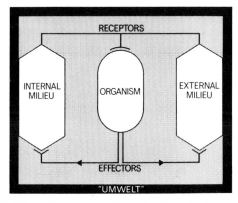

Fig. 4.4. Schematic representation of the Umwelt of an organism.

This Umwelt includes both an internal and an external component, which are closely interconnected. Any question concerning the housing and care of a certain species should first consider the Umwelt of males, females, and juveniles of the species.

The Umwelt of an animal is not comparable to ours, and therefore seemingly small changes in a housing system (i.e. ventilation, hygiene, care, etc.), may often have a drastic effect on the animals. For experimental animals, such as rats and mice, odours are an essential component of their Umwelt. Changes in the pattern of scentmarks in their environment may elicit reactions in the animals which are similar to those elicited by other unfamiliar factors. Not only physical but also social aspects, such as the relationship between individuals of a species, belong to their Umwelt. Such relationships are apparent as some animals will seek contact with each other whilst avoiding others. The way in which this works often communicates the idea that animals know each other individually, as illustrated by the mother-child relationship. Clearly a bond exists between the two that not only covers the nursing and safety of the child, but is also stress reducing. When such a bond is disrupted, several emotional expressions such as behavioural agitation and neuroendocrine stress responses will emerge, both in the mother and in the child.

Apart from the mother-child interactions, relationships may exist between individual animals of a certain species which are not only strongly emotional in nature, but are also strongly stabilizing. For example, specific male–female combinations of tree shrews (*Tupaia*) almost immediately form a harmonious pair-bond. In such a pair, both partners show a persistent reduction in heart rate and catecholamine levels in their blood, an improved immunological resistance, decreased physiological responses to external stressful stimuli and optimal reproductive success. This is in direct contrast to the non-harmonious pairs which have to be separated to prevent serious stress-related pathology. Clearly individuals of a certain species may like or dislike certain conspecifics. It is vital to take this into account when groups of animals are formed and put into a stable or cage. The individual differences in a group may be so great that it cannot be maintained in that specific composition. So far, little knowledge is available on the factors involved in the stability of social groups. Possibly the distinction between types of individuals (such as the active and passive copers mentioned later on) plays a role. Such a distinction can be important to the development of a social hierarchy, because the two types of animals seem to have a different predisposition to be either the dominant or the subordinates in a social group.

It is often questioned to what an extent such stabilizing or disrupting factors exist in the relationship between animals and human beings. There is evidence to show that they do exist, for instance, in pig husbandry, a human factor appears to be involved in the growth and reproduction of the animals.

In laboratory rats, handling has also been shown to affect age-related changes in behaviour and physiology. Although more experiments are needed in this field, these results would seem to indicate that the way humans interact with animals may affect the health of these animals, and hence the quality of the experimental results.

To summarize, the social contacts amongst animals as well as those between animals and human beings may be important to the health and well-being of the animals. With this in mind, animals who live in social groups should only be housed in isolation when it is unavoidable due to the nature of the experiment. It should also be taken into account that non-human vertebrates are individuals and come to the experimental procedures with their own, unique background.

Animals have not only knowledge of spatial aspects of their environment, but also of the way in which events precede or follow on from each other. As mentioned in the paragraph on learning, this knowledge is based on stimulus and operant conditioning. Stimulus conditioning allows the animal to predict certain events in its environment, for example the entrance of the animal caretaker predicts food. By means of operant conditioning the animal learns which behaviour will cause significant changes in its Umwelt, e.g. obtaining food or avoiding a rival. This process of reasoning implies that animals have expectations about future events. These expectations are not, however, always realized. It is possible to observe emotional expressions when the reality appears to differ from what was expected. Emotional expressions can be seen

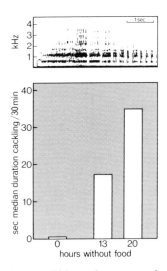

Fig. 4.5. Below: whenever hungry chickens do not get the expected food, they perform "cackling". Upper figure: sonogram of one "cackle".

for example in dogs by tail wagging, piloerection, various facial expressions, vocalizations such as yelping or screaming, along with physiological reactions such as heart-rate changes. These emotional expressions will emerge when the organism's certainty of its environment changes. One good example of this is given in fig. 4.5 which illustrates the fact that whenever an expected event does not occur, chickens will cackle as a form of emotional expression. These emotional expressions also sometimes have a signalling function with regard to conspecifics.

Predictability and controllability

Central to modern stress research are the terms controllability and predictability. The importance of these terms can be illustrated by a classical experiment. The experimental conditions are given in fig. 4.6. Three rats are put into three identical cages with their tails extending through the back wall. Electrodes are connected to the tails. For the animals 1 and 2 the electrodes are then connected to a shock generator. The wiring of the system is such, that weak electric shocks can be given which are identical in frequency, duration, intensity and occurrence. Rat number 3 serves as a control animal and therefore does not receive any electric shocks. Each rat has in front of them a light which can go on and off and a wheel which can move. In the case of rat 1 the light was presented at certain intervals which was followed by a shock after 10 seconds (stimulus conditioning, see above). The same number of signals and shocks were also presented to rat 2, but without a clear relationship between the signals and the adverse shocks. In a different experiment, rat 1 can switch

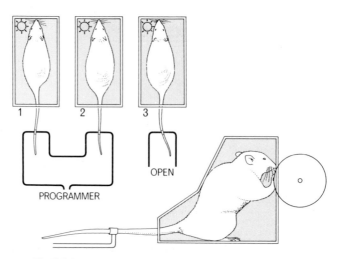

Fig. 4.6. Layout of the experiments by Weiss. See text.

off the shock by turning the wheel (operant conditioning, see above), whereas rat 2 also has a wheel, but one which is not connected to the shock generator. With these conditions the predictability and the controllability of the stressor can be manipulated during the experiment.

Although rats 1 and 2 received exactly the same number and intensity of shocks, the stress symptoms varied considerably. Rat number 2 who could not predict and had no control over the electric shock, suffered from severe damage to its stomach wall, showed signs of immunosuppression, and had the largest rise of plasma corticosterone (see also below). In fact rat 1, who could control or predict the stressor showed only minor differences in stress symptoms compared with rat number 3 who received no shocks at all. It can be concluded then, that it is the degree to which a stressor can be controlled or predicted which will determine the severity of stress symptoms, and not the stressor in itself.

Using this type of data as a basis, the following definitions of stress can be formulated:

– acute stress is the state of an organism which occurs after a sudden decrease in the predictability and/or the controllability of relevant environmental changes.

– chronic stress is the state of an organism when relevant environmental aspects have a low predictability and/or are not or not very well controllable over a long period of time.

The distinction between predictability and controllability is significant. While predictability is closely associated with stimulus conditioning, controllability is the result of operant conditioning. Controllability itself implies predictability, whereas the reverse is not necessarily true. For example, animals in certain housing systems may easily be able to predict the delivery of food, but this event may be totally outside the control of the animals. The absence of control over an aspect of life as important as food can be an important stress-eliciting factor within some housing systems.

Conflict behaviour and behavioural pathology

When acute stress is defined as a state induced by a situation of increased uncertainty, it is conceivable that these situations will induce a type of conflict. Conflict situations are part of daily life, and the accompanying conflict behaviour has been described extensively in ethology. Conflict behaviours falls in a group which includes certain agonistic behaviours (a mixture of aggression and flight), ambivalent behaviour, redirected behaviour, and adjunctive or displacement behaviour.

– Agonistic behaviour may occur when an organism is prevented from reaching its goal. An animal may for example attack an innocent conspecific given a situation in which a lever which after been pressed usually resulted in a food reward, suddenly did not deliver food any more.

– Ambivalent behaviour may occur when an organism has both a tendency to approach or to avoid a goal situation. When the two tendencies are equally strong this may result in circling movements around the goal, in which the side which tends towards the goal wants to approach, whereas the side tending away from the goal wants to avoid. In this uncertain situation, both tendencies are expressed simultaneously.

– Redirected behaviour can be observed when an organism cannot reach the goal or when it is afraid of the goal. In this situation, behaviour may be directed towards a replacement object.

– Adjunctive behaviour is characterized by the fact that it has seemingly little or no relationship to the conflict. For example, during a fight, cocks may suddenly start grooming or pecking the ground as if to start feeding. Adjunctive behaviour is often situation specific and may therefore have a signal value to conspecifics.

These conflict behaviours are often characterized by the fact that their duration span is short and their intensity is exaggerated, which is typical for acute stress situations, such as the emotional expressions mentioned above.

In a situation where such conflicts cannot be resolved, and are of a more permanent nature, chronic stress will occur. The evidence available indicates that the original conflict behaviour will modify into deviant behaviour. The best known pathological forms of behaviour are behavioural stereotypes and behaviour which causes damage to the animal itself or to its conspecifics. Damaging behaviours such as feather pecking in chickens housed on grid floors, tail biting of pigs housed on a concrete floor, and the grazing of oneanother's fur in mice, seems to stem from redirected behaviour. Similarly, socially isolated monkeys may bite their fingers, and mink used in the commercial fur farming are often reported as to be seriously damaging their tails, due to continuous sucking. Although the origin of this deviant behaviour is not always known, the conclusion can be drawn that it indicates serious shortcomings with regard to housing conditions and care.

A second group of behavioural pathologies, the stereotypes, are frequently observed in different animal species kept in captivity for example zoo animals, farm animals, pets and laboratory animals. Stereotypes are characterized as follows:
– they have a relatively simple construction and are constant
– they are repeated frequently
– they seem to have no specific purpose
– the form and expression of stereotypes are characteristic to the individual.

Stereotypes can be considered to be ritualizations of conflict behaviours. Studies using tethered sows, or voles kept in small cages showed that these stereotypes can be reduced through the use of the opioid antagonist naloxone. This would suggest that the occurrence of stereotypes is in some way associated with the release from the central nervous system of endorphin, which has an analgesic action. This finding may elucidate the functional significance of stereotypes. When taking this view, stereotypes may be biologically significant to the animal but one has to realize that the incidence of stereotypes indicates that the animals have been (or still are) in a state of chronic stress. Hence, housing conditions within which stereotypes develop, should be avoided.

The ability to cope and individual differentiation

The question as to whether an animal can control the situation successfully, i.e. can cope with the environmental demands or not, depends upon the mechanisms the animal has available to deal with the environmental challenge and upon the individual appraisal of the situation. When the situation is considered to threaten homeostasis (predictability), mechanisms are activated to cope with or to control the situation. Both the appraisal and the available coping mechanisms will depend upon the genotype and the phenotype of the individual. Not only the reaction to a stressor will vary, but also the type of reaction seems to differ amongst individuals. In a number of animal species, including human beings, different methods of coping can be seen.

In rats and mice, and presumably in a number of other species, two extremes of reactions can be seen. One group of animals react with an active coping style, characterized by attempts actively to control the environment. This can be seen, for example, in the form of the active defense of the home territory, flight in the presence of a dominant and active avoidance of shock. This type of stress response was originally described as the fight/flight response. A second type of coping style is characterized by a predominantly passive acceptance of the situation. For example, these animals will not defend territory, will freeze when approached by a dominant and are poor at avoiding aversive stimuli. This passive style of coping is also called the conservation-withdrawal response. Recent studies indicate that these two styles may appear to be alternative solutions to a problem but that both may lead to some kind of environmental control. For example, as far as the avoidance of attacks by a dominant male is concerned, active escape has in the short term the same result as quietly hiding in the corner of a cage.

Animals employing an active coping style are usually the ones that are active in social groups and may be found in the dominant and subdominant positions. Animals with a passive coping style are usually the subordinate animals in a given group. It can be presumed that individual differentiation is in principle present in every socially living vertebrate. The degree to which this differentiation will be expressed in captivity will depend upon the degree to which the housing system allows for the formation of social groups. In this context, factors such as group size and composition, sex-ratio, and available space are important.

Social relationships will always contribute to the variation between experimental animals. It is important to realize that this variation is not only of a quantitative but also of a qualitative nature. Reduction of this natural variation will implicate a form of selection of the experimental results.

Interaction between environment and physiology

Behaviour is an important way to obtain and maintain homeostasis of both the internal and external milieu. Physiological processes, however, also play an important role. For example, when an animal is put into a cold environment, it will reduce its heat loss not only by building a nest, but also by reducing its peripheral blood flow. In addition to this, it will increase heat production by shivering and by increasing its metabolism. An environmental challenge (stressor) will therefore always induce a strongly integrated behavioural and physiological response. This integrated response is initiated and coordinated by the central nervous system (CNS). With regard to the physiological response, the CNS has two major pathways at its disposal; the autonomic nervous system and the endocrine system (see fig. 4.7).

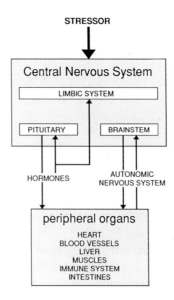

Fig. 4.7. Interaction between the central nervous system and peripheral physiology.

The autonomic nervous system

The autonomic nervous system has two major subdivisions; the (ortho-) sympathetic and the parasympathetic branches. With only a few exceptions, all organs are innervated by these two systems. At the beginning of this century, it was Cannon who recognized the importance of the sympathetic nervous system and its innervation of the adrenal medulla in the physiological response to stressors. A stressor may result in a sympathetic mass discharge, i.e. a virtually total activation of the whole sympathetic nervous system. Due to the widespread distribution of sympathetic nerve fibres, this mass discharge will be seen in a wide variety of physiological parameters such as an increase in plasma adrenaline and noradrenaline levels, an increase in heart-rate and blood pressure, an elevation of body temperature and changes in the immune system. Cannon called this pattern of reactions the fight-flight response because the whole pattern is consistent with the physiological preparation for physical activity. The sympathetic mass discharge will only emerge in the most extreme cases. Recent studies show that sympathetic activity can also be restricted to within certain parts of the system. For example psychological stressors usually result in an increase in plasma adrenaline due to the selective activation of the adrenal medulla, whereas noradrenaline released from the sympathetic nerve endings is generally associated with physical activity.

Both the sympathetic branch and the parasympathetic branch of the autonomic nervous system are active in reaction to a stressor. The fact that the two systems are generally balanced in their activity can be seen by the cardiovascular response to a stressor. The handling of an animal usually results in an increase in heart-rate and an increase in plasma catecholamines, which indicates an increase in sympathetic activity. When the animal is subsequently placed in a cage where it had previously experienced an aversive event, a sudden drop in heart-rate may occur even though the levels of plasma catecholamines may have continued rising. This relative decrease in heart-rate or bradycardia is due to an increased parasympathetic activity. This can be seen by the disappearance of the bradycardia response, having blocked cholinergic neurotransmission by means of atropine. This example illustrates the general presence of a balance in activity between the two components of the autonomic nervous system, and also how the two can be activated separately by specific stressors.

The neuroendocrine system

The hypothalamus-pituitary system generally determines the neuroendocrine response to stressors. The system that is classically involved in the neuroendocrine stress response is the hypothalamus-pituitary-adrenocortical (HPA) axis. Selye was the first to demonstrate that a wide variety of stressors such as heat, cold, or tissue damage are able to activate this system. This led to the formulation of the General Adaptation Syndrome (GAS) in 1950. Three different phases are distinguishable when an animal is chronically exposed to stressors. The first is the alarm phase which is the direct physiological reaction to a stressor. After a while this reaction modifies into the second phase, that of resistance. In this phase, the animal adapts its physiology to the continuous presence of the stressor. The increased excretion of adrenocortical hormones (mainly cortisol and corticosterone) may result in a hypertrophy of the adrenal cortex. In this situation, according to the Selyean stress concept, the animal has an enhanced resistance to the stressor. In the third phase, a state of exhaustion may occur, particularly when the animal is continuously exposed to rather severe stressors. In this phase, the physiological capacity of the animal is not sufficient in meeting the environmental demands, and the animal will die of stomach ulcers, infections, etc. In case of chronically extreme stress, the symptoms of the GAS, as elaborated by Selye, are clearly distinguishable. However, in present day housing conditions for laboratory animals, such extreme situations are rare. For this reason a great deal of research focuses on the activity of the pituitary-adrenocortical system in reaction to less severe environmental challenges. It would appear that the activity of the HPA axis is related to the predictability and controllability of the stressor. In the experiment which involved either predictable or controllable electric shocks in rats as described above, the plasma levels of corticosterone were highest in the animals which could not predict or control the stressor.

The pituitary hormone which activates the adrenal cortex in secreting corticosterone is ACTH (adrenocorticotropic hormone). This hormone is synthesized from a large precursor molecule known as pro-opiomelanocortin. A number of other stress hormones are derived from this precursor molecule. One of them is β-endorphin, an endogenous opiate. Studies taking place in recent decades have revealed that many neuroendocrine systems respond in reaction to a stressor. These include not only systems involved in the regulation of the adrenals (corticotropin-releasing hormone, vasopressin, ACTH), but also in reproduction (FSH, LH, testosterone, oestrogen, prolactin), in metabolism (growth hormone, thyrotropin, thyroxine, insulin) and in the regulation of blood pressure and body fluids (vasopressin, oxytocin). The effects of stress on these neuroendocrine systems may be direct, but they can also be indirect through the interaction with other neuroendocrine systems.

To summarize, it seems that a stressor induces a complex pattern of physiological changes. This complexity is only partially understood in terms of the underlying mechanisms and its functional significance. An important consequence, however, is that a wide variety of neuroendocrine and physiological parameters depend upon the degree to which an animal is exposed to stressors, i.e. they depend upon the predictability and controllability of the environment. This phenomenon can be seen as an important source of variation in animal experiments.

Functional significance of physiological stress responses

Physiological parameters, such as enhanced plasma levels of catecholamines or corticosteroids, are frequently used as indicators of an animal's lack of well-being. However, it should be noted that these parameters are adaptive and necessary for the organism to cope with the present (stressful) conditions, and to survive in the situation.

The physiological changes in reaction to a stressor are important on two organizational levels of the organism (see fig. 4.7). Both the autonomic nervous system, as well as the different neuroendocrine systems, affect peripheral organs such as the heart, blood vessels, immune system, etc. It can be stated, in general, that the function of this is the preparation of the peripheral physiological processes such as blood pressure, blood distribution, metabolism, immunocompetence, etc. in producing an adequate behavioural and physiological stress response. Not only peripheral organs are affected, the central nervous system is also an important organ targeted by the products of neuroendocrine systems. Several hormones, such as the steroids, cross the blood-brain barrier and bind themselves to specific receptors in certain areas of the brain. Other hormones affect the CNS via pathways which are still unknown, possibly through specific receptors on afferent autonomic nerve fibres.

This feedback of hormones to the CNS has several functions. With regard to the hypothalamus and the pituitary, it is involved in classical neuroendocrine feedback mechanisms. When looking at the higher limbic structures such as the hippocampus and the amygdala, however, hormones may affect behaviour. Many hormones which are released in reaction to a stressor, such as adrenaline, ACTH, corticosterone, vasopressin, β-endorphin, etc., are reported to affect both the learning and the memory processes. For example, the plasma concentration of adrenaline immediately after the acquisition of a learning task will greatly affect memory consolidation.

In summary, it can be said that the acute physiological stress responses have two functions: They organize the organism to cope behaviourally and physiologically with the challenge and, at the same time, they facilitate learning and memory processes which allow the animal to react more adequately to a similar stressor in the future. In fact, these physiological and neuroendocrine mechanisms can be considered as the basic mechanisms underlying all types of behaviour. Therefore, they can only be used as parameters indicative of the disturbed well-being of the organism when they show long term deviations from normal values.

Pathophysiology

The previous section was mainly devoted to acute stress responses and their significance for homeostasis. An organism may, however, reach a state of chronic stress when the homeostatic mechanisms are insufficient; in other words when relevant aspects of the environment are hardly, or are not, predictable and/or controllable.

The significance of chronic stress to the condition of laboratory animals has been illustrated by some experiments on male tree shrews. The males of this animal species live a solitary existence in large territories, where they may occasionally meet their neighbours. In a laboratory experiment, two males were allowed to have a short fight leading to a dominance relationship between the two. If the animals were separated for the rest of the day by a wooden partition, this situation had no negative consequences on physiology and behaviour of the winner and the loser, even when the daily fights were repeated for weeks. If, however, both animals were separated after the fight by a wire-mesh partition, so that the loser could not be attacked by the winner but could see him constantly, he rapidly lost bodyweight and died after a few days as the result of dramatic physiological stress responses, while the winner even gained weight and improved its health. This means that the dramatic physiological responses of the losers and their death are not the consequences of the physical exertions during the fights or of wounding, but of the constant presence of the potentially dangerous rival. It would seem that the possibility to actively escape from the presence of the dominant (controllability), outweighed the high number of fights to which the subordinate male was subjected.

Pathophysiological changes are not only observed in laboratory or animal husbandry conditions. In natural conditions, signs of disease can also be observed. In a study carried out on wild Australian marsupials (*Antechinus*) a high incidence of lethal infectious disease was observed in aggressive, territorial males during the mating season. These infectious diseases were due to the immunosuppressive action of high plasma levels of corticosteroids. These levels were enhanced during the mating season, mainly due to the intensive aggressive interactions of the territorial males. Similarly, high blood pressure and atherosclerosis were found in dominant or subdominant males in colonies of mice, rats, or monkeys, depending upon the stability of the social structure. The relationship between position in the social structure and the incidence of stress-related pathology, appears also to depend upon an individual differentiation in coping style as mentioned above. Animals which react with an active coping style, predominantly react with a sympathetic response, whereas animals using a passive coping style have a more reactive HPA system and show parasympathetic stress responses. Due to the differential involvement of these physiological systems in various types of pathology, this may also indicate an individual differentiation in susceptibility to stress pathology.

The distinction between physiology and pathophysiology is very difficult to define. In the event of less extreme circumstances, it is better to think in terms of susceptibility to certain stress-related diseases. As has been previously mentioned, the phenotype of an individual is the result of a continuous interaction between the genotype and its own life history. Many events which occur in life can account for some more or less permanent changes in behaviour and physiology. For example, the levels of plasma corticosterone during nursing will determine the activity and reactivity of the HPA axis at an adult age. Variation in corticosterone levels during nursing in the rat may either be due to the fact that the pups are confronted with a stressor, or by stress in the mother, because corticosteroids can be transmitted from the mother to the pup via the milk. During adulthood, permanent changes in the HPA axis may also be induced. A strongly activated HPA axis may lead to a permanent decrease of corticosterone receptors in the hippocampus. Due to the fact that these CNS corticosterone receptors are not only involved in behaviour, but also in the neuroendocrine feedback, i.e. the height and the duration of the response, a sort of spiral will develop in which a period of elevated adrenocortical activity will increase the likelihood of subsequent elevations. It seems, in general, to be the case for both neuroendocrine and neurotransmitter systems that the receptors will adjust to the concentration of the ligand (receptor up- and down regulation). This is an important fundamental principle in the dynamic adaptation mechanisms of the organism. It means that every individual, along with its appraisal of the situation, is a product of its own history. This is one of the factors involved in the individual differentiation of behavioural and physiological reactivity to stressors.

The dynamic interaction between environment, central nervous system and peripheral physiology, determines vulnerability to certain diseases. Long term sympathetic activation will, for example, enhance the risks of cardiovascular diseases such as hypertension and atherosclerosis, whereas a more chronic increase in adrenocortical activity will increase the risk of infection. A large parasympathetic activation will enhance the risks of heart rhythm disturbances and of sudden cardiac death. A serious stressor is, as a rule, not pathogenic in itself, but merely enhances the vulnerability and greatly potentiates pathogenic processes when other risk factors are also present. In stress-induced cardiovascular pathology, this may be seen in a high level of serum cholesterol or a reduced glucose tolerance, whereas stress-induced immunosuppression will only ever lead to pathology when infectious agents or malignant cells are also present.

It may therefore be concluded that the individual history of animals determines their behavioural, physiological and neuroendocrine state. This

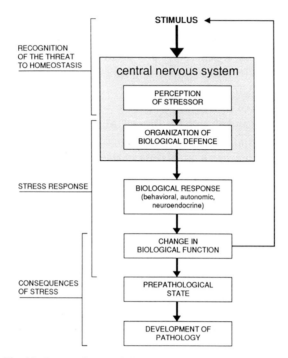

Fig. 4.8. Course of events induced by a stressor (after Moberg, 1985).

"state" determines the reactivity of an animal to certain challenges and the outcome of animal experiments, as well as its susceptibility to stress-related diseases. Therefore, it is important to know the degree to which the processes mentioned above play a role not only in the housing and care of experimental animals but also during the actual animal experiments.

A summary of the processes leading to pathology is schematically shown in fig. 4.8. In this model the response to a stressor is divided into three categories: the recognition or appraisal of a stimulus as a threat to homeostasis, the behavioural and physiological response, and the consequences of this response.

Well-being

Clearly, adaptation can only occur within the genotypic and phenotypic limits of the individual. The wider the regulatory range of homeostatic mechanisms, in terms of both behaviour and physiology, the better the guarantee for the well-being of the animals. Extreme conditions, such as low environmental temperatures, will not affect the well-being of the animal, so long as the conditions are controllable by means of the full repertoire of adaptation mechanisms i.e. nestbuilding, metabolism, shivering, etc. A judgement of the degree to which well-being may be affected under certain conditions has to be based, therefore, on a thorough knowledge of the animal species involved. Depending on the animal species and its normal social organization, environmental factors such as cage size and structure, light (intensity, wavelength, photoperiod, flicker-frequency), sounds, ventilation, etc. are as important as the presence or absence of conspecifics, their sex, and the predictability and controllability of the environment. There is a certain danger of anthropomorphism in the judgement of the relative importance of these factors. Conditions that are good for human well-being are not necessarily good for animals as well. This also holds for a comparison between different animal species, and between the strains of a single species.

This problem can be tackled by measuring the preference of an animal for certain environmental conditions, using a preference test. In this system, test animals are offered a choice of various conditions such as housing systems, bedding material, food, etc. (see fig. 4.9). When the choices are combined with detailed behavioural observations, information can be obtained on the relative importance of environmental factors. Care must be taken, however, when interpreting the obtained results in terms of well-being. The choice may, in fact, be biased due to previous experience, or an animal may not be able to judge which choice might be good for its own well-being in the long term.

Another way to approach animal well-being is by using a scoring system for signs of stress or suffering, based upon behavioural and clinical parameters. Morton and Griffiths were the first to develop a list of indicators such

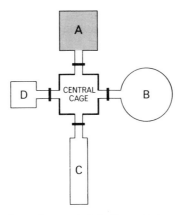

Fig. 4.9. Experimental layout of a preference test. In the central cage, the animal can make a choice out of four different housing systems. The duration of the stay in the various systems can be detected by photocells and used as a measure of preference.

as piloerection, reduced body weight, increased heart rate, diarrhoea, etc. Additional scoring systems for animal suffering have been developed since then. Each of these systems is aimed at estimating the degree of suffering based upon clinical, physiological and behavioural parameters. Although most of these parameters can be determined objectively, the question of to what extent they are indicators of well-being will remain a matter of interpretation.

Concluding remarks

Animals are highly dynamic, information-processing organisms, which continuously try to adapt themselves to the environmental conditions using behavioural and physiological mechanisms. Due to the nature of these mechanisms, each individual is a product of its own unique history. The regulatory range of these adaptive, homeostatic mechanisms is limited and fiercely determined by both genotypic and phenotypic constraints. Animals used by human beings, either as pets, in animal experimentation or in animal husbandry, are subject to the conditions offered by the responsible persons. Inevitably this will mean that their decisions on the housing and care greatly influence the well-being of the animals. In view of the dynamics in behaviour and physiology, as mentioned above, this also implies that in animal research these decisions also influence the quality of the experimental results. Due to the fact that the laboratory or husbandry conditions are unavoidably limited in comparison with the richness and the variations in nature, it has to be considered as to which part of the wide spectrum of natural variation is studied in the particular species under the limited and standardized experimental conditions. Standardization of housing and care of experimental animals is essential for the reliability and reproducibility of experimental results. However, very often at the same time, standardization also means restricting the extent to which animals can fulfil their behavioural and physiological needs. In every experiment, therefore, one should consider the question whether and/or to what extent the chosen housing and experimental conditions will affect the state of the animals in terms of their behaviour, physiology and well-being.

Literature

Benus R F, Bohus B, Koolhaas J M, Oortmerssen G A van. Heritable variation in aggression as a reflection of individual coping strategies. Experientia 1991; 47: 1008–1019.

Bohus B, Koolhaas J M. Psychoimmunology of social factors in rodents and other subprimate vertebrates. In: Ader R, Felten DL, Cohen N, eds. Psychoneuroimmunology. New York: Academic Press Inc., 1990: 807–830.

Bohus B, Koolhaas J M, Nyakas C, Steffens A B, Fokkema D S, Scheurink A J W. Physiology of stress:A behavioural view. In: Wiepkema PR, Adrichem PWM van, eds. Biology of stress in farm animals: an integrative approach. Dordrecht: Nijhoff Publ., 1987: 57–70.

Calhoun J B. The ecology and sociology of the Norway rat. Washington DC: Governement Printing Office, 1962.

Halliday T R, Slater P J B, eds. Animal behaviour. Oxford: Blackwell Scient. Publ., 1983.

Henry J P, Stephens P M. Stress, health and the social environment: A sociobiological approach to medicine. Berlin: Springer Verlag, 1977.

Holst D von. Vegetative and somatic components of tree shrew's behaviour. J Auton Nerv Syst, suppl 1986: 657–670.

Koolhaas J M, Bohus B. Social control in relation to neuroendocrine and immunological responses. In: Steptoe A, Appels A, eds. Stress,personal control and health. Brussels: John Wiley & Sons Ltd., 1989: 295–304.

Levine S, Ursin H. What is stress? In: Brown M R, Koob G F, Rivier C, eds. Stress: neurobiology and neuroendocrinology. New York: Marcel Dekker, Inc., 1991: 3–21.

Moberg G B, ed. Animal stress. Bethesda: American Physiological Society, 1985.

Morton D B. Adverse effects in animals and their relevance to refining scientific procedures. ATLA 1990; 18: 29–39.

Morton D B, Griffiths P H M. Guidelines on the recognition of pain, distress and discomfort in experimental animals and a hypothesis for assessment. Vet Rec 1985; 116: 431–436.

Sapolsky R M. Stress in the wild. Scientific American 1990; 262: 106–113.

Selye H. The physiology and pathology of exposures to stress. Montreal: Acta Medica Publ., 1950.

Stamp-Dawkins M. Animal suffering. London: Chapman and Hall, 1980.

Uexkull J von. Streifzüge durch die Umwelten von Tieren und Menschen. Rohwolt: Hamburg, 1956.

Wiepkema P R, Adrichem P W M van, eds. Biology of stress in farm animals. Dordrecht: Nijhoff Publ., 1987.

Wiepkema P R, Schouten W G P. Mechanisms of coping in social situations. In: Zayan R, Dantzer R eds. Social stress in domestic animals. Dordrecht: Kluwer Academic Press, 1989: 8–24.

5   Standardization of animal experimentation

Introduction

Standardization of animal experimentation can be taken in this context to mean the defining of the properties of any given animal (or animal population) and its environment, together with the subsequent task of keeping the properties constant or regulating them. The aim of standardization is to increase the reproducibility of group mean results from one experiment to another within the limits set out in chapter 4. This will improve comparability of results within and between laboratories. Standardization also often aims to reduce the variation in quantitative measurement values in apparently identical animals within a given experiment. From a statistical point of view, a reduced inter-individual variation of measured values lowers the number of animals needed per experiment (see chapter 12). It is implicit within standardization that reported results should be accompanied by a careful description of the potential sources of variation, such as the animals themselves, their environment and the experimental procedures employed.

Standardization of animal experiments can only involve the potential sources of variation that are known at the time. Variation in measured values can occur at two levels, the first being between apparently identical experiments known as between-experiment variation. Secondly it may occur between apparently identical animals within a given experiment known as within-experiment variation or inter-individual variation. In essence, both types of variation can be as a result of the same sources, i.e. the variable properties of animals and their environment along with other influences including experimental procedures. The observed inter-individual variation may be divided into various components (see chapter 12). What can be achieved by the standardization of potential sources of variation along with its limitations will be discussed here.

Between-experiment variation

Repetition of a given experiment, with the same or a different group of animals, will result in varied group mean measured values. The treatment effect, which refers to differences between the group averages for the control group and the test group, will vary therefore between experiments. This between-experiment variation is subject to two fluctuating components; the variation in measurement values between individual animals and the differences in experimental conditions. If interaction takes place between the treatment effect and the experimental conditions, then there is an extra cause for the treatment effect to vary per experiment. This may lead to a false interpretation of the results. In order accurately to assess the treatment effect, it is necessary to repeat experiments. The treatment effect is thus composed of the true effect either reduced or augmented by a systematical error and/or noise term.

Decreasing the between-experiment variation of treatment effects will reduce the need repeatedly to perform the same experiments and will therefore contribute to a reduction of the use of laboratory animals. From a scientific point of view, experimental results need to be reproducible and therefore independent of both time and place. A hypothesis for further research must be based upon reproducible experimental results.

Within-experiment variation

Quantitative measurements between apparently identical animals within an experiment will, however, be subject to inter-individual variation. This within-experiment variation can be summed up as the variation in the execution of experimental procedures, the analytical variation, the *intra*-individual variation and the intrinsic *inter*-individual variation (see chapter 12). The intrinsic *inter*-individual variation is a result of the contribution of each individual animal to the measured value. The intrinsic contribution will differ per animal and will basically be independent of the type of treatment to which the animal will be subjected. The *intra*-individual variation consists of non-standardizable variations within an animal which will result in day-to-day fluctuations of the measured value.

If the statistical power (i.e. the chance of detecting a true effect) is to remain constant given an increasing inter-individual variation in measured values (i.e. increasing standard deviation), then the number of animals required per experiment will increase. It is possible to reduce this number by decreasing the apparent inter-individual variation of results. This has important economical, practical and ethical consequences.

Sources of between- and within-experiment variations

An important source of variation within animal experiments is the animal itself. Differences between animals in one treatment group or between two groups of animals could involve differences in age, body weight, number of litter mates during the suckling period and other differences that may exist prior to the experiment. Such differences can increase either the within- and/or the between-experiment variations in measured values. Differences in characteristics (other than the intentional treatment) between control and test group may influence the treatment effect. Inter-individual differences in genotype, including differences in gender, can also increase the variation in measured values. Uncontrolled fluctuations in (micro)biological (pressure of infections, oestrus cycle etc.), physical (light, temperature etc.), chemical (nutrition, bedding etc.) and social (number of animals per cage, interactions with personnel etc.) environmental factors can increase the between- and within-experiment variations of the results. Such fluctuations may thus also affect the treatment effect.

The measured value obtained in an animal experiment is determined fundamentally by genotype-environment interactions. The response to treatment will also be influenced by this interaction. There are various degrees to which the environment can interact with the genotype of the animal. Environmental influences from the fertilization of an egg and the fetal stage through to sexual maturity are referred to as the primary milieu. The interaction between this milieu and the genotype will give rise to the phenotype. The phenotypical properties will subsequently be influenced by the pre-experiment conditions which are referred to as the secondary milieu. As a result, the dramatype is formed. Furthermore the laboratory animal will be affected by experimental procedures and treatments known as the tertiary milieu.

The diagram below illustrates the potential sources of variation within the results of animal experimentation.

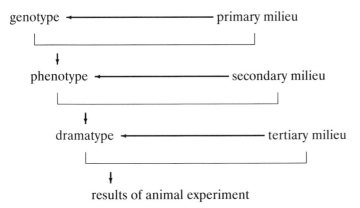

Depending on the type of measured values, the interactions between genotype and milieu, can have a variable influence upon the within- and between-experiment variations, including the treatment effect. Chapter 12 describes how the systematic errors and noise terms within observed treatment effects can be diminished.

Standardization of the animal and its environment

In theory, inter-individual differences in the genotype can be eliminated by using genetically uniform animals. The individuals of an inbred strain or F_1 hybrid (see chapter 7) are virtually genetically identical and as a result will on the whole show a smaller inter-individual variation in measured values (before and after treatment) than genetically non-uniform animals (i.e. random-bred or outbred animals). The interactions as depicted in the above diagram, however, illustrate that the genetic background of the animals is only one of the factors influencing the measured value. For instance, for the variation in body weight of mice of the same sex and age it has been shown that about 20% of the total variance may result from differences in pre- and post-natal environment and about 30% of the total variation may relate to analytical error and so-called intangible variance. The latter remains in genetically uniform animals, even after equalizing the controllable environment for each animal. The intangible variance is caused by uncontrollable genotype-environment interactions at various developmental levels, including that of ontogenesis.

Given adequate genetic quality control, it is possible to work with animals with a constant genotype when moving from one experiment to another, but not all experiments require animals to react identically. Certain experiments (e.g. toxicity tests) rather require some degree of genetic variation (see chapter 7).

The microbiological quality of laboratory animals can be of influence upon various types of measured values. Pressure of infection (latent infections) can markedly increase the inter-individual variation within an experiment and can also vary between experiments. Differences in microbiological environment of control and test animals can affect the treatment effect. This type of variation can be eliminated to a certain extent by using microbiologically defined animals. The status of these animals must be maintained by adequate hygienic measures. Microbiological quality control must be seen here as a prerequisite (see chapter 8).

Transportation involves changes in environment that can have a major impact on laboratory animals. Prior to arrival in the animal house, animals purchased from commercial breeders may have been transported by car, train and/or aircraft for many hours. Transportation by itself causes endocrine and metabolic responses that require up to one week for a new steady state to be reached. This so-called transportation stress may affect different individuals to a different extent and thus raises inter-individual variation of certain measured values, at least until a new steady state is reached. Transporting of animals from one place to another may involve changes in chemical, physical, microbiological and social environmental factors. The altered environment will cause changes in certain measured values, whether transient or not, and will at the same time raise inter-individual variation. Depending on the type of measurements to be carried out in projected experiments, transported animals must generally be given a period of adaptation of up to three weeks before being used in an experiment.

In practice, it is not possible to house individual animals under identical environmental conditions. Within any given animal house there are as a rule a number of animals housed either individually or in groups. Local differences in environmental conditions are inevitable and a few are mentioned here. Depending upon the type of ventilation system, the temperature at 1.5 m can be 3 to 4°C higher than it is at 0.5 m. The location of a cage in a rack will as a result influence the temperature within the cage (micro-climate). The micro-climate will also be affected by the number of animals per cage, relative humidity and the type of bedding material. Group housing of rats or mice can raise the temperature within the cage by up to 5°C, compared with room temperature. Fluorescent tubes, which are commonly used for lighting suspended from the ceiling, will cause a higher light intensity in the cages at the top of the rack. The difference between light intensity between cages at the top or the bottom of a rack can be four-fold.

Table 5.1 illustrates the influence of the number of animals per cage on food intake. The food intake of the mice falls markedly as cage occupation increases. Mice housed in groups generally huddle together which reduces heat loss, resulting in a depressed energy requirement.

Table 5.1

Influence of cage occupation upon food intake

Number of animals per cage	Food intake, g/mouse/day	
	Males	Females
1	7.6	6.8
2	6.2	5.9
4	4.9	4.6
8	4.2	3.6

After Chvédoff et al. (1980).

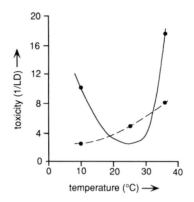

Fig. 5.1. Relationship between toxicity (1/LD, LD (= lethal dose) in g/kg body weight) and room temperature for salicylate (●———●) and ephedrin (●- - -●) administered intraperitoneally to rats.

Fig. 5.1 shows another example of an environmental factor which will affect experimental results, i.e. the effect of environmental temperature on the toxicity of the pharmacological agents, salicylate and ephedrin. Toxicity of salicylate, expressed as a lethal dose, shows a U-shaped correlation with room temperature. Similar relationships have been shown in connection with atropine, chloropromazin and pentobarbital. There is a direct relationship between ephedrin toxicity and room temperature, i.e. toxicity rises with temperature increase. Other correlations can be made between temperature and diphenyl-hydramin, pentachlorophenol and kinidin-sulphate. Therefore, in order, to reduce between-experiment variation in toxicity of drugs, room temperature should be standardized.

Differences between individual housing conditions should be equally distributed between control and test groups during an experiment. As a consequence, the treatment effect will not be biased by differences in housing conditions between the control and the test groups. The local differences in environmental conditions within animal rooms should be constant for the different experiments. Ideally, all environmental factors should be constant from one experiment to another.

Standardization of environmental factors is essential when justifying the use of laboratory animals. The practical realization of such standardization is not so straight forward and questions need to be answered. To which degree should environmental factors be standardized? Should the level be constant or rhythmic? Upon which criteria should the ideal level of environmental factors be based? These criteria may be a combination of optimal welfare of the animals and ergonomical considerations. The level of a given environmental factor formed on the basis of these criteria is not, by definition, associated with a small within-experiment variation of measured values. The Council of

Europe and the E.C., in their attempt to stay ahead, have already formulated recommendations for the housing and care of laboratory animals despite the lack of sufficient experimental data. These recommendations are based upon current knowledge, whether or not scientifically substantiated, and upon common practice.

Standardization of experiments and extrapolation of results

In principle, experimental results only hold for the conditions (animals, environmental factors) under which the experiment has been carried out. For validated routine testing, e.g. for the control of vaccines, this is not a problem. However, there are experiments from which it should be possible to generalize the outcome. Standardization of experiments implies a specialization of experimental conditions. Therefore, standardization is not identifiable with generalization of experimental results. The first question to be answered is to what extent are the animals used representatives of all comparable animals? Even if it is acceptable that the animals used are indeed representing a given population, the results will still only have a bearing upon this (limited) population (animals of the same strain, of the same sex, with the same body weight etc) and upon limited conditions (the biological, physical and chemical properties of the environment). It becomes even more complicated when the results obtained from working with laboratory animals must be "extrapolated" to other species, in particular to man. Clearly, caution must be the watchword here. The range over which results can be extrapolated from experiment to practice or, in particular, from one species to another, is actually rather wide in relation to any limitation of generalization of results due to standardization. Therefore the need for extrapolating results should not be an excuse for ignoring standardization.

Efficacy of standardization

The aim of standardization, i.e. the reduction of between-experiment variation and often also of within-experiment variation, is only to a certain extent empirically substantiated and then only for specific, quantitative values. In certain cases, standardization can have an opposite effect, i.e. an increase in within-experiment variation. Nevertheless it is a fact that standardization improves the comparability of results between laboratories, because, by its very nature, standardization implies careful reporting of experimental conditions.

Concluding remarks

It is clear that many questions concerning standardization remain unanswered. In particular, it is not known which aspects of standardization require the most attention and exactly how standardization should be implemented in practice. It is of course essential that standardization does not have a negative influence on the animal's welfare. This implies that in striving towards standardization, the physiological and ethological needs of the animal should be taken into account. If this is not the case then standardization could even be counterproductive.

The experimenter generally has to rely upon commercial suppliers when acquiring animals, and cannot therefore determine and/or control standardization prior to the experiment. However, certain demands can be placed upon the supplier in the areas of genetic quality or microbiological status with regard to the animals. A reliable supplier will inform the researcher about changes which have been introduced regarding housing and care of the animals, as well as their genetic and microbiological status.

In the following chapters, the influence of nutrition upon experimental results and the possibilities of genetic and microbiological standardization of laboratory animals will be described in detail.

Literature

Beynen A C. The basis for standardization of animal experimentation. Scand J Lab Anim Sci 1991; 18: 95–99

Chvédoff M, Clarke M R, Irisarri E, Faccini J M, Monro A M. Effects of housing conditions on food intake, body weight and spontaneous lesions in mice. A review of the literature and results of an 18-month study. Fd Cosmet Toxicol 1980; 18: 517–522.

Clough G. Environmental effects on animals used in biomedical research. Biol Rev 1982; 57: 487–523.

Gärtner K. A third component causing random variability beside environment and genotype. Lab Anim 1990; 24: 71–77.

Lang C M, Vesell E S. Environmental and genetic factors affecting laboratory animals: impact in biomedical research. Fed Proc 1976; 35: 1123–1124.

Newton W M. Environmental impact on laboratory animals. Adv Vet Sci Comp Med 1978; 22: 1–28.

Rao G N. Significance of environmental factors on the test systems. In: Hoover BK, et al., eds. Managing, conduct and data quality of toxicology studies. Princeton: Princeton Scientific Publishers, 1986.

6   Nutrition and experimental results

Introduction

The health status, performance and metabolism of experimental animals are influenced by the composition of the diet and the feeding practice. Thus, nutrition not only affects the well-being of the animals but also the outcome of experiments. Nutritional studies focus upon deliberate alterations to diets and the effects this has. The results, however, of some animal experiments can be affected unintentionally by the composition of the diet. Such effects can be brought about, for example, by undesirable and unknown variations in the dietary constituents, which can adversely affect the accuracy and precision of experimental results. This can lead to unnecessary sacrifice of animals and to wastage of time and resources. As part of an experiment food intake may differ between control and experimental groups. This can create biased results and lead to a false interpretation of the data. Should this occur, the use of animals can be considered unwarranted. This chapter focuses on nutrition as a potentially interfering factor within animal experimentation.

Nutrient requirements

The most critical aspect of formulating experimental diets is ensuring the presence of all the essential nutrients in the required concentrations. There is a considerable amount of published data regarding the nutrient requirements of laboratory animals. These data are periodically reviewed by committees established by the U.S. National Research Council, and reports are issued containing the estimated nutrient requirements. One such report in the series (National Research Council 1978) contains extensive estimates of the nutrient requirements for normal growth and reproduction. Absolute figures for nutrient requirements cannot be established and thus any requirement set always remains debatable.

When determining nutrient requirements, criteria such as growth, repro-duction, nutrient storage, enzyme activity and morphological and histological characteristics are taken into account. In general it is only possible to establish the minimum requirement of any given nutrient. The minimum requirement is the lowest amount of a given nutrient which can be present without showing signs of deficiency, or it can refer to the amount which just allows equilibrium between intake and excretion, or to the maintenance of normal levels of certain metabolites in the blood or urine. The various criteria for determining the minimum requirement do not necessarily reflect the same nutritional status. Therefore, the given minimum requirement for a nutrient is related to the criterion which was used when it was established.

When the minimum requirement of a nutrient is being ingested, the animal is in a critical state. A small increase in need, for instance due to sub-clinical infection, may induce deficiency. When formulating laboratory animal diets, recommended nutrient allowances are followed, which differ according to the animal species. The recommended allowances refer to the assessed amounts of nutrients to be ingested guaranteeing the optimum functioning of most individual animals. Clearly, the recommended allowance is greater than the minimum requirement. Maximum growth is often used as the criterion for determining the recommended requirements for laboratory animals. However, maximum growth has a negative impact on health at advanced age and certainly in the case of rodents, it can also reduce longevity.

Table 6.1 shows recommended nutrient allowances for the mouse, rat, hamster, guinea pig and rabbit. The recommendations are given for growing animals, as these are the most frequently used in experiments. Adult animal values are less well established or even unknown, but are likely to be lower than those for growing or breeding animals. The nutrient requirements are expressed in amounts (g or mg) per kg diet. The recommended nutrient requirements are given as guidelines and must be treated as such. The values are based upon observations made at different laboratories operating different conditions for the preparation and storage of diets, housing of the animals etc.

The amount of food ingested by the majority of laboratory animals will be determined by the animals' energy requirements and therefore the energy density of the diet is crucial. Dietary energy is in the form of fats, carbo-hydrates, protein and fermentable fibre. The animal's energy requirement is expressed in terms of a unit of heat, the MJ (1 MJ = 1000 kJ = 240 kcal). Not all of the energy in the diet, i.e. total combustible energy, can be utilized by the animal. Some of the dietary energy will remain undigested or will be lost in the form of flatulence or urinary products. Metabolizable energy is the available energy left after faecal, urinary, and gaseous losses have been

Table 6.1

Recommended nutrient allowances for growing animals fed *ad libitum* (expressed per kg feed consisting of 90% dry matter) [1]

	Mouse	Rat	Hamster	Guinea pig	Rabbit
Digestible energy [2] (kJ/g)	16.8	16.0	17.6	12.6	10.5
Fat (g/kg)	s.u.	50	50	s.u.	20
Fibre (g/kg)	r.u.	r.u.	s.u.	100	110
Protein (g/kg)	180	120 [3]	150	180	160
Arginine (g/kg)	3	6	7.6	s.u.	6
Asparagine (g/kg)	s.u.	4	s.u.	s.u.	s.u.
Glutamic acid (g/kg)	s.u.	40	s.u.	s.u.	s.u.
Histidine (g/kg)	2	3	4	s.u.	3
Isoleucine (g/kg)	4	5	8.9	s.u.	6
Leucine (g/kg)	7	7.5	13.9	s.u.	11
Lysine (g/kg)	4	7	12	s.u.	6.5
Methionine + Cystine (g/kg)	5	6	3.2	s.u.	6
Phenylalanine + Tyrosine (g/kg)	4	8	14	s.u.	11
Proline (g/kg)	s.u.	4	s.u.	s.u.	s.u.
Threonine (g/kg)	4	5	7	s.u.	6
Tryptophan (g/kg)	1	1.5	3.4	s.u.	2
Valine (g/kg)	5	6	9.1	s.u.	7
Glycine (g/kg)	s.u.	s.u.	s.u.	s.u.	r.u.
Minerals and trace elements					
Calcium (g/kg)	4	5	5.9	9	4
Chloride (g/kg)	r.u.	0.5	s.u.	s.u.	3
Magnesium (g/kg)	0.5	0.4	0.6	2	0.35
Phosphorus (g/kg)	4	4	3	5.5	2.2
Potassium (g/kg)	2	3.6	6.1	9.5	6
Sodium (g/kg)	r.u.	0.5	1.5	s.u.	2
Sulphur (g/kg)	s.u.	0.3	s.u.	s.u.	s.u.
Chromium (mg/kg)	2	0.3	s.u.	0.6	s.u.
Copper (mg/kg)	4.5	5	1.6	6	3
Fluoride (mg/kg)	s.u.	1	0.024	s.u.	s.u.
Iodine (mg/kg)	0.25	0.15	1.6	1	0.2
Iron (mg/kg)	25	35	140	50	r.u.
Manganese (mg/kg)	45	50	3.65	40	8.5
Selenium (mg/kg)	r.u.	0.1	0.1	0.1	s.u.
Zinc (mg/kg)	30	12	9.2	20	r.u.
Vitamins					
Retinol (mg/kg)	0.15	1.2	1.1	7.0	0.17
Cholecalciferol (μg/kg)	4	25	62	25	r.u.
DL-α-tocopheryl acetate (mg/kg)	18	27	2.7	45	36
Menadione (mg/kg)	3	0.05	4	5	r.u.
Thiamin (mg/kg)	5	4	20	2	r.u.
Riboflavin (mg/kg)	7	3	15	3	s.u.
Pyridoxine (mg/kg)	1	6	6	3	39
Cyanocobalamine (μg/kg)	10	50	10	10	n.r.
Nicotinic acid (mg/kg)	10	20	90	10	180
Folic acid (mg/kg)	0.5	1	2	4	s.u.

Table 6.1 (continued)

	Mouse	Rat	Hamster	Guinea pig	Rabbit
Biotin (mg/kg)	0.2	s.u.	0.6	0.3	r.u.
Pantothenic acid (mg/kg)	10	8	40	20	s.u.
Choline (mg/kg)	600	1000	2000	1000	1200
Inositol (mg/kg)	r.u.	n.r.	100	n.r.	s.u.
Ascorbic acid (mg/kg)	n.r.	n.r.	n.r.	200	n.r.

[1] As described in the text, absolute figures for nutrient allowances cannot be given, and different committees propose different allowances (see also Clarke *et al.*, 1977).
[2] Metabolizable energy generally varies from 90 to 95 percent of digestible energy.
[3] Recommended allowance for so-called ideal protein.
n.r. = not required; r.u. = required, but requirement unknown; s.u. = status unknown.
Based on NRC Nutrient Requirements of Laboratory Animals (1978) and NRC Nutrient Requirements of Rabbits (1977).

accounted for. The energy value biologically available to the body is 16.8 kJ per g for carbohydrates and protein, whilst dietary fats provide 37.8 kJ per g. The quantity required of diets with high energy density, expressed as g of feed, is lower than that of low-energy diets. Table 6.1 shows, therefore, the recommended nutrient allowances of diets for specified energy densities.

Care must be taken when using the recommended nutrient allowances. There are, for example, differences in minimum requirements between inbred strains of rats and mice. These differences have not been taken into account by the recommendations. It must be stressed that the recommendations do not necessarily hold for germ-free animals. Vitamins K and B12, for example, will be synthesized by the gut flora of conventional rats and mice and will be sufficiently ingested as a result of coprophagy. For SPF animals it is a wise precaution to include higher supplements of vitamins B and K, as their microflora may not contain the full complement of vitamin-synthesizing organisms.

Under certain conditions, the recommended requirement of a given nutrient in a diet may be insufficient. This may relate to the availability of the nutrient, i.e. the extent to which the nutrient is actually absorbed. Nutrient availability may be depressed when it is present in a poorly digestible form or when it interacts with other dietary components. The recommendations do not take these factors into account. For example, if a diet contains large amounts of soya bean protein concentrate and/or cereal products, the required concentration of zinc in the diet increases. These products contain phytate which forms an insoluble compound with zinc in the intestinal lumen so that the availability of zinc is reduced. Housing conditions can also influence the required concentration of zinc in the diet. The recommended requirement of zinc for the rat is 12 mg/kg diet (energy density = 16 kJ/g diet). When rats are housed in galvanized cages, they will lick the zinc and therefore, the required concentration of zinc in the diet will fall to 2–4 mg/kg.

Types of laboratory animal diets

Diets for laboratory animals are classified according to the degree of the refinement of the ingredients. They are known as: natural-ingredient, purified, or chemically defined diets.

Natural-ingredient diets

These are formulated with natural ingredients such as oats, corn, soya bean meal, and fish meal. They are the most economical and the most widely used diets. Nutrient concentration can vary considerably due to changes in the source of ingredients used in the manufacture of the diet. This is due to the fact that nutrient concentrations of natural ingredients are not fixed. Information on the ingredient composition of most commercial food is not readily available as it is the property of the manufacturer marketing the product under a trade name. The commercial closed-formula diets are the most readily available, the most economical and the most widely used. They are formulated with the aim of providing all known nutrient requirements for the growth of the species. The quantitative nutrient concentration range of a closed-formula diet is generally available from the manufacturer. Diets of known ingredient composition, open-formula diets, have been published for rodents kept in conventional environments, as well as for those reared in environments requiring sterilized food (National Research Council 1978). Formulations of existing open-formula diets can be modified, or new diets made, to meet the requirements of specific research programmes.

Chemically defined diets

These are formulated with pure chemicals. For instance, individual amino acids are supplied in place of whole proteins and carbohydrates are provided by specific sugars. Chemically defined diets are, however, expensive. At the time of manufacture, the nutrient concentrations in these diets are theoretically fixed; but just as for natural ingredients, the availability of nutrients may be altered due to, for instance, oxidation or interactions between nutrients. The formulation of these diets is dependent upon the knowledge of the nutrient requirements of the animals involved. Problems can occur associated with palatability.

Purified diets

These are formulated with a combination of natural ingredients, pure chemicals, and ingredients of varying degrees of refinement (e.g. protein may be supplied by casein). These diets are relatively inexpensive and, under most conditions, their nutrient concentrations are more stable than those of chemically defined diets.

The diet is a potential source of microorganisms that can be pathogenic to laboratory animals. Food for gnotobionts must be sterilized by either autoclaving or by gamma-radiation, and diets for SPF animals (see chapter 8) are usually sterilized. Autoclaving causes some destruction of most of the vitamins and may denature proteins. Radiation is less damaging, although it causes some loss of vitamins, particularly vitamin K. Losses on irradiation are much greater in the presence of water. Moist diets or aqueous solutions should not be sterilized by gamma-radiation.

Variation in diet composition

Variation in the concentration of dietary components, nutrients and contaminants, can cause clinical signs of deficiency or toxicity, which can be readily observed. When such a variation occurs, although it may be harmful to the animals, no biased results will appear in the literature as the experiment will be stopped. Comparatively small variations in the diet, which occur more frequently, however, are not always so obvious. Nevertheless, the metabolism on the cellular level of the animals may be affected, which in turn may influence the outcome of the experiment. Small variations in diet might unknowingly cause undesirable and biased results to appear in scientific journals.

Two types of diet variation need to be distinguished: one being differences occurring between diets from different manufacturers and the other where differences occur between batches of one particular brand. Table 6.2 illustrates the magnitude of the between-brand variation that may occur between commercial rat diets based upon natural ingredients. Essentially all diets were of the closed-formula type. It is clear from the table that commercial rat diets can differ considerably with respect to their composition.

Different batches of one brand of diet based on natural ingredients can also differ markedly in their composition (see table 6.3). It is important to note that the variation in protein concentration can be much higher than that indicated on the lable. It has been found in certain cases, after correction for analytical error, to be as high as 12% (expressed as relative standard deviation). Different batches of an open-formula diet also show

Table 6.2

Table showing the variation in the composition of natural-ingredient, commercial rat diets from different manufacturers

Component	Number of manufacturers	Mean ± SD	Range
Protein (g/kg)	4	206 ± 40	155–268
Riboflavin (mg/kg)	4		9–56
Calcium (g/kg)	4	8.9 ± 4.1	4.1–13.0
Zinc (mg/kg)	4	149 ± 67	56–233
Selenium (mg/kg)	3	0.08 ± 0.04	0.03–0.11
Lignin (g/kg)	5	18.5 ± 3.4	14.5–22.4
DDT (mg/kg)	3	1.2 ± 1.0	0–2.5

Based on Beynen (1987).

Table 6.3

Table showing the variation in the composition of different batches of one brand of a natural-ingredient, commercial rat diet

Component	Number of batches	Mean ± SD	Range
Protein (g/kg)	65	198 ± 0.7	182–213
Calcium (g/kg)	65	10.4 ± 0.1	8.0–14.0
Zinc (mg/kg)	65	50 ± 10	24–77
Selenium (mg/kg)	148	0.34 ± 0.15	0.04–0.66
DDT (mg/kg)	148	0.03 ± 0.05	0–0.3
Cadmium (mg/kg)	65	0.43 ± 0.16	0–0.9
Nitrosodimethylamine (μg/kg)	6		0.2–21.3

Based on Beynen (1987).

considerable variation in composition. Fluctuations in the composition of dietary components are likely to be minimal when using purified diets based on refined, standardized ingredients.

Variations in the diet of one brand, as shown in table 6.3, can be caused by errors occurring during the preparation of the diets, by changing the source and quality of the ingredients and/or by differences in the processing and storage conditions. Different manufacturers use different formulas and therefore produce foods with different nutrient compositions as shown in table 6.2. Researchers should not choose a brand of commercial diet purely on the basis of catalogue values, since such values generally do not conform with chemical analyses (see table 6.4).

Table 6.4

Zinc concentrations in four different commercial rat diets according to chemical analysis and catalogue values

Diet	Zinc (mg/kg)	
	Catalogue	Analysis
1	38	46
2	84	47
3	39	72
4	36	84

Based on Wise and Gilburt (1981).

Impact of variation in diet composition

Commercial laboratory animal diets can vary markedly between brands. If these differences in diet composition affect experimental results, the use of different brands may introduce a bias in the results. The use of a certain diet can either enhance or mask the response of animals to a given stimulus. This in turn can lead to incorrect interpretation of the results. From a scientific point of view this is undesirable. A variable diet- induced bias of experimental results implies that the results of different experiments are not comparable. This will increase the need to repeat experiments. A variable diet-induced bias of results essentially invalidates the comparison of experiments between different laboratories. If, however, during the course of a particular study or research programme the brand of the diet is altered, this bias can be reflected in experimental results obtained within one laboratory. Between-batch variation within a series of one type of experiment can decrease the precision of results. In other words, the standard deviation increases, which lowers the statistical power. This will result in the use of more animals in order to obtain valid information.

The feeding of different commercial diets to animals is likely to give rise to different results. For instance, with rats growth rates may differ, and the brand of diet has also been shown to affect the outcome of potency tests of bacterial vaccines and toxicity tests. Biological effects can be evoked by altering the concentrations of dietary components within their range of fluctuation in practical situations. For example, the protein content of the food (within the range 30–300 g/kg) affects demethylation and hydroxylation of certain xenobiotics by liver homogenates from the rat. Dietary selenium (within the range 0–0.1 mg/kg) affects growth performance and glutathione peroxidase activity in erythrocytes and liver of rats. Cadmium intake (within the range 0–1 mg/kg of diet) affects systolic blood pressure and renal vasculature in rats. Residues of DDT in the diet (within the range 0-1 mg/kg) influence the activity of

Table 6.5

Specification of rat diets in Vol. 210 (1983) of The Biochemical Journal

	Number of papers
Total	144
Rats used	65
No specification of diet	45
Trade name of diet given	17
Specification of diet composition	3

After Beynen (1985).

certain hepatic microsomal enzymes of the rat. Thus, unknown fluctuations of diet within certain studies can lead to an incorrect interpretation of the experimental results.

Diet standardization?

Clearly a standard diet for rats (and other laboratory animals) does not exist. It is also the case that many researchers do not specify the diet of their rats, probably due to the fact that they believe it to be standard. Table 6.5 highlights this problem. Should the diet affect the experimental results, it is difficult, if not impossible, to duplicate the experiments with comparable results without adequately describing the diet.

This leads to the question of whether efforts should be made to design guidelines in order to produce an international, standardized diet. However, when using natural ingredients it is not possible to produce a standard diet. Even with the use of purified ingredients, a standard diet over any period of time cannot be reliable. The constantly changing source and quality of ingredients excludes the possibility of a true standard diet, and of course specific research programmes may require specific diets. The standardization of laboratory animal diets should involve the concept of reference diets rather than a single set diet. This would allow for flexibility with regard to changing the concentrations of one or more components, whilst keeping the remainder of the diet relatively constant.

Practical approach to diet variation

Depending upon the parameters being studied, the results in many experiments may not be affected by small changes in the concentrations of dietary components. However, one must be aware of the possibility of adverse influences caused by variations in the composition of animal diets. How then should this problem be addressed? Researchers should initially search through the literature and identify components of the diet which may affect the parameters to be measured in the experiment. The diet to be used should also be analyzed to measure the concentrations of the components which have been identified. The concentrations of these components should then be kept constant throughout the experiment. In addition the diets of experimental animals should be described as extensively as possible in scientific papers. Repetition of experiments can only be meaningful if these guidelines are followed. It would then be possible to track down the part played by diet, if any, when it is apparent that experiments cannot be reproduced.

Diet forms

Diets for laboratory rodents can be provided in different physical forms. Experimental procedures will generally determine the most advantageous form for any given study. For example, when highly toxic compounds are added to the diet, a form should be selected that will produce a minimum amount of dust.

Generally speaking, pellets are the most efficient form of food for laboratory rodents as they are easy to handle, store and to administer. Only minimal amounts of these products are wasted by the animals. Food additives or test compounds cannot however be added after completion of the pelleting process, unless the pellets are reground.

Meal is a very inefficient form of food for rodents because they have a tendency to waste large amounts. When storage conditions are less than ideal, there is a tendency for meal to cake together and special equipment is required for feeding. Diets will be fed in meal form when food additives or test compounds are incorporated after the manufacturing process has been completed.

Semi-moist or gel form diets are efficient to use when dusty or highly toxic test compounds are to be incorporated. They are usually much more palatable than dry food. Diets in this form are, however, more susceptible to bacterial growth, they must be administered frequently, and large quantities are bulky and hard to handle.

Energy requirements and feed intake

Table 6.6 lists the energy requirements of rats under various physiological conditions. Growth and lactation for example, impose heavy demands on

Table 6.6

Estimated requirements of metabolizable energy and food intake in rats

Physiological status	Body weight (g)	Energy requirement (MJ/day)	*Ad libitum* food intake[1] (g/day)
Growth	100	0.21	15
Growth	200	0.36	25
Growth	300	0.49	34
Maintenance	400	0.23	16
Pregnancy	400	0.30	21
Lactation	400	0.65	46

[1] Energy density of diet: 14.5 kJ/g

energy. As energy requirements are related to metabolic weight, i.e. body weight kg$^{0.75}$, individual animals and strains with different body weights will have different energy requirements. The estimated energy requirements are related to metabolic body weight and metabolizable energy in the following way (Clarke *et al.*, 1977):

- Maintenance requirement = $0.45 \times$ body weight$^{0.75}$
- Growth requirement = $1.20 \times$ body weight$^{0.75}$
- Pregnancy requirement = $0.60 \times$ body weight$^{0.75}$
- Lactation requirement = $1.30 \times$ body weight$^{0.75}$

All requirements are expressed as a daily intake of metabolizable energy in MJ; body weight is expressed in kg. It should be stressed here that the estimates obtained assume a minimal expenditure of energy for physical activity, and are not applicable to animals from which any sustained work output is expected. Furthermore, no extra heat generation has been allowed for to compensate for low environmental temperature as it has been assumed that the animals are housed under conditions of thermal comfort or thermal neutrality.

Natural-ingredient diets may contain the following amounts of energy sources (expressed as weight percentages): 50% carbohydrates, 25% protein and 5% fat. The energy density of this diet is then 14.5 kJ/g. The contribution made by fibre to dietary energy is negligible. On the basis of the energy requirement of the animal and the energy density of the diet, the expected *ad libitum* food intake can be calculated (Table 6.6).

Along with body weight and physiological status, the condition of the animal must also be taken into consideration when considering food intake, e.g. sick animals generally consume less food. The energy density of a diet is an important determinant of food intake. Dietary characteristics which influence palatability may also determine food intake.

Variable energy density of diets

Various groups of animals showing the same gender and breed or strain with similar body weight, age, health status etc, will have a similar energy requirement. Regardless of the composition of the diet, the animals will generally consume an almost constant amount of energy, provided that they are fed *ad libitum*. This is because laboratory animals tend to adjust their food intake to satisfy their energy requirements. Therefore, if the energy density of the diet increases, the animals will consume less food and *vice versa*. This implies that, when diets are being used which have different compositions within one experiment, the concentrations of the components, which must not vary between experimental groups, must be identical when expressed relative to dietary energy. If this is not done, then the intakes of these components will differ between the control and the test animals when they have free access to food. This must be taken into account when formulating diets with different compositions.

It is of course the case that researchers will sometimes wish to make variations to the content of a nutrient or ingredient in an experimental diet. Such modification may result in changes in the consumption of other components of the diet. Natural-ingredient diets can be misused in studies where test diets are formulated by adding large amounts of one ingredient such as fat or sugar. What generally then occurs is that the natural-ingredient diet, which was originally formulated as a complete diet, is considered to be the control diet. This causes the problem then that the test and control diets contain different concentrations of all nutrients, because those in the test diet have been diluted by the addition which has been made. When the concentrations of energy are different, then different amounts of diet will be consumed by animals fed with the test or the control diets. It is impossible to achieve a valid interpretation of data collected from such a study, since observed differences in animal response could be due to the matter of interest in, or to other differences in the constitution of the test and the control diets. This problem can be kept to an absolute minimum when the test diet is formulated by adding minute amounts of a compound to the complete, natural-ingredient diet.

Control and test diets can both be prepared by adding control and test supplements to a commercial, natural-ingredient diet. However, the problem still exists of reducing the intake of essential nutrients. Commercial, natural-ingredient diets generally contain sufficiently high amounts of essential nutrients to permit dilution without producing serious imbalances. As a rule of thumb, natural-ingredient diets can be diluted by 10–20 percent with supplements. The possible effects of such dilutions must be evaluated carefully for any given experiment. It must be taken into account that the

Table 6.7

Examples of expected results of low and high-fat diet formulations when fed to rats

Diet ingredient	Diet 1: Low-fat	Diet 2: High-fat	Diet 3: High-fat, adjusted	Diet 4: High-fat, adjusted
Protein (g)	20	20	20	20
Carbohydrate (g)	60	40	15	15
Fat (g)	10	30	30	30
Fibre (g)	4	4	4	4
Mineral mix (g)	4	4	4	4
Vitamin mix (g)	1	1	1	1
Test compound (g)	1	1	1	1
"Inert" compound (g)	–	–	–	25
Total (g)	100	100	75	100
Energy value (kcal/g)	4.10	5.10	5.47	4.10
Expected intake				
Energy (MJ/day)	0.34	0.34	0.34	0.34
Food (g/day)	20	16	15	20
Protein (g/day)	4	3.2	4	4
Carbohydrate (g/day)	12	6.4	3	3
Fat (g/day)	2	4.8	6	6
Fibre (g)	0.8	0.64	0.8	0.8
Mineral mix (g/day)	0.8	0.64	0.8	0.8
Vitamin mix (g/day)	0.2	0.16	0.2	0.2
Test compound (g/day)	0.2	0.16	0.2	0.2
"Inert" compound (g/day)	–	–	–	5

background composition of the diet, i.e. the natural-ingredient diet, is poorly characterized and subject to variation. Accurate nutritional control includes both standardization and characterization of the ingredients used to make up the experimental diets. For this reason, purified diets are generally used for nutritional experiments with small animals.

Table 6.7 shows the potential effects from certain low-fat and high-fat dietary formulations. In this example, the low-fat diet (Diet 1) contains 10 percent fat, 20 percent protein, 60 percent carbohydrates, fibre, vitamin and mineral mixes, and a test compound. The high-fat diet (diet 2), is formulated by adding 20 percent fat, deleting an equal weight of carbohydrates, whilst maintaining the same level of other components. The expected effects on nutrient intake are shown on the table underneath the diet formulation. The high-fat diet will have a 24 percent higher energy concentration than the low-fat diet. It can be presumed that the caloric intake of rats consuming these diets under *ad libitum* conditions would be essentially the same i.e. that the rats will consume a constant amount of energy. One would therefore presume that the weight of food consumed by rats fed the high-fat diet would be considerably lower than that consumed by rats fed the low-fat diet. In addition to the changes in fat and carbohydrate intake, the intake of protein, mineral mix, vitamin mix, fibre and the test compound will subsequently all be lower with the rats fed on the high-fat diet. Thus, the change in food intake is also important when a test compound is being administered in the diet. In the example given, there would be a 20 percent difference in the intake of the test compound.

One method which would eliminate some of these problems is illustrated by Diet 3. Fat and carbohydrates have been exchanged isocalorically: some carbohydrate is omitted to compensate for the increase in calories resulting from the addition of extra fat. This adjusted high-fat diet ensures an intake of protein, vitamins, minerals, and fibre comparable with that of Diet 1. Although the components of Diet 3 do not add up to 100 g, and the expected food intake is lower than with Diet 1, the intake of the test compound and of all nutrients except for fat and carbohydrate will be the same.

Apart from the fat and carbohydrate intake, rats fed Diets 1 and 3 would also show differences in actual food intake, i.e. the quantity of the intake. This alone could produce a difference in experimental results between the groups. In another approach to diet formulation (Diet 4), a relatively inert ingredient, such as cellulose, may be added to bring the ingredients up to 100 g. Diet 4 is isocaloric with Diet 1, and the nutrient intake should also be the same. This approach would appear to be satisfactory, but for the fact that inert compounds do not exist. Therefore, one would have to elect for the formulation of a high-fat diet as illustrated by Diet 3.

A similar example could be given for fibre-enriched diets at the expense of carbohydrates. The high-fibre, low-carbohydrate diet would be expected to have a lower energy value than the low-fibre, high-carbohydrate diet. The consumption, therefore, of the high-fibre diet could be expected to be greater. Here again, there would be changes in the intake of other nutrients, and comparisons between animals fed the high- and low-fibre diets would become very difficult.

Feeding regimes

Various feeding regimes can be applied to laboratory animals. The choice of feeding regime will depend upon practical and scientific criteria.

Ad libitum feeding. With this regime the animals have free access to food any time of the day or night. Under *ad libitum* conditions, rodents and rabbits consume most of their food during the dark phase. A rat will take approximately 12 meals per day of which 8 meals will be taken during the dark phase.

Meal feeding. During fixed time periods, one or more periods per day, the animals are allowed to consume as much food as they like. Meal feeding can be controlled by a feeding apparatus. This feeding regime is used for experiments requiring a strictly controlled nutritional state, such as a certain number of hours postprandially.

Restricted feeding. This regime involves limiting the food intake or under-feeding, but is not equivalent to malnutrition or the induction of nutrient deficiency. Restricted feeding generally refers to both nutrient and energy restriction. It can be used to equalize food intake of different animals, for instance those in control and test groups.

Pair feeding. This is a specific form of restricted feeding. It involves the measurement of the amount of food consumed by animals with depressed food intake, (e.g. treated animals), whilst giving the same amount to animals in the non-treated control group. By doing this, the food intake of control and test animals will be equalized. When employing this procedure, each animal in the test group must be assigned its own control counterpart. The amount of food consumed by the treated group will be offered to the control group one day later.

Restricted feeding brings with it various practical implications. Under *ad libitum* conditions, the animals may be given food once every two to four days. When animals are fed restrictedly, food has to be provided daily either manually or automatically, and animals have to be housed individually. If the animals are housed in groups, the dominant ones may almost be able to carry out *ad libitum*-feeding. It is a fact that restricted feeding reduces diet costs.

When carrying out either pair feeding or restricted feeding studies, a third group should always be fed the identical control diet *ad libitum*, as an additional control. Researchers should take into account that pair-fed control animals are usually underfed and will therefore consume their food faster than animals with an unrestricted intake. Various techniques can be used to partially compensate for this difference in consumption pattern, e.g. feeding control animals their daily ration in divided batches. Each experiment, should have its food consumption determined and have it reported on periodically.

Variation in food intake within experiments

In certain experiments with animals fed *ad libitum*, food intake of the test animals may be lower than that of the control animals. Reduced food intake in the test animals can be due to intoxication with the compound under study, irrespective of whether it is given with the food or not, or to deficiency of a nutrient. Food intake can also be depressed due to the fact that the compound under study has of itself anorexic activity. The difference of food intake between the control and the test groups would imply that comparison of the measured parameters is not straightforward. If and when both the treatment and the food intake exert an independent influence upon the parameter under study, then the effect of the treatment cannot be interpreted unequivocally. The observed effect will have been caused partly by the difference between the control and the test treatment, and partly by the difference in food intake between the control and the test group. If the research requires insight into a specific effect of the test treatment, then the variation in food intake should be overcome. This can either be done by the administration of restricted amounts of food or by employing the paired feeding technique.

It has been demonstrated repeatedly that food restriction inhibits the development of spontaneous tumours and prolongs life in rats and mice. The impact, therefore, of depressed food intake in test animals on the interpretation of results has been especially relevant in cancer bioassay feeding studies with rats. When rats are treated with a carcinogenic substance together with a reduced food intake, then the carcinogenic activity of the test compound will be underestimated. In fact, this has occurred frequently in cancer bioassay studies in which the rats were fed *ad libitum*. Table 6.8 shows hypothetical outcomes of a carcinogenesis bioassay in which control and test rats were fed *ad libitum*. The test compound reduces food intake by 20%, which frequently occurs in practice. Of the control rats, 30% will develop tumours, whilst a food restriction of 20% will reduce tumour incidence to 10%. In experiment A, the test compound increases tumour incidence to 40%. When this is compared with the incidence rate in control rats fed *ad libitum*, one could presume that the compound causes cancer. However, the carcinogenic activity of the compound is underestimated, and this becomes clear when test animals are compared with control animals which are fed restrictedly. In experiments B and C with both control and test rats fed *ad libitum*, the incorrect conclusions would be drawn that the test compound is not carcinogenic, or that it indeed protects against carcinogenesis. The latter has occurred in practice. It is clear that carcinogenicity testing with rats fed *ad libitum* will not yield results from which conclusive interpretations can

Table 6.8

Hypothetical results of a cancer bioassay

Treatment	Feeding regime	Food intake	Percentage of rats with tumours			
			A	B	C	D
Control	*ad libitum*	100%	30	30	30	30
Test	*ad libitum*	80%	40	30	20	10
Control	restricted	80%	10	10	10	10

be drawn. Ideally, both control and test rats should be fed restrictedly so that feed intakes are identical, or the technique of paired feeding should be applied.

Literature

Beynen A C. Biochemists and the diet of their rats. Trends Biochem Sci 1985;10: 108–109.

Beynen A C. Laboratory animal nutrition and experimental results. Scand J Lab Anim Sci 1987;14: 89–97.

Beynen AC. Ad libitum versus restricted feeding: Pros and cons. Scand J Lab Anim Sci 1992;19: 19–22.

Clarke H E, Coates M E, Eva J K, Ford D J, Milner C K, O'Donoghue P N, Scott P P, Ward R J. Dietary standards for laboratory animals: report of the Laboratory Animals Centre Diets Advisory Committee. Lab Anim 1977;11: 1–28.

Committee on Laboratory Animal Diets. Control of diets in laboratory animal experimentation. ILAR News 1978:21:A1-12 and Nutr Abstr Rev B 1979; 49: 413–419.

National Research Council. Nutrient requirements of rabbits. Washington: National Academy of Sciences, 1977.

National Research Council. Nutrient requirements of laboratory animals. Washington: National Academy of Sciences, 1978.

Wise A, Gilburt, D J. Variation of minerals and trace elements in laboratory animal diets. Lab Anim 1981;15: 299–303.

7   Genetic standardization

Introduction

A major factor contributing to the variation of the results in animal experiments is the genetic background of the animals. In certain types of tests genetic differences between the individuals of a test group are acceptable or even preferable, e.g. when results are to be extrapolated to other species, such as in toxicity tests. Other experiments require a uniform animal population. Whatever the requirements of the tests are, it must be possible to reproduce the results. For this reason the genetic background of the animals should be standardized. This can be achieved with specific breeding programmes or by biotechnological manipulations. Both techniques have resulted in the production of animal populations with a standardized genetic variation. In this chapter, the breeding systems applied for generating groups of genetically standardized animals will be discussed. Different aspects of genetic quality control, when dealing with these populations, will also be covered.

Genetic uniformity

Monozygotic animals

Littermates usually have different genotypes but there are certain species where genetic uniformity of littermates exists, e.g. the siblings of the nine-banded armadillo *(Dasypus novemcinctus)* are all genetically identical. This primitive mammal, found in Southern and Central America, is mainly used as a test animal for leprosy research. The armadillo produces four monozygotic offspring per litter (i.e. derived from one fertilized egg). The birth of monozygotic twins is not an unusual event in several other mammalian species. Genetic uniformity does not mean that the animals will be phenotypically

127

identical, or that their response when submitted to the same experimental procedure will be exactly the same. When comparing calves which have been born as monozygotic twins, minor differences may be visible in their coat patterns. Subtle differences in the environment during the intra-uterine development may have caused variation in the migration of melanocytes from the neural tube to the peripheral parts of the body, resulting in differences in pigmentation. Slight differences may be found both in the morphological and the physiological characteristics of genetically identical twins. The differences will of course be smaller than with littermates exhibiting different genotypes. If genetic uniformity is required, monozygotic individuals should be the animals of choice; however only a limited number of these animals are available for use in research. Although it is possible to produce such animals by cloning, the traditional and still the most frequently used method for the production of genetically uniform animals is inbreeding. A large number of inbred strains of both mice and rats are available at present.

Inbred strains

Inbreeding, or the crossing of closely related animals, increases homozygosity in the offspring. The degree of inbreeding is expressed by the coefficient of inbreeding (F). F is the fraction of the original heterozygous genes which have become fixed in a homozygous state due to inbreeding. F will increase with the number of generations of inbreeding. The increase in F per generation (ΔF) is dependent upon the degree of consanguinity of the ancestors (see fig. 7.1).

   The production of inbred strains commenced at the beginning of this century, mainly due to the need for genetically identical animals for cancer research. Tumour tissues were maintained by successively transplanting (passaging) the neoplasm onto different individuals from the same species. This method was sometimes successful, but very often the neoplasms were rejected by the recipients shortly upon grafting. The reason for this remained unclear until 1903, when Carl Jensen succeeded in maintaining a lung tumour in an inbred population of albino mice through 15 generations. The tolerance or the rejection of transplants seemed to be a genetically controlled process. This discovery led to an increase in the production of inbred strains. At present there are over 1000 genetically defined strains of mice and over 400 genetically defined strains of rats available. According to the "Committee on Standardized Nomenclature for Inbred Strains of Mice" a population may only be defined as an inbred strain after a minimum of 20 successive generations of either brother-sister (bxs) mating, or mating between offspring and the youngest parent. At that point (i.e. 21st generation) the coefficient of inbreeding will be 98.4%, which means on average 98.4% of the originally heterozygous loci have become fixed in a homozygous state. Although it is

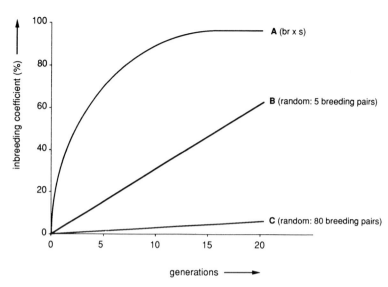

Fig. 7.1. The increase of inbreeding per generation depends upon the relationship between the individual partners of a breeding pair. Brother–sister matings (cf. A) result in a steep increase of the inbreeding coefficient. With random matings the increase depends upon the size of the population, or more specifically upon the number of breeding pairs (cf. B and C).

possible that small variations still occur within an inbred strain, it may be considered to be a genetically uniform group of animals, and therefore may be regarded as isogenic.

According to the rules for the nomenclature of genetically defined strains, an inbred strain is designated by a code which consists of between one and four capital letters (e.g. A; DBA; WAG). The only exceptions to this rule are names of some old strains (e.g. C3H; C57BL; 129) which were already widely accepted and recognized when the rules were established.

Inbred strains can be separated into two or more substrains. If after between 8 and 19 generations of bxs mating a strain is split into parallel lines, these lines can be regarded as substrains. Furthermore, strains shall be regarded as substrains if differences are detected between parallel lines of an established inbred strain or if a branch is separated and maintained at a different laboratory. It must be mentioned that the rules for the nomenclature of substrains are not consistent when comparing the literature for the various species. Substrain designations are appended to the strain's name. Strain symbol and substrain designation are separated by a slash (e.g. C57BL/6J or C57BL/1OScSn).

In order to facilitate a true comparison of experimental results between laboratories, it is essential to use the correct strain nomenclature when reporting experiments.

Inbred strains are frequently used in biomedical research not only because of their uniformity but also because several strains carry specific genetic characteristics or disorders which also occur in man.

Inbreeding can result in decreased vigour, having a negative effect upon growth, survival or fertility. However, most inbred strains are not seriously affected and possess normal viability. This can be explained as follows. In any natural population most animals carry a number of detrimental recessive alleles, which are not expressed in the phenotype. This is due to the fact that each one is accompanied by a dominant counterpart. The chances of a descendant being homozygous for one or more of these recessive alleles is rather small in the case of random matings, but this will increase, however, when the parents are related. Inbreeding depression due to an increased chance of homozygosity of harmful alleles will occur mainly during the first 4–10 generations. Gradually, the less favourable combinations of alleles will be eliminated (i.e. the respective lines will decease), whereas the more favourable combinations will be propagated (i.e. will survive). Therefore, a fully inbred strain usually possesses a gene pool which is balanced, enabling normal development of the animals.

It was long presumed that genetic uniformity of an inbred strain would also guarantee a uniform response when the animals were submitted to the same experimental conditions. However, as long ago as 1956, McLaren and Michie demonstrated otherwise. They showed that offspring from mice of a cross between two inbred strains responded more uniformly when exposed to the anaesthetic pentobarbital, compared with either of the two parental inbred strains. There have been many other examples reported since that date to support this phenomenon.

F_1 hybrids.

F_1 hybrids are animals resulting from a cross between two inbred strains. All F_1 hybrids are genetically uniform and heterozygous for all the genes for which the two parental strains differ (fig. 7.2). The finding that a more uniform response to an experimental procedure is more likely to occur with a F_1 hybrid, than with the parental strains, may be explained by the larger number of alleles present in the F_1 hybrids. A larger pool of alleles provides the animal with a sturdier buffer when compensating for minor environmental fluctuations. However, this decreased sensitivity to environmental influences is not always desirable. Certain experiments require animals that are highly sensitive.

Under certain circumstances, F_1 hybrids may show a less uniform response than individuals from the parental inbred strains. This may be due to the improved ability of the F_1 hybrids to adapt. This phenomenon is known as the

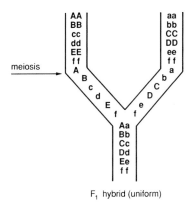

F₁ hybrid (uniform)

Fig. 7.2. The F₁ hybrid is uniform but heterozygous for all genes for which the parental strains differ.

"Tryon-effect" after R.C. Tryon who was the first person in 1940 to describe this variation using F_1 animals of "maze-bright" and "maze-dull" rats.

F_1 hybrids generally show a more uniform response when a morphological parameter is being studied, and a more variable response when behavioural characteristics are under investigation. There are, however, no general rules which can be applied as would be noticeable, for example when studying communication between animals where behaviour would present itself rather uniformly, like a morphological trait. Functionally speaking this seems logical as a variation in communicative behaviour could easily lead to misinterpretation.

Coisogenic strains

Occasionally mutants are found among the individuals of an established inbred strain. If the mutant represents a genetic model for a human disease, or if the mutation involves a gene of general interest, then a subline of the inbred strain carrying the mutant gene, may be established. A subline which differs from the original inbred strain by only one gene, is termed coisogenic. Such a strain may be extremely useful as it enables the comparison of two isogenic strains which only differ at the locus of interest. The symbol for a coisogenic strain must consist of the full strain and substrain designation, followed by a dash and an indication of the mutant gene (e.g. BALB/cRij-*nu*, which means a BALB/c strain carrying the "nude" allele (*nu*), and maintained at TNO in Rijswijk (Rij), The Netherlands).

Sometimes it may prove difficult to maintain a coisogenic strain. This is, of course, particularly so when the mutation involves a recessive allele which causes infertility or which is lethal for the progeny. In such cases the mutant gene can only be maintained in the heterozygous state.

Congenic strains

It is possible to introduce a genetic trait into an inbred strain by backcrossing repeatedly. Several of these breeding schemes, using repeated backcrossing, have been designed. The choice of which scheme to use will depend upon whether the differential locus is dominant, co-dominant or recessive. A system (cross–intercross–backcross system), which is used frequently for the introduction of a recessive mutant, is shown in fig. 7.3. Here, after an initial cross, a cycle of intercrossing–backcrossing is repeated at least 10 times, whilst ensuring that the animals selected for the backcross carry the gene of interest (donor gene, *mm*). As a result of crossing-over during meiosis, and the selection of the proper backcross animals, the donor gene is introduced into the genome of strain A (recipient strain). The resultant strain is congenic. This strain is genetically similar to the original strain A but it contains the donor gene as well as some concomitant passenger genes on either side of the locus of interest. The number of retained adjacent genes is reduced with successive generations of backcrossing.

The designation of congenic strains is similar to the designation of coisogenic strains. However, if congenic strains differ at the major histocompatibility locus it is acceptable to give an abbreviated strain name, followed by a full

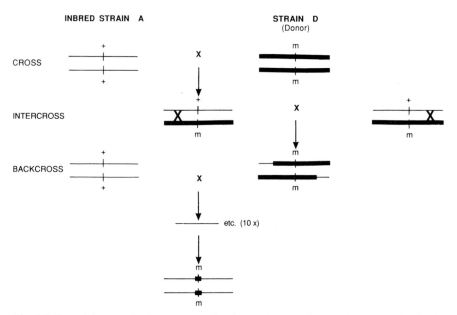

Fig. 7.3. Cross–intercross–backcross system for the production of congenic strains. The dominant gene ($++$) is replaced by the recessive gene (*mm*).

stop and the abbreviation of the name of the donor strain (e.g. B10.D2, which refers to a C57BL/10 carrying the H-2 haplotype of the DBA/2 inbred strain).

Recombinant inbred strains

Recombinant inbred strains are produced by bxs mating of individuals from the F_2 generation of a cross between two (unrelated) inbred strains, termed progenitor strains. Preferably a large number of strains is derived from these two progenitor strains in parallel and independently (see fig. 7.4). The RI strains can be regarded as established after a minimum of 20 generations of bxs matings and will then form a set or series of RI strains. They are designated by combining abbreviated names of both the parental strains which are separated by a capital X. The parallel lines are given numbers (e.g. B6XH-1 which is the first recombinant inbred strain derived from the progenitor strains C57BL/6J and C3H/HeJ). RI strains represent a fixed set of randomly assorted genes of both progenitors. These strains are very valuable for genetic research, in particular for studies on linkage analysis and for the identification and genetic analysis of complex genetic traits.

Recombinant congenic strains

Recombinant congenic strains represent a series of inbred strains, which are derived from the second or third backcross generation of two unrelated inbred progenitor strains, one serving as background the other as donor strain.

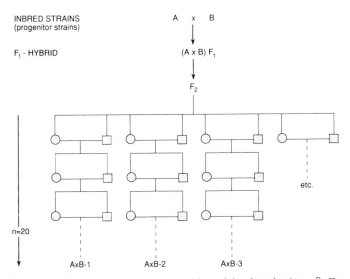

Fig. 7.4. Scheme for the production of recombinant inbred strains (○ = ♀; □ = ♂).

After 20 generations of bxs inbreeding, the genome of each of the resulting recombinant congenic inbred strains will primarily contain genomic material from the background strain, plus a small proportion of the donor genome (when the process of inbreeding starts after 2 backcrosses this is on average the equivalent of 12.5% of the donor genome). The genomic material of the donor strain is unevenly dispersed over the genome of the background strain. When comparing recombinant congenic strains, the various chromosomal segments of the donor strain will show some overlap. Therefore, some 20–25 parallel lines will be necessary in order to cover at least 95% of the donor strain's genome.

Recombinant congenic strains are usually expressed by the prefix RCS and the abbreviated names of the progenitor inbred strains, separated by a small c (e.g. RCS CcS-1 which means the first recombinant congenic strain from the parental strains BALB/c and STS; BALB/c is the recipient strain and STS the donor strain).

Recombinant congenic strains have been developed for the study of the genetic background of quantitative traits, such as susceptibility to tumour development or disease resistance.

Transgenic animals

A transgenic strain is created by the introduction of a foreign gene (insert) into the germ line of an animal from an established inbred strain. It is possible to introduce cloned DNA or a modified retrovirus directly into the pronucleus of a zygote by means of micro-injection.

The general procedure for the production of a transgenic strain would involve the following. Approximately twelve hours after mating fertilized eggs should be collected from the oviduct. At this stage the male and female pronuclei have yet to fuse. Cloned DNA, containing the gene of interest, should be micro-injected into one of the pronuclei. To achieve this, a specially designed injection pipette (2–3 microns in diameter) must be used. The injected zygote should then be transferred into the oviduct of a female which has been made pseudopregnant after being mated with a vasectomized male. This takes place either shortly ($\sim$2 hrs) after microinjection (approximately 20–40 embryos per recipient) or after a cultivation period of $\sim$48 hrs (5–10 normal developed 8-cell embryos). After birth, littermates have to be screened for integration into the genome using Southern blot analysis or PCR (see later). In subsequent generations, it has to be verified that the integration is stable. Each animal derived by microinjection will serve as the founder of a transgenic strain, since integration sites will not be alike for any one construct. Once the DNA has been integrated into the genome, it will be present in all nucleated cells, including gametes, and will therefore be inherited in a normal

Mendelian fashion. On average, not more than 5% of the micro-injected zygotes will incorporate the transgene. In only a fraction of these cases will the transgene be expressed. Both undesirable and harmful side effects may result as a consequence of this manipulation, whether it is successful or not (in terms of transgene expression). An increased susceptibility to arthritis or stress, together with decreased fertility as a result of this, and other defects, have been reported. Despite these drawbacks, transgenics are powerful tools not only for genetic analyses but also for designing specific models of human diseases.

Transgenic strains are indicated by the name of the strain, followed by the transgene symbol, e.g. C57BL/6J–TgN(XX)Y, where Tg = transgene, N = non-homologous insertion, XX = insert designation and Y = laboratory code.

Examples of their use include the study of the regulation of gene expression, and the study of the process by which normal cells undergo transformation. This technique is also being applied in livestock breeding aiming at increased productivity, improved disease resistance, and to produce, for example, recombinant pharmaceutical proteins in the mammary gland.

Genetic variation

Random bred colonies and outbred stocks

As mentioned above, it may be preferable to have a certain degree of genetic heterogeneity within a group of animals e.g. as the base population in selection experiments, or as the background population for deleterious mutants (e.g. nude gene in mice and rats). It is, however, more difficult to maintain a given level of variation within an animal colony than it is to maintain its uniformity. If less than an infinite number of breeding animals are used for propagation of the colony, inbreeding is inevitable, causing a loss of alleles in subsequent generations. When matings occur at random, ΔF is $1/8 n_f + 1/8 n_m$, where n_f is the number of female breeders and n_m the number of male breeders. If $n_f = n_m$ then $\Delta F = 1/2N$, where N is the total number of breeding animals. This means that if a population consists of 50 female and 50 male breeding animals $\Delta F = 0.5\%$, and if there are only 10 breeding pairs $\Delta F = 2.5\%$.

If the inbreeding coefficient of a random bred colony increases, the gene pool will correspondingly decrease. This process may be accelerated if the breeding population of the colony has been temporarily reduced in size, e.g. when a conventional colony is changed into an SPF colony by the performance of hysterectomies (bottle-neck effect).

If offspring of as many parents as possible are being used for breeding purposes, then the reduction of the gene pool of the colony will be kept to a minimum. The matings may be at random, or better, should be arranged in such a way that breeding partners are only distantly related. Rotation schemes which have been designed for this purpose may reduce the increase of the inbreeding coefficient by 50%. Thus, consistent breeding according to a rotation scheme may result in a reduction of ΔF ($1/4N$ instead of $1/2N$ per generation).

It is obvious that, when using animals from a random bred colony, or from a population which has been propagated by the system of minimal inbreeding, the reproducibility of the results of successive experiments will be limited. The gene pool will gradually change over time and eventually it will become impossible to compile a group of test animals with exactly the same genetic background as previous experimental groups.

If a random bred colony is maintained as a closed population for at least four generations, and if the number of breeding animals is sufficient to guarantee that $\Delta F < 1\%$, then the colony may be designated as an outbred stock. An outbred stock is not subject to artificial directional selection for any characteristic, apart from breeding performance. Following the rules of nomenclature, the designation of an outbred stock consists of a symbol indicating the current breeder/holder of the stock, followed by a colon and the stock symbol consisting of between one and four capital letters (e.g. Ola:SPRD; Han:NMRI).

Mosaic population: inbred strains and their F_1 hybrids

During long term experiments, in particular if consistent genetic variation is essential, the use of an outbred stock is inadequate due to the gradual change of the gene pool. The genetic variation can be standardized by using

Table 7.1

Standardization of the genetic variation by hybridizing inbred strains (mosaic population). A, B, C and D are inbred strains

♀ \ ♂	A	B	C	D
A	A	(AB)F1	(AC)F1	(AD)F1
B	(BA)F1	B	(BC)F1	(BD)F1
C	(CA)F1	(CB)F1	C	(CD)F1
D	(DA)F1	(DB)F1	(DC)F1	D

reciprocal crosses of a number of inbred strains (see table 7.1). With four inbred strains A, B, C and D at least 10 different genotypes can be produced. Where n = number of inbred strains, $n + (n^2 - n)/2$ different genotypes can be produced. If the reciprocal F_1 hybrids such as $(AB) F_1$ and $(BA) F_1$ are considered to be non-identical, then even more genotypes are generated. A mosaic population or a population of inbred strains and their hybrids will result. A group of test animals and a group of control animals with identical genetic variation can be collected by taking one or two (one of each sex) animals from each entry of the breeding scheme. The same genetic variation can be generated at a later stage, provided that the inbred strains are still free from genetic contamination. This requires an accurate breeding programme, and a monitoring system for controlling the genetic quality of the inbred strains.

Genetic quality control

Genetic contamination, which is the inadvertent outcrossing (miscegenation) of an inbred strain, can go undetected for some time. In the case of miscegenation occurring between two different albino inbred strains, the phenotypes of the offspring cannot be distinguished from the parental phenotypes. Several reports have been published indicating that certain inbred strains have become genetically contaminated. Some groups report up to 20% of the strains which have been tested as being contaminated.

Also unintentional exchange of tags with strain designation may occur e.g. during transportation of two strains which are phenotypically alike. Both strains may still be uniform, but are then designated with wrong names.

It is imperative to check both uniformity and authenticity of inbred strains regularly.

Strain uniformity can be tested by skin grafting. The acceptance or rejection of grafts will largely depend upon the compatibility of the MHC (major histocompatibility complex) haplotypes between the donor and the recipient. Although isohistogenicity is a sensitive method to verify uniformity, it is certainly not the method of choice to determine authenticity.

Genetic monitoring of inbred strains should be a common practice to all who breed and maintain defined strains. Quite often breeders, and/or holders rely merely on published data of strains with identical names. The establishment of an appropriate system for monitoring both uniformity and authenticity first requires the establishment of a genetic strain profile, including biochemical and DNA markers, or, depending upon the strains maintained, immunological, morphological, pathophysiological and cytogenetic markers. Subsequently a critical subset of these markers, differentiating between strains maintained in the same unit, must be selected.

Biochemical markers

Isozymes, which are variants of the same enzyme, occurring in blood and tissue samples, are both accurate and sensitive markers for genetic quality control. Electrophoretic techniques are used to separate these variants. An example can be used to illustrate this point. For the mouse gene coding for the enzyme isocitrate dehydrogenase-1 (*Idh-1*; E.C.1.1.1.41.), two co-dominant alleles *Idh-1^a* and *Idh-1^b* have been identified. Each of these code for a different form of the protein. Each isozyme exhibits a different mobility when subjected to electrophoresis resulting in two distinct zones following activity-specific staining. In the homozygous animals (*aa* or *bb*) only one form of the protein (A or B) can be detected. In the heterozygous animals (*ab*) both zone A and zone B are present.

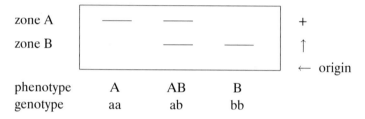

phenotype	A	AB	B
genotype	aa	ab	bb

The number of protein markers which are now available for genetic quality control exceeds 50, and is still increasing.

DNA markers

Polymorphism at the DNA level is becoming increasingly important for the genetic characterization of inbred strains. RFLP (restriction fragment length polymorphism) and in particular SSLP (simple sequence length polymorphism) are being used for this purpose.

Restriction enzymes are being used for generating RFLP's. A restriction enzyme is an endonuclease which cleaves DNA at a specific nucleotide sequence. RFLP represents variation in the length of DNA fragments due to a mutation at a recognition site for the enzyme, resulting in non-cleavage. Polymorphisms are then detected using the Southern blot technique. DNA from two strains, which differ at a recognition site for a particular restriction enzyme, will give rise to fragments of different sizes when digested with this enzyme. The fragments are then separated by agarose gel electrophoresis and are subsequently transferred ("blotted") onto a nitrocellulose membrane. The DNA fragments are denatured and hybridized to a radio-labelled sequence (probe). The fragments are made visible by exposing the membrane to photographic film (autoradiograph).

SSLP's have arisen through the existence of microsatellites. These are fragments of DNA which consist of tandem-repeats of 2–4 nucleotides (e.g. $(CA)_{18}$ or $(GGC)_{15}$). There are at least 10^5 sequences containing $(CA)_n$ repeats in both mouse and human genomes, where n is between 9 and 30. There are perhaps half as many $(GA)_n$ microsatellites. At any specific locus, the number of repeats may vary between inbred strains. These differences between inbred strains can be visualized using the polymerase chain reaction (PCR), combined with agarose or polyacrylamide gel electrophoresis (PAGE). PCR results in the amplification of the selected DNA fragment. Oligo-nucleotides (primers), complementary to the (unique) regions flanking the microsatellite, are hybridized to denatured genomic DNA (annealing). Taking the oligonucleotides as starting points, new DNA strands are synthesized in the presence of Taq-polymerase and a mixture of nucleotides (extension), thereby doubling the number of strands at any specific locus. After repeated denaturation, annealing and extension, sufficient of the product will accumulate so as to be made visible on a gel after staining with ethidium bromide (fig. 7.5). Differences in product size as minimal as one repeat unit, will result in detectable differences in mobility after electrophoresis.

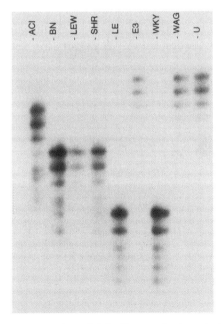

Fig. 7.5. DNA markers are extremely useful for the genetic characterization of inbred strains. The different positions of the bands indicate a difference in length of the microsatellites (tandem repeat) in the inbred strains. The SSLP (simple sequence length polymorphism) is made visible through the combination of PCR (polymerase chain reaction) and gel electrophoresis.

Microsatellites undergo Mendelian inheritance. Their presence in abundance in the mammalian genome, together with the fact that they are highly polymorphic, makes them extremely valuable for the genetic quality control of inbred strains.

It is now possible to characterize each inbred strain and to establish a genetic profile based upon the allele distribution of a given set of protein and/or DNA markers.

Monitoring procedures need to be repeated at certain intervals. Routine verification of the genetic profile of old breeding pairs, or of a representative sample from an inbred strain each 3–4 generation, gives insight into the genetic stability of the colony.

The genetic profile should ideally include markers covering the entire genome. In reality, only part of the genome will be covered in genetic monitoring programmes. Therefore, the stability of a genetic profile should not be interpreted as if the entire genome had remained unchanged. Genetic quality control is not aimed at tracing minor changes, but is executed primarily to detect genetic contamination at an early stage.

Genetic relationship between inbred strains

The origin of an inbred strain and the interrelationship between different inbred strains is not always known. However, for certain purposes it is

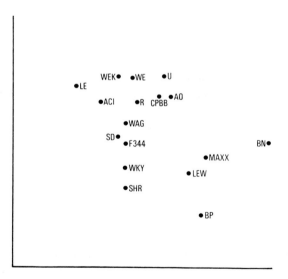

Fig. 7.6. Diagram of the "genetic distance" between 17 rat inbred strains. The genetic distance is estimated from the degree of allelic concordancy (discrepancy) for about 50 marker genes.

essential to have knowledge of the origin of the strain and to be able to determine the genetic distance between strains. Examples here would include studies aimed at choosing strains to be used in comparative tests, or where a cross is to be set up between two distantly related strains.

Strains which have similar genetic profiles are likely to be more closely related than strains with profiles that differ to a large extent. Therefore, comparison of the genetic profiles of inbred strains is sometimes used in order to estimate the relationship between inbred strains (fig. 7.6).

Cryopreservation

Mammalian embryos can be conserved through the use of special techniques involving freezing and storing. This is referred to as cryopreservation. This technique offers the possibility of storing embryos in a "bank". Embryo-banking is considered to prevent the extinction of valuable inbred strains that could occur as a result of a fatal disease or an accident. It also is thought to prevent genetic drift and guarantees the constant availability of strains which are fluctuating in demand, without the need for maintaining the strain as a vital breeding nucleus.

After mating, preimplantation embryos are collected from pregnant females and are subjected to a defined procedure of freezing (slow freezing; fast two-step freezing; vitrification). Embryos are then stored in liquid nitrogen ($-196°C$). After thawing, the embryos may be implanted into a recipient female. The survival rate of embryos depends upon the vigour of the strain, and on the procedures employed for freezing and thawing. Generally speaking not more than 20–30% of frozen embryos will develop into normal foetuses following implantation.

Re-derivation of a strain via embryo transfer excludes the chance of intrauterine contamination during pregnancy, which is reported to occur for a variety of bacterial and viral infections. Thus, this technique can also be used to start up a germ-free or SPF colony (see chapter 8) or to transfer a strain from one laboratory to another.

Literature

Altman P L, Katz D D, eds. Inbred and genetically defined strains of laboratory animals. Vol 1-2. Bethesda: FASEB, 1979.

Festing M F W. Inbred strains in biomedical research. London: McMillan, 1979.

Festing M F W. Genetic contamination of laboratory animal colonies: an increasingly serious problem. ILAR 1982; 25: 6–10.

Festing M F W. International index of laboratory animals. Carshalton: Lion Litho Ltd, 1993.

Green E L. Genetics and probability in animal breeding. London: McMillan, 1981.

Grosveld F, Kollias G, eds. Transgenic animals. London: Academic Press, 1992.

Hedrich H J, ed. Genetic monitoring of inbred strains of rats. Stuttgart: Fischer Verlag, 1990.

Lyon M F, Searle AG. Genetic variants and strains of the laboratory mouse. Oxford: Oxford University Press, 1989.

Tryon R C. Genetic differences in maze-learning ability in rats. Yb. Natn. Soc. Stud. Educ. 1940; 39: 111–119.

Zutphen L F M van. Genetics of laboratory animals. In: Ruitenberg J, Peters P, eds. World animal science. Amsterdam: Elsevier Science Publishers, 1986: 47–84.

8   Microbiological standardization

Introduction

Microbiological quality assurance of laboratory animals aims to produce animals that meet with preset requirements of microbiological quality, and the maintenance of this quality during the experiments. Microbiological quality assurance is a prerequisite for microbiological standardization of laboratory animals.

Reasons for microbiological quality assurance of laboratory animals

Disease and mortality in laboratory animals

The occurrence of outbreaks of infectious diseases in groups of animals makes apparent a reason for paying attention to their microbiological quality. In rodents and rabbits, the most commonly used laboratory animal species, infectious pathology is frequently found in the respiratory tract, the intestinal tract and the liver. These organ systems can be affected by several groups of microorganisms such as viruses, mycoplasmas, bacteria and parasites. Individual species, or combinations of microorganisms, can cause high morbidity and mortality. Different strains of an animal species can show genetically based differences in their susceptibility to infectious pathology from any given microorganism. Contamination by mouse pox virus is, in some mouse strains, followed by lethal infection, but other strains are almost totally resistant to clinical disease (see chapter 9). Lewis rats for example are more susceptible to *Mycoplasma pulmonis* infection than are Fisher (F344) rats. Several genetic factors (Ity, Lsh and xid) influence the susceptibility of mice to *Salmonella* infection. Similarly, C57BL/6 mice are more susceptible to *Streptobacillus moniliformis* infection than other strains.

Table 8.1

Estimation of the number of microorganisms associated with diseases in laboratory rodents and rabbits

	Mouse	Rat	Guinea pig	Rabbit
Viruses	25	20	15	10
Mycoplasmas	3	3	2	2
Bacteria	25	20	15	15
Parasites	25	35	20	25

Contamination is not necessarily followed by clinical symptoms (latent or subclinical infection). The number of microorganisms considered to be (potentially) pathogenic for laboratory animals, amounts to several dozens (table 8.1) and every year "new" pathogens, notably viruses are being discovered. Studies on the pathogenesis of viral and bacterial respiratory and intestinal infections, have shown that, generally, contamination with both a virus and a bacterium is necessary before a clinical disease will develop. Rodents can carry *Pasteurella pneumotropica* or *Mycoplasma pulmonis* for their whole life without showing clinical symptoms. During Sendai virus infection, however, they are at serious risk of dying from secondary bacterial pneumonia. Respiratory viruses presumably inhibit various activities of the lung macrophages, which as a result are no longer able to remove inhaled bacteria from the lower airways. Severe pneumonia is likely to develop. Non-respiratory viruses can also induce a secondary bacterial infection in the respiratory tract. Reo 3 virus infection, which causes among other things hepatitis in rodents, can also lead to an impairment of the local immunological defense system of the lungs. Non-microbiological factors may also have a role in the development of clinical disease. Relatively high concentrations of ammonia can inhibit ciliary movement in the respiratory tract, and thereby limit the elimination of microorganisms.

The association of microorganisms with disease and mortality in laboratory animals, has made a considerable contribution to the introduction and use of animals that are free of specified (potentially) pathogenic microorganisms (Specified Pathogen Free or SPF animals; see page 154).

Interference with results of experiments

Most viral, bacterial and parasitic contaminations do not lead to overt clinical symptoms, but to latent infection. However, these latent infections can have a considerable impact upon the outcome of animal experiments. The subtle effects of latent infections became apparent with the increase in the use of SPF animals. This reduced the frequency with which disease outbreaks occurred.

There are numerous examples of influences of microorganisms on the physiology of the laboratory animal and hence of the interference of latent infections with results of animal experiments. For instance, Sendai virus infection, which is associated with a decreased B-cell and T-cell response after antigenic stimulation. The virus enhances the production of interferon, and decreases the serum level of the 3rd complement factor (C3). Infection by mouse hepatitis virus (MHV) is, amongst other things, associated with the suppression of the phagocytic activity of the reticulo-endothelial system. The virus inhibits the cytotoxic activity of lymphoid cells, and induces a clear increase in the serum levels of a number of liver enzymes such as aspartate-transaminase (ASAT) and alanine-transaminase (ALAT). Lactate dehydrogenase elevating virus (LDHV), which is one of the most frequently observed contaminating viruses of transplantable tumours of laboratory animals, induces a serious increase in the lactate dehydrogenase and corticosteroid levels in plasma, and delays the rejection of skin transplants. These examples illustrate that latent infections can influence the outcome of animal experiments. It is essential, therefore, that the presence of microorganisms which might modulate the animal's response during experimentation, is known.

Zoonoses

Some of the microorganisms which may be present in laboratory animals, can also affect man (zoonoses). Zoonoses can stem from members of all groups of microorganisms and zoonoses can present themselves along the range from subclinical to lethal infections. Conventional animals are the most likely to harbour microorganisms which can cause disease in man. Laboratory animals that have never been rederived by hysterectomy and animals that have been trapped in the wild, should be considered as potential reservoirs of zoonotic microorganisms. It is rather unlikely for SPF animals to be contaminated by these microorganisms. However, zoonotic microorganisms have been detected in rederived animal populations, e.g. *Streptobacillus moniliformis*, a bacterial species which can be cultivated from the nasopharynx of healthy conventional rats. In man, *S.moniliformis* can cause rat-bite fever if transmitted through an animal bite, or Haverhill fever if transmitted via contaminated water or milk. Untreated rat-bite fever can be a fatal disease. The occurrence of the bacterium in laboratory animals is possibly underestimated. *S. moniliformis* is quite difficult to cultivate and serological methods for the detection of antibodies to the bacterium in rats are not yet in common use, although they are available.

Trichophytosis which occurs quite frequently, is a fungal zoonosis, mainly caused by *Trichophyton* sp and *Microsporum* sp, and can be present in a variety of mammals. The infection is mostly subclinical. In man, trichophytosis manifests itself as a localized skin disease, with circular or ringlike skin lesions (ringworm).

An important latent infection in rats is Hanta virus infection. The virus is transmitted via respiratory and intestinal secretions and excretions, and via the urine. Man can become easily contaminated through both direct and indirect contact with contaminated animals, biological products, materials and equipment. Hanta virus infection in humans can present itself as a serious acute interstitial nephritis (haemorraghic fever with renal syndrome — HFRS), causing the complete loss of the functional capacity of the kidneys, and can occasionally lead to death.

Laboratory animals that have been experimentally inoculated with zoonotic microorganisms, are certainly a source of human pathogenic microorganisms, but risks are limited by the use of preventive hygienic measures (see below).

Quality of biological products

The risk of zoonotic infections has led to quality requirements for products that are made with the use of laboratory animals. All sera, vaccines and other biological products to be used in humans have to be safe. It is obvious that the administration of, for example, live or attenuated viral vaccines, which are produced in cells of contaminated animals, can result in zoonotic infections, despite having taken stringent purification steps. Therefore, the production of vaccines and other biological products is governed by strict precautionary regulations. These "Good Manufacturing Practise" (GMP) rules, aim to fully control all production steps, finally resulting in a product of a good, i.e. safe, quality. Laboratory animals that are used for production purposes, must originate from an animal colony that is free from a number of specified pathogenic microorganisms, notably those which have zoonotic potential.

SPF animals are also used in vaccine control experiments. These experiments are performed to assess the potency and safety of the given product. Safety testing of, for example, viral vaccines is amongst other things, aimed at excluding the presence of extraneous viruses, including human pathogenic ones. The experiments are performed by injecting laboratory animals with the vaccine and examining their sera for antibodies to various undesired viruses. During the study, intercurrent contamination of the animals from other sources must be excluded.

Sources and paths of contamination

Laboratory animals can become contaminated with (potentially) pathogenic microorganisms from several sources and through different paths. The most important sources of contamination are other laboratory animals, biological materials derived from them, pet animals, staff and materials and equipment used for breeding and experimentation.

Laboratory animals

Contaminated laboratory animals are an important source of undesired microorganisms. Despite all the efforts made to maintain their microbiological quality, buying animals from breeding colonies frequently causes the introduction of (potentially) pathogenic microorganisms into a laboratory. The frequency with which the various (potentially) pathogenic microorganisms occur in animal colonies varies with time. However, in general, two groups of undesired viruses can be distinguished: those which are only rarely reported, and those which occur widely in animal colonies. Examination of animals for the presence of microorganisms belonging to the latter group, is very useful for gaining a quick first impression of the animal's microbiological quality.

In comparison with breeding colonies, in experimental colonies less attention is generally paid to preventive hygienic measures. In experimental colonies, animals from different sources are often housed together. In addition, experimental laboratories, as a rule harbour experiments which overlap each other in time, thereby maintaining infections which have been introduced. This implies, therefore, that animals in an experimental laboratory are quite likely to contain several (potentially) pathogenic microorganisms. The introduction, therefore, of animals from another experimental colony brings with it the serious risk of introducing contamination. Most of the experimental colonies are generally not monitored as of yet, for the presence of undesired microorganisms.

Biological material

In modern biomedical research, laboratory animals are frequently used as a source of biological material such as sera, ascites, cells, tissues and organs. Animals are also used as a source of microorganisms, that can to date not be cultivated *in vitro*. Laboratory animals can become contaminated by the administration of biological materials which have been derived from contaminated animals.

In principle, biological materials can contain the same, notably intracellular microorganisms, that are present in live animals. Most contaminations are viral, but also mycoplasmas and intracellular bacteria, including *Bacillus piliformis*, have been found to be contaminants. Studies in the USA showed that more than 90% of the transplantable tumours and more than 70% of the viral reagents examined, were contaminated by one or more viruses. Contamination with several infectious microorganisms can result from serial passage of biological materials in animals. As a result of serial passage, a tumour cell line can become consecutively contaminated with several contaminants present in the animals used. Serial passage of a *Treponema pallidum* strain, for example, that was presumably contaminated with a Coronavirus, was accompanied by intercurrent death (up to 40%) in rabbits. The introduction of biological materials is presently the most important cause of outbreaks of Ectromelia virus infection.

The risk of a zoonosis also exists when biological materials are used *in vitro*. Homogenization of contaminated tumour material has led to Hanta virus infection. Contamination by Lymphocytic choriomeningitis (LCM) virus has been detected in *Toxoplasma* strains that were passed on serially in mice.

The presence of contaminating microorganisms in biological materials can be detected by the examination of sera from animals that were previously injected with the material (e.g. Mouse Antibody Production test or MAP test). Contamination of the animals from other sources during the study must be excluded. Therefore, antibody production tests should be performed preferably within isolators.

Pet animals

Pet animals can constitute a serious risk of contamination for laboratory animals. For those individuals involved in the care and treatment of laboratory animals, the keeping of pet animals, especially of the common laboratory animal species, must be discouraged. In some breeding colonies, the keeping of pet animals by animal technicians and staff and their families is forbidden. This seems reasonable, given that contamination has serious (financial) consequences for the breeder.

Personnel

Despite the above mentioned preventive hygienic measures, man is, without doubt, the most important factor in the transmission of contaminating microorganisms between groups of animals. Man can act as a vector after contact with contaminated animals, and can also temporarily be the host of microorganisms that are (potentially) pathogenic for laboratory animals. It is advisable to have separate personnel working with laboratory animals of different microbiological qualities. For instance, those involved in breeding should not enter experimental laboratories. Even personnel who do not have contact with contaminated laboratory animals, can be a source of contamination. Tuberculosis for example can be transmitted to almost all mammalian species. The transmission of, for example, *Salmonella* species and

Campylobacter jejuni, as a result of food poisoning, is more likely. Several conditions in man, especially those showing an increased spread of (potentially) pathogenic microorganisms, increase the risk of contaminating laboratory animals, e.g. diarrhea, skin rashes, chronic respiratory disease.

Individuals who carry and shed *Salmonella* species and *Staphylococcus aureus* can initiate some problems. SPF animals are more susceptible to staphylococcal disease than conventional ones, due to their rederivation and the consequent loss of their "normal" microflora (see below).

One may presume that various microorganisms which are pathogenic to man are not able to propagate well in laboratory animals on account of the species barrier. However, contamination by these microorganisms can cause a small group of the animals to temporarily develop antibodies against them. These antibodies may react with antigens that are used for the serological monitoring of laboratory animals (see below).

Materials and equipment

Materials and equipment can serve as a vector in the contamination process. Food and bedding can become contaminated by feral rodents at times of production, harvesting and storage. The animals' bedding can be sterilized by autoclaving. Their food is usually supplied in pelleted form. During the pellet-making process, the temperature rises up to 70 to 80°C, which kills off most of the microorganisms. In short-term experiments, pelleted diets are used without further treatment. Food to be used in SPF breeding units has to satisfy more stringent demands and is often additionally treated by gamma-irradiation or by autoclaving, in order to eliminate all (potentially) pathogenic microorganisms (pasteurization).

Water can also be a source of contamination for laboratory animals, for example *Pseudomonas aeruginosa,* which can lead to infection, whilst the animals' resistance is low as a result of for example sublethal total body irradiation. Bacterial growth in water bottles can be prevented by acidifying (pH 2–3) or by chlorinating (15–20 ppm active chloride) the drinking water.

The cages and surgical equipment used, can also act as a vector for contamination, but they can be sterilized or disinfected (see below). Generally speaking the air is filtrated. There are various types of filters in use. When air has to be sterilized, the so called HEPA filters offer the best results.

Microbiological qualities

Laboratory animals can be arbitrarily classified according to a number of different microbiological qualities (fig. 8.1). The first animal experiments

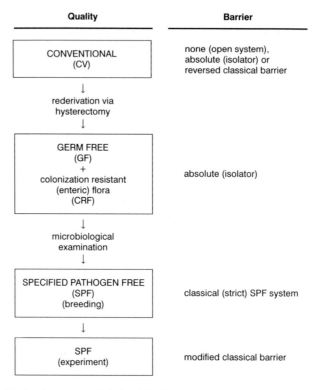

Fig. 8.1. Quality-barrier system: Relationship between microbiological qualities of laboratory animals and their barrier systems.

were performed upon conventional (CV) animals. These animals can harbour "by nature" the whole range of infectious microorganisms, since they are kept without the application of preventive hygienic measures. At the other end of the quality scale, germ-free (GF) animals exist. These animals can be obtained from CV counterparts by performing a hysterectomy (rederivation) and are kept under sterile conditions within isolators. GF animals are very susceptible to infections by microorganisms that are only rarely the cause of disease in CV animals. Therefore GF animals can not be housed without problems under conventional conditions. To provide GF animals with some resistance to opportunistic infections, they are deliberately given a flora, which provides the formerly GF animal with a general resistance to the growth of other bacteria (colonization resistance). An example of this approach is the use of mouse derived enteric colonization resistant (mCRF) flora. CRF animals are housed as GF animals within isolators and some animal species will even breed in this microbiological status. Frequently CRF animals are used to start SPF breeding

colonies (see page 154). For large-scale breeding, CRF animals are introduced into units where a wide range of protective hygienic measures, aiming
at preventing undesired microbial contaminations (barrier system), are operational.

Gnotobiotic animals

Gnotobiotic animals harbour a "fully" known microflora and/or fauna (gno-
tos = known; biota = flora and fauna), and are therefore microbiologically
standardized animals. If no detectable microorganisms are present, the animal
is considered to be GF. Both GF animals and GF animals having one or more
known microorganisms, are gnotobiotic animals. CRF associated animals are
also said to be gnotobiotic animals. The exact composition of the flora of CRF
animals is unknown, but they are housed under the same conditions as their
GF counterparts.

Rederivation. This is a technique which is used to create a nucleus of
animals for starting a colony free from (potentially) pathogenic microorganisms. Rederivation of laboratory animals is mainly performed by an aseptic
hysterectomy on pregnant mothers, prior to normal delivery. During this procedure the closed uterus is removed from the donor-animal, and aseptically
introduced into a sterile isolator passing through a dunk tank, containing
a disinfecting solution. Finally the young are born by opening the uterus.
Rederivation can also be performed by Caesarean section, in which the uterus
is opened *in situ* and the young are isolated immediately after operative birth.
Animals obtained by hysterectomy or through Caesarean section are reared
by hand or are fostered by lactating animals (foster mothers).

   Since the early sixties the most common species, i.e. mouse and rat, and
related strains, have been rederived. Rederivation of other animal species has
been done on a limited scale only. This is due partly to economic reasons
but also to zootechnical problems. Rabbits for instance, have to be raised by
hand. Rederivation of hamsters and gerbils has been found to be extremely
difficult, and many attempts have failed due to enteric infections.

Vertical transmission of microorganisms. Hysterectomy or Caesarean section
mostly yields GF animals. However occasionally the offspring is found to be
contaminated with one or (more rarely) several microbial species, which have
been transmitted during pregnancy to the young, through the placenta or via
another means (vertical contamination). Vertical transmission, i.e. passing on
to the next generation, can occur if the mother suffers from an active infection
during pregnancy, accompanied by the presence of microorganisms in the
bloodstream and concomitant penetration of the placental barrier.

Autochthonous or normal microflora. In conventional animals, the skin and the mucous membranes of the mouth, the respiratory tract, the urogenital system and the gastro-intestinal tract, harbour apathogenic, so called "normal" or autochthonous flora. This flora contributes to the animals' resistance against (potentially) pathogenic microorganisms. This microbial based resistance to colonization by pathogens has been described as bacterial antagonism, bacterial interference and colonization resistance.

The number of bacterial species which make up the normal flora is unknown. It is estimated that the mouse intestinal flora may contain 500 species. Bacterial counts in the intestinal contents can be up to 10^{10} to 10^{11} per gram. Which bacterial species inhabit other parts of the body is largely unknown. The intestinal bacterial flora lives in a very intimate fashion with its host (fig. 8.2), and both host and bacterial flora benefit from this relationship

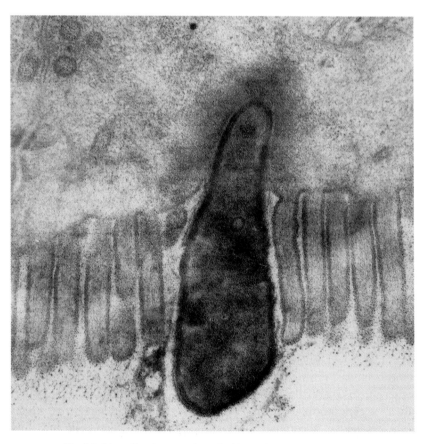

Fig. 8.2. Mutualism between intestinal bacterium and enterocyte.

(mutualism). The importance of this mutualism for the host is apparent when making a comparison between CV and GF animals.

Anatomical and physiological characteristics. GF animals show a variety of morphological and physiological "abnormalities", when compared with CV animals. Intestinal parameters show striking differences between the two groups. In GF animals the caecum is considerably enlarged and its contents are rather liquid. The intestinal wall is thin and less well developed than that of CV animals. GF animals produce faeces which have a soft consistency.

An inevitable consequence of rederivation via hysterectomy, is the loss of all "normal" flora. To compensate for this loss of autochthonous (notably intestinal) flora, GF animals were administered with aerobic and facultatively anaerobic bacterial species. This approach very often gave bad results. In GF guinea pigs that were associated with *Escherichia coli*, *Streptococcus fecalis* and lactobacilli, 75% of the animals died. Most animals were lost from enteric infections due to the bacterial species administered to them.

Since more than 99% of the "normal" enteric flora of animals consists of strictly anaerobic bacteria, GF animals have also been associated with such anaerobes. The so called Schaedler flora, which has been given to mice and rats, partly consists of such anaerobic bacteria. Animals given such a flora have, however, been found to be rather susceptible to enteric infections. The bacteria which can be cultivated from the affected gut are aerobic and facultatively anaerobic species, which are only rarely present in infections in CV animals. Infections by these opportunistic pathogens, e.g. *S. aureus* and *P. aeruginosa*, can be found in CV animals, but only after debilitating treatments such as sublethal body-irradiation or the administration of antibiotics, have taken place.

In SPF breeding colonies, opportunistic infections usually increase in frequency some time after the establishment of the colony. The number of infectious processes can increase rapidly, but problems usually gradually disappear. This is presumably due to the introduction into the colony of bacterial species which partly contribute to colonization resistance in the intestinal tract and other parts of the body.

Strictly anaerobic flora has been used in different laboratory animal species. For mice and rats, a mouse derived enteric flora (mCRF), was sufficient to "normalize" the GF animals. In both species the size of the caecum was clearly reduced and an acceptable colonization resistance was also obtained.

The autochthonous enteric flora is at least partly species specific. In rodents and rabbits, species specific flora has been found to "normalize" GF abnormalities better than flora from another animal species. The next few years will certainly see more attention paid to the development and improvement of species specific (enteric) flora. Such flora is a prerequisite for the development of microbiologically fully standardized animals.

Use.   Gnotobiotic animals are used for different purposes. One such an application is the production of viral vaccines. Animals which are to be used as a donor of cells to be used for the production of vaccines for use in humans, have to be taken from animal colonies that are free from adventitious infections. Gnotobiotic animals meet with this requirement. Gnotobiotic animals which have been associated with a more or less complex enteric flora, can be used to study the role of bacteria(l species) in the transformation of orally administered compounds (biotransformation). Another example is the study of the effects of sublethal total body irradiation or other immunosuppressive methods applied during cancer research. This type of research is almost impossible to perform using conventional or sometimes even SPF animals, due to disturbing opportunistic infections. Research on intestinal ecology, including the pathogenesis of infections, the role of the local intestinal immune system and the "normal" flora, would not be possible without the use of gnotobiotic animals.

SPF animals

Specified pathogen free (SPF) animals are those which have been found to be free from a number of specified (potentially) pathogenic microorganisms. SPF animals are not kept under conditions guaranteeing a full separation from the environment. Therefore, the animals used to start the colony (mostly CRF), will be colonized in time by a wide variety of microorganisms. Some of these microorganisms will inevitably be introduced by animal caretakers. Colonization is not of itself a problem, as long as the animals are not colonized by undesired microorganisms. It could be argued that the more heavily the animals are colonized by apathogenic species, the more likely it is that species will be present which contribute to the resistance of the animal to opportunistic pathogens.

   SPF animals can hardly be considered to be standardized animals. The most one can expect is that examination of the animals for the presence of (potentially) pathogenic microorganisms, will show which species are presumably not present within the colony. With the lifetime of the SPF colony, the anatomical and physiological characteristics of the animals will gradually "normalize" towards those of the CV animal.

Use.   There are various reasons why SPF animals are used; for example, the testing for the safety of products, and the performance of animal experiments with no interference from infections (ultimately all experiments).

The duration of experiments partly determines the likelihood of contamination. Long-term experiments are at greater risk than short-term ones. The use of SPF animals in very expensive (semi)chronic toxicological studies is strongly advised. Ageing-research (gerontology) clearly is also a field in which SPF animals have to be used. The median survival time (MST) of rats, and hence the frequency of tumours in the animals, can be seriously affected by intercurrent infections. The life-span of SPF animals generally exceeds that of conventional animals. SPF animals are also used in studies in which the animals' immunological capacity is decreased by immunosuppressive regimes, or by its genetic constitution, as in T-cell deficient nude animals and both T- and B-cell deficient SCID (Severe Combined Immuno Deficient) mice.

Conventional animals

Conventional animals are still widely used in biomedical research. They are suitable for particular types of experiments. Animals should be considered as conventional animals, if their microbiological status is unknown or questionable. As a rule, these animals (notably rodents and rabbits), are "quarantined" for a period of time. The length of this period is based upon the longest incubation time required for excluding infections. This implies the expectation that the "quarantine" period would reveal certain clinical symptoms in the animals. However, most infections in laboratory animals are latent.

"Quarantining" of animals could be used as part of a strict quality assurance programme. Release of the animals from "quarantine" should then be based upon the results of screening and diagnostic examinations performed on them, not yielding any indication of the presence of specified pathogens. Screening is time-consuming and costly, and often animals have to be sacrificed for a thorough examination. Therefore this approach is only rarely applied. A better alternative seems to be to perform experiments in "quarantine units" (isolators), or to use the period merely for acclimatization. Dogs and cats for example could be vaccinated and de-wormed during such a period.

Barrier systems

The barrier concept is a basic principle in the quality assurance of laboratory animals. A barrier consists of a wider or lesser range of preventive hygienic measures. The range will depend upon the microbiological requirements set for the animals.

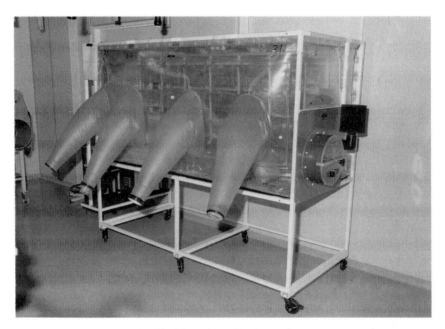

Fig. 8.3. Isolator (Trexler type).

Absolute barrier (isolator)

The microbiological status of gnotobiotic animals can be maintained only if the animals are kept fully separated from the environment. For this an absolute barrier (isolator), is required. Several types of isolators have been developed. All types, including the most commonly used Trexler (plastic) and Gustafsson (steel) isolators, have a similar construction (fig. 8.3). All equipment, such as cages and materials, food and bedding, are sterilized and introduced through a dunk tank or via a lock which can be sterilized using peracetic acid vapour.

Although CRF animals are not gnotobiotic, since the composition of their flora is not exactly known, they must be kept under gnotobiotic conditions to prevent the introduction of other flora. CRF animals that are maintained in isolators for any length of time, seem for some reason, to loose part of their flora.

Classical SPF barrier

The preventive hygienic measures taken to protect SPF animals in breeding units, are less strict than those for gnotobiotic animals. Here only the introduction of (potentially) pathogenic microorganisms has to be prevented, so disinfection instead of sterilization, of materials and equipment will (theoretically) be sufficient. Generally, however, sterilization of materials and equipment is carried out, since it is by far the safest. Special care is taken with personnel. The number of people entering the unit, is limited to the absolute minimum. Taking a shower is considered essential before commencing work within the "clean" area. Although showering increases the shedding of resident bacteria from the skin, it also removes the far more important transient (potentially) pathogenic microorganisms. Sterilized working clothes, a mouth mask, gloves etc., should be worn. Within the "clean" area, positive pressure is maintained towards the environment.

Modified barrier systems

The preventive measures which aim at protecting SPF animals during experimentation, are derived from those of the classical barrier system. Which measures are taken will depend upon insights into the risks of contamination and according to the consequences of a barrier breakdown. For long-term toxicological experiments, the barrier system may imitate the classical SPF barrier, but in short-term pharmacological experiments, preventive measures need hardly be taken. Animals can be housed in cages provided with protective hoods (filter top), which are only removed when the animals have to be handled. These cages are preferably only opened within Laminar Air Flow (LAF) cabinets (fig. 8.4).

Reversed classical barrier (isolation units)

Sometimes the environment has to be protected against contamination by microorganisms carried by the animal. Animals can be housed in a barrier system (infection unit), which is actually a "reversed" version of the classical barrier system. Waste material is disinfected and personnel take a shower upon leaving the area. Microorganisms can be classified into "pathogen groups". There are different classifications in use, but all are based upon the potential consequences of contamination in man. For each pathogen group, a series of containment or restrictive measures are operational (physical containment level). For work with harmless microorganisms, no special measures are necessary. Animal experiments in which microorganisms are involved, that can have serious consequences for individuals, but not for the community, such as HIV, can be performed within a gnotobiology department. Animals are kept within isolators which have a negative pressure compared with the environment. Exhaustive air is filtered until sterile. If very dangerous pathogens are involved, i.e. microorganisms that constitute a serious risk to the community, there must be absolute certainty that no single microorganism

Fig. 8.4. Laminar flow cabinet.

reaches the environment. Experiments with, for example, the hemorraghic fever associated viruses, must be performed in separate buildings. Laboratory animals used for these experiments are housed within isolators, in order to guarantee a full physical separation between the research personnel and the microorganisms.

Experimental infections with serious laboratory animal pathogens, such as Ectromelia virus, are also performed under strict conditions providing a containment of the microorganisms (isolators).

Individual barrier measures

Basically all measures are aimed at reducing, as far as possible, the number of (potentially) pathogenic microorganisms that could be passed to the animals through contact with personnel, materials or equipment. A variety of methods involving one of the following approaches such as cleaning, disinfection and sterilization, can be used.

Cleaning. Animal rooms, cages, drinking bottles etc., should be periodically cleaned. Animal rooms are cleaned using large quantities of hot water, if possible with the aid of high-pressure equipment. Soiled bedding is removed from cages, which are then cleaned in a special type of washing machine. The washing-steps, using hot water and detergents, are aimed at removing any remaining dirty material. Drinking bottles are thoroughly cleaned by rinsing and scale is mechanically removed. The most important purpose of the cleaning is a reduction in the number of microorganisms. Cleaning makes disinfection and sterilization more effective.

Disinfection and sterilization methods. For the elimination of (potentially) pathogenic microorganisms, i.e. disinfection, or of all living microorganisms, i.e. sterilization, essentially the same approaches are used. Disinfection needs less intensive treatment than sterilization. If it is possible to apply both approaches, then sterilization is preferable. The disinfection methods do not guarantee the killing of all (potentially) pathogenic microorganisms.

Physical and chemical methods exist for disinfection and sterilization. Food can be disinfected using 0.9 Mrad gamma-irradiation, whereas 2.5 Mrad is needed for sterilization. Whether the intended goal can be achieved or not, will depend upon the number of microorganisms initially present, since a particular treatment will lead to a fixed decimal reduction in the number of microorganisms. Upon heating, the intensity, i.e. the combination of time and temperature, will determine whether disinfection or sterilization results. Disinfection will result from short-term heating at, for example, 70°C, whereas sterilization will need more intensive heating under positive pressure at 121°C.

The ease with which microorganisms are killed varies according to the particular treatment. The decimal reduction time is the time needed to reduce the number of microorganisms by a factor of 10. This time also differs according to the method applied.

In chemical disinfection (decontamination), the killing of microorganisms is determined by several factors, such as the concentration of the disinfectant, the temperature and pH during treatment and the presence of organic material. The disinfectant of choice, will depend upon the nature of the material that has to be treated, and on the groups and/or species of microorganisms to be eliminated. The working spectrum of the various groups of disinfectants such as alcoholic solutions, halogens, phenols, aldehydes and biguanides, differs. Halogens whose activity is based, for example, on free chlorine, are effective against several groups of microorganisms, but biguanides, such as chlorhexidin, are only active against vegetative bacteria (except mycobacteria). Peracetic acid is a very potent antimicrobial substance and can be considered as a sterilant. Peracetic acid vapour is commonly used in gnotobiotic technology. Chemical disinfectants and sterilizing agents have to be used with care as all substances (of course depending on their concentration), are basically harmful to mammalian species, including man.

The effect of cleaning and disinfection can be monitored using agar plates, on which the number of bacterial colonies can be counted, after an appropriate incubation. Autoclaving can be monitored by recording temperature, pressure and humidity which were present during treatment. The process can also be monitored by the simultaneous autoclaving of strips showing a temperature dependant colour-change. Spore strips which are incubated after processing, can also be used.

Quality control

Microbiological quality control can be divided into the control of the barrier system and the control of the laboratory animal. The latter is dominant in many laboratories, where it is assumed that the absence of contamination in the animals will indicate that the integrity of the barrier system has been fully maintained.

Control of the barrier system (process control)

The series of preventive hygienic measures constituting the barrier, can be monitored using both microbiological and physical methods. Autoclaving can be monitored by examining whether test organisms were killed by the treatment or not, but also by recording the time, temperature and pressure. The number of microorganisms present in food, air and on surfaces can be estimated. Air pressure in different areas can be recorded and can, in the case of deviation from preset requirements, be reported and even be automatically adjusted.

Control of the laboratory animal (product control)

The examination of animals for the presence of (potentially) pathogenic microorganisms is of considerable importance. Most attention is paid to the periodic examination of healthy animals (screening). Postmortem examinations are performed on diseased and dead animals (diagnosis), to clarify the various causes. In the event of a presumed microbial involvement in disease problems observed, the microorganism(s) could be sought for using a "direct"

Table 8.2

Methods for diagnosis in and screening of laboratory animals for the presence of (potentially) pathogenic microorganisms

Microorganisms	Material	Screening	Diagnostics
Viruses	serum	CF, HAI, SN IF, ELISA	
	organs		isolation IF on histologic preparations IEM
Mycoplasmas	serum	ELISA	
	organs	selective cultivation	cultivation
Bacteria	serum	MA, IF, ELISA	
	organs	selective cultivation	cultivation
Parasites	serum	IF, ELISA	
	organs/feces	microscopy of native or fixated material	microscopy on native native or fixated material

CF = complement fixation test; HAI = hemagglutination inhibition test; SN = serum neutralization test; IF = immunofluorescence test; ELISA = enzyme-linked immunosorbent assay; MA = micro-agglutination test; IEM = immuno-electron microscopy.

approach, e.g. by microscopy or cultivation. An alternative approach could be the examination of sera for antibodies to these microorganisms (serology). The various methods used for screening and diagnosis in laboratory animals, are summarized in table 8.2. The examination of laboratory animals for the presence of the various (potentially) pathogenic microorganisms should preferably be left to the specialist.

Gnotobiotic animals. Gnotobiotic animals are animals with a "completely" known microflora. This is an operational definition, since this "completeness" depends upon the examination methods used. This means that, if the methods used did not reveal the presence of microorganisms, or only revealed those deliberately given to the animal, the animal is considered to be gnotobiotic.

The microbiological examination of gnotobiotic animals which are to be used to start SPF colonies, can vary. If animals have been obtained by rederivation from an SPF colony that did not contain undesired microorganisms, the likelihood of vertical transmission of these microorganisms is, of course, very low. If rederivation was performed on CV animals, the examination must be much broader to detect a wide range of microorganisms, since numerous species can be present and vertically transmitted. If there are no indications showing that vertical contamination exists, then further examinations could be limited to those microorganisms which are most likely to be introduced in the event of a barrier breakdown (e.g. spore forming bacteria).

In the sera of hysterectomy derived animals, antibodies to various microorganisms that were present in their mothers, can be detected in the first two to three months of life. These antibodies will be mostly of maternal origin, but these have to be differentiated from antibodies produced by the young themselves. The levels of the latter, one may presume, increase with time or remain more or less stable if the young are contaminated. On the contrary, maternal antibodies will gradually disappear. The examination therefore of paired sera, taken with an interval of at least two weeks from individual animals, is sometimes necessary in order to reach definite conclusions.

SPF breeding populations.   SPF breeding colonies are monitored periodically for the presence of (potentially) pathogenic microorganisms. The frequency of examination ranges between 2 and 12 times per year. The number of animals that are examined on each occasion also varies, but falls mostly between 5 and 25. The sample size seems to be on average 10 animals or sera. The size of the sample taken will basically determine the likelihood with which a contamination present in the colony, will be detected (table 8.3). A sample size of 5 implies that the detection level is only about 50%. This means that contaminations having an incidence of lesser than 50% will, with 95% probability, not be detected.

Table 8.3

The sample size needed to detect a contaminated animal depends on the percentage of contaminated animals in the colony.

Percentage contaminated animals (incidence)	Sample size
5	59
10	29
20	14
30	9
40	6
50	5
70	3
100	1

Calculated as

$$S = \frac{\log p}{\log N}$$

where S is the sample size, p the likelihood of error of result (here 5%) and N is the percentage of uncontaminated animals.

The list of microorganisms sought for during routine monitoring, varies between colonies, and contains only part of the microorganisms that are associated with disease, mortality or other interferences during research. This seems reasonable since, in rederived colonies, maintained under classical SPF conditions, a wide range of (potentially) pathogenic microorganisms will never arise. A number of microorganisms will be very difficult, if not impossible, to detect in healthy animals. The presence of other microorganisms will probably be detected on postmortem examination, and not by the examination of healthy animals. Laboratory methods used show a wide range of variability, and studies to outline the suitability of different methods in detecting particular microorganisms, are rather scarce.

The above mentioned reasons point to the fact that records of health monitoring data, indicating the microbiological status of the animals, are very difficult to interpret. When analyzing the data, one has to take into account all the barrier measures which apply to the colony. Breeding records can give some information on the possible presence of adventitious microorganisms within the colony. Infections can be accompanied or followed by a dip in production. The interpretation of health monitoring data is complicated and should therefore be left to the specialist.

SPF animals in experiments. In general, animal experiments follow a less strict hygienic regimen than that of breeding colonies. Therefore, contaminations occur more frequently during experiments than within breeding stock. During long-term experiments, SPF animals can become more or less conventional. This "conventionalization" can have various effects on the physiology of the animal, and thereby influence the outcome of the experiments.

The degree of conventionalization of animals during experiments, can be estimated by examining them repeatedly during the study, using the methods described for within the breeding colonies. On the whole, the examinations are limited to a small number of microorganisms. The values of various physiological parameters in control animals during successive experiments, can provide very useful additional information on the possible interferences upon the outcome of the experiment. During (immuno)toxicological research, counts of the total number of white blood cells and the various cell types, immunoglobulin levels (IgM and IgG) and the relative weight of lymphoid organs (thymus, spleen), are assessed regularly. If there is a considerable variation in the values for these parameters in animals of control groups of successive experiments, there is a clear indication of the fact that intercurrent infections are present.

Vaccination and therapy

Vaccination of laboratory animals is, as a rule, limited to the larger laboratory animals, i.e. cats and dogs. It is possible to vaccinate rodents and rabbits against a small number of viral diseases, for example mouse pox, Sendai and myxomatosis, but there is some doubt as to its effectiveness. Clinical disease can occur in spite of the fact that vaccination has been performed. Vaccination leads to the development of antibodies, which can seriously interfere with serological monitoring. It is virtually impossible to differentiate between antibodies which have been caused as a result of vaccination or contamination.

In the case of an outbreak of disease, the administration of antibiotics should be considered in order to save a valuable experiment. The use of antibiotics, however, is certainly not without risks. In some rodents, for example guinea pigs and in rabbits, the normal intestinal flora is easily disturbed, leading to severe enteric pathology caused by toxigenic bacteria. Preventive medicine can be given to animals via their food or drinking water, but any medication can, of course, influence the results of experiments (see chapter 9)

The taking of therapeutic measures in animals that are infected by a zoonotic microorganism, is to be discouraged. It is also the case that animals which are contaminated by microorganisms, that can cause devastating problems within laboratory animal colonies, will usually have to be destroyed. The implications of, for example, Sendai- or mouse pox virus infection is always more important to the research community as a whole, than for any individual study.

Organization of quality assurance and quality control

Microbiological quality assurance of laboratory animals and animal experiments is primarily based on spatial and personal separation of animals possessing different microbiological qualities. Classification of animals according to different qualities is, of course, arbitrary. It should be based upon a thorough knowledge of the microbiological quality of all the sources of animals and groups of animals in experimental laboratories.

The ordering of animals should be centrally based and carried out under the guidance of a veterinary microbiologist. The microbiologist must have insight into all planned experiments, since the introduction of infectious microorganisms or contaminated biological materials into animals, can have serious risks of infection for other laboratory animals. Finally he/she can give advice on methods of preventive hygiene and the interpretation of results of the microbiological monitoring of laboratory animals.

Literature

Bhatt P N, Jacoby R O, Morse H C & New A E eds. Viral and mycoplasmal infections of laboratory rodents: effects on biomedical research. New York: Academic Press, 1986.

Block S S. Disinfection, sterilization and preservation. Philadelphia: Lea & Febiger, 1983.

Coates M E & Gustafsson B E, eds. The germ-free animal in biomedical research. Laboratory Animal Handbooks 9. London: Laboratory Animals Ltd, 1984.

Fox J G, Cohen B J & Loew F M, eds. Laboratory animal medicine. London: Academic Press Inc., 1984.

Hamm T E, ed. Complications of viral and mycoplasmal infections in rodents to toxicology research and testing. Washington: Hemisphere Publishing Corporation, 1986.

Kunstýř I, ed. List of pathogens for specification in SPF laboratory animals. Biberach a/d Riss: Gesellschaft für Versuchstierkunde (SOLAS), 1988.

Kunstýř I, ed. Diagnostic microbiology for laboratory animals. Viruses, bacteria, chlamydia, fungi and parasites. Stuttgart: Fischer Verlag, 1992.

Schulz K D, ed. Hygiene recommendations for laboratory animal houses. Vol 1 & 2. Biberach a/d Riss: Gesellschaft für Versuchstierkunde (SOLAS), 1978.

Steele J H, ed. CRC Handbook series in zoonoses. Vol. 1-3. Boca Raton: CRC Press Inc. 1979-1984.

9 Diseases in laboratory animals

Introduction

Diseases and pathological lesions in laboratory animals can be divided into
two groups:
– Induced diseases (induced pathology):
  Generally speaking these experimentally induced diseases are the subject
  of a particular study. Genetically selected diseases in inbred strains (genetic
  models) and diseases induced by toxicity testing also belong to this group.
– Non-induced diseases (spontaneous pathology):
  In reality these are not diseases which occur spontaneously but are abnormalities which occur unintentionally, for example with aging. In many
  cases, their cause is unknown.
  This chapter only deals with non-induced lesions which generally have a
negative effect upon the quality of the animal experiment. The main focus of
this chapter is an overview of the procedures and available methods that are
suitable to detect whether disease is present in (a group of) animals and, if
so, to determine the cause(s) of this disease. First, however, some definitions
pertaining to disease and pathology are presented and the impact of disease
on animal experiments as well as the cause of disease are briefly discussed.
The chapter ends with a short description of possibilities and limitations of
therapeutical intervention in diseased experimental animals.

Definitions

Disease

A normal healthy organism (man, animal) is confined to a narrow range of
functional and structural characteristics, whereby it is in a steady state balance

with all environmental influences known as homeostasis. In order to maintain this homeostatic balance, the physiological processes within the organism are subjected to feed-back and compensatory regulating mechanisms. This results in the continuous adaptation of the organism to environmental changes. When circumstances are normal, these physiological adaptations are in a dynamic balance with the external factors. When external factors change, for example, due to the occurrence of pathogenic micro-organisms, a new balance is achieved brought about by adaptations within the organism. Changes or abnormalities within the organism itself may influence its adaptability and will therefore have an effect on the homeostatic balance between the organism and its environment. Despite the fact that in such situations potentially harmful conditions are present within the organism, clinical manifestation of disease may be absent. Manifest disease, as a result of organic dysfunction, will only occur when the adaptive capacity of the organism to (a combination of) harmful external influences is exceeded, and/or when the regulating mechanism itself is defective or alterations within the organism itself result in a decreasing capacity to adapt.

Depending upon the degree of organic dysfunction, there may be clinical signs of disease and associated macroscopical or histological lesions may be present in the affected organs. Such lesions are not always visible; for example there may be alterations in biochemical processes without any histologically detectable associated lesions. Clinical disease is always the result of interactions between external (the environment) and internal factors. Appreciation of the complex and dynamic nature of the homeostasis which underlies the balance between health and disease also provides insight into the phenomenon of disease within groups of animals.

Pathology

Pathology is the study of disease: the causes of cell and tissue injury, the mechanisms of injury, and the responses of cells, tissues and organisms to injury. Pathology as a science is concerned with disease processes from the onset of injury and cellular and tissue abnormalities through to their disappearance; a sequence of events also known as pathogenesis. This study encompasses functional, metabolic, molecular and morphological phenomena. This complexity of disease processes necessitates a multidisciplinary approach. Thus disease can not be understood purely by a clinical, histological, biochemical or microbiological approach. Pathology, therefore, includes not only post-mortem studies (gross pathology, histopathology, microbiology, biochemistry, molecular biology) but also includes the study of the living animal (clinical studies, cytology, clinical chemistry, haematology). In order to understand the pathophysiological processes which lead to or which are the result of disease, knowledge from all these different areas has to be integrated. The term "pathology" is also often used when referring to a specific area of pathology, for example clinical pathology, histopathology, background pathology etc.

Intercurrent disease

Those non-induced diseases which manifest themselves during the course of a given experiment are intercurrent diseases. The course the disease takes will vary:
  – If the disease is deadly, then its significance is recorded by a *mortality* figure, which indicates the number of animals lost.
  – If the disease is clinically manifest, but does not result in mortality, then the term *morbidity* is applied. This refers to the percentage of clinically diseased animals. Such a disease may be transitory, but may also result in persistent lesions. For example, corneal inflammation in rats caused by a SDAV (sialo-dacryo-adenitis virus) infection will disappear after a short period. Retarded cerebellar development (hypocerebellism) in rats neonatally infected with KRV (Kilham Rat Virus), however, is an example of a persistent lesion.
  – If the disease takes a subclinical course, no manifest clinical signs are present. For instance, many bacterial and viral infections occur in rodents without any detectable signs of disease. In the field of animal experimentation, it is important to be aware of the presence of such infections, since experiment-associated stress or immuno-suppression can result in the clinical manifestation of a disease due to such an infection. Tyzzer's disease, caused by *Bacillus piliformis*, is a well documented complication occurring due to experimental stress in a variety of laboratory animal species. Above all, subclinical diseases often have an influence upon immunological, biochemical and/or haematological parameters that are measured in the experiment. Examples of subclinical diseases which interfere with experimental parameters are viral infections such as Sendai, MHV (mouse hepatitis virus) and LDH (lactate-dehydrogenase) virus. When faced with unexpected and aberrant experimental results, it must be taken into account that these might be the result of such a latent infection. Microbiological monitoring of the animals may lead to recognition of the causal factor.

Background pathology

Besides manifest diseases, pathological lesions may also occur that have no detectable adverse influence on animal health or on experimental results. Yet it is of great value to the researcher when animal breeders keep records of the frequency of macroscopic and histologic lesions, as part of their animal quality

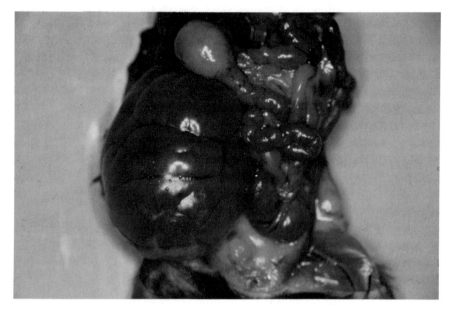

Fig. 9.1. Severe hydronephrosis in a C57Bl/6 mouse.

monitoring programs. This enables the researcher to anticipate the spectrum of lesions, along with the incidence, with which they can be expected. In other words, the researcher will know what is "normal" for the species and strain under study. Background pathology is therefore the study of the nature and incidence of spontaneously occurring lesions, ranging from bald spots in rats or mice acquired due to excessive grooming, to congenital lesions such as atrophy of the optical nerve associated with microphthalmia in rats, to chronic degenerative renal disease or to hydronephrosis (fig. 9.1). Another important aspect of background pathology is the recording of the onset and course of lesion development and pathophysiological significance of these lesions. An example of this would be the age at which in rats degenerative and inflammatory renal lesions are first histologically observed and at what stage of their development these lesions result in functional alterations. The importance of the availability of background pathology data when selecting animal species and strains for specific experimental purposes, can not be overemphasized. Due to genetic drift and dynamic interactions between the animal and its environment, background pathology will not be entirely consistent in every detail, and variations will occur between experiments. Therefore, necropsies and complete histopathologic examination are always carried out in the context of subchronic and chronic toxicity tests on the exposed as well as the control groups. These control animals also provide some insight into the background pathology of the strain. Laboratory animal breeders invest a great deal of effort in keeping the animal's environment as constant as possible. A shift in the pattern of lesions may be an indication that a change in environmental conditions has occurred. For instance, an increased incidence of biting injuries may be associated with disturbances in the animal room, which could be attributable to, for example, the start of nearby construction activities. An increased incidence of renal calcification in rats may indicate that a change in diet composition has occurred. Similarly, a change in the incidence of congenital lesions, such as microphthalmia, may be a result of inaccurate breeding or selection procedures. Thus, background pathology information is often valuable when evaluating the influence of (changes in) environmental factors on laboratory animals and on experimental parameters measured in these.

Causes of disease

The causes of disease (etiology) can have a genetic and/or environmental basis. Disease is rarely a result of a single causal factor, i.e., the cause of most diseases is multifactorial in nature.

Genetic factors are important determinants of the susceptibility of animals to disease. For example, there are large differences amongst mouse strains with regard to the occurrence of tumours, renal disease and myocardial calcification to name but a few lesions. Infection with mouse pox virus results in high mortality in the DBA/1, DBA/2, BALB/c and C3H strains, for example, whereas the morbidity/mortality in strains such as C57BL/6 and AKR is much lower. Genetic factors are also involved in hereditable diseases and some, but not all, congenital abnormalities.

Environmental factors such as infections, chemical and physical agents, as well as nutrition, husbandry, and housing, have an enormous influence on health and disease. Errors in animal care and nutrition alone, or these in combination with infections, can have very serious consequences for animal and experiment. The handling and treatment of the animal during the experiment always has either a direct or an indirect influence upon the physiological balance of the animal. Pathologic lesions may also be caused by inadequate experimental techniques. Blood sampling by inexperienced personnel can result, for example, in haemorrhage (bleeding) and local inflammation, complications of blood sampling by puncturing the orbital sinus may result in the complete loss of the eye. Adverse side effects of cardiac puncture may be haemopericardium (presence of blood within the pericardial cavety), haemothorax (presence of blood within the pleural cavety) or damage to lung tissue. If injection fluid is administered extra-vasally during an attempted intravenous injection, tissue necrosis (cell death) and concomitant inflammation can occur. All such complications may not only have a local effect but can also give rise to generalized reactions for instance in the immune and/or the circulatory system. Many diseases and lesions in laboratory animals are caused by infectious environmental factors. Due to improvements both in standards of hygiene and in the microbiological status of the animals, the incidence of infectious diseases has been greatly reduced over recent decades. As a result, non-infectious environmental factors, which can lead to disease and/or affect results of experiments, become more prominent and are receiving more attention from the researcher.

Diagnosis of disease

The aim of diagnostic examination is to detect latent diseases and lesions and to define clinically manifest pathological problems. Having made a correct diagnosis, it is possible to estimate morbidity and mortality together with the potential spread to other (groups of) animals and the possible risks involved for exposed personnel. Having made a diagnosis, it will be possible to assess the consequences of the disease and, if required, the therapy for the animal as well as the consequences for the experiment and the animal facility of a research institute. Precautions can be taken to prevent spreading of the disease and against it reoccurring. Sick or dead individuals must be given as much attention as massive outbreaks of disease in laboratory animal breeding colonies and in experimental groups. A single diseased animal may be the precursor of a massive disease outbreak, or it may indicate the presence of latent disease. On the whole, making a correct diagnosis requires considerable experience, and the cooperation of specialists in the field of laboratory animal pathology and medicine is invaluable. Both the scientist responsible for the experiment and the animal technician involved in it need to be able to recognize signs of disease/abnormality at an early stage. In order to do this, they must have some knowledge of the diagnostic procedures and methods available.

Diagnostic examination

A complete diagnostic investigation must include the history of the disease and the background of the animal and physical, laboratory and postmortem examinations. For the successful completion of such examinations, appropriate laboratory facilities are needed. Sometimes it is possible to make a correct diagnosis with a simple physical examination, whilst in other cases, even after carrying out all possible investigations and tests, it is not possible to arrive at a definitive diagnosis. In the next sections, various diagnostic procedures and methods will be discussed. Special attention is given to infectious diseases as they can easily lead to severe problems within a laboratory animal colony. However, the detection of the presence of an infectious agent does not necessarily imply that the agent is the causal factor. Infection may be secondary to a disease that is brought about by other factors.

An in-depth review of the diagnostic techniques which are available and the interpretation of the results is beyond the scope of this chapter. For such highly specialized information the reader is referred to references at the end of this chapter.

History. At the first sign of a problem, as much information as possible should be collected about the history of the disease and the background of the animals before starting any examinations. This is to avoid loss of information that may be important to the diagnostic process. The following check-list gives an overview of some of the important disease history and background features.

General information about the group of animals:
- species; strain; sex; age
- microbiological status (germ-free; gnotobiotic; specific pathogen free; conventional; microbiological monitoring procedures used)
- origin and source; date of delivery
- use (breeding; stock; experiment)
- experimental procedures.

Information about the environment, both present and past:
- animal room
- quarantine and barrier procedures
- type and size of cage; number of animals per cage
- diet and drinking water
- bedding (nature; amount; chemical quality; microbiological quality)
- hygiene (procedures and actual situation); vermin
- possible recent disturbances amongst the group; recent other changes (e.g. new animals)
- light-dark regime; ventilation; air quality; relative humidity; temperature
- possible relationship between diseased animals and specific cages, position on the racks, position of the rack in the room, animal technicians, investigators.

History of the disease and accompanying clinical signs (anamnesis):
- nature of clinical signs and observed abnormalities (onset and duration;

number of animals affected; morbidity; mortality; age and sex of the
affected animals)
- previous disease and treatment
- breeding results (fertility; litter size; litter viability)
- possible seasonal associations
- abnormalities in experimental results.

Clinical examination.   First and foremost in clinically examining a living
animal, is the close observation of the animals appearance and behaviour.
Any abnormalities recorded at this stage will give the first and often critical
leads when making a diagnosis. Further examinations can then be carried
out targeted at presumed causes of the observed abnormalities. It is essential
to be familiar with the normal appearance and behaviour of animals of the
species and strain in question. Differentiation between normal and abnormal
in the sense of general appearance and behaviour is otherwise not possible. In
general, animal technicians who have daily contact with the animals will often
be the first to notice that something is wrong. Clinical examination consists of
a systematic review of the various organ systems in order to ascertain which
system has been affected and to narrow down the number of possible diseases
or lesions.
   The following list outlines a number of important aspects to check:
- general condition (behaviour; appearance and development; body weight;
  body temperature; temperature (and colour) of extremities and ears)
- respiratory system (frequency and type of respiratory movements)
- circulatory system (heart beat frequency; colour of mucous membranes;
  possible oedema)
- digestive system (food intake; possible malocclusion; production of faeces
  and its appearance; inspection of the mouth; abdominal palpation; possible
  wetness around anus)
- urinary system (drinking; production of urine and its colour and appearance; abdominal palpation of kidneys and/or bladder)
- skin (inspection; determination of turgor to assess possible dehydration;
  possible wounds or lesions)
- musculo-skeletal system (posture; locomotion; possible muscular weakness
  or fractures; abnormalities of joints or feet and toes)
- nervous system (behaviour; possible paralysis or seizures; reaction to
  environmental stimuli).

Clinical examination is more difficult to carry out in small animal species such
as rodents than it is in larger animals. Normal reference values of physiological parameters are often not well defined and have such a wide variation
that they are only really useful when looking at marked abnormalities. Apart

from this, the handling of these animals may cause considerable changes in the respiratory, cardiac and endocrine systems. The initial, and perhaps most important, contributions to a clinical examination of rodents is the careful observation of the animals in their own cages by experienced staff in combination with reliable information about the environmental conditions and the history of the animal group.

Additional examinations.   When the history of the illness together with a clinical examination, is still insufficient to make a diagnosis, then additional examinations are necessary. Depending upon the animal species, the type of problem and the circumstances i.e. whether the animals are in experiment or not, it may be possible in some cases to collect blood and other samples from the animals whereas in other cases animals may need to be sacrificed for further diagnostic examination. Scrape samples of skin, fur, faeces and urine can be collected for parasitological, mycological, bacteriological and biochemical tests. Samples can be taken from the mucous surfaces of nose, throat, vagina and from the rectum for microbiological tests. Often very valuable haematological, biochemical and serological information can be obtained by taking blood samples. Other diagnostic tests used in veterinary medicine, such as X-ray echography and biopsies, can be used, depending again on the animal species and the problem in question.

Postmortem examination.   Postmortem examination is an often invaluable diagnostic tool for establishing the cause of disease or the cause of death of animals. When performing an autopsy, changes in tissues and/or organs which had as yet not manifested themselves in clinically apparent symptoms, can be discovered. Postmortem examination is frequently used when problems occur in rodents.

The diagnostic possibilities of a postmortem investigation will largely depend upon the interval between the death of the animal and the autopsy. The autopsy should be carried out as soon as possible after the death of the animal, by an experienced person. Autolysis and bacterial putrefaction commence immediately after death and progress rapidly at room temperature. Within as little as one hour, the mucous membranes of the intestinal tract may be unusable for histological examination. In rabbits, the bacterial production of gases can cause a rupture of the stomach within a few hours after death. Autolysis and bacterial putrefaction can be delayed by keeping the carcases cool. The dead animal should be made wet using cold water, which diminishes the insulation capacity of the fur, and then it should be placed in a sealed plastic bag in a refrigerator at about 4°C. The plastic bag will retain the ectoparasites, which tend to leave a dead animal, and ensures that they are not missed during the postmortem investigation.

When it is not possible to perform a complete postmortem investigation the same day or the next, it may be advantageous to keep (certain parts of) the dead animal in some form of temporary storage. Fixation in a buffered 4% (v/v) formaldehyde solution of the entire animal (rodents) following opening of the abdominal and thoracic cavities is one possibility. Formalin only penetrates slowly into the tissues, extracts water and disinfects. Organs and tissues preserved in formalin can really only be used for histological investigations. Freezing of the entire animal at $-20°C$ (rodents) is another means of preserving (parts of larger) animals. Freezing permits some microbiological examinations. However, freezing causes destruction of the cellular plasma membrane due to crystallization of salts within the cells, which may impede macroscopic examination of these (parts of the) animals and markedly interferes with microscopic examination. Alternatively, small tissue samples, not be larger than a few cubic centimetres, could be frozen in liquid nitrogen, and can be used for histological examination (cryostat sections) and for some microbiological examinations.

Problems caused by autolysis and/or bacterial putrefaction are not a factor when living animals are submitted for postmortem investigations. The animals can be subjected to a clinical examination prior to the autopsy and blood can also be collected for further investigations. It must be taken into account here that transportation and a new environment (necropsy room) cause behavioural changes and may affect the clinical parameters which are to be assessed. The fresher a corpse is, the easier the autopsy, the higher the quality of the tissue samples preserved for histology, and the better the resemblance of the microbial flora to the flora of the living animal. It is, for example, much easier to find motile protozoa (flagellates) in the enteric contents of a fresh corpse than it is to find their cysts in the enteric contents of a corpse which has cooled down.

Finally, of course, when submitting living animals for postmortem investigation, it is possible to choose the time and the method for euthanizing the animal(s). It is important to realise that the method of euthanasia chosen will influence the appearance of tissues and organs at the postmortem investigation and may affect the results of laboratory tests. The use of barbiturates, for example, causes dilatation of blood vessels and in dogs, cats and horses, it results in a severe splenomegaly (enlargement of the spleen). Injection of euthanasia drugs into the abdominal or thoracic cavity may cause acute inflammatory changes and/or haemorrhages if blood vessels are damaged. Exsanguination will cause a macroscopically visible anaemia, but may facilitate microscopical examination for the presence of subtle changes.

Submission of animals for a postmortem investigation should be accompanied by a clear history of the disease and, if possible, the results of a clinical investigation. This will often greatly facilitate the identification of the disease and/or cause of death.

A postmortem investigation begins with a macroscopic inspection of the outside of the animal, in the course of which the fur should be checked for the presence of ectoparasites. A magnifying glass or a stereo-microscope may be necessary when examining animals for ectoparasites such as mites. Postmortems should be conducted on a surface which can be easily cleaned and disinfected or discarded, small laboratory animals fixed belly side up and larger non ruminant animals lying on the right side. The fur of the ventral surface of the (small laboratory) animal should be dampened from the chin to the tail with disinfectant. This is to diminish problems caused by loose hairs and to reduce the risk of bacterial contamination. The skin should be removed from the ventral side commencing with a mid-line incision and working towards the dorsal side. The amount and colour of subcutaneous fat, the hydration state of the subcutis and the appearance of the subcutaneous lymph nodes and mammary glands should be examined. The joints of the limbs need to be opened in order to inspect the articular surfaces and the synovia; this is difficult in small animals and is routinely only done in larger species. The thoracic, abdominal, oral and cranial cavities should be opened to check and the size, colour and location of the organs and the presence of lesions should be determined, as well as the possible presence of abnormal contents and changes in the lining of the cavities. Finally, all organs should be removed from these cavities and examined individually.

In some cases, macroscopic examination of the corpse and the organs is sufficient to make a diagnosis. More often, however, additional microscopical and microbiological investigations will be necessary. For example, microscopical examination is needed to determine whether an observed tissue mass is a neoplasm, and, if so, what type of tumor it is. A correct diagnosis of most macroscopically visible alterations in laboratory animals requires microscopical examination. A number of diseases results in changes which are only visible through microscopic examination. A complete postmortem examination of laboratory animals should always include a microscopic examination of a selected number of organs, particularly in the case of toxicological studies. Information collected from postmortems of control groups and intercurrent deaths will give an indication of the expected range of background pathology within the researcher's own laboratory animal colony.

Depending upon the results obtained from the macroscopic examination, it will be possible to decide whether additional histological, microbiological, parasitological, clinical, chemical, haematological and/or serological investigations need to be performed. The organs which are to be used for histological examination should be kept in a fixative or frozen, using liquid nitrogen. The choice of the method (formalin, Bouin's solution, glutaraldehyde) will depend upon the kind of investigation to be performed. Materials for microbiological studies should be collected and sampled in such a way that contamination can not occur, i.e. bacteriological, serological and mycological materials must be sterile and sampling sites should be desinfected with the exception of the g.i. tract, nose, oropharynx and vagina. Photographs taken of abnormalities along with descriptions can be useful at a later stage when discussing cases or as documentation.

Methods of microbiological examination

Microbiological investigations must be performed to determine if the cause of a disease is infection with a micro-organism and, if so, which micro-organism is the cause. The more certain and the more focused the diagnosis, the greater the effectiveness of the measures which can be taken. Depending upon which micro-organism is involved, the following diagnostic techniques can be employed:

– Direct techniques: visualization of a causative agent by means of histological examination (Gram staining, immunofluorescence techniques, electron microscopy) or of isolation followed by cultivation.

– Indirect techniques: detection of the presence of antibodies against an infectious agent or the presence of products from a causative agent (e.g. toxins from *Clostridium botulinum*).

An important difference between these two groups of diagnostic techniques is that a positive result using an indirect test does not mean that the etiological agent is still present. It is even possible that it was never present, for example, the presence of antibodies against parvo virus in cats does not necessarily mean that the cats are or were ever infected with parvo virus. Vaccinations and antibodies present in young animals received from the mother, may also be the cause of positive antibody titres. Negative results, in both direct and indirect tests do not always exclude the presence of an infection. Every technique employed has its own detection limit, below which an existing infection will not be detectable and which determines the sensitivity of the test. It takes some time (generally a number of days, sometimes much longer) after the initial contact with an antigen, before the amount of antibodies in the blood serum will exceed the detection limit of a test. By studying the amount (titre) and the type (IgG, IgM or IgE) of antibodies present, it is sometimes possible to ascertain whether an infection is recent or has been present for a while. To perform this type of investigation (known as "paired sera"), it is necessary to collect, over a two to three week period, a number of serum samples taken from the same animal.

A brief description of a number of microbiological methods for detection of infection with the various microbial agents is presented in the following (see also chapter 8).

Viruses

In the absence of complicating secondary, often bacterial, infections, most viral infections do not cause clinical symptoms within otherwise healthy adult small laboratory animals (an exception is e.g. the ectromelia virus in mice). They are more likely to cause disease in neonates (e.g. the Sendai virus in mice). Another reason for suspecting a viral infection would be a negative change in breeding results within an animal colony. The presence of a viral infection is, however, usually detected by means of serological examinations which are performed as part of a health-monitoring program or with experimental results when problems occur (see chapter 8). In larger laboratory animal species, a number of viruses, for example, the parvo virus in dogs and cats and viral haemorrhagic disease in rabbits, may cause severe clinical problems and even lead to death. When dealing with such clinically evident viral diseases, results of clinical and postmortem investigations (macroscopical and/or microscopical) generally provide sufficient information to arrive at a preliminary diagnosis. Such an initial diagnosis can usually be confirmed relatively quickly, by means of a microbiological method, preferably a direct one by detecting the presence of viral antigen.

Intracellular or intranuclear inclusion bodies, detectable using histological examination, occur in the course of a number of viral infections. Detectability of such inclusion bodies can be increased by applying specific staining techniques. Viral antigens can be visualised in tissues using an immuno-histochemical method by means of (group-)specific antisera. Tissue which is to be investigated by this method must be collected as soon as possible after death, frozen for histologic examination in liquid nitrogen and stored at $-70°C$. The isolation of a virus can be performed using cell cultures, laboratory animals, or embryonated eggs. Virus isolation is generally only applied when the direct immunological detection techniques have not been satisfactory, or if the presence is suspected of viruses which have as yet not been characterized or for which there are no antibodies available. Materials which are to be used for such investigations should be frozen at $-70°C$ or should be stored in liquid nitrogen.

Bacteria (including Mycoplasmata)

The detection of bacterial infections can be done using a variety of techniques. Various direct techniques allow the determination of the specific morphology of bacteria and to their staining characteristics using Gram and other staining

methods. Additional information can be derived from their growth pattern
on agar plates and to their metabolic characteristics (biochemical reactions)
using selective culture media. Serology, an indirect technique, can also be
employed and involves the detection of antibodies against bacterial antigens
which provide evidence of (previous) infection. New specific methods for
detecting an increasing number of bacteria are constantly being developed.

Morphology of bacteria.   It is relatively quick and easy to demonstrate the
presence of bacteria by microscopical examination of smears, tissue imprints
or histological sections, which are stained using a variety of stains. Bacteria
can be subdivided according to their shape into bacilli (rods), cocci, spirilla
and vibrios. They can also be classified according to their staining properties,

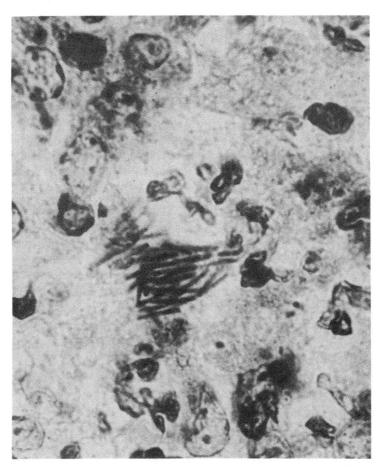

Fig. 9.2. Intracellular *Bacillus piliformis* bacteria.

for example, positive or negative when using the Gram stain, acid resistance in the Ziehl-Neelsen staining reaction, and whether they are encapsulated or not.

A variety of other characteristics can in addition be examined, such as endospore production, division pattern (budding or true branching) and motility. For a number of bacteria, which do not multiply in broth or on agar plates (e.g. *Bacillus piliformis*), histological examination of affected tissues and organs is the most important diagnostic approach (fig. 9.2). Although special histological staining techniques may be necessary, microscopic inspection of smears of organs which normally are free from bacteria, is generally both quick and satisfactory. This method provides direct information about the presence or absence of bacteria, and it will also give information about their quantity and morphology.

Growth on culture media. Most bacteria can be cultured in the laboratory employing appropriate techniques. Culture media contain the nutrients necessary for the bacteria to grow and multiply, and they exist in solid (agar plates) as well as liquid (broth) form. Cultivation on agar media (generally at 37°C for a period of at least 24 hours) should reveal characteristics of the resulting bacterial colonies such as growth rate, shape, colour and whether swarming occurs. Together with colony size and smell, all these factors are helpful in discriminating characteristics in identifying bacteria.

Biochemical characteristics. The growth of bacteria is a biological process which requires nutrients and which produces metabolites. Determination of the nutrients required, and identification of the metabolites produced by cultured bacteria provides useful information for identification purposes. This is often achieved by the addition of indicators to the medium which change colour when a particular type of bacteria grows. By varying the type and amount of components of a medium, it is possible to produce so-called elective, selective or non-selective media. *Non-selective* media contain all the necessary nutrients for growth of many types of bacteria. The bacterial colonies that are suspected to be relevant, are isolated from a non-selective agar plate in order to grow a pure culture from which the bacterium can be identified. The composition of *elective* media allows certain (types of) bacteria to grow faster than others. *Selective* media only allow the growth of selected bacteria. Selective media can be produced, for example, by adding restricting antibiotics which inhibit growth of all except a few types of bacteria. An example of a selective medium is the medium used for isolation of *Mycoplasma* spp..

The isolation and identification of the most common pathogenic bacteria can usually be completed in a matter of days, providing the suitable culturing media and identification techniques are available. Multitest systems which require the inoculation of a limited number of media have been developed and are commercially available.

Immunological tests.   For some bacteria, it is difficult or very time consuming to carry out direct identification techniques. The presence of some bacteria can be determined using serological methods which detect the presence of antibodies. Such tests are carried out as a matter of routine when screening for a.o. *Mycoplasma pulmonis* in rodents, *Corynebacterium pseudotuberculosis* (causes lymphadenitis in goats and other species), and *Leptospira* spp. in various animal species. Serological methods are relatively cheap, fast and reliable and, as such, this type of screening will probably be widely used in the near future for the detection of a growing number of bacterial infections (see Table 8-2). Frequently, however, the sensitivity and/or specificity of serological methods are insufficient. If an animal or a colony is seropositive for a certain bacterium, it is advisable to obtain confirmation by isolating the bacterium in question.

Protozoa

Certain protozoan organisms can infect animals and cause lesions within different organs. For example *Encephalitozoon cuniculi* (Nosema) may cause inflammatory lesions in brain and kidney in both rabbits and guinea pigs. *Toxoplasma gondii* cysts can be found in almost any part of the body of infected (laboratory) animals, just as they can in man. *Eimeria stiedei* causes macroscopically visible changes of the bile ducts in rabbits. All these examples of protozoan infections can be diagnosed by conducting a postmortem and a histopathological examination, supplemented where necessary by the use of immunological methods (IFA, ELISA).

Most protozoan infections occur within the intestinal tract (e.g. coccidia, flagellates); a number of these will only appear in a specific part of the intestine. Flagellates, sarcodines and ciliates can be recognized by their motility characteristics in fresh, wet smears of the enteric contents, or in a fresh sample scraped of the enteric wall for examination. These samples need to be kept at approximately body temperature. Samples can be preserved for further investigation and/or identification in Bouin's fixative. Cysts of, for example, coccidia, can be detected in direct wet faecal preparations by microscopical examination at a magnification of 40×, provided that they are excreted via the faeces in sufficiently large numbers. It is possible to detect smaller numbers of cysts using an enrichment method, such as sedimentation or flotation methods.

Fungi

Dermatophytes and deep fungi may be the cause of opportunistic infections in laboratory animals, but they are not primary pathogens. Dermal lesions caused by fungi may, however, occur and can be divided into two groups: the superficial and the deep skin mycoses. The incidence of dermal mycosis in laboratory animals which are kept in adequate conditions, is minimal. If it does occur, it is generally caused by *Microsporum* spp. or *Trichophyton* spp.. Superficial skin mycoses can be diagnosed by the microscopical examination of hairs and skin scrapings which have been taken from the border line between normal and the macroscopically altered skin regions. In the event of a *Microsporum canis* infection, the infected hairs and skin will show up bright green under the ultraviolet light of a Woods-lamp. If deep skin mycoses or internal fungal diseases are suspected, microscopical examination of exudate and/or tissue biopsies will be necessary, using special staining techniques such as PAS (periodic acid Schiff) or methamine silver histological examination.

The tracing of carrier animals of subclinical fungal disease, and the identification of dermatophyte or internal fungus, requires the use of culture methods. The materials under investigation should be inoculated in specific media developed for fungi (Sabouraud or malt agar plates). Generally, two identical plates will be inoculated, one incubated at 37°C and the other at 20°C (room temperature). After inoculation, the plates should be kept in the dark. As soon as growth occurs, which can take from a number of days to a few weeks, the mould or yeast can be identified by examining morphological and biochemical characteristics of the organism cultured.

Helminths

Helminths particularly occur in the intestinal tract of laboratory animals. Nematodes such as oxyurids (pinworms) found in rats, mice and rabbits and cestodes (tapeworms) can be detected by macroscopical and microscopical examination of the intestinal contents in the course of a postmortem. The oxyurids of rats, mice and rabbits occur in the caecum and colon. Whilst the host animal is resting, the females of these worms deposit their eggs around the anus (rat or mouse), or in the mucosal crypts of the colon (rabbits). The eggs of the oxyurids, in the rabbit, hatch within the enteric crypts, whilst those of the rodents hatch outside the animal. Therefore, it may be difficult to find eggs of oxyurids in the faeces of rats, mice or rabbits. An alternative diagnostic method, used for the screening of oxyurids in living rats and mice, is to press a piece of transparent adhesive tape against the anal region of the animal during the first half of the afternoon i.e. the middle of the host's resting. The presence of other (egg producing) intestinal helminths can be determined by searching for eggs in the faeces by carrying out microscopic examinations (magnification 40×) of direct or enriched (sedimentation/flotation) wet preparations.

Helminths can also occur in the blood, lungs, urinary bladder or indeed anywhere in the body. Diagnostic techniques employed include those of macroscopic and microscopic postmortem inspection, direct immunofluorescence techniques for the detection of antigens, serology and isolation using culturing methods.

Ectoparasites

Ectoparasites, such as fleas, mites and lice, generally cause clinical abnormalities such as itching (pruritus), alopecia and/or inflammatory lesions of the

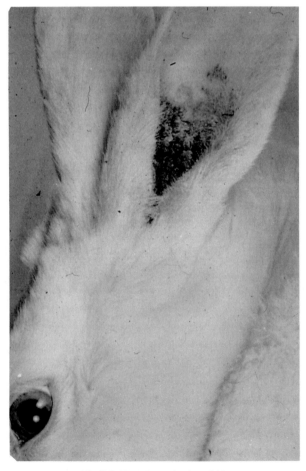

Fig. 9.3. Ear mange in the rabbit.

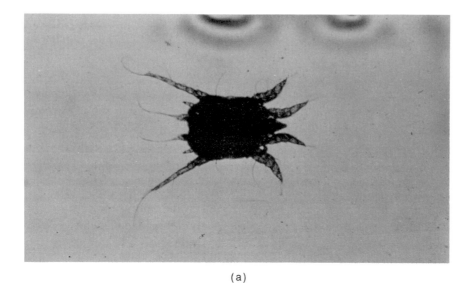

(a)

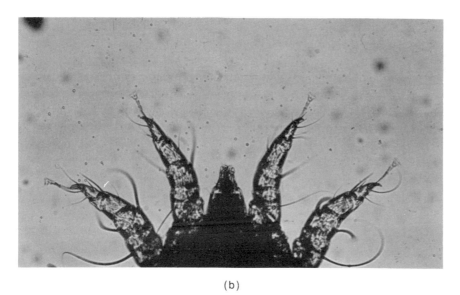

(b)

Fig. 9.4. (a) Ear mite *Psoroptes cuniculi* with suckers at the end of their legs (b).

skin. Often, the parasites or their products, namely the faeces of fleas and the eggs of lice or mites, are visible upon close inspection with the naked eye, or can be seen with the aid of a magnifying glass or stereomicroscope.

There are also ectoparasites which do not live on the surface of the skin but, for example, in the external auditory canal (such as *Psoroptes cuniculi* which causes ear mange in the rabbit, see figs. 9.3 and 9.4a, b) or in the skin (such as *Demodex* spp. in the hamster and dog or *Trixacarus caviae* found in the guinea pig). These parasites can be diagnosed by microscopic examination of excreta (earwax of the rabbit) and skin scrapings. The presence of ectoparasites under the skin or inside the body, for example, in the respiratory or digestive tract, can be detected in the course of a macroscopical postmortem or a histological examination.

Interpretation of results of diagnostic examinations

Having obtained all the relevant information, a diagnostic decision should be made by combining and evaluating the results of the various diagnostic tests. This task is best carried out by specialists in laboratory animal medicine, who will present their conclusions along with advice for action to the breeder or user of the animals. The interpretation of the combined information is a delicate process with many pitfalls. Many diseases are caused by a combination of factors, and the overestimation of the importance of factors such as opportunistic infections may lead to a wrong diagnosis. The identification of a single pathogenic agent does not mean that this is the only or primary cause of the disease. The interaction with, and the importance of, environmental factors must not be underestimated. In addition, contamination during sampling and the occurrence of commensal micro-organisms can lead to diagnostic errors. Comparison of the data from the diagnostic tests with reference data obtained from healthy animals, kept under the same circumstances, can be of great value.

Therapeutical interventions

When the cause of the disease has been established, the choice has to be made of accepting the situation without further action, applying therapy or euthanasia of the affected animals or of the entire experiment, colony or group. Therapy, generally, is the first choice considered. There are, however, risks involved when applying therapy both for the animals and for the experiment. The risk of transmission of an infectious disease to other animal groups within the institute is another serious factor which has to be taken into account. The fear of the spread of the infection to other animal rooms, or to other experimental groups, is usually dominant when discussing what actions need to be taken, and often leads to the conclusion that groups of infected animals must be eliminated. There are certain experiments, particularly toxicity testing studies, which fall under stringent guidelines, leaving little room for treating sick animals. According to some of these regulations, sick animals may only be treated if therapy is proven not to interfere with the experiment. It is, however, often difficult and sometimes even impossible to guarantee that a therapy will not influence test results. When the application of treatment is justified, the most effective therapy has to be selected. For larger animals such as dogs, cats and pigs, sufficient information to help in the decision making process is available from veterinary medicine. Information about the therapeutic effect and side effects of drugs is, however, not always readily available, especially regarding small laboratory animals. Therapeutic information from other animal species or from man often has to be relied upon. Differences in species-specific susceptibility may pose considerable problems, however. A particular dose of antibiotic may be used without much risk in man or dogs, whilst the same drug may cause disease or even death in rodents as a result of disturbing the microbial balance within the intestinal tract.

An important factor to be considered is the degree to which the treatment produces resolution of the disease without remnants. Often, in one or more of the internal organs, persistent lesions may occur, which may influence experiments. An infectious disease often persists latently in clinically healthy animals which puts them and their environment at risk. All of the above mentioned factors and consequences must be considered before a decision is made about the type of treatment. Logistic considerations, such as the number of animals that need treatment, also need to be taken into account. Furthermore, it will have to be decided whether the treatment should be restricted to the diseased animals, whether it should include all animals (including controls) of the particular experiment, or whether it should be applied to the animal colony or facility as a whole.

It is beyond the scope of this book to deal with the question what therapy is indicated in a given situation. This decision should be left by the veterinarian who is specialized in the field of laboratory animal science.

The problems involved when weighing and administering therapeutic treatment to laboratory animals may demonstrate the extraordinary importance of preventive measures and microbiological and husbandry standardization when breeding or experimenting with these animals.

Literature

Baker H J, Lindsey J R, Weisbroth S H, eds. The laboratory rat. vol. I. Biology and diseases. New York: Academic Press, 1979.

Bhatt P W, Jacoby R O, Morse H C, New A E, eds. Viral and mycoplasmal infections of laboratory rodents: effects on biomedical research; Proceedings of a conference held at the National Institute of Health, Bethesda, Maryland on October 24–26, 1984. Orlando: Academic Press, 1986.

Foster H L, Small J D, Fox J G, eds. The mouse in biomedical research. Vol. 2. Diseases. New York: Academic Press, 1982.

Fox J G, Cohen B J, Loew F M, eds. Laboratory animal medicine. London: Academic Press, 1984.

Hamm T E, ed. Complications of viral and mycoplasmal infections in rodents to toxicological research and testing. Washington: Hemisphere, 1986.

Harkness J E, Wagner J E, eds. The biology and medicine of rabbits and rodents. Philadelphia: Saunders, 1989.

Hsu C K, New A E, Mayo J G. Quality Assurance of rodent models. In: Animal quality and models in biomedical research. Spiegel A, Erichsen S, Solleveld HA (eds) p 17–28. Stuttgart: Gustav Fischer Verlag, 1980.

Kunstýř I ed. Diagnostic microbiology for laboratory animals. Stuttgart: Gustav Fischer Verlag, 1992.

Marcato P S, Rosmini R, eds. Pathology of the rabbit and hare, a colour atlas and compendium. Bologna: Società Editrice Esculapio, 1986.

National Research Council. Infectious diseases of mice and rats. Washington, DC: National Academy Press, 1991.

National Research Council. Companion guide to infectious diseases of mice and rats. Washington, DC: National Academy Press, 1991.

Walvoort H C. Assessment of distress through pathological examination. In: Replacement, reduction and refinement: present possibilities and future prospects. Hendriksen CFM, Koëter HBWM (eds) p 265–272. Amsterdam: Elsevier Science Publishers B.V., 1991.

Wagner J E, Manning P J, eds. The biology of the guinea pig. New York: Academic Press, 1976.

Weisbroth S H, Flat R E, Kraus A L, eds. The biology of the laboratory rabbit. New York: Academic Press, 1974.

Whittaker D. The importance and difficulties encountered with diagnosis of disease in laboratory animals. Anim Technol 1989; 40: 23–29.

10 Animal models

Introduction

Important decisions have to be taken when planning experiments and selecting experimental methodology, equipment and materials. Medical and biological research projects will generally employ at least one of the following categories:
- human volunteers
- experimental animals
- embryos, organs, tissues or cells having either plant, animal or human origin
- bacteria, fungi, protozoa
- inanimate models such as computer programmes, physical or chemical products.

Experimental material should be chosen with the purpose of solving the case being studied in the simplest possible way. Together with the scientific considerations, there are also legal and ethical matters which have to be taken into account when selecting test material (see chapter 18).

This chapter deals with the general aspects involved when using laboratory animals as models of man or indeed of other animal species. It is often the case that ethical, practical and/or financial reasons prevent the use of human volunteers or the target animal species for these studies. This chapter does not set out to list the various animal models which are currently available. Rather, the aim here is to describe the basic strategy required when selecting an animal model.

The use of experimental animals

One way in which laboratory animals are used for research or medical purposes is as the providers of biological products, such as hormones or antibodies. Some examples here would be the production of the pregnant mare's serum for the treatment of reduced fertility, and the production of polyclonal and monoclonal antibodies, which are mainly used for scientific purposes but which may also be used for therapeutic and diagnostic reasons. The researcher should aim to select the animal most suited to producing the required product in both sufficient quantities and in the purest possible form.

Animals are also used within science as models for the study of biological responses. Here the researcher employs physiological, pathophysiological or behavioural parameters to study the responses of the animal, having administered compounds or stimuli. This is necessary when monitoring the pharmacological and toxic effects of certain compounds, when measuring the concentration of drugs and when establishing the efficacy and safety of vaccines. Responses also need to be studied when testing the implantation of foreign elements, e.g. artificial organs and also in microbiological diagnostics. The animals used within these studies serve as a sentient "measuring device" or as a "biological instrument".

The demands which the test animal has to fulfil, when employed as a measuring device, will depend upon the type of measurements required. Ideally the test animal should react unequivocally to the given stimulus. With regard to diagnostic procedures, for example the use of mice for toxoplasmosis testing, only a positive or a negative reaction is required. Neither false-positive nor false-negative reactions should occur. The test animal must be sufficiently sensitive to enable its reaction to be both specific and clearly discernible. In the case of other bioassays, such as calibration tests for the determination of hormone concentrations or for the efficacy testing of vaccines, the researcher should also select an animal which will show a consistent, dose-dependent relationship. The use of defined animals within a controlled environment is vitally important. When an experiment is undertaken with the aim of finding the pharmacological or toxic effects of compounds, it is of paramount importance that the test animal's reactions can be extrapolated to those of other species, including man.

Animals are also used within research for the study of biological processes. In this area of study, scientists attempt to gain insight into the physiological and pathophysiological or the ethological processes within the animal. Examples here would include the development and growth of organs, regulatory processes such as circulation, respiration and the production of urine, immunological processes, the development of tumours, metabolic disorders, behaviour etc. With other processes, more specific, morphological, metabolic and/or pathophysiological functions may play a role (e.g. muscular dystrophy, hypertension, diabetes). In both these cases it should be possible to generalize the findings and extrapolate them to other animal species or man.

Research with laboratory animals is also carried out in order to improve the welfare, health and quality of the animals and their environment.

The concepts of animal models

Most of our knowledge regarding general biochemistry, physiology and endocrinology stems from animal experiments, which ideally should be extrapolated to man. In most experiments the animal, therefore, serves as a substitute for man and is referred to as an animal model. It is important here to define the term "laboratory animal model". One definition would be a model in which normative biology or behaviour can be studied, or in which a spontaneous or induced pathological process can be investigated, and in which the phenomenon resembles in at least one respect, the same phenomenon in human or other species of animal. This definition includes the use of animals as models for studies of normative biology and behaviour, but most laboratory animal models are developed and used to study the cause, nature and cure of human disorders.

The significance of results from animal experiments is dependent upon the selection of a suitable animal model. The extent to which the results can be "extrapolated" depends upon the type of animal model and the nature of the research. There are no rules regarding the choice of a proper animal model, nor are there rules for the extrapolation of results from the model to another animal species or man. It is, however, very valuable to have knowledge of relevant comparative biomedical aspects.

Animal models used in the study of human disease can be divided into four groups: induced models, spontaneous models, negative models and orphan models. The induced and spontaneous models are the most important.

With *induced animal models*, a disease or disorder is induced experimentally, either surgically or by the administration of biologically active substances, so that a corresponding likeness is obtained with regard to symptoms and etiology from those which would be expected in the target species. By interfering with the environmental, dietary, endocrine, immunological or infectious status of animals, models have been created for a plethora of human diseases and malfunctions. A new group of induced animal models in this field is transgenic animals (see chapter 7). To date mice are the preferred transgenic animals for research purposes, although other species, including fish, are receiving considerable attention. The production of transgenic animals containing foreign genes may result in hitherto unrecognized welfare problems, and researchers must be alert to signs of distress and pain in these animals.

Spontaneous animal models of human disease are those which exhibit naturally occurring genetic variants, and hundreds of strains/stocks of animals have been analyzed and categorized showing spontaneous diseases reflecting those of man. Migaki (1982) has listed 206 diseases in animals which are attributed to non-experimentally induced inborn errors of metabolism. It is possible to obtain spontaneous models either from inbred strains (genetically uniform) or from random-bred populations (heterogeneous) where a high percentage of the animals are affected by the disease.

Negative models are species, breeds or strains in which a certain disease does not develop. This term may also be given to a model which is insensitive to a certain stimulus which would usually have an effect on other species or strains. The underlying mechanisms of insensitivity can however be studied with a view to providing further insight into the given area of research.

Orphan animal models refer to models where a disease is initially recognized and studied in an animal species, with the knowledge that a human counterpart could be identified at a later stage. Papilloma viruses in malignant epithelial tumours, and Mareks disease virus as a lymphoproliferative agent, are two examples of orphan animal models.

Only rarely, however, do animal models fully mirror the human state in health or disease. It is often sufficient to determine the selection of an animal model given a similarity between man and animal with regard to only one aspect of the phenomenon under study. A number of different spontaneous and induced models of the same condition should be employed to scrutinize the different, possible mechanisms involved.

Extrapolation

When selecting an animal model for use, it is important to consider the desired range of generalization of the results to be obtained. The rationale for extrapolating results to other species is based on homology. Homology refers to the evolutionary similarity between morphological structures and physiological processes amongst different animal species but also between animals and man. Despite the fact that wide divergences have occurred during evolution, there are still many similarities amongst the varied animal species and between animals and man. When embarking upon the study of specific features, it is necessary to select the species or strain that displays total conformity with regard to the specific anatomical or physiological features with the species to which the results are to be extrapolated.

Extrapolation can take two forms; it may be qualitative or quantitative. Qualitative extrapolation deals with an animal's (patho-physiological) processes and its reactions to stimuli extrapolated to other animals or man. Quantitative extrapolation involves assessing, on the basis of animal tests, the dosage of a certain compound which would be beneficial or harmful to man or the target animal. Qualitative differences between species together with possible quantitative differences in physiological processes have a role to play here. Rates of basal metabolism and conversion of compounds in warm-blooded animals are proportional to body surface i.e. the smaller the organism, the larger its relative body surface and therefore the more intense its metabolism. In smaller animals, a higher percentage of the body weight is taken up by the liver, the kidneys and the heart. Therefore, it is advisable to relate dosage to body surface or metabolic weight (= body weight$^{0.75}$) rather than to body weight.

The extrapolatability of results may also be affected by the degree of discomfort felt by the test animal. Table 10.1 gives a general indication of the extrapolatability of results from animal experiments, taking into account the degree of similarity between animal model and target animal, and also the degree of discomfort inflicted by experimental procedures during the experiments. When extrapolating results within the same species, one of the main differences recorded will be discomfort due to experimental procedures. Extrapolation may also be hampered by differences in genotype, sex, age and physiological status. The effect of differences in genotypes will be even more pronounced when the data is to be extrapolated to another species or to man. This is due to the differences in morphological and biochemical characteristics, to the response to substances and other stimuli, or to differences in the pathophysiological reaction patterns which exist between species.

Extrapolation from animal to man should always be carried out with reservation. Test results obtained from animals will ultimately have to be verified in studies with humans. This means that it generally remains a matter of hindsight as to what extent extrapolation from animal to man was justified. It is often not possible to verify animal data in humans. In can only be suggested that, given this situation, animal tests can reduce risks imposed on man. Animal experiments for example set up to assess the safety of drugs and synthetic substances employed in agriculture, industry and food

Table 10.1

Extrapolatability of results from animal experiments

Animal model and target animal	Discomfort during experiment	Type of extrapolation	
		Qualitative	Quantitative
Animal model matches target animal	slight	+++	+++
	severe	+++	++
Animal model does not match target animal	slight	++	+
	severe	++	+

+ = low degree of extrapolatability; +++ = high degree of extrapolatability.

processing, reduce the risks involved for humans, even though toxicity data from test animals can never guarantee complete safety for human beings. The risk of false extrapolation can be minimized by using several species of animals in the experiments. This is the case in toxicological screening, where the authorities usually require the use of two species, one of which is to be a non-rodent. When carrying out research into the etiology and therapy of diseases, extrapolatability from an animal model is enhanced when the diseases under study have a common origin in both man and the experimental animal. Animal tests can speed up the progress of research undertaken to combat sickness in man. Whilst observation of phenomena in animals provides ideas for directional research in humans, it also makes such research safer.

The selection of animal models

The selection of an animal model for research requires careful, indeed meticulous, planning. Before commencing, the key question or hypothesis must be clear, as this will determine the choice of animal model. Only when the key question has been clearly defined will it be possible to ascertain which "key substrate" is necessary to provide the answer i.e. a particular type of cell, tissue, an organ, or the interaction between organs. The substrate then has to be defined. Should the substrate be healthy or ill, growing, adult or old? If the decision is taken that the substrate should be ill, the question then arises as to whether an induced model or a spontaneous one would suffice. The key substrate might be a single affected cell type, but could equally be a complete system of organs.

Having clearly defined the key substrate, it is then possible to look for species or strains which are suitably endowed with the required characteristics. The next step is to determine whether the key substrate is to be examined as such (e.g. as an *in vitro* organ) or whether the intact live animal should be used as a carrier of the key substrate. The latter may allow studies of longer duration and will also permit the investigation of interactions between organs.

The steps taken in the selection of an animal model can be summed up briefly:
1. define the key question
2. decide on the key substrate
3. determine in which animal species/strains this key substrate is found
4. establish which animal species/strains possessing the key substrate are the most advantageous from the technical point of view and which cause the minimum discomfort in the animals

5. establish which practical factors should be decisive i.e. availability, accommodation, care, tractability, equipment, published information, expertise, expense
6. select the animal model on the basis of scientific, practical and ethical considerations.

Scanning available literature will indicate species used within the topic of interest, but often these species are used more out of habit than the fact that they are chosen on the basis of comparative studies. There are obvious practical reasons which favour the use of the common laboratory animal species such as mice and rats. For the study of specific diseases, the available literature can disclose availability of spontaneous and/or induced models. When a suitable animal model is not readily available, the researcher may have to consider developing a model, but this is very time consuming. Apart from the model's desired properties, the researcher has to study pathophysiological reactions and possible infringements on the animal's welfare. This applies both to induced and to spontaneous models. The developed model then has to be validated to demonstrate that it can indeed act as a model for man or for the target animal.

The commonly used species of experimental animals, such as mice, rats, hamsters, guinea pigs and rabbits, usually present no problem as far as supply is concerned. They are often bred on the research premises, or can be purchased from commercial breeders. Random-bred animals and, generally speaking, the most widely used genetically defined animals can also be obtained from these sources. When planning research it must be taken into account that delivery periods grow longer as the specifications multiply or the number of animals on the order increases. With regard to inbred strains, which must show specific characteristics (genetic models), it is often necessary to turn to another research institute from where it is possible to purchase a few pairs of animals for breeding purposes.

The majority of inbred strains and genetic models have been registered in international catalogues and it is relatively easy, therefore, to locate any one particular inbred strain. Preference should be given, wherever possible, to specialized laboratory animal breeders; this is due to the fact that the animals on offer are generally kept under constant control with regard to microbiological status and genetic quality. Sometimes there are certain legal provisions which place restrictions on the methods of acquiring animals for experimental purposes. These provisions may differ between countries. This may also apply to the purchase of dogs and cats. These types of animals can be obtained from commercial laboratory animal breeders, but it may also be possible to buy them from authorised dealers. Non-human primates may be subject to certain jurisdictions, which means that permission is required from governmental authorities for trade, as well as for research purposes.

The large-scale import of monkeys practised a few decades ago has almost been abolished. In several countries monkeys are now being bred in specially organized centres for primates.

More than a hundred animal species are being used for research and, apart from the more commonly used laboratory animals and farm animals, this includes a variety of birds, reptiles, amphibians and fish. In most countries the importation of animals is subject to a number of rules and regulations designed to control contagious diseases and to protect certain species. When animals are purchased with no background health knowledge, or have been caught in the wild, there is a risk that they are infected with pathogens. Depending upon the animal species, the researcher should place the acquired animals in quarantine (see chapter 8) before introducing them to rooms where animals are already resident. Supervision during this quarantine period should be carried out by a veterinarian.

Literature

Andrews E J, Ward B C, eds. Spontaneous animal models of human disease. Vol 1. New York: Academic Press, 1979.

Andrews E J, Ward B C, Altman N H, eds. Spontaneous animal models of human disease. Vol 2. New York: Academic Press, 1979.

Calabrese E J. Principles of animal extrapolation. New York: John Wiley & Sons Inc., 1983.

Desnick R J, Patterson D F, Scarpelli D G, eds. Animal models of inherited metabolic diseases. Prog Clin Biol Res 1982; 94.

Festing M F W. Inbred strains in biomedical research. London: The Macmillan Press Ltd. 1979.

Festing M F W. International index on laboratory animals, 6th ed. Carshalton: Medical Research Council, 1992.

Hau J, ed. Laboratory animal models. Scand. J. Lab. Anim. Sci. 16, Suppl. 1, 1989.

Jones T C, ed. A handbook: Animal models of human disease. Washington: The Registry of Comparative Pathology; Armed Forces Institute of Pathology, 1972–1987. Fasc 1–16.

Migaki G. Compendium of inherited metabolic diseases in animals. Animal models for inherited metabolic diseases, 473–501. New York: Alan R Liss, 1982.

Mitruka B M, Rawnsley H M, Vadehra D V. Animals for medical research: Models for the study of human disease. New York: Wiley, 1976.

Schmidt-Nielsen, K. Animal physiology. Cambridge: Cambridge University Press, 1975.

11 Phases in an animal experiment

Introduction

Animal experimentation plays an important part in many branches of natural science. Animals are used to investigate, describe, explain and predict biological phenomena and effects. Statements on the basis of experiments must be in keeping with the empirical data. These data must in turn be methodologically correct. This chapter presents an introduction to the philosophy and methodology of animal experimentation, discussed in relation to the phases in an animal experiment.

Descriptive and experimental research

Scientific information is gained in two ways: by systematic observation and by experimentation. In the former case, known as "descriptive research", emphasis is placed on determination of amounts or relationships. For instance, estimation of the average age of people from different countries, or the number of people who die each year as a result of coronary heart disease, etc. With descriptive research, cause-effect relationships, such as those between smoking and lung cancer, can be inferred, but are difficult to prove beyond reasonable doubt.

In experimental research the approach is quite different. Here, research involves the design and analysis of experiments with populations to which different treatments are assigned during the course of the experiment. In this case causal relationships are much more easily demonstrated. This chapter is restricted to a discussion of experimental research, particularly that carried out with animals. Experimental research is usually based on the results of descriptive research or earlier experimental research. It may be basic research, aimed at a deeper understanding of biological systems, or it could be carried out because of legal obligations. For instance, prior to launching a drug on the market, the risk of the drug causing harmful side effects at dose levels appropriate to human exposure must have been investigated and considered to be acceptably low.

Philosophers do not entirely agree on how new knowledge is acquired, and at least three different philosophies have been accepted by working scientists. Briefly, these are:

(1) *The inductive–hypothetico–deductive philosophy.* According to this philosophy new theories or hypotheses are formulated by observing all possible facts in order to gather relevant data from which an hypothesis is developed by a process of inductive reasoning. Inductive reasoning is a process whereby a general law is formulated on the basis of repeated observation of a particular phenomenon. Once the hypothesis has been formulated, experiments may be carried out with a view to finding support for it. The problem with this approach is that inductive reasoning does not seem to be an entirely logical process. The 18th century philosopher David Hume stated that we are not justified in reasoning from (repeated) instances of which we have experience to other instances (conclusions) of which we have no experience. "The reason why we do have expectations in which we have great confidence is custom or habit; that is because we are conditioned by repetitions and by the mechanism of association of ideas...". This led him to the conclusion that argument or reason plays only a minor part in our understanding, and that "our knowledge is unmasked as being not only of the nature of a belief, but of rationally indefensible belief — of an irrational faith". Thus the scientific method, the most powerful intellectual tool devised by humans, appeared to him to be logically unjustifiable.

(2) *The deductive philosophy of Karl Popper.* Popper put forward an alternative philosophical approach which he claims overcomes the problems associated with inductive reasoning and which he claims we do not need to justify because it is a process which we do not in fact use. His approach is now widely accepted by many working scientists.

According to Popper *no hypothesis or theory can ever be shown to be true,* but *it can sometimes be shown to be false.* If we are unable to falsify a theory, we can provisionally accept it. According to him, good theories are ones which can easily be falsified and, at any one time, there may be several competing theories, among which we must choose. Very briefly, he states that "the method of science is the method of bold conjectures and ingenious and severe attempts to refute them".

Bold theories are ones which have a high level of generality and a high truth content. Such bold theories should be the most easily tested. If they can be shown to be false, then a competing theory would have to be developed. The more rigorously we can test a theory, the more confidence we can have in it, but it can never be proved to be true. The most that we can claim is that the theory is *a better approximation of the truth* than any competing theory.

(3) *The paradigm shift philosophy of Thomas Kuhn.* According to Kuhn, science progresses by a process of sudden change, followed by a period of consolidation. Most "normal science" consists of experiments and observations based around existing hypotheses. As information gradually accumulates, it may become clear that these existing hypotheses are not entirely satisfactory. At some stage the existing hypothesis may become untenable, and an entirely new hypothesis may emerge. Kuhn terms this a "paradigm shift". The emergence of this new hypothesis may lead to rapid scientific advance, but this eventually settles down again to another period of "normal science", until the next paradigm shift.

With any of the three philosophies noted above, when experimental research is based on earlier investigations, the various observations are studied to develop one or more explanatory theories. Logic and intuition play an important role here. According to the inductive-hypothetico-deductive philosophy, it is at this stage that inductive reasoning is used. For instance, when a group of analogous chemicals fails to induce cancer in various laboratory animals species, inductive inference might lead to the general hypothesis that all similar chemicals are non-carcinogenic in all animal species, including man. However, it is possible that certain animal species do not fit into the generalization or that the new chemical does not comply with it. On the basis of the general hypothesis a specific or working hypothesis can be formulated. For instance, the new chemical does not cause cancer in humans, or it is non-carcinogenic in the rat. This hypothesis contains the inference (prediction) that administration of the compound to man or rats does not cause cancer. The inferring of predictions from an hypothesis is called the process of deduction.

However, according to Popper, a working hypothesis is arrived at not by a process of induction, but by a process of choosing among competing hypotheses, many of which can be discarded because they have already been shown to be false. With the above example, the hypothesis might be that the chemical is a non-carcinogen in all mammals. This is a testable hypothesis because it can be administered to mammals of various species and, if it causes cancer, then the hypothesis would be rejected. In practice, the two philosophies lead to a working hypothesis that appears quite similar and must usually be tested by experimentation. Here, Popper places great emphasis on the need to try to *falsify* the hypothesis, whereas other philosophical approaches tend to seek data to *support* rather than refute the hypothesis.

The hypothesis can now be put to the test in an experiment. When the hypothesis is not rejected on the basis of the experimental results, it is accepted for the time being. Experimental results, often also including the concurrent serendipitous observations, may contribute to a completely new spiral of induction-hypothesizing-deduction-experimentation-induction (according to one philosophy), or the rejection of the current hypothesis and the formulation of a new one (according to Popper).

Below the various phases in an animal experiment are described in chronological order. The case is put that the objective of the experiment is to test a certain hypothesis. The various phases illustrate the general course of such an animal experiment. Clearly, depending on the actual problem, there will be deviations from the following outline. However, prior to this, there is a brief discussion of whether the philosophical underpinnings of the scientific method are of any great importance to research workers working with animals.

Does scientific philosophy matter?

The practical consequences of all three philosophies noted above superficially appear to be very similar. An hypothesis is arrived at by a process of (1) inductive reasoning or (2) discarding competing hypotheses or (3) as a result of the last paradigm shift in the particular discipline. Whatever the process, the next step is the formulation of an appropriate set of experiments to test the hypothesis and gather new data. Many scientists can spend their whole career making a valuable contribution to their branch of science, without really being aware of any of the above philosophies.

However, there are some occasions on which a clear idea of the underlying philosophy is useful. In animal research, a concept that is often poorly understood is that of *"extrapolation from animals to humans"*. According to some scientists, research is carried out on animals, and then the results are extrapolated to humans. Exactly how this is done is rarely stated. However, the underlying philosophy is that of inductive inference, or arguing from a particular set of observations of which we have experience (for example that a drug is safe in rats and dogs) to another set of which we have no experience (that it is safe in humans). This is exactly the problem faced by Hume, who concluded that the whole process is illogical. It also seems illogical to many anti-vivisectionists who can point to specific instances where tests in animals gave results which were not of predictive value in humans (e.g. the fact that penicillin kills guinea-pigs). It would seem that the modern trend towards the use of *in-vitro* techniques would be even more difficult to justify. If it is difficult to explain how one extrapolates from rats to humans, how much more difficult is it to explain how one can justify extrapolating from bacteria to humans, as appears to be necessary in the case of the Ames test (see chapter 17).

However, according to Popper's philosophy, there is no need to explain how to extrapolate from bacteria or animals to humans, because it does not happen. A toxicologist would set up a series of hypotheses, and proceed to test them experimentally. The first hypothesis might be that the compound is not genotoxic. This can be tested using the Ames test and other *in-vitro* techniques. Failure to show that it is genotoxic would mean that the hypothesis is provisionally accepted. The testing would, of course, need to be as rigorous as possible. From this, another hypothesis might be developed that the compound is not a mammalian carcinogen. This could be tested in rats and other laboratory species. If it were shown to be a rat carcinogen then the hypothesis would have to be rejected. In most cases the compound would then be discarded. However, it would be possible to continue with another hypothesis that the chemical is not a carcinogen in animals which metabolize it by route X–Y–Z (as in humans), provided an animal which uses such metabolic pathways can be found. It will be seen that according to this philosophy, there is no extrapolation. A hypothesis suggests certain experiments which can be used to test it, and *suitable action is decided before the experiment is even started.*

There appear to be many advantages in considering animal experiments in the light of Popper's philosophy. Extrapolation does not need to be explained, and the place of *in-vitro* tests and lower organisms in testing hypotheses can be seen more clearly, so that pressure to use more primates could well be reduced.

Selection of research topic

The selection of the research topic, in its broadest sense, is determined by social scientific or practical relevance (for instance, environmental factors in relation to the development of cancer). In a narrower sense (for instance, the influence of specific dietary constituents on development of a specific form of cancer), the selection of research topic is also determined by the possibilities and objectives of the research institution and/or the interest of the investigator.

Animal tests may also be carried out by order of industries or government. There are legal guidelines for the admission of new chemicals (colouring matters, drugs etc) on the market. Within this framework, testing on animals is compulsory before the compound is sold. The manufacturers of new compounds frequently commission research. In the course of the development of new chemicals, industries also carry out their own research.

Formulation of hypotheses

Ideally, the three following stages should precede the formulation of an hypothesis.
1. Observing and recording all relevant information.
2. Analysis and classification of this information.
3. The development of general hypotheses based on such information.
In practice, it is difficult to decide what information is relevant. This must be judged subjectively, and intuition may play an important role. A thorough search of the literature is usually necessary. This can be done efficiently with the use of computer programs and literature banks.

The relevant information has to be analyzed and classified. Provisional hypotheses will already have been developed. *"The critical discussion of competing theories which is characteristic of good science goes (as a rule) far beyond the kind of thing with which we are perfectly satisfied in ordinary life"* (Popper 1972). A creative, imaginative faculty is essential.

A general hypothesis involves making a guess at the relationship between observed phenomena and their possible causes. Great inventiveness is needed, and this is especially so when this hypothesis implies a radical break with conventional notions. Remember that, according to Popper, bold conjectures are preferred, because these are most easily tested. A bold conjecture is a theory with a greater truth content than the one which we are hoping that it will replace.

The ways of developing fruitful hypotheses are quite diverse and sometimes appear very unscientific. This is quite acceptable provided rigorous procedures are used to choose among, or test, competing theories.

Experiments are used to test the validity of the preferred hypothesis, and great care must be taken to ensure that the chosen experiment will in fact fulfil this function. The predicted experimental results should be carefully considered. If this is not done, it may be found that, after having obtained the experimental results, it is not possible to use them to refute the preferred hypothesis.

For instance, the duration of treatment for an effect to be perceptible should be indicated prior to execution of the experiment. Otherwise, it might be concluded by hindsight that the experiment did not last long enough, and that the experiment was incapable of doing what it was designed to do. Fortuitous observations are of scientific interest when they are used for the generation of hypotheses that are subsequently tested in experiments deliberately designed to do so. However, in rare cases, they may lead to a rejection of the current hypothesis, in which case they may be of critical importance.

The relevance of a prediction is determined by at least three factors.

(1) *The degree of specialization that took place to render the hypothesis testable.* For instance, the experiment may involve using a specific strain of rats or duration of the treatment. A failure to disprove the hypothesis (for example that a compound is not toxic to rats) in this case may be because the wrong strain of rats was used. Well designed experiments may take account of such problems by including more than one species or strain of animals, exposure duration, different diets, husbandry conditions etc., in order to increase the generality of the results.

(2) *The power of the experiment.* A very small or badly designed experiment, using very variable material, may not be capable of detecting subtle effects which are still of biological importance and relevance to the hypothesis being tested. Remember that the method of science involves bold conjectures but also *severe and ingenious attempts to refute them.* This implies rigorous, well designed experiments with sufficient power to detect any treatment effect of sufficient magnitude to be of biological interest.

(3) *How critical the experiment is to the hypothesis.* If the results of the experiment lead to a total rejection of the current hypothesis, this is of much more interest than if all that is required is a minor adjustment in the scope of the hypothesis.

The hypothesis must be made operational. This is a purely practical point. At this stage, the parameters to be measured are defined and the measuring apparatus selected. Validity (lack of bias) and reproducibility (high precision) of the analytical methods are crucial here.

Selection of test material

When selecting suitable test material, many alternatives should be considered, including alternatives to living organisms and even humans. Here, we consider the situation in which an animal model is chosen. Within the framework of the inductive philosophy, the choice of animal is extremely important in relation to later generalization of the experimental results, especially for extrapolation of the results to another animal species, including humans (see chapter 10).

Preparation of research protocol

In the process of formulating the hypothesis, the practical possibilities of testing should be taken into account. The researcher is usually quite free to choose the most appropriate methods. However, the size of the experiment is determined by the statistical verification standards which have been set (see chapter 12). Limiting factors are often of a practical nature. For instance, the choice of animal may be determined by experience concerning experimental techniques in a given animal species. The size of the animal or availability of a specific disease model may be critical.

The next step is to draft the research protocol. It may list the following:

1. Facts and inferences that led to the general hypothesis.
2. Formulation of the working hypothesis.
3. Exact deductive arguments that lead to the prediction to be verified.
4. Schematic design of the experiment, including treatments (see chapter 12).
5. Description of operational definitions and measuring methods.
   Criteria on which the choice of animal model is based should be indicated as well as the arguments speaking against the use of alternatives to living organisms. The validity and reproducibility of the analytical methods should be discussed, as well as the units in which the results are to be expressed.
6. A description of the anticipated discomfort of the animals (see chapter 14).
7. Number of animals to be used and statistical and methodological considerations on which this number is based should be given. This implies that the choice of effect considered to be relevant, statistical analyses, statistical power, acceptable chance of type I error and experimental design (see chapter 12) are discussed.
8. A description of logistics, i.e. the ways of collecting, processing and analyzing the data.
9. Practical aspects, such as personnel required, name of research leader, costs etc. (see chapter 13).

The research protocol serves several purposes. It is useful for assessing the ethical acceptability of the proposed experiment (see chapter 18). It may be used as working paper to be scrutinized by colleagues. It can be submitted to potential funding bodies. It is useful in preparing a detailed protocol (see below) and it forms the basis for the evaluation and reporting of the experimental results (see below).

Detailed protocol for the execution of the experiment

What is needed next is a paper describing the practical actions to be undertaken. In a simple and clearly structured way, the course of the experiment must be described. Such aspects as choice of species, and strain, and the housing of the animals, must be noted. Their nutrition, the method and timing of the collection, processing and/or storage of biological samples and any euthanasia of the animals should be accurately described. The detailed protocol provides a guide both for the investigator and the animal and laboratory technicians. The investigator must continue to watch over the conditions that are used in order to verify the scientific prediction.

When the animal experiment is finished and all the data has been collected, it must be analyzed using the appropriate mathematical and statistical methods. Finally, the results must be interpreted in the context of the original hypothesis.

Evaluation and reporting

On the basis of the experimental results and statistical analysis conclusions are drawn as to validity of the original working hypothesis. This may be difficult, especially for the more general hypothesis.

It is not always easy to be sure that any given experiment will give a rigorous test of the working hypothesis. In practice, an experiment will often be carried out in a specific animal house, using a particular species and strain of animals, under a particular husbandry regimen, using a particular diet, and measuring a particular set of end-points. If the experiment shows that the working hypothesis is clearly wrong, then the experiment can be judged to have been successful. However, if it fails to falsify the hypothesis, there is always the suspicion that had a different strain, diet, or set of end-points been measured, a different result may have been obtained. A really rigorous test of the working hypothesis might include testing under a wide range of different conditions, such as with different species and strains, different diets etc. This is particularly true if the hypothesis is one such as "this compound is non-carcinogenic in all mammals (including humans)". This is a testable hypothesis in that, if it could be shown to be a carcinogen in rats, the hypothesis would be disproved. However, it is difficult to test severely without using several species, strains, modes of administration etc. This may require a whole series of experiments.

The final phase is reporting and interpreting the results of the experiment or series of experiments. This can be done in the form of an internal report or publication in a scientific journal. In the latter case, the lay-out of the publication is determined by the journal to which it will be submitted. A general lay-out is as follows.

1. *Title and authors (with affiliation)*. Generally, individuals should not be included as authors unless they have made a substantial contribution to the work. All authors carry responsibility for the validity of the work.
2. *Summary*. Brief description of the aims of the experiment and the hypotheses tested, experimental design and conclusions.
3. *Introduction*. Summary of existing knowledge and possible working hy-

potheses, with a statement of the results to be expected if the hypotheses are not true.

4. *Materials and methods.* Results of animal experiments should be reproducible in other laboratories. Thus, when reporting the results, the animals used and their environment should be carefully described so that the experiment can be repeated under similar conditions (see chapter 5). The following experimental details should be given.

a. Animals:

Origin, species, breed, strain (inbred, outbred, any genetic quality control) and proper nomenclature, specific properties as model, age, sex, body weight, microbial status (with indication of procedures used to test this).

b. Housing:

Type of animal room (barrier, isolator, laminar flow), temperature, relative humidity, ventilation, lighting (intensity, day-night cycle), cage type (size, model, material, presence of a filter top), number of animals per cage, bedding (type, frequency of changing), transport, acclimatization period.

c. Nutrition:

Diet (manufacturer, composition, form, sterilization, any quality control procedures), feeding regimen (*ad libitum*, restricted, pair feeding), drinking water (*ad libitum*, automatic supply, bottles, sterilization, quality).

d. Experimental procedures:

Chemicals, drugs (dose, manufacturer, purity, additives), time point (time during the day, season, oestrus cycle, nutritional status), route of administration of drugs (orally, intravenously), sampling methods (blood, urine, faeces), anaesthesia (premedication, type of anaesthetic, dose, duration, route of administration), execution of experimental techniques, euthanasia (method), collection, processing and storage of organs.

e. The experimental design:

Formal layout (completely randomized, randomized block, Latin square, factorial), measuring methods and method of statistical analysis (parametric; *t*-test, analysis of variance, regression, correlation; non-parametric) should also be stated. It may also be noted that the experimental protocol had been approved by an animal experiments committee (see chapter 18).

5. *Results.* Well-organized presentation of results in the form of figures, tables and words.

6. *Discussion.* Description of the results in the light of earlier work, implications for the working hypothesis being disproved or provisionally accepted,

generalization of the outcome, suggestions for further research.

7. *Acknowledgements.* Names of persons and institutions that contributed to the investigation, but did not justify being an author, names of funding agencies.

8. *Literature cited.* List of literature cited in the text. No paper should be cited unless it has been studied by one or more of the authors.

A manuscript will not usually be published immediately. The editorial board of the journal refers it to a number of anonymous experts who judge its quality on the basis of the methods used and their relevance to the working hypothesis, the way that the experiment has been conducted, and the interpretation of the outcome. In most cases the manuscript will be returned to the authors with suggestions for ways in which it could be improved, or pointing out areas where the referee does not agree with the conclusions. It is then for the authors either to modify the manuscript, or defend their original submission.

This evaluation attempts to prevent publication of papers based on poorly conducted experiments. Moreover, the referee system will encourage investigators to design and execute their experiments properly; only then does the investigator have a reasonable chance that his/her work can be published in a respected journal.

After publication in an international journal, preferably in English, the results of the experiment are available to any interested person. The article can then either trigger the formulation of new hypotheses, or of experiments designed to test the existing hypotheses even more rigorously, or the results contribute to formulating aspects of policies in relation to public health.

Literature

Popper K R. The logic of scientific discovery. London: 1959.

Working committee for the biological characterization of laboratory animals/GV-SOLAS. Guidelines for specification of animals and husbandry methods when reporting the results of animal experiments. Laboratory Animals, 1985; 19: 106–108.

12 Design of animal experiments

Introduction

Animal experiments should be designed and executed so that the results are as informative as possible. It is wrong to use too few animals as the experiment may lack the power to detect some biologically meaningful effects. Such experiments will be a waste of time and resources, and an unnecessary sacrifice of animals. Likewise, it is wrong to use more animals than are required to detect a treatment effect. In order to prevent the use of either too few or too many animals, it is essential to consider, prior to execution of the experiment, the experimental design and the number of animals needed.

In an animal experiment, treatments are applied to groups of laboratory animals. Despite accurate execution of the experiment, individual animals from identically treated groups will give different results or measured values. This is due to uncontrollable variation between individual animals.

Variation between apparently identical animals, i.e. animals belonging to the same treatment group, is caused by factors that cannot be made identical for all animals. These factors involve individually determined genetic or microbial status, developmental accidents and environmental influences and interactions between them, including interactions with the experimental treatment. If an experiment is repeated with the same or other animals but under identical conditions different group mean values will be obtained. As a result, the observed treatment effects will also be different.

Statistical analysis of the results is usually required to account for this variability. The process of statistical analysis should ideally be done according to an experimental specification (see chapter 11) that was set prior to starting the experiment.

This specification should include:
a. the minimum magnitude of treatment effect that is considered to be of interest;

b. the chance of failing to detect such an effect, if it truly exists, i.e. the chance of obtaining a false–negative result;

c. the chance of obtaining a false–positive result (i.e. there may be no true treatment effect, but by chance the means may differ to such an extent that it appears as though there is). This is usually specified as the significance level that will be accepted.

This specification, together with data on expected inter-individual variability, makes it possible to estimate the number of animals needed to detect the specified treatment effect with a suitably low probability of obtaining a false–positive or false–negative result.

In most experiments, the objective is to determine the effect of different treatments. This has to be done against a background of uncontrollable variation which should be reduced as far as possible, and distributed at random among the treatment groups. As a result, any uncontrolled variation will have a minimal impact on the treatment effect.

This chapter presents an introduction to various elementary aspects of the design of animal experiments. Details and more complex aspects belong to the domain of statisticians rather than of biomedical researchers.

Testing of hypotheses

The testing of hypotheses is a formalized procedure for drawing conclusions. In its simplest form, an experiment consists of two groups of animals: a control and test group. The usual hypothesis to be tested is the "null hypothesis", *that there is no difference between treated and control groups.* An "alternative hypothesis" should also be specified. Commonly, this would be *that there is a difference between treated and control groups,* though sometimes it would take the form that the treatment reduces (or increases) the effect of interest. A formal procedure, based on probability calculations, is used either to accept the null hypothesis, or reject it in favour of the alternative hypothesis.

The first step is to choose a "significance level". This is the probability that the treated and control groups will be judged to be different when in fact there is no true treatment effect. Clearly, this probability should be quite low otherwise many differences will be judged to be due to a treatment effect when in fact they have risen simply by chance allocation of variable animals to the two groups. By convention, a significance level of 5% is often chosen, although other levels could also be justified.

The next step is to calculate the probability that the observed, or even larger, differences between the treated and control groups could have arisen by chance. This is done by means of a statistical test such as Student's *t*-test or the analysis of variance. If this test is done using a computer it is likely that the result will be a "*p*-value", which is the probability that we are seeking. This is the probability that a difference as large as, or greater than, the observed difference could have arisen by chance if the two groups are in fact random samples from the same population. This *p*-value is then compared with the pre-determined significance level. If the *p*-value is less than the significance level, then it is unlikely that the observed difference could have arisen by chance and the null hypothesis is rejected. If it is larger, then the observed difference may well have arisen by chance, and the null hypothesis is not rejected.

As an example, assume that one wishes to examine the effect of a drug on blood pressure in rats. Rats are allocated at random to the control group or to the test group, which receives the drug. Assume that the researcher predicts that the new drug affects blood pressure, and sets the significance level at the 5% probability level. At the end of the experiment the data is entered into an appropriate computer program and a *t*-test is used to compare the treated and control groups. Suppose a "*p*-value" of 0.03 is obtained. As this is less than the pre-determined probability level, the null hypothesis would be rejected, and the alternative hypothesis accepted.

Suppose, however, that the "*p*-value" was 0.06. As this is larger than the 0.05 pre-determined significance level, the null hypothesis would not be rejected, and it would be concluded that *according to this experiment there is no evidence that the drug has an effect*. In this case, the observed *p*-value was not very different from the significance level. It might be suspected that the treatment really does have an effect, but that this experiment failed to detect it, possibly because the sample size was too small, or the variability of the animals was too great. Failure to reject the null hypothesis does not necessarily mean that it is true, only that in a particular experiment there was no evidence for a particular treatment effect.

In most cases, this procedure will lead to the correct decision being made. However, false decisions may sometimes occur, as suspected in the above example. Table 12.1 illustrates this. A *type I* error (*false positive* result) is made when on the basis of statistical analysis a true null hypothesis is rejected. The probability of a type I error is identical to the significance of the test. In other words, by accepting a 5% significance level, the research worker is accepting

Table 12.1

Possible decisions when testing hypotheses

Decision	Reality	
	Null hypothesis, correct	Null hypothesis, incorrect
Accept null hypothesis	Right	Type II error
Reject null hypothesis	Type I error	Right

that on 5% of occasions the experiment will lead to a false positive result. A *type II* error (*false negative* result) is made when an invalid null hypothesis does not get rejected; this happens when a true treatment effect did not induce a sufficiently "clear" difference between control and test group in the experiment.

As noted above, rejection or acceptance of the null hypothesis is based on the *p*-value for the experiment (i.e. the chance of observing a treatment effect of this magnitude, or even larger, given that the null hypothesis is true) in relation to the chosen significance level. As a rule, significance levels of 5% or 1% are usually used. If smaller levels are chosen it will increase the chance of a false negative result (failure to detect a true treatment effect, or type II error).

Experimental data can take many forms. Most commonly it arises as a result of a *measurement* such as body weight or the concentration of an enzyme in the blood. In other cases, it may be a *count* such as the number of animals with or without a tumour, or it may even involve some sort of subjective *classification* such as the degree of necrosis of a tissue, scored as 0, +, ++, and +++. The type of statistical test used in assessing the treatment effect may depend critically of the type of data.

Assume, for the moment, that the experiment involves measurement data. Assume also that, under the null hypothesis, both the control and treated group represent a random sample of animals from a hypothetical infinite population in which the character of interest has a so-called *normal*, or *Gaussian* distribution. Such a distribution, which is extremely common in nature, is shown in fig. 12.1. It is specified by two "parameters", the mean (a measure of location) and the standard deviation (a measure of the variation about the mean). These are the only two items of information that are needed to specify the distribution with complete accuracy. The distribution is symmetrical and bell-shaped.

The alternative hypothesis must be stated clearly, as it will determine whether a "two-sided" or a "one-sided" test is to be used. Sometimes it is not relevant or known whether the treatment should increase or decrease the mean value so the null hypothesis is that *there is no treatment effect*, and the alternative is that *there is a treatment effect*. As the treatment effect can go in either direction, a two-sided test is appropriate. However, if the alternative hypothesis is that the treatment reduces the mean (say), and it would be inconceivable that it could increase it, then a one-sided test is appropriate. This directly influences the required number of animals in test and control groups (see later).

There are many statistical tests to evaluate the results of experiments. The choice of test to be used is determined by the nature of the observations and design of the experiment. The most widely used statistical tests require theoretically that the deviations from the mean values are normally distributed.

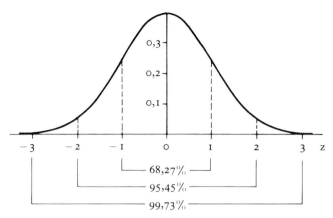

Fig. 12.1. Standardized normal distribution. The standardized variable z on the horizontal axis is obtained by subtracting each measured value from the population mean (μ) then dividing by the population standard deviation (σ). For a random measurement, there is a probability of 95% that the value will fall in the interval between $z = -1.960$ and $+1.960$. When a z value for a given probability of exceeding is defined as z_p, then some corresponding values are: $z_{0.025} = +1.960$, $z_{0.5} = 0$, and $z_{0.975} = -1.960$. In other words, 2.5% of z values are greater than 1.96, 50% are greater than 0 and 97.5% of values are greater than -1.96. The solid vertical line indicates the relative frequency of the population.

However, small departures from this do not cause any problems. In practice, measured values seldom conform to a perfect normal distribution. Sometimes the distribution is skewed. Often the data can be transformed (e.g conversion into their logarithmic values) to a more normal distribution. When this is not possible, so-called "non-parametric" statistical tests may be used. In certain cases, the experimental design, and consequently also the statistical analysis, can be very complex, so a statistician should be consulted prior to starting the experiment.

The probability of a type II error cannot easily be controlled as it depends on the true difference between control and test group, the variability (standard deviation) of the material and the number of animals used. When there is substantial variation between animals, and when the number of animals is small, then there is a high probability of a type II error. Such an experiment is said to lack "power". This also holds true in case of a small difference in mean measured values between control and test group.

Identification of the "experimental unit"

So far, it has been assumed that the whole animal is the "experimental unit", defined as the unit *which can be assigned independently to one of the treatments*. This is the unit which will be subjected to statistical analysis. However, the experimental unit may be part of an animal, or a group of animals. The experimental unit must be identified precisely; failure to do so may result in an experiment which cannot be statistically analyzed. This point can best be explained by giving some examples:

(a) A rat is used as a source of hepatocytes, obtained by perfusion of the liver with a collagenase solution. The hepatocytes are plated out in Petri dishes, and each dish is assigned at random to one of the treatments. The experiment is repeated on 6 rats.

In this case, the experimental unit is clearly the *Petri dish*. The individual rats represent replications of the experiment. The appropriate statistical analysis would recognise this structure.

(b) Twenty mice are used in a nutrition experiment, to compare two pelleted dietary formulations. The mice are assigned at random to two large cages with ten mice per cage. One cage is fed dietary formulation A and the other formulation B. Data is collected on growth and body composition of each mouse.

In this case, the cage (not the individual mouse) is the experimental unit. Although mice were assigned at random to the two cages, the two diets could not be assigned at random to individual mice, since all mice in the same cage had to have the same diet. Thus, once a diet had been allocated to the first mouse in the first cage, the diet of all other mice would automatically follow. All other mice in the same cage would have to have the same diet, and all mice in the other cage the other diet. The mice within a box are not independent replications of the treatment groups. As there are only two experimental units, and they have different treatments, this is an example of an experiment which can never be correctly analyzed, and is virtually useless, scientifically. True, at the end of the experiment it would be possible to use a *t*-test to compare body weight (say) in the two groups. But if this differs between the groups, it would never be known whether this is due to the treatment or to some other effect such as fighting among the animals in one cage, or to different locations of the two cages.

(c) Forty mice are used in a nutrition experiment to compare the effects of four different vitamin solutions given by intra-peritoneal injection. The mice, identified by an ear punch, are housed four to a box. Within each box, a mouse is assigned at random to each of the four treatments.

In this case, the mouse is the experimental unit, as mice can be independently assigned to each treatment. However, the statistical analysis should take account of the particular structure of the experiment, with the boxes each representing a replication of the four experimental treatments.

(d) A pharmacologist uses anaesthetized rats to study the effects of various drugs, administered intravenously, on the heart. Ten compounds can be studied sequentially on each rat, and these are tested in a random order. Five rats are used in a particular study.

In this case, the experimental unit is a rat for a period of time, so that each rat provides ten experimental units. The structure of the experiment using five rats would need to be taken into account in the final statistical analysis.

Determining the size of an experiment

There are several ways of determining how large an experiment needs to be. The three main methods are listed below; the method based on mathematical equations and the "resource equation" method are discussed in more detail in the following sections.

(a) *Determining sample size from mathematical equations.* For relatively simple experiments, it may be possible to calculate exactly the number of experimental units (usually, but not always whole animals) which are needed to attain specified objectives. With appropriate computer programs, even more complex designs may be planned in this way. This approach is particularly useful for long-term and expensive experiments such as clinical trials of new drugs.

(b) *The "resource equation method".* With more complex experiments, the "resource equation" approach suggested by Mead (1988) is recommended. It is based on arbitrary rules for the number of treatments and the number of units to be assigned to the estimation of "experimental error", but is a sensible and logical approach. It is the method which is probably used by most statisticians for short-term and complex experiments which are not particularly expensive to conduct.

(c) *Methods based on previous experience.* Frequently, the size of an experiment is determined by previous experience. The disadvantage of this method is that it may be too large (or too small), leading to a waste of resources and animals. In some cases, such as toxicity testing, the size of an experiment is determined by regulatory authorities, who also appear to have relied on past experience. An individual faced with this sort of experiment must follow the guidelines. However, a critical examination of the size of experiments based on past experience should be made periodically using method (a) or (b) above.

Determining sample size from mathematical equations

The explanations below are applicable to experiments consisting of a control and test group with the objective being to detect a specified treatment effect, if it exists, with a pre-established probability (power). The principles described here, however, hold for all types of experiments. The method is described in detail by Cohen (1988), and a computer program (Piantadosi, 1990) is available which covers a wide range of designs, though it has been written for the professional statistician rather than the experimenter.

Suppose that an experiment is to be designed to investigate the effect of a newly developed drug on blood pressure in rats. The difference between the blood pressure measurements at the start and end of the experiment is calculated so that for each animal there is a difference measurement. One group of animals receives the drug in between the initial and final measurement (test group) and the other group of equal size receives a placebo. How many animals per group have to be used?

Prior to starting the experiment the objectives must be defined. These include:

a. the significance level to be used (probability of a type I error), typically set at the 5% level;
b. the required statistical power (1 − the probability of a type II error), often set at 90%;
c. the minimum treatment effect (difference in mean of control and test group) considered to be of interest.

In addition, an estimate of the anticipated variation (standard deviation) between individual measurements with respect to difference of final and starting value is needed, and the type of statistical test must be specified. In this case, the data will consist of quantitative measures of blood pressure change, and a *t*-test would be the appropriate method of statistical analysis.

From this information it is possible to calculate the number of animals needed in each group as follows:

(a) It is assumed that a type I error of 5% and power of 90% is to be specified (thus, the probability of a type II error is 10%).

(b) The size of the treatment effect of interest (the biologically meaningful difference between the treated and control group) is determined on the basis of physiological, clinical, public health or economical considerations. For example, it may be that the new drug should have a higher efficacy than those already being used. If current drugs lower blood pressure in rats by 25% when compared with controls, the new drug should lower blood pressure by more than 25%. A smaller effect, even if it truly exists, may not be of interest. The minimum effect to be detected now is 25%. At this stage, interest is not primarily directed towards a good estimate of the magnitude of the true effect. We merely wish to detect, as statistically significant, a treatment effect at least this large when it exists. Should the observed difference turn out not to be statistically significant, the conclusion will be that a possible treatment effect is less than 25%. It is possible, however, that there is a true treatment effect which is smaller.

(c) The anticipated individual variation (standard deviation, σ) must be estimated. This can be done from earlier experiments or data from the literature. When this is not possible, σ can be estimated from a small pilot study. Pilot studies are often necessary anyway in order to validate the experimental protocol. We will assume that the σ of the control and test group are identical.

When σ is known, the size n of each group (assuming equal numbers of treated and control subjects) with two-sided testing is given by the formula:

$$n = 2 \left[\frac{(z_{\alpha/2} - z_\pi)^2}{[(\mu_1 - \mu_2)/\sigma]^2} \right]$$

For one-sided testing the equation is:

$$n = 2 \left[\frac{(z_\alpha - z_\pi)^2}{[(\mu_1 - \mu_2)/\sigma]^2} \right]$$

The values of z come from the standardized normal distribution, depending on the chosen significance level and power. The right z points of the standardised normal distribution (fig. 12.1) are: $z_{0.10} = 1.282$; $z_{0.05} = 1.645$; $z_{0.025} = 1.960$; $z_{0.01} = 2.326$; $z_{0.001} = 3.090$. The complement of the right z point is negative; thus if $z_{0.10} = 1.282$ then $z_{0.90} = -1.282$, etc.

In the example above, the reference drug produces a blood pressure lowering of 25% ($= \mu_1$). Let us say that the effect of a new drug should be considered statistically significant with a high probability when its blood pressure lowering effect is at least 35% ($= \mu_2$). Assume that in a comparable experiment the coefficient of variation ($[\sigma/\mu] \times 100$) of blood pressure reduction was 14%. Suppose that the chance of a type I error is set at $\alpha = 5\%$ and the chance of a type II error at $\beta = 10\%$, so power (π) is 90% The desired group size can then be calculated using the above formula, by using the following values:

$\alpha = 0.05$; $\quad z_{\alpha/2} = 1.645$; $\qquad \pi = 0.9$; $\quad z_\pi = -1.282$ and

$$\frac{(\mu_1 - \mu_2)}{\sigma} = \frac{(35 - 25)}{14}.$$

Therefore,

$$n = 2 \left[\frac{(1.645 + 1.282)^2}{(10/14)^2} \right] = 33.6, \text{ that is } n = 34 \text{ per group.}$$

Note that, in this example, the data is presented in terms of the percentage reduction in blood pressure, and the coefficient of variation, rather than the actual numerical reduction and standard deviation. However, the same result would have been obtained had the actual values been used.

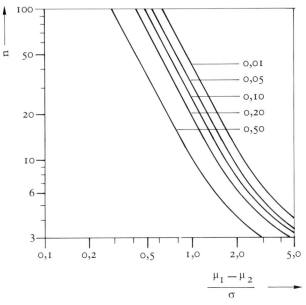

Fig. 12.2. Sample size (*n*; number of experimental units for each of the two treatments) as function of the difference considered meaningful expressed as multiple of the standard deviation $((\mu_1 - \mu_2)/\sigma)$. The lines are constructed under the following assumptions: normally distributed measured values; a two-sided test for treatment means $(\mu_1 - \mu_2)$; use of Student's *t*-test for evaluating the difference of two group mean measurement values with type I error probability (α) of 0.05. The standard deviation, σ, is estimated using the data. The lines have as inscription the probability of concluding "no clear difference"; this is the complement of the power (π) so that the indicated values for π are 0.50, 0.80, 0.90, 0.95 and 0.99. The tangents to the curves from above would illustrate the relationship under conditions of known σ.

If one cannot assume that σ is known, the relationship between n, $(\mu_1 - \mu_2)$, α and π is given in fig. 12.2. This figure holds for $\alpha = 0.05$ (two-sided) and has the quantity $(\mu_1 - \mu_2)/\sigma$ on the horizontal scale, n on the vertical scale and the probability of a type II error $(1-\pi)$ with the lines.

For other combinations of α and π, when the question to be addressed is one-sided, n has to be multiplied with the factor $(z_\alpha - z_\pi)^2/(z_{0.05} - z_{0.90})^2$. Table 12.2 illustrates the dependency of α and π on this factor. In the above-mentioned example, lowering of α to a value of 1% and raising the desired power to 95% leads to a required number of animals per group of $n = 1.84 \times 33.6 = 62$.

When several parameters are measured on each animal, a different number of animals may be required for each parameter. The various group sizes should be combined, depending on the importance of each end-point, so that one number of animals is obtained. When more than two treatments are to be compared, the analysis of variance rather than the *t*-test is indicated, and

Table 12.2

Relationships between required numbers of animals per group with variable type I error probability (α) and power (π) but with constant difference considered meaningful and expressed as multiple of the variation coefficient (σ)

α	$\pi = 0.50$	$\pi = 0.70$	$\pi = 0.80$	$\pi = 0.90$	$\pi = 0.95$
0.10	0.19	0.38	0.53	0.77	1
0.05	0.32	0.55	0.72	1	1.26
0.02	0.49	0.78	0.98	1.30	1.60
0.01	0.63	0.95	1.17	1.52	1.84

The table is exact with a normal distribution and knowledge of σ for one- and two-sided testing and is a good estimate with σ to be assessed in combination with Student's t test. In the table values for $(z_\alpha - z_\pi)^2 / (z_{0.05} - z_{0.90})^2 = 0.1167(z_\alpha - z_\pi)^2$ are presented.

calculation of the required group size becomes more complicated. However, for $\alpha = 0.05$ and $\pi = 0.90$, the number of animals estimated to be necessary to compare two groups will be a reasonable estimate.

To estimate the number of animals needed for a two-sample situation, Table 12.3 can be used. This table has been constructed for $\alpha = 5\%$ (two-sided testing) and $\pi = 90\%$. Suppose that it is considered meaningful from a physiological point of view, if the true treatment effect (difference between control and test group) is 20% or more. The coefficient of variation in the projected experiment is estimated to be 15%. According to the table a minimum of 26 animals (13 per group) is needed to detect, as statistically significant, an effect of 20%. The table shows that the group size required falls with decreasing coefficient of variation, at constant effect to be detected.

Table 12.3

Required sample size (n; number of animals per group) to detect a statistically significant effect when using a two-sided Student's t-test for two samples with type I error probability (α) of 0.05 (or 0.025 for one-sided testing) and power (π) of 0.90

Difference considered meaningful (%)	Anticipated coefficient of variation (%)			
	5	10	15	20
5	23	86	191	338
10	7	23	49	86
15	4	11	23	39
20	3	7	13	23
25	3	5	9	15
30	3	4	7	11

The figures in the table (n) are based on the theory underlying fig. 12.2.

The resource equation method

Methods of estimating the sample size from mathematical equations have certain disadvantages. If many end-points are involved, then:

a. it is often difficult to specify the size of treatment effect which would be of biological interest;
b. there may not be any useful estimates of the standard deviation of each character;
c. the calculations are difficult to perform and interpret with complex experiments such as those involving several treatments and factors;
d. different sample sizes may be needed for each character, and these may be difficult to reconcile across all characters.

It may still be well worthwhile using above mentioned method for expensive and time-consuming experiments with important consequences, such as clinical trials of a new drug. However, for most short-term animal experiments, an easier method is needed.

The "resource equation" method proposed by Mead (1988) is probably the method used by most statisticians when designing relatively inexpensive experiments. What Mead has done is to express usual practice explicitly, and give some justification for it. In this discussion, it is assumed that the end-point is measured data (not discrete dead/alive data), and it is assumed that the experiment will be analyzed by the analysis of variance, though this would not always be essential.

If there are N experimental units, then Mead's resource equation is:

$$N - 1 = T + B + E$$

where T is the number of degrees of freedom associated with treatments (i.e. the number of treatments -1), B the number associated with blocks and other methods (e.g. the analysis of covariance, not discussed here) of allowing for environmental variation (i.e. B is the number of blocks plus covariates -1), and E is the number associated with error (obtained by subtraction of T and B from N).

All that this equation states is that the number of degrees of freedom can be added together. What Mead has done is to suggest the number of degrees of freedom that *should* be associated, in particular, with treatments and error.

Mead suggests that in a "good" experiment, the number of treatments or treatment combinations (e.g. with a factorial experiment, described later) should be between 10 and 50. He suggests that to have fewer than 10 treatments is wasteful of resources. To have more than 50 would be to make the experiment too complex. In fact, many biological experiments do have fewer than 10 treatments, and are therefore not as efficient in terms of the use

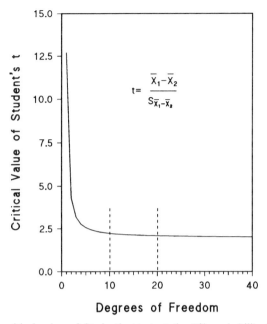

Fig. 12.3. The critical value of Student's *t*-test at the 5% probability level, plotted against degrees of freedom. Note the rapid decline as the degrees of freedom increase from one to about 10, followed by little further decline up to 40 degrees of freedom and beyond (not shown). Vertical lines have been drawn at 10 and 20 degrees of freedom, corresponding to the range suggested by Mead (1988) as being suitable for well-designed experiments. Below 10 degrees of freedom, experiments are likely to lack power. Above 20 degrees of freedom, there is little gain in precision without a substantial increase in sample size, so experiments will tend to be wasteful of resources.

of resources (animals) as they might be. Generally, research workers should be asking many more questions in their experiments than they are doing at present. With factorial designs (see below) it is relatively easy to have a large number of treatment combinations.

Mead also suggests that E, the number of degrees of freedom associated with experimental error should be between about 10 and 20. This can be justified by examination of fig. 12.3, which shows the critical value of Student's t plotted against the degrees of freedom. Note that, as the number of degrees of freedom increases from one to ten, the critical value of t declines steeply. This implies that the size of biological effect that can be detected declines rapidly and substantially as the error degrees of freedom increases from one to ten. In other words, the experiment becomes substantially more powerful, and sensitive to a small treatment difference. It is a matter of debate whether the curve is sufficiently flat at 10 degrees of freedom, or whether it would be better to draw the line at 15 degrees of freedom. However, there is very little further decline from that point onwards. The experiment would have to be made very substantially larger to gain any useful increase in statistical power. In many cases, this would not be worthwhile. In fact, Mead suggests that to have more than 20 degrees of freedom for error would, in most cases, be a waste of resources.

Mead points out that it would be possible to keep the number of degrees of freedom between 10 and 20 by performing several small experiments, rather than one large one. However, this would be inefficient because of the need to estimate the standard deviation within each experiment. He states that "The experimenter should identify clearly the questions he (*or she*) wishes the experiment to cover, and he should also consider carefully if he is asking enough questions to use the experimental resources efficiently".

Note that Mead's suggestions are only guidelines. Where experimental units and measurements are cheap (e.g. Petri dishes of hepatocytes when one rat may produce enough cells to fill hundreds of dishes, and the end-point is easily determined) it may be worthwhile doing larger experiments than he suggests. Also, in cases where very small biological effects may still be important (say in toxicology), it may be worth designing experiments with 25–40 degrees of freedom for error.

Mead makes no particular comments about B, the degrees of freedom associated with blocking. At first sight, it would seem that blocking would lead to an increase in the size of the experiment. However, the loss of a few error degrees of freedom for blocks is usually more than compensated for by the reduction in over-all variation and the consequent increase in statistical power. The important point is to identify possible sources of variation that can be controlled by blocking.

In conclusion, using this method, all the experimenter has to do is decide on the number of treatments to be used, and whether any variation can usefully be eliminated by using blocks. He or she will then need a total number of experimental units to ensure that there are 10–20 degrees of freedom left over to estimate error. Such an experiment should detect all "large" treatment effects. It may not be able to detect "small" treatment effects, but these could, in any case, only be detected by a very large experiment.

As an example, consider a hypothetical experiment to determine whether low levels of heavy metals in the diet influence the growth, health and behaviour of rats. Four dose levels are to be given, and, as the response may be genetically determined, it has been decided to use three strains of rats. Thus there are $4 \times 3 = 12$ treatment combinations, which is within the range 10–50 suggested by Mead. The rats are to be fed the diets in individual cages, they are to be weighed regularly, blood samples are to be taken at certain intervals for estimation of heavy metal loads, and the rats are to be subjected to a battery of behavioural tests such as activity and learning ability. Finally, at the end of the experiment the rats are to be killed, and organs are to be removed for chemical analysis and histology.

In view of the range of different end-points to be determined, it is felt that over-all variation could be minimised by doing the experiment in blocks of 12 rats (corresponding to the 12 treatment combinations). How large should the experiment be?

Using the resource equation, with 2 blocks, $N = 24$, $T = (12 - 1) = 11$, $B = (2 - 1) = 1$, so $E = 24 - 11 - 1 - 1 = 11$. The experiment might just be large enough with 24 rats in total. However, if some of the effects are quite subtle, it may be worth using three blocks (36 rats in total), in which case E is 23, which is not far above the number recommended by Mead. Note that it is essential that an experiment of this sort is analyzed by the correct method. It would be quite wrong (and almost impossible) to attempt to use Student's t-test to compare the different treatments. It is essential that a single over-all estimate of the standard deviation is estimated for each character, and this can be done most appropriately using the analysis of variance.

Intra-individual variation and the value of multiple measurements

The variation among individuals treated alike is measured by the within-group standard deviation. This *inter-individual* variation or "error" is made up of two components:
1. variation due to analytical errors and "time" effects at the time that the measurements are made;
2. intrinsic individual variability.

If the inter-individual variation is large, then the precision of the various treatment means will be low, and the experiment will lack power. Obviously, the experimental units should be as uniform as possible. Some ways of achieving this, by controlling the intrinsic variability such as the use of disease-free and inbred animals, as well as techniques such as stratification or blocking, are discussed later. This section discusses briefly the reduction of variation due to analytical errors and time effects.

Suppose that a fully developed rat is weighed daily. The recorded weight will vary, depending on small errors in reading the balance and rounding the numbers, and on whether or not the animal has recently eaten, drunk some water, defecated or urinated. Thus, daily weighing will result in small fluctuations in apparent body weight, which will be in addition to the intrinsic "real" body weight differences between individuals. In the case of body weight, such fluctuations are usually so small that they can be ignored. However, for other characters, this within-unit variation may be substantial. In such circumstances, making the measurement two or more times may be well worthwhile. Thus, chemical determinations may be made on duplicate or triplicate samples, behaviour may be assessed by observing the animals or measuring their activity on several occasions etc. However, it is important to remember that the use of duplicate samples does not remove the intrinsic variation between individuals. It can only reduce that part of the variation associated with analytical errors and time effects.

Whether or not it is worthwhile making more than one measurement on each experimental unit will depend on the relative magnitude of the two types of variation, and the cost of measurement versus the cost of increasing the total size of the experiment. This is discussed in more detail by Snedecor and Cochran (1980). Generally, it is only worthwhile doing duplicate measurements if the measurement error is high in relation to the intrinsic error. However, if each measurement is expensive (e.g. in the use of radioactive reagents), but experimental units are cheap (e.g. Petri-dishes of cultured cells), then it may be better to have more experimental units, and do a single measurement on each. In contrast, if experimental units are expensive (e.g. dogs), and measurement is relatively cheap (e.g. simple clinical biochemistry), and measurement error is large, then multiple measurements may be well worthwhile.

Where two or more samples are taken from an individual, the results should be averaged before starting the statistical analysis. Variation within an individual should never be used as a measure of the within-group standard deviation. A small experiment involving, for example, five mice in each of two treatment groups should never be made into a larger experiment by doing duplicate determinations of the end-point in each mouse, and analyzing the 20 observations rather than the 10 that would result from averaging the duplicate measurements. Enlarging an experiment in this way will lead to too many false positive results.

In conclusion, if there is substantial intra-individual variation as a result of fluctuations over time, or analytical errors, then it may be worthwhile making several measurements of the chosen end-point. However, the use of resources in this way has to be balanced against the possibility of adding more experimental units, which may increase the power of the experiment even more by reducing the standard error associated with intrinsic differences between individuals.

Intrinsic variation among individuals and errors in assessing the treatment effect

Usually, the results of an animal experiment are expressed in the form of numbers, such as the difference between the means of a character in the control and test group. The importance of these numbers is determined by the variation or "error" within the experiment. Low variation leads to high precision, so that smaller biological effects can be detected for a given size of experiment. The previous section dealt with reduction of the error using multiple measurements. This section deals with the reduction of intrinsic variability between experimental units. Having minimised both measurement and intrinsic variability, it may be possible to reduce variation still further by stratification or "blocking". This is discussed in a separate section.

Intrinsic variability can be reduced in a number of ways, including the following (see also chapter 5):

(a) *Use of isogenic strains.* Variability can often be reduced by using genetically uniform animals of an inbred strain or, an F1 hybrid, where they are available (e.g. particularly with mice and rats).

(b) *Use of SPF animals.* Sub-clinical infection can drastically increase the variability of the animals because each animal is likely to be at a different stage in the disease process, and chance will play a large part in determining the exposure of each individual to the disease-causing organisms.

(c) *Environmental and nutritional control.* The environmental conditions (temperature, humidity, lighting, bedding material, type of cage etc) and nutrition should be well controlled and optimal for each species. Sub-optimal environments have been observed to lead to increased variability for a wide range of characters.

(d) *Selection for uniformity.* Variation can be reduced by selecting animals which are uniform on the basis of observable characteristics, such as age, body weight etc., whether or not in combination with genetic and microbial status. Animals which are excessively large or small should always be eliminated as they may be intrinsically unhealthy.

(e) *Acclimatization.* Moving animals from one environment to another may lead to increased variability, as each animal acclimatizes at its own individual rate. Animals should not be used for experimental purposes for 2–3 weeks after a major change of environment.

In conclusion, all research workers should aim to use animals of a defined (preferably isogenic) strain, free of pathogens, and maintained in a defined optimal environment. This will lead to low over-all variability. The result is either that fewer animals are needed to achieve the same level of statistical precision or, if the same number of animals is used, then the precision of the experiment is increased. An added advantage is that an experiment of this sort should be much more repeatable, as the conditions under which it was carried out have been closely defined.

Reduction in error by stratification or blocking

Having reduced inter-individual variation as much as possible by using defined animals with a controlled environment, and having considered whether
multiple measurements of the end-points is worthwhile, it may still be possible
to increase precision by the use of stratification or blocking.

Stratification involves dividing the animals into groups (blocks) on the
basis of certain known present or future characteristics. Within each block the
animals are randomly assigned to treatment groups. For instance, the animals
from one litter have a high degree of genetic and environmental similarity. If
there are four treated groups, each litter could be divided into groups of four
animals of the same sex, one of which could be assigned to each treated group
at random. Each set of four would then represent a "block". Within each
block the animals would be as similar as possible except for any treatment
effect.

One great advantage of blocking is that the experiment can be conveniently
divided up into small sections, which can spread the work load while at
the same time increasing precision. In the section describing the "resource
equation" method of deciding on the size of an experiment, an example was
given of an experiment with four dose levels of heavy metals, and three
strains of rats, giving 12 treatment combinations. It was suggested that such
an experiment could be done as either 2 or 3 blocks. In this case, the 12
animals of a block would be treated as a group. The first group of 12 animals
may be put on to the experiment during the first week, the second on the next
week, and so on. Measurements of the 12 animals within a block would all be
done at the same time (though in random order), which may be convenient
if one step involves, say, centrifugation of samples, and there are only 12
slots available in the centrifuge. Any differences that arise between blocks
are eliminated during the statistical analysis, and do not inflate the over-all
variation. There are many occasions when splitting the experiment up in this
way is administratively convenient, but without a stratified design of this sort,
it is not always easy to see how this can be done.

Preventing bias in the treatment means

During the course of the experiment, care should be taken to prevent interfering factors having dissimilar influences on control and test groups, thereby
causing *biassed* results. Control and test animals must be housed identically at
least on a group basis. Cages of control and test animals should be distributed
over the racks, either randomly or in blocks, according to some known or presumed environmental influence such as illumination or temperature. When

a test group receives a certain compound by intravenous administration, the control group should be given the solvent intravenously. This will exclude bias due to any effects of the solvent and/or the procedure of intravenous administration. With oral administration of a test compound, the control group may be given a placebo, i.e. the carrier material without the test compound. When the influence of a surgical intervention is studied, the control group should undergo a so-called sham operation. The control animals then are subjected to all surgical procedures (anaesthesia, laparotomy, suturing, after-care) except for the actual experimental procedure.

Generally, the experimental data for each individual is obtained through objective laboratory techniques. However, to ensure that there can be no possibility of bias, the animals should still be processed in random order, preferably as numbered samples without any indication of which treatment group they belong to. If the control animals were processed on one day, and the treated animals on another, any differences in calibration of the equipment, composition of the reagents or skill of the staff, could be misinterpreted as being due to the effects of the treatment.

For measurements that are intrinsically subjective, this is even more important. Suppose that the effect of a compound on hair loss is to be measured. The degree of hair loss may be classified in four categories: none, little, moderate, much. The categories must be defined as carefully as possible using sketches or photographs. Nevertheless, it is often difficult to decide whether a given animal has little or moderate hair loss. In such experiments, the control and test group must be evaluated by a person who is blinded to treatment group. Thus, the assessor cannot be influenced by any prejudice (bias) which would cause a systematic error. It is also important that the animals from the two groups are evaluated in random order. This will prevent the influence of any gradually changing standards during assessment, for instance due to changing attitude of the assessor, which could otherwise cause a systematic error in the scores.

Determination of treatment effects with little or no systematic errors allows unequivocal interpretation. Cancelling out variable, interfering influences, so as to obtain accurate and unbiased treatment effects, will enhance the reproducibility of results of animal experimentation within and between laboratories. The need to repeat animal experiments will thus be reduced, leading to responsible animal use.

Randomization

If the aim is to compare the effects of control and test treatments in animals, and there is no information about individual responses, the available animals (or other experimental units) should be assigned randomly either to control or test group (randomization). This process will divide the inter-individual variation approximately equally between control and test group.

For each animal a piece of paper may be numbered and drawn blindly from a box producing man-made random numbers. The animals are allocated to control and test groups in rotation. Tables of random numbers or random allocation on the basis of computer-generated random numbers can also be used.

In some cases, it may be impossible to assign treatments to animals in a random manner. For example, if the aim is to see whether males and females, or animals of different strains have similar levels of a particular hormone, the treatment is the sex or strain of the animal, which clearly can not be assigned at random. In this case, the study is more of a survey of sex or strain characteristics, although in all other respects it should be regarded as a formal experiment.

Note that, following randomization, it would be possible to perform a statistical test for a character such as body weight and find a "significant" difference between groups. By definition, such a result could be expected 5% of the time if a 5% significance level is used, and 1% of the time with a 1% significance level, in the case of no real effect at all. If the measured character (e.g. body weight) is thought to be an important contributor to the final measured end-point (say liver weight), then a correction can be made using a technique such as the analysis of covariance. Strictly, one should accept the results of a randomization of this sort. In practice, if body weight were the end-point of interest, and the two groups differed significantly for body weight following randomization, then most individuals would make a second randomization. In many cases, however, it will not be possible to measure the character of interest until the end of the experiment.

Even if the differences in a character, such as initial body weight, do not differ significantly between groups, research workers are sometimes tempted to "improve" on the random allocation of animals by re-arranging individuals so that mean weights are exactly identical. However, this can not be recommended. By reducing the variability *between* groups, the variability *within*-groups is automatically increased. This reduces the power of the experiment. If variation in body weight, or some other measurable character, is believed to contribute to over-all variability, and if the animals are more variable than would be ideal, then this effect should be removed by stratification or blocking.

Replication

The use of more than one experimental unit (for example animal, part of an animal or cage of animals) per group ensures that the magnitude of the treatment effect can be assessed more accurately. Replication is also essential in order to estimate the within-group variability of experimental units in terms of the standard deviation.

Some experimental designs

The design of an experiment is the way in which the experimental units (for example individual animals) are arranged with regard to the treatments and possible interfering influences. The accuracy of experimental results is greatly affected by experimental design. The researcher can select from a wide range of designs, but in each case the appropriate statistical tests must be used. However, the principle is always the same. The probability of observing a treatment effect as large as or greater than that which has been observed is calculated. If this is less than the pre-chosen significance level, then the null hypothesis is rejected and the alternative hypothesis is accepted. In most cases a test statistic such as Student's t-test or a variance ratio is calculated and compared with the value in a table appropriate to the pre-determined significance level. However, many computer programs give a direct estimate of the probability (p-value).

Most designs involving measurement data can be analyzed by the analysis of variance. The design and statistical analysis of certain experiments can be extremely complex. We restrict ourselves here to relatively simple designs which are commonly used. In most cases, these can be analyzed quite simply using widely available computer programs. However, it is not possible to explain the analysis of variance, or the assumptions (such as a normal distribution for measured values, independence between experimental units, and similar variances in each group) which are necessary if the data are to be correctly analyzed. Emphasis here is on the design of experiments. A well chosen design is the first step towards obtaining results which are unbiased and have high statistical precision, leading to a powerful experiment.

The statistical analysis of the data is carried out according to a fixed procedure. Any set of measured values can be analyzed statistically. However, the statement "statistically significant" is relevant only when the measured values had been collected using a proper experimental design. In this case, it is possible to assume a causal relationship between the imposition of a treatment, and the difference in treatment means.

Experimental designs may be divided into several categories. The main formal designs are described briefly below.

Completely randomized or "parallel" designs

These are designs in which each animal is subjected to one treatment only (though there may be several different treatments), with all animals undergoing the various treatments simultaneously. In this case, possible time influences cannot act as confounding factors: control and test groups are exposed to the same time influences. These simultaneous or parallel designs have a number of advantages. A large number of treatments can be investigated simultaneously while the duration of the experiment is limited to the duration of one treatment. For statistical analysis, inter-individual variation can be substantial.

In completely randomized designs the animals (or other experimental units) are randomly assigned to the various treatments (or vice-versa). These designs may be modified in different ways. Figure 12.4 illustrates this for an experiment that compares three treatments (or two test treatments and one control treatment). Each treatment (A, B or C) is applied to a different set of animals; the number of animals per set is not necessarily identical. In scheme 1 (fig. 12.4), only at the end of the test period are individual measured values established (indicated with arrow).

In the statistical analysis, the values are averaged over each treatment and the differences between treatment means represents estimates of the treatment effects. The process of randomization makes it unlikely that animals with different intrinsic contributions to the measured value are unequally distributed between the treatment groups.

The disadvantage of scheme 1 is that inter-individual variation for a character, such as body weight, contributes to the standard deviation of the treatment means. This reduces the statistical power. In scheme 2 (fig. 12.4), individual measured values are established both at the beginning and end of the test period (clearly, this is not technically feasible for characters such as kidney weight which involve killing the animal). The change in measured value during the course of the test period can now be calculated for each animal and averaged for each treatment. The difference between the mean changes of two groups equals the treatment effect. When compared with scheme 1, the advantage of scheme 2 is that some inter-individual variation is eliminated from the standard deviation of the treatment means. In scheme 2, randomizing guarantees that inter-individual variation in the initial measurement, and thus also in the difference between initial and final measured value, is distributed with equal probability between all treatment groups. Part of the inter-individual variation in initial values may be caused by

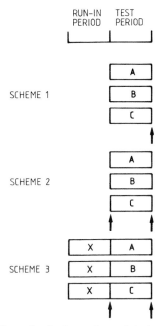

Fig. 12.4. Examples of fully randomized experimental designs to compare three treatments: A, B and C. Treatment X is a pre-experimental treatment. The time points at which measurements are done and/or samples are taken are indicated with an arrow. Scheme 1: measurements are done at the end of the test period; scheme 2: measurements are performed at the beginning and end of the test period; scheme 3: the test period is preceded by a run-in period and the measurements are performed at the beginning and end of the test period.

differences in past history between the animals. Scheme 3 takes into account such differences. The scheme is identical to scheme 2, but the test period is preceded by a run-in or acclimatization period X, which is identical for all animals. Even during this pre-experimental period, environmental conditions should be identical for each animal.

Randomized block designs

With parallel randomized blocks, the animals are grouped into blocks on the basis of certain characteristics such as initial body weight, or because they come from the same litter. It may also depend on the way that the data is collected or the cages are arranged on the animal house shelf. In some cases, blocks are separated in time. For example, four short-term treatments may be compared in four animals, repeated on six different days. The days would represent blocks.

Formation of blocks, on the basis of certain characteristics, is especially desirable when the measured values are known to be influenced by these characteristics. Typically, the size of the blocks is the same as the number of treatments, or some multiple of this number. In exceptional circumstances, blocks may need to be smaller than the number of treatments, leading to a class of design called "incomplete blocks", which is not discussed here. This situation also shows up when, for example, the number of treatments exceeds the number of individuals within a litter. As far as possible, animals from one block should have almost identical characteristics (e.g. weight, same litter, concentrations of blood constituents, measurements taken on the same day, etc.) and are assigned randomly to the various treatments. In the absence of a treatment effect, all animals from one block would ideally give identical measured values; between the blocks the mean measured values may be different. Figure 12.5 illustrates this. In this example, each block contains three animals, and there are three treatments labelled A, B and C. Assuming that the design is balanced (i.e. there are equal numbers of animals on each treatment and within each block), the treatments are averaged across all

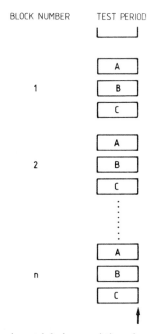

Fig. 12.5. Example of an experimental design consisting of randomized blocks to compare three treatments: A, B and C. The time point of measurement and/or sampling is indicated by an arrow. The animals are assigned to the blocks on the basis of observed (e.g. body weight) or future (e.g. time at which the end-point is measured) characteristics; within each block the animals are as comparable as possible but between blocks there are differences. Within each block the animals are randomly allocated to one of the treatments.

blocks. The averages are estimates of the treatment effects. The between-block variation is eliminated because comparison of the treatments is always done within each block of animals. This is readily achieved using a two-way analysis of variance without interaction. The precision of such designs is high because inter-individual variation within each block is relatively small due to the selective formation of the blocks.

The success of block designs is determined by proper block formation. It should be clear that block formation is based on obvious characteristics of the animals and/or in the way that the data is to be collected. Inter-individual variation cannot be eliminated completely. Randomized block designs are particularly useful for large experiments. In such cases a completely random-ized design becomes inefficient because it is difficult to obtain enough animals which are in all respects reasonably identical, house them all under identical conditions, and process the samples or collect the data in a short period.

Cross-over designs

These are designs in which the animals undergo different treatments consec-utively. In this case, the experimental unit is the animal for a certain time period. It is clear that such designs cannot be applied when the animals have to be killed to obtain the measured values, or when endpoints such as chronic diseases are to be studied. However, when, for instance, studying concentrations of blood components, these designs may be highly efficient. Inter-individual variation is eliminated automatically because each animal acts as its own control. An important advantage is that fewer animals are usu-ally needed than in parallel designs, because treatments are compared within the same animal. Cross-over designs are in fact randomized block designs in which the individual animal is the block, and as noted above, the experimental unit is the animal for a brief time period.

The simplest form of cross-over design is presented in fig. 12.6. Each treatment (A, B or C) is applied (in random order) to one animal for a pre-defined period, followed by the next treatment. The differences between

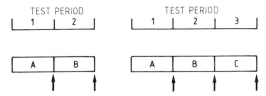

Fig. 12.6. Examples of cross-over designs. All animals are subjected to each treatment (A, B or C) in the same order. The arrows indicate the time points at which measurements are carried out and/or samples are taken.

measured values at the end of each test period are the estimates of the treatment effects. The treatment effect must not carry over into the next period. An advantage of the design is that intrinsic inter-individual variation is eliminated because the comparison of treatments is done within the same animal.

Latin square designs

In the example given above, one disadvantage of cross-over designs is that correction for time trends is not possible, as the treatments are applied in random order. To take account of both inter-individual variation and time influences, a Latin square design may be applied (fig. 12.7).

In such a design the number of treatments, time periods and minimum number of animals (using the above example) must be equal. Thus, a 4×4 Latin square might have four animals, four time periods per animal and four treatments. However, the treatments are applied to each animal in a pre-defined order so as to eliminate time trend effects. Although there is an element of randomization in Latin squares, it is restricted in such a way that time trends are still eliminated. Latin square designs might also be used to eliminate a time trend or heterogeneity within one day (say animals have to be measured consecutively over a period of a whole day) and across several days (say the experiment lasts a week). In the latter case, heterogeneity may arise over a period of several days if there is a subjective element in assessing the data and/or if the assessment is done by a different person each day.

Although a Latin square design provides high precision due to the elimination of two sources of variation (inter-individual and between time periods in

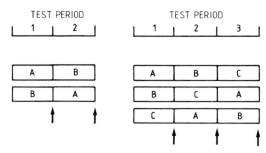

Fig. 12.7. Latin squares for the comparison of two or three treatments (A, B, C). Each group of animals undergoes the treatments in a different order. These experimental designs can be used to eliminate inter-individual variation and time influences, given an appropriate experimental unit (see text). The animals are assigned to one of the sequences of treatments at random. The arrows indicate the time points at which measurements are carried out and/or samples are taken.

the above example), a major limitation is that squares with less than about five treatments (i.e. 5×5 squares) are too small and may lack statistical power. A 4×4 Latin square only has 6 degrees of freedom for the error term. Squares larger than 7×7 may be too large to manage easily. Smaller squares may be replicated, which leads to a more complex statistical analysis.

The designs discussed do not allow corrections for carry-over effects. These effects imply that treatments not only have effects during active treatment but that there is also an after-effect into the following test period. Such an after-effect contributes to the measuring value in the next period when another treatment is applied. In this case, a design should be used in which all different treatments follow one another an equal number of times during the entire course of the experiment. The 2×2 Latin square already satisfies this requirement: the sequences A–B and B–A each occur once. When three treatments are investigated, a Latin square is unsatisfactory. The sequences A–B and B–A now must occur twice each. It is necessary to extend the 3×3 Latin square (fig. 12.8) so that each measuring value will be influenced by the after-effect of each treatment except for the measuring values at the end of the first test period. The estimated treatments effects will be relatively accurate, but the standard deviation is overestimated because the after-effect goes in it. Carry-over effects are best eliminated by separating the test periods from one another by a wash-out period. During the wash-out period all animals receive a control treatment. The wash-out periods should be sufficiently long so that after-effects of the previous treatments are not present. By incorporation of wash-out periods, the duration of the experiment

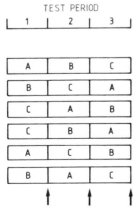

Fig. 12.8. Cross-over design for comparing three treatments (A, B and C), while correcting for possible after-effects of the treatments. Each order of treatments occurs twice. The animals are assigned randomly to each sequence of treatments. The arrows indicate at which time points measurements are performed and/or samples are taken.

is prolonged. It is also possible to quantify and eliminate after-effects by applying multiple linear regression to the data.

Factorial designs involving more than one treatment factor

Factorial designs study the combined effect of two or more treatment effects (factors). Such designs are highly efficient. They are widely used in agricultural research, and should be more widely used in research involving laboratory animals.

Table 12.4 shows an example of a $2 \times 2 \times 2$ or 2^3 factorial scheme: there are three factors (A, B and C) each at two levels (high or low), giving 8 treatment combinations. These could represent, for example, two drug treatments, two mouse strains and two time periods. Each square presents one combination of treatments which is applied to one or more experimental units.

One of the advantages of factorial designs is that they increase the generality of the results, without increasing the size of the experiment. In the above example, the main aim may be to compare the two drug treatments. However, by using two strains it is possible to determine whether the result is "general" across both strains, or whether it is "specific" to a single mouse strain, with the other strain showing no effect. If the effect can be generalised (i.e. both strains respond equally), then there will have been virtually no loss of precision in comparing the two drugs. However, if the strains behave differently, then this information may be of great importance, as it will show that the results obtained with one mouse strain cannot be generalised to other strains.

It is unfortunate that many research workers are taught to vary only a single factor at a time. In fact, experiments aimed at exploring the inter-relationships between two or more factors are highly efficient in terms of use of experimental resources, provided they are carefully planned and correctly analyzed.

More factors and/or more levels can be used, though the number of animals needed may become rather large. An experiment with three factors at three levels (3^3) involves 27 treatment combinations, involving at least

Table 12.4

Example of a 2^3 factorial scheme

	A, low		A, high	
	B, low	B, high	B, low	B, high
C, low	☐	☐	☐	☐
C, high	☐	☐	☐	☐

Each square indicates a treatment group of animals.

54 animals if there are two animals in each treatment group to allow for replication to give an estimate of experimental error. Such an experiment may be too large to be entirely practical, although smaller factorial designs do not cause any particular problems.

Factorial experiments are often designed as randomized blocks: each set of treatment combinations is represented by one block, so this experiment would involve, say, two blocks each with 27 animals. Factorial schemes can also be carried out as completely randomized designs. The statistical analysis of factorial experiments is described in detail in most text books; also computer programs are readily available.

Split-plot or repeated measures designs, with more than one type of experimental unit

In the designs discussed, above the experimental unit is the same for each factor being studied. Often it is a cage of animals, a single animal, or part of an animal. However, in some circumstances, two different experimental units may be used in the same experiment.

Assume, for example, that the effect of two dermal administrated creams is to be investigated using animals with an induced skin disorder. The compounds are to be administered to each animal at symmetrical locations on the body (for example the left and right flank, assigned to treatment A or B at random). In this case, the experimental unit is the patch of skin on an animal and each animal acts as a homogeneous block. Suppose also that a factor only applicable to whole animals, for instance nutrition, is incorporated into the experiment (say diet X and Y). Whole animals will then act as the experimental unit for the factor nutrition and animal parts as the experimental unit for the factor skin cream.

Designs based on this principle were originally developed for agricultural research and are called split-plot or repeated measures designs. The main plot (i.e. one animal) can be assigned to a whole-plot treatment. It can also be split into parts to which the sub-plot treatments are randomly assigned. If the split plots represent a time factor, then the experiment is regarded as a repeated measures design. For example, animals may be assigned to four nutritional treatments. Growth rate may then be studied over a number of time periods, with a view to studying trends in growth rate during these periods. Each time period then represents a sub-plot. Admittedly, in this example "time" is not a variable that can be assigned at random. However, in some cases, the sub-plots may have the status of a crossover design, with genuine random allocation of time periods to a treatment such as a psychometric drug. The interest in this case would be in comparing the drug effects on animals of different nutritional status.

For the factor applied to the whole plots, the inter-individual variation is present, while for the factor applied to the sub-plots the inter-individual variation is eliminated, leaving only the intra-individual variation. Thus the sub-plot treatments effects are usually measured with considerable precision, while comparisons among main-plot treatment effects are much less precise. For an extensive description of these designs and appropriate methods of statistical analysis see the list of recommended literature.

In some cases, the dividing line between characters, experimental units and measurements is not entirely clear. Consider body weight of a rat measured at, for example, 3, 6 and 9 months of age. It might be argued that these three body weights represent different characters in the same way as body weight and liver weight are clearly different characters. In this case, they should be analyzed separately, or by an appropriate multivariate analysis (discussion of which is beyond the scope of this chapter). On the other hand, it may be argued that these represent three determinations of the same character "body weight". In this case, they should be averaged prior to statistical analysis. Finally, it may be that the aim is to study a trend in body weight over time. In this case, they would represent repeated measures, and a split-plot analysis would be used. Also, weight differences could be calculated for each rat, and analyzed accordingly. It is up to the individual research worker to make the appropriate interpretation, depending exactly on the circumstances.

Conclusion

The choice of experimental design depends on many factors, such as possibility of subjecting one animal to more than one treatment and/or measurement, the number of available animals, the number of treatments to be examined and available time and finances. The most important consideration should be the anticipated number and type of interfering influences, and the type of treatment structure (simple or factorial). Precision can usually be improved by better experimental design, so that the same result can be obtained with fewer animals. Thus, paying careful attention to the experimental design and statistical analysis prior to starting the experiment can contribute substantially to a responsible use of animals and to a reduction of animal use.

Literature

Cochran W G, Cox G M. Experimental designs, 2nd ed. New York: Wiley, 1957.

Cohen J. Statistical power analysis for the behavioral sciences. Hillsdale, New Jersey: Lawrence Erlbaum Associates, 1988.

Cox D R. Planning of experiments, New York: Wiley, 1957.

Festing M F W. Experimental design. In: De Boer J, Archibald J, Downie HG, eds. An introduction to experimental surgery. Amsterdam: Excerpta Medica, 1975: 5–45.

Mead R. The design of experiments. Cambridge, New York: Cambridge University Press, 1988.

Owen D B. Handbook of statistical tables. Reading: Addison Wesley, 1962.

Piantadosi S. "Clinical trials design program". Ferguson, Missouri /Cambridge, U.K.: Biosoft, 1990.

Snedecor G W, Cochran W G. Statistical methods. Ames: Iowa State University, 1980.

Van Raaij J M A. Influence of human diets containing casein, soy protein isolate, and soy protein concentrate on serum cholesterol and lipoproteins in humans, rabbits and rats. Wageningen: Pudoc, 1982.

13 Organization and management of animal experiments

Introduction

Research is, as a rule, not conducted by individuals working in isolation. Biomedical research projects usually involve a great number of people and many kinds of processes and structures. All of these are interrelated and influence all the participants, including the researcher him/herself. If the researcher does not master the management of the processes, there will be a negative effect on research as a whole: animals or materials will not be made correctly available, experimental results will be unreliable and the whole process will be to no avail.

A successful researcher, just like the successful leader and manager, uses the positive forces within the organization and knows how to limit those that are potentially negative. In order to achieve this, the researcher must have an understanding of the structures (organization) and the processes (management) that are important when carrying out research.

Organization

At some point, the workload becomes so extensive that it can no longer be carried out by one person. It has so many aspects that it becomes expedient to subdivide the tasks and allocate them to persons with varying degrees of specialization. For example, within a growing research group, the ordering of chemicals will no longer be the task of each individual. One (preferably specialized) person will be put in charge of this task. Specialization implies that certain techniques will be mastered, and therefore carried out, by only one (or a few) of many co-workers. Along with the actual allocation of research tasks, there will also be a separation of competence. Budgetary consent will often be handled by persons without a direct scientific interest in the project. A further aspect is the influence of legal provisions which increasingly dictate that interventions on animals may only be carried out by competent persons authorized for particular procedures. Definition of competence inevitably brings about a division of responsibility. The researcher is responsible for the correct design and progress of the project. He/she publishes the results or reports to the research director. Laboratory technicians and animal technicians are responsible for correctly carrying out laboratory- and animal procedures. The tasks of the laboratory animal welfare officer (laboratory animal veterinarian or biologist) are to advise the researchers, to oversee the well-being of the animals and to answer to the governing board of the institution or to the national authority.

Management

The term "management" embraces all activities within an organization which are necessary to allow an effective and efficient operation to function, using the personnel and materials that are available. This includes the administrative aspects as well as quality control (accuracy) and follow-up. Professional management is needed in order to enable a process to run smoothly, especially if an existing project is threatened with failure. Failure can be caused by many factors and include illness, sudden and unexpected changes in deliveries, product specification, or supplier. Division of tasks according to competence and level of responsibility requires procedural discipline on the part of all the participants. Everyone must know what to do and when to do it. The person responsible for the chemical stock, orders new chemicals once a week and must therefore be informed in time to be able to fulfil an order. As a rule, animals are not delivered on a daily basis. Numbers and specifications of animals must be given on time to the person in charge of coordinating the orders. It is clear that agreed fixed procedures will prevent mistakes and avoid frustration. Division of tasks necessitates agreements on the timing and execution of the different phases of the project. All agreements should be in writing and listed in a procedure protocol. It may seem that there is much paperwork (written protocols, grant application, animal order form, reagent order forms etc.) and that the number of different forms is excessive. However, if used correctly, they will facilitate coordination, lead to higher efficiency and prevent mistakes.

Organization of research as a dynamic process

More attention should be paid to management when an organization becomes more complex, when changes in procedures or in the structure of the organization occur more frequently, or when workload pressure increases. This is not uncommon when working in scientific research, particularly when working within university or similar research institutions. These institutions have a research activity profile that is characterized by rapid changes in project types and staff turnover, and many short-term projects. In comparison, industrial research has a long history of working with project plans, in which goals, methods, time schedules, personnel requirements and material costs are defined in advance and then monitored during the project. In academic research environments, researchers are used to a great deal of liberty, both in the choice of research topic and the scientific approach to its solution. Budget constraints within non-commercial research institutes have been the most important single driving force for change and have prompted analysis of whether planning and monitoring of research could lead to higher efficiency.

Since the 1980's, there have been major changes in the way scientific research is structured within many universities. More than ever before, the financing of research, and consequently, the survival of academic research groups is increasingly dependent upon scientific output and quality. Research projects are being designed in such a way that the risk of failure is minimized. These changes have their own drawbacks. Planning and rigidity may hamper the flexibility and creativity to move along with new ideas and could hamper the response to unexpected findings and results. The situation is by no means stable. There will always be pressure on research organizations, academic and industrial, continuously to adapt and adjust the organization of research.

Conditions specific to animal experiments

As stated above, the organization of research is changing, mainly due to efforts to optimise the use of personnel and material resources. Animal experiments have an extra dimension that extends beyond personnel and material needs. When planning experiments that use animals, in addition to efficiency requirements, there is a need to limit the number of animals used and to avoid pain and distress. These added requirements have brought about special legislation in most countries. Ethics committees that regulate the welfare aspect of research have been established (see chapters 2 and 18). The researcher is ethically bound to plan his/her experiment so that whenever possible alternatives to animals are used, the numbers of animals used are kept to a minimum, and the methods and techniques are refined wherever possible. There are many ways to achieve these goals. Improved exchange of information between institutes, the use of dead instead of live animals for training, and through the use of experienced and skilled animal caretakers and technicians. Log books, required by legislation in many countries, will prevent unnecessary and uncontrollable research being done. This will ensure that the progress of research is recorded, the objectives of the experiment and the numbers of animals registered, and the expected degree of distress estimated. The log book will also record the protocol for the experiment together with the amount of compound administered, all surgical interventions performed, all observations, and ultimately the results of the procedures.

Ethics committees have been established in several countries and are being proposed in others. Their purpose is to deal with the question of whether the scientific objectives of an experiment justify the use and possible suffering of animals. Protocols for new animal experiments must be presented to, and approved by, an ethics committee beforehand. The project leader must therefore be aware of relevant legislation as well as undertake an ethical evaluation when planning an experiment (table 13.1).

Legal requirements in most countries are in a process of change as animal welfare concerns play an increasingly leading role. There is a general trend towards higher qualification requirements on the part of all persons engaged in experimentation with animals. This is true at all levels: designing, caretaking and performing experiments.

The factors described in table 13.1 place extensive demands on the organization and management of animal experiments. Compliance with most if not all of these will, however, also benefit the researcher *per se*. A well designed protocol will lead to good science as well as avoid the use of too many

Table 13.1

Checklist of legal aspects that may be involved in animal experiments

---

1. Is the procedure an experiment according to the national law? (In several countries not all procedures involving animals are considered to be experiments.)
2. Is the institute accredited (licensed) by an authorised accreditation organisation to carry out experiments with animals?
3. Is the researcher qualified (competent) and authorised (licensed) to design and/or carry out an animal experiment?
4. Is there an adequate research plan whereby the inevitability of the use of animals, instead of alternatives, is clear?
5. Are there sufficiently qualified support staff (caretakers, technicians, analysts) to permit the project to be successfully carried out?
6. Are the animals obtained from an accredited source?
7. Does the animal facility meet the requirements? (Housing and husbandry conditions.)
8. Is there appropriate equipment for anaesthesia and euthanasia and do all relevant personnel know how to use it?
9. Have the appropriate animal welfare authorities (local animal welfare officer, responsible person, or central authority) been informed about the experiment. Has this been done in good time before the experiment is to be started?
10. Has the research project been presented before an ethics committee (in those countries where this is appropriate)?
11. Is the use of laboratory animals recorded and is a log book being kept?

animals. This has an ethical as well as a time/cost benefit. Good and efficient research will automatically meet many of the demands indicated in table 13.1.

Factors influencing the results of animal experiments

The reproducibility of animal experiments is highly dependent upon the degree of standardization of the factors that can influence the reaction pattern of the animal (see chapter 5). When designing an experiment with animals, the factors mentioned in table 13.2 should match the requirements

Table 13.2

Factors which could influence the results of animal experiments

factor	watch for
genetic quality	– strain/stock – breeding system – quality breeder/supplier
biological status	– sex – age – body weight
health status	– quality breeder/supplier – constant level of quality – hygienic barrier in maintenance
nutrition	– quality supplier – constant composition (lot-nr.) – quality drinking water
maintenance – cage	– type (dimensions) – bedding – number of animals per cage
– animal room	– ventilation – temperature – relative humidity – lighting – noise – other animals
transportation	– means of transportation – transport-cage – food supply
animal care	– qualification of animal caretaker
experimental techniques	– qualification of animal technician – standardization of techniques – time of intervention

of the experiment with as little variation as possible. Standardization implies, wherever possible, the same supplier of animals, the same caretakers and technicians, the same animal room, the same experimental procedure at the same time each day etc. This means tight and close cooperation between the researcher and support personnel. Support personnel (caretakers and technicians) can contribute substantially to the quality of research because of their direct and daily experience with the animals. They will often know where to place priorities, and how to deal with specific problems.

Good Laboratory Practice (GLP)

One special field of research that involves the use of animals, and in which organization and management are of great importance, is the area of research, which has to meet the standards required for the registration of substances (chemicals, drugs, etc.). This type of experimentation has to be carried out according to procedures set by governmental guidelines. A growing number of countries also demand that this research fulfils the management principles of GLP (good laboratory practice). These GLP principles were first presented at the end of the 1970's by the American Food and Drug Administration (FDA). They refer exclusively to the methods of conduct and management of the research and to the circumstances under which it is carried out. They are there to stimulate accuracy in the conducting and reporting of animal experiments. For example, according to GLP, prior to commencing research, a clear-cut studyplan must be available, detailing the nature and scope of the experiments including all the procedures designed to achieve the pre-set objective. It should also contain the name and qualifications of the researcher responsible for the experiment, together with who will carry out the procedures and when, plus a record of all the observations. All procedures must be described in detail, stating the work instructions and the SOP's (standard operating procedure). There must be SOP's for animal maintenance, experimental techniques, laboratory measurements, hygienic procedures, examination of the animals, collection and processing of data, etc. GLP principles also take into account the layout and equipment of laboratories and animal rooms. GLP sets out guidelines regarding the construction of the animal rooms and the environmental conditions, under which the laboratory animals must be kept. The animals themselves must meet quality requirements, specified by the researcher. Documentation must be kept which confirms all these conditions.

Although GLP regulations are primarily meant to guarantee accuracy in toxicity research, their application to other areas of research involving the use of animals, can contribute towards standardization and hence towards the reproducibility of research results. The application of these rules does not, however, guarantee that the required level of standardization will be achieved for each experiment. Each type of experiment has its own specific demands with regard to standardization.

Centralization of animal experiments

Many institutions have some form of centralization for both spatial and personnel facilities with regard to animal experiments. Centralization may include:

(a) Joint purchase and breeding, housing in quarantine and stocking of animals: the "*laboratory animals supply facility*".

(b) As (a), but also housing and maintenance of animals in experiments: "*the laboratory animal hotel*". This concept may refer to joint facilities for less commonly used animals and/or animals which have special housing demands, such as sheep, dogs, cats and primates. It may also refer to the housing of all animals during experiments. In this case, the research departments do not have animal rooms in their own buildings, but make use of a centralized facility. Animals would still be removed for special interventions such as surgery, irradiation, X-ray, etc.

(c) The most extreme form of centralization is the one, in which not only the activities mentioned under a and b are centralized, but also all (surgical) interventions are carried out at the central facility. In this case all personnel, including the animal technicians, are employed by the facility: the *central animal institute*.

For the researcher, centralization implies that co-workers, rooms, and other facilities no longer belong to his/her own department. This is often seen as a disadvantage and often implies an extra consultation step in that the facility management will have to be involved in the decisions and action process. It is essential that co-workers who work within the facility are motivated, informed and are consulted when contributing to animal experiments. Equal time and attention should be given to both animal facility co-workers and workers from the associated user research institute. Giving time and attention to the facility co-workers will ensure that they are informed about the demands placed on the care and health status requirements of the animals that are used in the project.

A central animal institute is faced with a great variety of research lines which differ from one institute to another, each with its own demands with regard to quality and health profiles of the animals that are needed. This inevitably will mean several suppliers, each of which may use different methods of quality assessment and control. Centralization also means that more personnel will be involved and consequently brings more problems with regard to the maintenance of hygienic conditions in the animal rooms. For practical reasons it is usually not possible to separate animals on the basis of supplier, demands of the experiment, etc. This means that the central institute, in the interest of all researchers, has to apply procedures and rules which may not always seem necessary to the individual researcher. This can have cost/budget implications and is sometimes the subject of debate and negotiations. Advantages of centralization lie in the greater volume of trained personnel available, which may lead to a more efficient allocation of tasks, to an increase in knowledge and skills over a wider range of techniques, to better opportunities for creating optimal spatial and technical facilities and to the more efficient use of animals. The concentration of expertise is also of benefit to the welfare of the animals. Within a central institute, researchers and research lines meet one another, and as a result researchers with related research questions, corresponding animal models and techniques come to know each other and can exchange information. This should be actively encouraged by the central institute management.

Optimal arrangement of research activities

In the preceding paragraphs, a number of restrictive conditions has been mentioned which the researcher has to deal with. One of the most crucial factors is time planning. Research activities must be organized in such a way, that the different reports (internal reports, articles, dissertations) are ready within a given period of time. This is conditional on all the research activities being carried out in the right sequence and in time. All the phases from the start, execution and end (the final report) of the research project must be taken into account (see chapter 11). In addition to general factors which apply to all types of experimentation, there are those which apply more specifically to animal experiments:

– Time must be allocated to obtaining the right number of animals. These must comply with the protocol needs regarding biological status (sex, age, body weight, strain/stock). This is especially the case when ordering animals from less commonly used strains or from non-commercial suppliers. The same also applies when the demand for animals from own breeding colonies increases. The size of the breeding stock has to be enlarged before animals can be delivered for research. Supplying aged animals will also imply considerable delays.

– An adequate quarantine period which is necessary to determine potentially undesirable contamination of animals of unknown health status must be built in (see chapter 8). The quarantine period is also needed to allow newly transported animals to adapt to the new environment. This includes moving animals within the central institute.

– Delays caused by unexpected and spontaneous death of animals.

– Time must be allowed to learn and master new techniques.

– Time for delivery of special diets.

– Pilot experiments are always a prerequisite when new methods, techniques, diets etc. are introduced.

– Time needed for the submission to, and approval by ethical committees or regulatory authorities.

Logistic resources necessary for successfully carrying out the experiment can also influence time planning:

– space in the animal rooms;

– availability of personnel (caretakers, technicians, analysts);

– funds for the purchase of animals, reagents etc.;

– availability of special equipment and apparatus (isolators, laminar airflow benches etc.).

The above mentioned factors all demand planning and coordination.

A well-founded estimate of costs and a plan of expenditure must be drafted. This is essential if appropriate funding is to be raised and budget constraints are met during the course of the research project. The animal technicians and animal institute leadership will make a valuable contribution to this process and must be consulted.

Cooperation — working with others

Almost every animal experiment involves interdisciplinary and cross-departmental cooperation. The researcher has to take the role of conductor and make sure that *all* the necessary actions take place in the *right way* and at the *right time* by the *designated persons* (see fig. 13.1). There is a greater chance for success if the following rules are implemented:

(1) Take decisions about activities that have to be performed by others only after deliberation with those concerned. They must be informed well in advance about what has to be done, how to do it, and when it has to be done. Their opinions should be taken into account when establishing policy that will influence a final decision.

(2) Motivate co-workers. Inform them about the aims of the research. Give them specific information about the significance of the role they will play. Tell them about the progress of the research and of the results as they appear (both positive and negative findings, as well as setbacks). Give reasons for changes to the protocol. Motivate also by asking advice and by giving

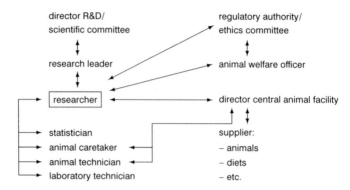

Fig. 13.1. Network of contacts in laboratory animal experiments

arguments when asking them to perform a procedure in a particular way.

(3) Keep a log and diary and minutes of all meetings:
– make a short written report of every consultation meeting, about the agreements that were reached (who agreed to what, how and when);
– make written protocols, signed by the technician concerned, covering the dates that techniques are to be carried out, the numbers of animals involved, doses to be administered, etc.;
– develop forms for dated recording of research data including information on the strain, sex, numbers of animals, body weight development, health status, tumour dimension, dates of death, anaesthesia, euthanasia, etc.;
– distribute copies of reports, protocols and forms to those concerned.

(4) Make agreements on time and change them as seldom as possible. Much time is wasted by ill-prepared and hasty work. If changes in the protocol are absolutely necessary, discuss them well before they are due to take place, and note them down in writing. Make sure that all the people concerned are informed and understand the changes.

(5) Keep your agreements and make sure that others do the same.

Safety in the animal house

The centralised management of an animals facility also has implications for comprehensive and extensive personnel and in house safety programmes. The manager of the institute, as a veterinarian or other suitably qualified person, will also be able to maintain an overview of activities that play a role in personnel safety. Planning scientific projects with animals involves factors not limited to the animals themselves. Researchers may bring in substances that could be hazardous to the technical or other staff. This is particularly the case when handling substances such as radioactive isotopes, carcinogens, cytostatics or other substances potentially hazardous to staff. The animals may be intentionally infected with infectious agents as a part of the experimental protocol or they may be infected with zoonoses that can cause disease in the members of staff. The protocol may require inoculating the animals with material of human origin. Alternatively the material could be of animal origin and carry undesirable infectious agents. Finally, the animals could represent a source of antigen causing allergic symptoms among sensitive staff members.

Planning a research project places demands on both researcher and the central institute manager. The researcher could often be ignorant of factors that could influence the general environment of the institute. This is particularly the case when disease causing organisms (virus, bacteria or parasites) are introduced. The degree of specialisation that may be necessary when planning research projects makes it difficult for an individual researcher to have a total overview of all aspects of the biology surrounding the chosen protocol. The staff of the central animal facility plays a crucial role in preventing inadvertent accidental contamination. There may be a need to contain or isolate animals for a period of time while special examinations are carried out and the microbiological quality of the animals or tissues established. Disease contamination is one of the most significant and serious setbacks in research with animals. It is therefore essential that projects are planned with this in mind and that the expertise of the institute's laboratory animal science specialists is included in planning.

There is also a significant cross-flow of specialities in preventing zoonoses. The vast majority of the most commonly used laboratory animals are bred and supplied from sources that are free from zoonoses. The situation is different when working with wild caught animals, primates in particular. Close collaboration between veterinary and human medical expertise is necessary when planning projects with these animals. There are significant and serious diseases that can pass from animal to human workers. These can have fatal consequences for the individuals concerned. It is therefore essential that the institute leadership plays an active role in a planning and advisory capacity when these animals are used. It should not be the sole responsibility of the researcher to decide what type of housing, handling and procedures should be used when using this type of animal.

Similar precautions need to be applied when working with substances as carcinogens, cytostatics and radioisotopes. There is often a chain of decision making when planning a procedure. The person who decides to include a substance in a protocol — and at the same time has the most information regarding the potential hazards associated with the use of the substance — is often not the person actually responsible for administering the substance.

There may also be a change in the toxicity of the substance in that metabolites excreted in the urine or faeces may be considerably more toxic than the parent substance. It is clear from this that each substage in the administration of a compound needs to be analyzed. Sets of written rules need to be prepared and safety procedures established with clear and easily understood standard operating procedures. At no time should there be any doubt as to what is being given, what the hazards are and who is or could be in contact with the substance. Responsible individuals must be appointed and they should be accessible in the case of accidents or doubt.

Immunisation procedures can have special hazards when administering antigens that could represent a hazard. An example worth noting is immunising animals with HIV or viral hepatitis antigens. Inadvertent self-injection with such antigens could at worst make a technician HIV or hepatitis positive with fatal results. It is therefore essential that there are clear descriptions of what is being given and what action to take in the event of an accidental self-injection. Such instructions should accompany all procedures involving any material of human origin.

Planning and experimental protocol should be extended to include factors that are of importance to safety planning. The leader of the animal facility should be included as a member of the team and there should be an interchange of expertise that covers this aspect of project planning. The institute's project registration scheme could be used to register potential hazard information. Any chemical substance that is to be given to the animals must be described. Carcinogenicity, cytotoxicity or radioactivity must be noted in full detail and copies of the information made available to all members of the team. Standard operating procedures should be drawn up. The staff of the animal facility should play an active role in gathering this type of information and make sure that all co-workers are fully informed before they are exposed to potentially hazardous procedures. Lines of responsibility should be clearly established and each member of the team must be made aware of who to report to in the event of an accident. Emergency medical personnel must be informed of procedures prior to an accident taking place. This is particularly necessary in the event of accidental self-injection. This type of accident often seems to be minor and superficial at the time of happening. Emergency department personnel must be trained as to what to do since the treatment that may be necessary might appear to be out of proportion to the degree of immediate damage. The special knowledge and expertise of the animal institute's staff will play a significant role in ensuring that procedures can be carried out with a minimum of risk to personnel and animals in the facility.

Literature

Clingerman K J. Laboratory animal facilities and management. Bibliography 1979–1990, Dept. Natl. Agric. Libr. US, Beltsville, Md. The Library 1991; 91–43, 48 p.

Hayden C C. How to increase employee participation in the lab animal environment. Lab Anim 1987; 16, 47–49.

Robbins S T. Management. New York: Prentice Hall, 1991.

14 Recognition of pain and distress

Introduction

Pain and distress are relatively vague concepts when applied to animals. As these terms refer to subjective states, they are strictly only applicable to humans. However, the sharing of common neural structures and physiological processes, and the existence of behavioural manifestations comparable to those seen in humans in states of pain and discomfort, make it plausible to assume that animals also experience pain and discomfort. It is ethically prudent to go one step further and to accept that animal suffering can at least be equivalent to the suffering of a human when both are subject to the same procedure. This *analogy postulate* should be accepted unless its invalidity has been proven in a specific case. The postulate can be the basis for making choices when using animals for research, although one should realize it has a weak scientific basis and should be used with caution. One cannot exclude the possibility that procedures which are comparatively harmless for human subjects are painful or stressful for certain animals, and vice versa.

It would be much more satisfactory if we could reliably estimate an animal's suffering from behavioural and physiological signs. But, as yet, there is no guarantee that states of pain and discomfort are properly recognized on the basis of presumed analogous behaviours. For one thing, our estimation of the intensity of such subjective states may be incorrect because of interspecific differences in the relations between states and behavioural manifestations and because the context influences this relation. Does the deafening squealing of a piglet which is physically restrained indicate that it is subject to more intense pain and suffering than the comparatively mute way in which a wildebeest undergoes being torn apart by Cape hunting dogs? When we move away from mammals to other vertebrates, such as fishes, and, especially, when we move to invertebrates, the inference of pain becomes progressively more problematic. The lack of recognized behavioural responses may unjustifiedly suggest the absence of pain perception and suffering. Nevertheless, in spite of some drawbacks, the analogy postulate remains our first and best principle.

The behavioural criteria for the recognition of states of pain and discomfort are discussed in this chapter. An evaluation of these criteria should be based on insight into the biological function of these supposed states and their behavioural correlates. We can subsequently arrive at some guiding principles, by recognizing that, in nature, discomfort and pain form adaptive monitoring systems playing an important role in the motivational structuring of behaviour, rather than being meaningless sources of suffering.

Discomfort and suffering

Discomfort is integral to animal life and, in regulating the priorities of the various functions to be executed by the organism, emotional correlates undoubtedly play a role. Although we cannot know the subjective experiences associated with these emotions in other animals, we recognize expressions that are similar to ours, especially in species that are phylogenetically close to us.

We know personally that there are "positive" emotional states, of pleasure, agreeability and satisfaction, that are the rewarding experiences associated with the successful execution of biological functions. Conversely there are various "negative" states of want, need and discomfort, reflecting a discrepancy between what is actually the case and the norm value of certain internal conditions or environmental relations. Such discrepancies are the motivational factors, driving the behaviours serving to correct these discrepancies and to reach and maintain the respective norm situations. Hunger, thirst, fatigue, the absence of a mate, the presence of a threat are obvious examples. These states respectively motivate the behaviours of feeding, drinking, sleeping, searching for mates and courting, and defense or avoidance. Within the natural boundaries of variation, such states can hardly be considered suffering. Discomfort turns into distress and suffering when such states persist at high intensities for long durations. This seems likely to occur in higher animals especially when the prospects of performing the appropriate corrective functions are unavailable and when the expectations of coping are low. Then, components of fear (a tendency to avoid specific objects, events and situations) and stressful anxiety (a more general and unfocused form of fearful arousal) make their contribution. The important role of expectancies and the predictability and controllability of variables which are relevant to the animal in the performance of its functions has become evident since the pioneering experiments of Weiss (see chapter 4).

This leads to the conclusion that various forms of activity may be indicators of discomfort and distress. Appetitive behaviours associated with different functional systems may signal discomfort if:

– their performance is unnaturally intense and prolonged,
– they do not lead to the consummatory or goal situations characteristic for the respective functions, and
– they lead to severe (possibly detrimental) deregulation of the hierarchy of priorities and of the time budget relations of biological functions.

The experiences of discomfort, need and hindrance must be regarded as biologically meaningful phenomena. Such experiences provide the impulse for the execution of behaviours by which these states are removed. If this does not ensue as a result of the behaviour in accordance with the animal's expectations, the animal may switch to other behavioural modes. As explained in chapter 4, pathological forms of behaviour, such as soothing stereotypes and directly damaging elements, may occur when animals are kept in a situation where conflicts cannot be solved and discomfort turns into stress. If no available behaviour delivers the "expected" result, the animal can also end up in a situation equivalent to depression or "learned helplessness". The animal loses the impulse to act, becomes passive, apathetic and listless. The switch to a "depressive" attitude may be seen as a biologically meaningful reaction. If coping attempts remain fruitless, or even are harmful, then a strategy may be preferable in which the animal resigns from the situation which is unmanageable, or suppresses all initiatives until the situation changes for the better. There is no point in wasting effort and running unnecessary risks. A similar apathetic attitude, characterized by depressed posture and unresponsiveness, can also be observed in cases of illness and chronic pain (see below).

Pain

Pain represents a special class of distress. A heterogeneous set of phenomena can be subsumed by this concept. It varies, for example, from the acute pain that is associated with certain forms of tissue damage, the aching of muscles associated with too much exercise leading to the accumulation of lactic acid, to various forms of often chronic neural pain. In some of its forms, at least, a sensoneural substrate specifically tuned to nociception can be distinguished.

Pain has always been regarded as a biologically-adaptive mechanism, the main function of which is to warn the organism that (part of) it is under potentially damaging stress or that damage has actually occurred. Learning psychologists have emphasized an additional function. In the conditioning of behaviour, two kinds of effects influence the future occurrence of a behaviour: rewards and punishments. The influence of the latter has customarily been studied by using mild electric shocks as a punishment. Here pain acts as an unconditional stimulus, releasing withdrawal and defensive responses. At the same time, learning psychologists point out, associations are formed with the stimulus characteristics of the pain provoking situation. These then act as conditional stimuli, releasing avoidance responses and fear towards that situation. Thus the animal learns to recognize danger. However true, this role should not lead to a generalized statement that fear is a conditional response to pain. The ethological literature abounds with examples showing that flight and avoidance may also be evoked as unconditional responses, for instance, by sudden "startling" stimuli, or, more specifically, to certain sign stimuli, such as those indicating a possible predator. Fear of predators cannot, as a rule, be a pain-conditioned response, because few animals have a second chance after a painful confrontation with a predator.

An important distinction is made between primary and secondary pain. This distinction is clearly recognisable in our own experience. The immediate sensation following a pain-inflicting stimulus is an acute, sharp and well-localized pain. This "primary pain" is mediated by thick, fast-conducting myelinated $A\delta$-fibres. The primary pain often subsides soon, to be followed later by "secondary pain". This is less localized and is generally of a chronic (or "tonic") nature, sometimes pulsating. Even though potentially hurting severely, its quality is "diffuse" and "aching" rather than "sharp". It is mediated by thin, slowly conducting unmyelated C-fibres. The relation between primary and secondary pain is complex. In the "gating theory" of Melzack and Wall (1965), a mechanism is proposed for the short-term regulation of the transmission of incoming signals from nociceptive neurons via the spinal cord to the brain. The signals of the fast-conducting fibres, responsible for the initial acute pain, are, at the same time, supposed to build up a self-inhibiting influence by clogging a spinal gate through which these signals are transmitted upwards. This would explain that the primary pain abates soon after its sharp onset. When, later, the signals of the slow-conducting C-fibres begin to come in, this counteracts the inhibition and the blockade of the gate is raised. Thus the nociceptive signals are transmitted once more to the brain. In addition to this short-term regulatory mechanism, there are other regulatory mechanisms of pain sensation, operating at more central levels under the influence of a diversity of motivational factors, for example via enkephalins (fig. 14.1). The transmission from the C-fibres appears to be very sensitive to opiate blockade; such an inhibitive influence has not been found for the fast $A\delta$-fibres.

Bolles and Fanselow (1980) have argued that the different forms of pain, rather than being separate sensations, represent functionally differentiated

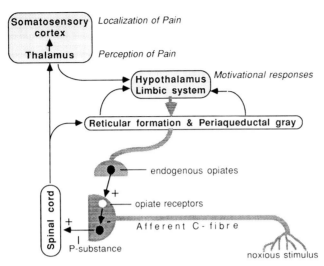

Fig. 14.1. Schematic representation of the pain pathway via C-fibres. A noxious stimulus of C-fibres is transmitted by means of a specific pain transmitter substance (the P-substance) to the dorsal horn of the spinal cord, and, further, to higher brain centres. In the higher brain centres perception and localization of pain occurs, and motivational changes and consequent behavioural responses are provoked. Via the reticular formation, motivational factors can generate feed-back influences on the transmission of pain signals by the secretion of endogenous opiates. These chemical signals are perceived by opiate receptors, which, in turn, inhibit the transmission of signals from the C-fibres (adapted after Sherwood R. Human Physiology, 1989).

aspects of an integral process of *pain behaviour* in response to tissue damage. They have distinguished three behavioural phases. The first two phases, the *perceptive* and *defensive* phases, are associated with the perception of primary pain. This triggers quick withdrawal responses of the organism or its affected body members, as well as defensive responses directed at warding off the pain-provoking agent. Reflex-like responses of this kind can partly remain after brain connections have been severed. It seems that the more direct and reflex-like the reaction, the more easily it can be dissociated from subjective experience, and the less trustworthy the reaction is as an objective measure of the pain experience. This also means that, although we can experience this pain, such experience is not necessary for the adaptive response. It also means that the occurrence of such responses in animals does not necessarily imply perception and concurrent suffering. In the perceptive phase the animal is also alerted to the pain-inflicting agent and conditioned to its stimulus characteristics. The third phase, the *recuperative* phase, begins after the onset of secondary pain. This pain produces a motivational reorganization of inhibiting activities that might interfere with recovery and allowing the animal to recuperate. The animal may look for a place to hide, rest, and lick its wounds. Other functions are suspended. Posture and movements are depressed, just as in the human patient who is ill or suffers from chronic pain and displays a listless and apathetic attitude. Such "depression" can be seen as a biologically-adaptive response enabling the animal to be quiet and wait until it has recovered or (in the case of "helplessness" after repeated failures) until the situation has improved. In the past, attention has been focused mainly on acute nociperception. Until recently, chronic pain in animals has received only limited attention. The LASA Working Party (1990) expressed their opinion that chronic pain or distress may often be more insidious, particularly in the early stages, than acute pain.

According to Bolles and Fanselow, pain behaviour is best regarded as a separate motivational system, interacting competitively with other motivational systems. This is in line with ethological theory which sees behaviour as a hierarchical structure of motivational systems, competing for hegemony of expression. When a particular system achieves hegemony and its behavioural functions take place, this largely inhibits other systems. This inhibition ensures that the programme of the activated function can be brought to completion, largely without interruption. Just as the state of pain can suppress other motivations interfering with the recuperative process, the reverse can be true (other motivations, when strong, can temporarily suppress the state of pain).

The recognition of pain

The recognition of pain can occur in two contexts. Pain can be induced intentionally by applying noxious stimuli in order to establish the effect of some experimental manipulation (drugs, such as analgesics, or stress factors) on pain perception. The methods used have mainly been focused on primary and acute forms of nociception, and not so much on chronic pain. Stimuli used most often include pinching, heat stimuli and electric shocks. Pain can also occur as a consequence of both intended or unintended procedures. An indication of the level of suffering experienced by the animal is needed in order to judge the acceptability of the procedures.

Valid judgements about the degree of suffering an animal experiences must be based on behavioural responses of the animal. Here it is important to realize that different types of reaction may be expected, according to the phase of the pain behaviour process:

(1) The reactions released by primary pain are generally withdrawal and protective responses. In addition, the sudden onset of a primary pain often evokes vocal responses in many species. The immediacy and conspicuousness of such responses makes them easily recognizable as symptoms. It is important

to note that the threshold and intensity of responding can be influenced by a diversity of motivational factors, such as stimuli relating to predation risk, social conflict, territoriality, sex, etc. (see also below "Social facilitation and inhibition").

(2) In the phase of recuperation, which follows when lasting damage has been inflicted, the responses are different and of a more heterogeneous nature:

a. Motor patterns and their coordination may be changed or performed in a slow and wary fashion to spare structures that have been damaged, e.g. limping. Such behavioural changes are not too difficult to recognize for the experienced observer, as most veterinarians can confirm. Changes in the locomotory activity of experimental animals may be valid criteria for estimating the degree of chronic pain. The same applies to behavioural elements such as cringing; these might be seen as attempts to escape from the pain sensation or to suppress it with "competing" stimulation.

b. Motivational changes, resulting, for instance, in withdrawal to a safe and quiet place and refraining from all but the most urgent actions. Low alertness, a "depressed" posture, subdued dynamics and low motivations for other, even vital behavioural functions (for example, anorexia) reflect a state of apathy and "depression".

Symptoms of apathy and "depression" are less easily appreciated than elements such as limping and cringing, and certainly not as easily as the primary pain responses. In addition, certain forms of chronic pain are not associated with any easily observable adjustments. Thus dental pains and certain abscesses may go unnoticed, even though we would expect them to be painful by analogy. Thus horses and pigs do not betray certain internal afflictions which we might consider painful on the basis of the analogy postulate.

(3) In addition, emotional expressions may occur. As indicated under 1. vocal reactions like screams and roars may be given in response to primary pain. Sighs, moans, groans and yelps may be responses to secondary pain. At least some of these are communicative signals, evolved to inform others, particularly conspecifics, about the state of the sender. Vocal signals are the most conspicuous to a human observer but many species also produce olfactory signals, for example the alarm substances effused by fishes of certain species when their skin is damaged. Many laboratory workers fail to appreciate that rodents and lagomorphs can also communicate pain and distress by odour, for instance, to conspecifics in neighbouring cages. We may expect such displays of pain and suffering to occur in social species where such informing can be ultimately beneficial for the sender by adaptively influencing the behaviour of receivers.

Significance of pain signals

In nature, screams given as a response to primary pain can, just as fear screams, alert conspecifics to the source of danger. This might evoke help in defense from these conspecifics. Even if the alarm brings no direct benefit to the sender, the sender can nevertheless profit in terms of "inclusive fitness". This can occur when there are relatives with a similar genetic background which can then avoid the danger more effectively, for instance, by learning about its nature.

Displays of pain and distress can also serve as signals of helplessness and need. Examples are the yelps and whines occurring in some species, such as dogs and wolves. They are derived from the infantile repertoire, where they release parental care and protection. In some species, care has come to be given also to certain adult animals. It has even become the concern of group members other than a parent. Examples include dolphins rendering support to incapacitated pod members in danger of drowning, or canids where pack members bring and regurgitate food, not only to cubs, but also to the adults staying with the cubs. In species such as these, signals of helplessness may release tolerance and even active support.

Species differences in pain expression

Varied forms of emotional expression of secondary pain are expected to be especially characteristic of species which have evolved cooperation, sharing, and communal brood care, e.g. in socially cooperative carnivores rather than in ungulates.

Social signals of primary pain are expected, especially in species where conspecifics can immediately and effectively adjust and avert the danger. Thus pigs are very "touchy" and react immediately and loudly when being squeezed. This is a very adaptive response in a species where body contact is common and the piglets need strong signals when in danger of being squashed by heavy adults. In contrast, many other ungulates, such as antelopes, are comparatively mute.

Social facilitation and inhibition

Little is known still about contextual and environmental factors that might influence the expression of pain in animals. *Concealment* of pain behaviours may be expected in species and in conditions where their display might be a hazard. Signs of injury or sickness might attract and direct the attention of predators to an easy prey; a limping individual in a herd of herbivores is an unmistakable signal. Also, in species with a social hierarchy, a display of weakness might tempt conspecifics to try and overthrow a dominant. Under such conditions of risk, other behavioural motivations might compete with the pain system and suppress it; this may consequently lead to increased pain thresholds. This reflects a trade-off in which certain short-term interests, for example momentary safety, are secured at the price of a retarded recuperation. The evidence for such phenomena in animals is still largely anecdotal and there is a need for systematic investigation.

There is more evidence that *social facilitation* of pain expression, well known in the human species, also occurs in some animal species. Such expression may be reinforced into "hypochondric" behaviour when an animal has learned that this brings social relief, tolerance or affection. In humans, conditioning processes may influence not only pain expression but also the thresholds of pain perception. Phenomena, reported especially for dogs, have been interpreted in this way, such as "sympathetic lameness", limping, asthmatic behaviour, and anorexia nervosa. Clearly this provides a further complication when judging signals of pain and distress, especially, when dealing with companion animals rather than experimental counterparts.

Concluding remarks

We have discussed various behavioural manifestations of pain and distress. It is clear that these may lead to underestimations of an animal's suffering in some cases and to overestimation in others. Our ethical obligation to the animals that may suffer as a result of our interference during experimentation, requires us to err at the side of the latter.

In addition to the behavioural parameters discussed above, physiological features can also be important. We can distinguish immediate and long-term physiological responses. Examples of the first are changes in pupillary dilation, cardiac rate, respiratory pattern, salivation, sweating, gastrointestinal motility and urination and defaecation. There are good reasons to believe that these reflect the actual experience of the animal. In some cases, such as certain internal afflictions in horses, these are the only ones visible. In other cases of suffering, long-term indicators may include impaired immune system functioning and increased levels of corticosteroids and catecholamines, which can be measured both in the blood and in the urine. These endocrine changes can inhibit gonadal activity and suppress reproductive functions. This can manifest itself behaviourally in inhibited sexual and nursing behaviours. Finally, growth may be impaired and body weight may even decrease. The measurement of some of these parameters demands invasive techniques, which can add, *per se*, to the disturbance. For example, the stress involved in collecting blood samples for hormone measurements may modify the endocrine effects which one wants to measure. In this instance, permanent cannulation of the jugular vein can be the solution, since it reduces the stress of handling during blood sampling.

Our moral obligation to animals placed in our custody is the most important factor in guiding decisions on whether or not to perform certain experiments, but avoidance or reduction of pain and distress in experimentation is also demanded for more practical reasons. Pain, fear, and anxiety, all have strong motivational and physiological consequences. These may substantially interfere with the results of the investigations. Also for this reason, a careful and thoughtful application of analgesics and anxiolytics is required (see also chapter 15). Such application should be informed, because effects may be complex. If the pain system competes with other motivational systems for its behavioural expression in terms of functional priorities, fear may inhibit pain, namely when the source of fear has nothing to do with the pain. Under different circumstances, namely when the fear is actually directed to a particular pain experience, the sensitivity to that stimulus may be enhanced. This complexity is exemplified nicely by the human experience of fearing the pain of the dentist's treatment. This fear can abolish the aching of the teeth that required the dental treatment in the first place. If pain is an unexpected result of a treatment which causes fear, the fear may inhibit the pain perception. Reducing the fear, for instance by applying anxiolytics, may actually restore the pain sensitivity. Appropriate treatments should reflect a complete and integrated view of the motivational organisation of a particular animal and its activation in given situations.

Literature

Bolles R C, Fanselow M S. Perceptual-defensive-recuperative model of fear and pain. Behav Brain Sci 1980; 3: 291–323.

Broom D M. Assessing welfare and suffering. Behav Proc 1991; 25: 117–23.

Colloquium on recognition and alleviation of animal pain and distress. J Am Vet Med Assoc 1987; 191: 1177–1344.

Fordyce W E. Learning processes in pain. In: Sternbach R A, ed., The psychology of pain. New York: Raven, 1987.

Hendriksen C F M, Koëter H, eds. Animals in biomedical research. Amsterdam: Elsevier, 1991.

Hooff J A R A M van. On the ethology of pain, its experience and expression. In: Beynen A C, Solleveld H A, eds. New developments in biosciences, their implications for laboratory animal science. Dordrecht: Nijhoff, 1988.

Keefe F J, Fillingim R B, Williams D A. Behavioral assessment of pain: Non-verbal measures in animals and humans. ILAR News 1991; 33: 3–13.

Kitchell R L, Johnson R D. Assessment of pain in animals. In: Moberg G, ed. Animal stress. Bethesda: Amer Physiol Soc, 1985.

Laboratory Animal Science Association Working Party. The assessment and control of severity of scientific procedures on laboratory animals. Lab Anim 1990; 124: 97–130.

Melzack R, Wall P D. Pain mechanisms: a new theory. Science 1965; 150: 971–979.

Morton D B, Griffiths P H M. The recognition and assessment of pain, distress and discomfort in experimental animals. Vet Rec 1985; 116: 431–436.

Recognition and alleviation of pain and distress in laboratory animals. National Research Council Washington DC: National Academy Press, 1992.

Sanford J, Ewbank R, Molony V, Tavenor W D, Uvarov O. Guidelines for the recognition and assessment of pain in animals. Potters Bar: Universities Federation for Animal Welfare, 1989.

Smith J A. A question of pain in invertebrates. ILAR News 1991; 33: 25–31.

Soma L R. Assessment of pain in experimental animals. Lab Anim Sci 1987; 37: 71–74.

15 Anaesthesia, analgesia and euthanasia

Introduction

Experiments in animals can result in pain and distress and, for both ethical and scientific reasons, this should be reduced to a minimum or eliminated. The ethical arguments for the humane treatment of animals are discussed in chapters 1 and 18. The scientific reasons become apparent when it is appreciated that pain and discomfort evoke a range of physiological responses affecting a large number of body systems. Eliminating or reducing pain can reduce the magnitude of these effects, and so improve the validity of an animal model.

Pain occurring during surgical procedures can be completely prevented by the use of appropriate anaesthetic techniques and these are discussed in detail below. It is important to realise that most anaesthetics affect many body systems, and so may interact with an experimental protocol. To minimise such interactions, anaesthetic regimens should be selected with care, after consideration of the pharmacology of the drugs involved. On the other hand, pain as such may also interact with the experimental procedures.

Post-operative pain, and pain occurring as a result of some non-surgical experimental procedures, can be alleviated by the administration of analgesics. In order to control pain effectively, it is essential to be able to assess the degree of pain that is being experienced by the animal. Pain is a subjective sensory/emotional experience. Establishing the presence of pain in animals, which cannot communicate with us verbally, is difficult. Nevertheless, comparison of the structure and function of the central nervous system in animals and man indicates that the necessary mechanisms for pain sensation (nociception) are present in animals. In addition, analgesics modify the responses of animals to procedures that are known to cause pain in man. These observations support the conclusion that noxious stimuli are likely to be unpleasant for animals, producing a sensation that is probably similar to pain in man. For further details on the recognition of pain in animals, see chapter 14.

Anaesthesia

Anaesthesia is a reversible and controllable condition in which the perception of noxious (painful) and other stimuli by the central nervous system is suppressed. Anaesthesia can be produced either by administration of drugs which produce a loss of consciousness (general anaesthetics), or localised areas of the body can be made insensitive using local anaesthetics. A variety of drugs can be used to anaesthetize animals. Tables 15.1–15.4 present dosage information for frequently used anaesthetics and related drugs in laboratory animals. The selection of a particular anaesthetic technique will be influenced by the animal species to be used, the type of procedure to be carried out, the duration of the procedure, the experience of the research worker and the purpose of the experiment. If a non-invasive, non-painful procedure is to be carried out, then either heavy sedation or hypnosis (sleep) may be sufficient. For invasive procedures, immobilization and effective pain relief are essential. If physiological data have to be collected, a very stable situation (steady state) will normally be required, in which changes in anaesthetic depth during the experiment are minimal. In addition, the anaesthetic selected should have minimal effects on the body system of interest.

An "ideal" anaesthetic should have the following characteristics: it should be easy to administer, induce a sufficient and stable state of anaesthesia, have no influence on physiological functions, be reversible and be safe for both animal and personnel. Unfortunately there is no anaesthetic technique available that meets all of these criteria. Thus compromises have to be made and for this reason it may be necessary to consult a specialist in animal anaesthesia for advice before starting an experiment.

General anaesthesia

Four components of general anaesthesia can be distinguished: analgesia, loss of consciousness, suppression of reflex activity and relaxation of skeletal muscles. General anaesthesia can be produced by the administration of one single drug, for example by the use of inhalational agents such as halothane or isoflurane, or by administration of injectable agents such as pentobarbitone or propofol. However, in any particular experiment, the degree of suppression of consciousness and reflex responses and the degree of analgesia that is required will vary. When only one drug is administered, it is not possible to adjust the individual components of anaesthesia independently. In contrast, if a separate drug is used for one or more components, then the degree of suppression can be tailored to the requirement of the particular experiment. Such an anaesthetic technique is called balanced anaesthesia. When using a balanced anaesthetic regimen, the dosage of each anaesthetic agent used can be relatively low, so there is less danger of a toxic overdose and the undesirable side-effects of each drug can be minimised. A potential disadvantage of balanced anaesthesia is that drug interactions are possible, and also each individual drug can have specific effects on the physiological processes of the animal. A thorough knowledge of the pharmacology of the drugs to be used is therefore needed.

Local anaesthesia (analgesia)

In contrast to general anaesthesia, local anaesthetics affect only part of the body, and the animal remains conscious. Local anaesthetics can be applied in a variety of ways, to achieve different degrees of anaesthesia (analgesia).

(i) Surface anaesthesia: Direct application of local anaesthetic gel or spray to mucous membranes, or application of local anaesthetic cream to intact skin, can produce localised areas of anaesthesia. This technique can be used for minor, superficial interventions, such as catheterisation of the urethra, or percutaneous placement of catheters into blood vessels.

(ii) Local infiltration: It is possible to desensitise deeper layers of tissues by infiltration of local anaesthetic into the tissues. This is a useful technique for minor surgical procedures such as skin biopsy.

(iii) Local nerve block: Large areas can be desensitised by injecting local anaesthetic around the nerves supplying a particular body part. This technique is especially useful for desensitising the lower limbs or tail, and enables extensive surgical procedures to be undertaken.

(iv) Regional anaesthesia: Even larger areas can be desensitized by administration of the local anaesthetic close to the spinal cord. If the drug is administered intrathecally, into the cerebrospinal fluid, the technique is termed spinal anaesthesia. If the drug is administered into the epidural space, i.e. before the dura mater is pierced, it is termed epidural anaesthesia. Spinal and epidural anaesthesia can be used to allow surgery to be carried out in the posterior part of the body, i.e. hind legs and abdomen. Although these techniques have been most widely used in larger animals, particularly sheep and cattle, they may also be used in small mammals such as rabbits.

The most widely used local anaesthetics are procaine, lidocaine, bupivacaine and prilocaine. In some cases, epinephrine or norepinephrine are added to cause local vasoconstriction and slow the absorption of the compound. This will prolong the anaesthetic effect, but can also lead to the typical cardiovascular responses seen after administration of catecholamines. The advantage of

Table 15.1

Rodent anaesthetic dose rates

	Mouse	Rat	Hamster
Premedication (anticholinergics)			
Atropine	0.05 mg/kg s.c.	0.05 mg/kg s.c.	0.05 mg/kg s.c.
Glycopyrrolate	–	–	–
Premedication (sedatives)			
Diazepam	5 mg/kg i.p.	2.5 mg/kg i.p.	5 mg/kg i.p.
Acepromazine	2.5 mg/kg s.c.	2.5 mg/kg s.c.	5 mg/kg s.c.
"Hypnorm" (fentanyl/fluanisone)	0.3 ml/kg i.p./s.c.	0.4 ml/kg i.p.	0.5 ml/kg i.p.
Xylazine	10 mg/kg s.c.	10 mg/kg s.c.	10 mg/kg s.c.
Medetomidine	–	0.5 mg/kg s.c.	–
Anaesthesia (short duration, 5–10 minutes)			
Alphaxalone/alphadolone	10–15 mg/kg i.v.	10–12mg/kg i.v.	–
Propofol	26 mg/kg i.v.	10 mg/kg i.v.	–
Thiopentone (20–25 min)	30–40 mg/kg i.v.	30 mg/kg i.v.	–
Methohexitone	10 mg/kg i.v.	7–10 mg/kg i.v.	–
Anaesthesia (medium duration, 20–60 minutes)			
"Hypnorm"/midazolam (1 part Hypnorm, 1 part midazolam and 2 parts water for injection)	4 ml/kg i.p.	2 ml/kg i.p.	6 ml/kg i.p.
Fentanyl/ etomidate	0.08 mg/kg i.p. 18 mg/kg i.p.	– –	– –
Fentanyl/ metomidate	0.08 mg/kg i.p. 60 mg/kg i.p.	– –	0.05 mg/kg i.p. 50 mg/kg i.p.
Ketamine/ xylazine	100 mg/kg i.p. 10 mg/kg i.p.	90 mg/kg i.p. 10 mg/kg i.p.	200 mg/kg i.p. 10 mg/kg i.p.
Ketamine/ medetomidine	75 mg/kg i.p. 1.0 mg/kg i.p.	75 mg/kg i.p. 0.5 mg/kg i.p.	–
Pentobarbitone	40–60 mg/kg i.p.	40–55 mg/kg i.p.	50 mg/kg i.p.
Anaesthesia (long duration, non-recovery)			
Chloralose	–	130 mg/kg i.p.	–
Urethane [1]	–	1–2 g/kg i.p.	1–2 g/kg i.p.
Anaesthesia (inhalation agents, short/medium/long duration)			
Ether	Induction concentration 15–20%		
Halothane	Induction concentration 4–5%		
Isoflurane	Induction concentration 4%		
Methoxyflurane	Induction concentration 4%		

[1] Urethane has been reported to be a carcinogenic drug.

local anaesthesia is that in general, it has less influence on normal physiological functions. However, especially following induction of spinal or epidural anaesthesia, extensive blockade of the sympathetic nervous system may occur, leading to vasodilation in the blocked area and resulting in systemic haemodynamic responses such as hypotension and tachycardia. Local anaesthetic drugs

	Gerbil	Guinea pig	Rabbit
Premedication (anticholinergics)			
Atropine	0.05 mg/kg s.c.	0.05 mg/kg s.c.	–
Glycopyrrolate	–	–	0.1 mg/kg s.c.
Premedication (sedatives)			
Diazepam	5 mg/kg i.p.	5 mg/kg i.p.	2 mg/kg i.v.
Acepromazine	5 mg/kg s.c.	2.5 mg/kg s.c.	1 mg/kg s.c.
"Hypnorm" (fentanyl/fluanisone)	0.5 ml/kg i.p.	1 ml/kg i.p.	0.5 ml/kg i.m.
Xylazine	5 mg/kg i.p.	5 mg/kg i.p.	5 mg/kg i.m.
Medetomidine	–	–	
Anaesthesia (short duration, 5–10 minutes)			
Alphaxalone/alphadolone	–	–	6–9mg/kgi.v.
Propofol	–	–	10 mg/kgi.v.
Thiopentone (20–25 min)	–	–	30 mg/kgi.v.
Methohexitone	–	–	10 mg/kgi.v.
Anaesthesia (medium duration, 20–60 minutes)			
"Hypnorm"/midazolam	4 ml/kg i.p.	2 ml/kg i.p.	0.3 ml/kg
(1 part Hypnorm, 1 part			i.m. (Hypnorm)
midazolam and 2 parts			2 mg/kg i.p. or
water for injection)			i.v. (midazolam)
Fentanyl/	–	–	0.03 mg/kg i.v.
etomidate	–	–	2 mg/kg i.v.
Fentanyl/	0.05 mg/kg i.p.	–	
metomidate	50 mg/kg i.p.	–	
Ketamine/	70 mg/kg i.p.	40 mg/kg i.p.	35 mg/kg i.m.
xylazine	3 mg/kg i.p.	5 mg/kg i.p.	5 mg/kg i.m.
Ketamine/	–	40 mg/kg i.p.	25 mg/kg i.m.
medetomidine		0.5 mg/kg i.p.	0.5 mg/kg i.m.
Pentobarbitone	60 mg/kg i.p.	37 mg/kg i.p.	45 mg/kg i.v.
Anaesthesia (long duration, non-recovery)			
Chloralose	–	70 mg/kg i.p.	80–100 mg/kg i.v.
Urethane [1]	–	0.5 g/kg i.p.	1 g/kg i.p. or i.v.
Anaesthesia (inhalation agents, short/medium/long duration)			
Ether	Maintenance concentration 5%		
Halothane	Maintenance concentration 1–2%		
Isoflurane	Maintenance concentration 1.5–3%		
Methoxyflurane	Maintenance concentration 0.5–1%		

may, depending on the concentration and volume administered, exert toxic effects. During local or regional anaesthesia the animal remains conscious, and this may be a major limitation of the technique in animals which have not been habituated to handling and restraint. Administration of a sedative may resolve this problem. Alternatively, local anaesthesia can be used to provide

Table 15.2

Dog, cat, ferret and larger species anaesthetic dose rates

	Dog	Cat	Ferret
Premedication (anticholinergics)			
Atropine	0.05 mg/kg s.c.	0.05 mg/kg s.c.	–
Glycopyrrolate	0.01 mg/kg s.c.	0.01 mg/kg s.c.	0.1 mg/kg s.c.
Premedication (sedatives)			
Diazepam	–	–	2 mg/kg i.m.
			1 mg/kg i.v.
Acepromazine	0.5 mg/kg i.m.	0.5 mg/kg i.m.	0.2 mg/kg i.m.
"Hypnorm" (fentanyl/fluanisone)	0.2 ml/kg i.m.	–	0.5 ml/kg i.m.
Xylazine	1–2 mg/kg i.m.	1–3 mg/kg i.m.	–
Medetomidine	0.1 mg/kg s.c.	0.1 mg/kg s.c.	–
Azaperon	–	–	–
Anaesthesia (short duration, 5–10 minutes)			
Alphaxalone/alphadolone	–	9–12 mg/kg i.v.	8–12 mg/kg i.v.
Propofol	5–7.5 mg/kg i.v.	7.5 mg/kg i.v.	–
Thiopentone	10–20 mg/kg i.v.	10–15 mg/kg i.v.	–
Methohexitone	4–8 mg/kg i.v.	4–8 mg/kg i.v.	–
Anaesthesia (medium duration, 20–60 minutes)			
Ketamine/	0.2 mg/kg i.v.	–	25 mg/kg i.m.
diazepam	0.2 mg/kg i.v.		2 mg/kg i.m.
Ketamine/	5 mg/kg i.v.	15 mg/kg i.m.	10 mg/kg i.m.
xylazine	1 mg/kg i.v.	1 mg/kg s.c.	0.5 mg/kg i.m.
Pentobarbitone	20–30 mg/kg i.v.	25 mg/kg i.v.	25–30 mg/kg i.v.
Anaesthesia (long duration, non-recovery)			
Chloralose	80–110 mg/kg i.v.	80–90 mg/kg i.v.	–
Urethane [1]	1 g/kg i.v.	1.25 g/kg i.v.	–
Anaesthesia (inhalation agents, short/medium/long duration)			
Ether	Induction with injectable anaesthetics		
Halothane	Induction with injectable anaesthetics		
Isoflurane	Induction with injectable anaesthetics		
Methoxyflurane	Induction with injectable anaesthetics		

[1] Urethane has been reported to be a carcinogenic drug.

analgesia in animals that have been rendered unconscious by administration of a low dose of a general anaesthetic.

Pre-anaesthetic preparations

Before inducing anaesthesia, a number of preparations are necessary. The most appropriate anaesthetic regimen should have been selected, and all of

	Sheep/Goat	Pig	Primate
Premedication (anticholinergics)			
Atropine	0.05 mg/kg s.c.	0.05 mg/kg s.c.	0.05 mg/kg s.c.
Glycopyrrolate	–	–	–
Premedication (sedatives)			
Diazepam	2 mg/kg i.m.,	1 mg/kg i.m.	1 mg/kg i.m.
Acepromazine	0.1 mg/kg i.m.	0.2 mg/kg i.m.	0.2 mg/kg i.m.
"Hypnorm" (fentanyl/fluanisone)	–	–	0.3 ml/kg i.m.
Xylazine	1 mg/kg i.m. (sheep) 0.05 mg/kg i.m. (goat)	–	–
Medetomidine	–	–	–
Azaperon	–	0.5 mg/kg s.c.	–
Anaesthesia (short duration, 5–10 minutes)			
Alphaxalone/alphadolone	2.2 mg/kg i.v. then 2 mg/kg i.v.	6 mg/kg i.m.	10–12 mg/kg i.v.
Propofol	3–4 mg/kg i.v.	3 mg/kg i.v.	–
Thiopentone	10–15 mg/kg i.v.	6–9 mg/kg i.v.	15–20 mg/kg i.v.
Methohexitone	4 mg/kg i.v.	5 mg/kg i.v.	10 mg/kg i.v.
Anaesthesia (medium duration, 20–60 minutes)			
Ketamine/	4 mg/kg i.v.	10 mg/kg i.m.	15 mg/kg i.m.
diazepam	1 mg/kg i.v.	2 mg/kg i.m.	1 mg/kg i.m.
Ketamine/	4 mg/kg i.v.	10 mg/kg i.m.	10 mg/kg i.m.
xylazine	1 mg/kg i.v. (sheep) 0.05 mg/kg i.v. (goats)	1 mg/kg i.m.	0.5 mg/kg i.m.
Pentobarbitone	30 mg/kg i.v.	30 mg/kg i.v.	5–15 mg/kg i.v.
Anaesthesia (long duration, non-recovery)			
Chloralose	–	–	60 mg/kg i.v.
Urethane [1]	–	–	–
Anaesthesia (inhalation agents, short/medium/long duration)			
Ether	Maintenance concentration 5%		
Halothane	Maintenance concentration 1–2%		
Isoflurane	Maintenance concentration 1.5–3%		
Methoxyflurane	Maintenance concentration 0.5–1%		

the equipment that will be required should be checked to ensure that it is intact and functioning correctly. Ensure that sufficient quantities of anaesthetic and emergency drugs are readily available. The animals which are to be anaesthetised should have undergone one to two weeks acclimatisation period and, during the immediate pre-operative period, their body weight and daily food and water consumption should have been recorded. The animals should be in good health and free from any clinical signs of disease. In some instances it may be appropriate to carry out laboratory investigations to confirm the health status of the subjects. Prior to major surgery, haematological and biochemical evaluations may be carried out in larger species. For example, a knowledge of the pre-operative haemoglobin content or haematocrit is helpful if these parameters are to be used to evaluate the degree of intra-operative haemorrhage.

If the animal is to recover from anaesthesia, then preparations for providing post-operative care should be made before commencing the procedure. A suitable recovery pen or incubator should be available, and equipment for maintaining body temperature post-operatively should be switched on to allow sufficient time for the temperature in the recovery area to stabilise.

When using an anaesthetic regimen for the first time, it is advisable to anaesthetise only one animal to ensure that an appropriate depth of anaesthesia is attained and that recovery is uneventful. The response of different strains of rodents to anaesthetic agents varies considerably, and the dose rates quoted in this chapter may need to be modified for use with certain strains of rodents.

During induction and recovery from anaesthesia, some species may vomit if they have been recently fed. To avoid this problem, dogs, cats, pigs and non-human primates should be fasted for 12–16 hours prior to anaesthesia. Pre-anaesthetic fasting is unnecessary and undesirable in small rodents and rabbits.

Pre-anaesthetic medication: It is sometimes useful to administer drugs prior to induction of anaesthesia, either to reduce possible side-effects of the anaesthetic agents, or to minimise the distress associated with induction and to ensure a smooth recovery from anaesthesia. Anticholinergic agents, such as atropine or glycopyrrolate, may be used to reduce the volume of bronchial and salivary secretions, and to block the undesirable autonomic responses to surgical manipulation of the viscera. Sedatives or tranquillisers may be used to reduce stress and make animals easy to restrain. Use of sedatives will also smooth the induction and recovery from anaesthesia. The majority of commonly used sedatives and tranquillisers have no analgesic action, and so additional medication will be required to control per- and post-operative pain. Suggestions for pre-anaesthetic medication and dose rates for different species are given in tables 15.1 and 15.2.

Induction and maintenance of general anaesthesia

General anaesthesia can be induced either by injection of one or more compounds by the intravenous, intramuscular or intraperitoneal routes, or volatile anaesthetics may be administered by inhalation. In small animals (< 1 kg), induction with volatile anaesthetics can be achieved using an induction chamber. With larger species, this is rarely practicable and the animal will need to be restrained and a face mask used to administer the anaesthetic. The animal may resent the procedure and so be difficult to restrain. To minimise stress during induction it is advisable either to administer a sedative prior to face mask induction, or to administer a short-acting injectable anaesthetic to produce loss of consciousness followed by administration of an inhalational agent to maintain anaesthesia for the desired period.

Inhalation agents have the advantage of allowing easy adjustment of the depth of anaesthesia. It is therefore easy to compensate for variations in the susceptibility of different individuals to the anaesthetic agent. Following short periods (< 30 min) of anaesthesia, recovery is very rapid. Because of their ease of administration to small rodents and the rapid recovery, inhalational agents are probably the agents of choice for most procedures in these species.

Anaesthetic agents

Inhalational agents

Isoflurane: This is a potent anaesthetic which produces rapid induction of anaesthesia, rapid recovery and can provide safe and effective anaesthesia in all mammalian and avian laboratory species. Isoflurane is non-flammable, non-explosive and non-irritant. This anaesthetic undergoes virtually no metabolism and is almost entirely removed from the animal by exhalation from the lungs. Because of this, it does not induce liver enzymes, and this minimises the risk of interference with experimental studies which involve drug metabolism. Because it is a potent anaesthetic, isoflurane should only be used with a calibrated vaporizer.

Halothane: Like isoflurane, halothane is a potent anaesthetic which must be used in a calibrated vaporizer. Induction and recovery are slightly less rapid in comparison with isoflurane. Halothane causes moderate hypotension at surgical planes of anaesthesia. The compound is extensively metabolised in addition to being exhaled through the lungs.

Methoxyflurane: Methoxyflurane is a potent anaesthetic but, because it is less easy to vaporize than halothane and isoflurane, it can be used safely in simple apparatus. If a vaporizer is unavailable, liquid methoxyflurane can be poured onto a cotton wool pad placed in an induction chamber. It is important to ensure that contact between the cotton wool pad and the animal is prevented by use of a metal grid or similar device, as the liquid anaesthetic is irritant. Methoxyflurane undergoes substantial metabolism, releasing inorganic fluoride ions which can cause damage to the kidney

Table 15.3

Anaesthetic dose rate in birds, reptiles, amphibians and fish

	Ketamine	Pentobarbitone	MS-222	Urethane	Halothane	Isoflurane	Remarks
Birds							combination in pigeons: ketamine 30 mg/kg + metomidate 10 mg/kg i.m. or pentobarbitone 10–20 mg/kg i.m. endotracheal intubation relatively easy
0.1 kg	10–20 mg/kg i.m.				2–4%	3–5%	
0.1–0.5 kg	5–10 mg/kg i.m.						
0.5–3 kg	2–5 mg/kg i.m.						
Snakes	20–80 mg/kg i.p.	15–30 mg/kg i.p.	200–400 mg/kg i.p.		3.5–6.5%	4.0–6.5%	metomidate 8–10 mg/kg i.p.; thiopentone 8–45 mg/kg i.p.
Lizards	15–70 mg/kg i.m.	10–25 mg/kg i.p.			4–5% for induction; 1–2% for maintenance	4–5% for induction; 2–3% for maintenance	induction lasts 10 minutes
Tortoises	60–120 mg/kg i.m.	10–30 mg/kg i.p.			4% for induction; 1.5% for maintenance	4% for induction; 2.0% for maintenance	induction lasts 10 minutes
Frogs		30–60 mg/kg in dorsal lymph sac	induction 1500 mg/l; maintenance 600 mg/l	20 ml/kg in dorsal lymph sac			chloralhydrate 10%; 1–2 ml dorsal lymph sac; MS-222 should be neutralised with 50 ml M 0.5 SoHCO$_3$/l
Fish			250–14,000 mg/l water	10–90 g/l water			Propanidid 0.2–1.5 mg/l

Table 15.4

Dose rates of muscle relaxants and antagonists in mg/kg

	Mouse	Rat	Guinea pig	Rabbit	Cat	Dog	Sheep	Goat	Pig
Muscle relaxants									
Pancuronium		2	0.06	0.1	0.06	0.06	0.06	0.06	0.06
Alcuronium					0.1	0.1			
Atracurium					0.5	0.5			
Vecuronium			0.1–0.2		0.1	0.1		0.15	0.15
Gallamine	1	1	0.1–0.2	1	1	1	1	4	2
d-Tubocurarine		0.4		0.4	0.4	0.4	0.4	0.3	
Guafenesin								start with 50 afterwards 220/hour	
Antagonists									
Opiate: naloxone	0.1	0.1	0.1	0.1	0.05–0.1	0.1	0.1	0.1	0.1
Alpha-2-adrenerge: atipamezole	0.2	0.1	0.1	0.1	0.1	0.1	0.1	0.1	

and so should not be used for studies of renal function. A disadvantage of methoxyflurane is the long recovery period.

Enflurane: Enflurane resembles halothane, but induction and recovery are slightly more rapid. It is less extensively metabolised than halothane, but it offers no significant advantages in comparison to halothane and isoflurane, and is rarely used in laboratory animals.

Ether: This irritant and inflammable anaesthetic forms explosive gas mixtures with oxygen and air. The irritant properties of ether vapour result in profuse salivation, increased bronchial secretions and occasional laryngospasm in animals. Irritation of the respiratory tract by ether can exacerbate pre-existing respiratory disease in rodents and rabbits. Despite these obvious disadvantages, ether is still used extensively to anaesthetise small rodents. It can be administered using simple apparatus, using a cotton wool pad in an anaesthetic chamber, and it is difficult to overdose an animal even when using such crude equipment. However, animal welfare concerns, and the significant safety hazard posed by ether, have resulted in many laboratories discarding this agent in favour of safer and more humane alternatives.

Nitrous oxide: This anaesthetic is supplied in compressed form in pressurised cylinders. It is delivered as a mixture with oxygen and, to avoid hypoxia, the relative proportions of the two gases should not exceed 65% nitrous oxide with 35% oxygen. In man, nitrous oxide is an effective analgesic which can produce unconsciousness when used as the sole anaesthetic agent. In laboratory mammals, it is considerably less potent, and will not produce unconsciousness, even when administered at high ($> 90\%$) concentrations.

Anaesthetic potency: The required inspiratory concentration of an inhalational anaesthetic needed to induce unconsciousness and anaesthesia depends upon the species and the anaesthetic agent used. The "minimal alveolar concentration" (MAC) is the concentration of an anaesthetic (as an inspired percentage concentration) at which 50% of the animals do not react to a standardized painful stimulus (table 15.5). To provide a surgical level of anaesthesia, 1.5 MAC is usually required, although some individuals may require 2 MAC or greater. Administration of injectable anaesthetics, analgesics and/or sedatives lowers the MAC-value of inhalational anaesthetics.

Gas scavenging: Chronic exposure to inhalational anaesthetics is believed to be detrimental to human subjects, and it is standard practice in most operating rooms to use apparatus to remove waste anaesthetic gases. Safety legislation in many countries now requires all users of inhalational anaesthetics to ensure effective scavenging of waste anaesthetic gas, and so reduce the degree of pollution of laboratories and operating rooms. A number of commercially produced devices are available. As a temporary measure, simple anaesthetic apparatus can be transferred to a fume cabinet, but this is rarely convenient in the long term.

Table 15.5

MAC-values in percentages for inhalational anaesthetics in different species

	Ether	Halothane	Enflurane	Isoflurane	Nitrous oxide
Human	1.92	0.75	1.68	1.15	105
Primate		1.15	1.84	1.28	200
Dog	3.04	0.87	2.20	1.41	188
Pig				1.45	
Sheep				1.58	
Cat	2.10	0.82	1.20	1.63	255
Rat	3.20	1.10		1.38	150
Mouse	3.20	0.95		1.41	275

Injectable anaesthetics

A large number of different injectable anaesthetic agents are available for use in laboratory animals. These are briefly summarised below, and suggested dose rates are listed in tables 15.1 through 15.3. It is important to emphasise the variation in response to anaesthetics that occurs between individual animals, and the even larger variation reported between animals of different strains. When first using a new anaesthetic regimen, it is essential to assess the regimen in one animal, before proceeding to anaesthetise larger groups. This problem is most frequently seen with small rodents, because anaesthetics are usually administered as a single intraperitoneal injection. This does not enable the anaesthetic to be administered gradually to achieve the desired effect. In rabbits and larger species, anaesthetics can be administered by the intravenous route and, after administration of approximately 50% of the predicted dose, the remaining drug can be injected more slowly to provide the appropriate depth of anaesthesia. Intravenous administration of anaesthetics in rats and mice is not especially difficult and the required expertise will be available in most research laboratories. Consideration should then be given to using this route of administration, especially if short (< 10 minute) periods of anaesthesia are required.

Barbiturates: Two short-acting agents (thiopentone and methohexitone) and a longer acting agent (pentobarbitone) are widely available for animal anaesthesia. All of these anaesthetics produce sleep (hypnosis), but are poor analgesics. Surgical anaesthesia is only attained at dose rates that cause significant cardiovascular and respiratory depression. If barbiturates are administered intravenously, the dose rate can be carefully adjusted and they can be used with relative safety. Intraperitoneal injection of short-acting agents has very unpredictable effects and is not recommended. Intraperitoneal administration of pentobarbitone can produce surgical anaesthesia, but the drug has a narrow safety margin and mortality may be high.

Dissociative anaesthetics: Ketamine and tiletamine are the most widely used dissociative anaesthetics. In larger species, particularly non-human primates, dissociative anaesthetics can provide light surgical anaesthesia, but the degree of muscle relaxation is poor. If the dissociative anaesthetic is combined with a sedative or tranquilliser, the quality of anaesthesia is greatly improved. The commercial preparation of tiletamine consists of a mixture of tiletamine and zolazepam (a benzodiazepine). Ketamine can be combined with a tranquilliser, such as acepromazine or diazepam, but is most effective when administered in combination with a sedative-analgesic such as xylazine or medetomidine. A particular advantage of these combinations is that the sedative-analgesic can be reversed with a specific antagonist (atipamezole, table 15.4), so considerably speeding recovery.

Neuroleptanalgesics: Neuroleptanalgesics are mixtures of a potent analgesic and a tranquilliser. The most widely used commercial preparations are fentanyl/fluanisone (= "Hypnorm"); fentanyl/droperidol (= "Innovar"); etorphine/methotrimeprazine and etorphine/acepromazine. When used alone, these compounds produce profound analgesia, but the degree of muscle relaxation is poor, and respiration is severely depressed. In several species it is possible to combine the use of fentanyl/fluanisone with a benzodiazepine, (diazepam or midazolam) and produce surgical anaesthesia, good muscle relaxation and only mild respiratory depression. Narcotic analgesics can be antagonized by naloxone (table 15.4).

Steroid anaesthetics: Alphaxalone/alphadolone ("Saffan") is a useful anaesthetic in most laboratory species. This anaesthetic should not be used in the dog, since the solubilising agent (Cremophor) present in the commercial preparation causes histamine release. In the rabbit, surgical planes of anaesthesia are produced only at dose rates that can cause respiratory arrest. In most other species, if administered by intravenous injection, alphaxalone/alphadolone produces moderate surgical anaesthesia lasting 5–15 minutes. Repeated injections, or a continuous infusion, can be use to prolong anaesthesia without unduly extending the recovery time.

Other agents

Propofol: This anaesthetic can be used to produce surgical anaesthesia in non-human primates, dogs, cats, sheep, pigs, rats and mice when administered intravenously. In rabbits the degree of analgesia produced is insufficient for major surgery. The duration of anaesthesia is short (< 10 min) and recovery is rapid. Repeated doses of propofol, or administration of a continuous infusion can be used to prolong anaesthesia without unduly extending the recovery time.

Tribromoethanol: This anaesthetic can be used in rodents, and produces surgical anaesthesia with good muscle relaxation. Decomposition of the solution can cause severe irritation on intraperitoneal administration, resulting in death of some animals. It is therefore essential that only freshly prepared solution should be used. Administration of this anaesthetic on a subsequent occasion in the same animal can cause gastrointestinal disturbances and death, even if a freshly prepared solution is used.

Assessment of depth of anaesthesia

Whatever anaesthetic is selected, it is important to be able to monitor the depth of anaesthesia to ensure that the animal does not become too lightly anaesthetised and so perceives painful stimuli, nor too deeply anaesthetised and so be in danger of death due to anaesthetic overdose. Reflex activity, changes in the pattern, rate and depth of respiration, alterations of heart rate and blood pressure and other reactions to painful stimuli are used to determine the depth of anaesthesia. Unfortunately the changes in these parameters at different depths of anaesthesia vary in different animal species and with different anaesthetic agents. It is also important to recognize that the transition from consciousness to complete surgical anaesthesia is a continuum, and not a series of discrete steps. Nevertheless, anaesthesia has traditionally been divided arbitrarily into four stages. These stages can be recognized most easily when anaesthesia is induced without the use of any premedication.

Stage 1, the induction stage: During this stage the animal is conscious and experiences a light state of analgesia and sedation.

Stage 2, the excitation stage: The animal is losing consciousness and shows exaggerated reflex activity and muscle movements. The pupils become dilated and there is an increase in tear and mucous production.

Stage 3, the surgical stage: The frequency of respiration is reduced, and its depth increases. The eyelid and corneal reflexes disappear, muscle tone and reflex responses decrease. There is no response to surgical or other stimulation.

Stage 4, the hypoxic (toxic) stage: The vital brain centres are depressed to such an extent that respiration and heart beat stop. The pupils become dilated and unresponsive to light. This stage is reached during euthanasia when an overdose of an anaesthetic is administered.

For most experiments the surgical stage is required. Unfortunately, there is considerable variation in the responses described above when different anaesthetic combinations are used. To determine whether the animal has sufficient anaesthesia, the following reflex responses can be assessed:

1. the righting reflex: the animal attempts to turn over to the prone position after being placed on its back;
2. the palpebral reflex: blinking when the inner or outer canthus of the eye is touched;
3. the pedal reflex: withdrawal and flexion of a leg when a digit or the interdigital skin is pinched;
4. the swallowing reflex: pulling the tongue or pressing the throat results in swallowing;
5. the tail pinch reflex: pinching the tail with finger-nails or a haemostat results in a flick of the tail and occasionally in vocalisation;
6. the ear pinch reflex: pinching the ear in rabbits and guinea pig produces a head shake response.

Loss of the righting reflex and the pedal withdrawal reflex are the most practically useful assessments that can be made in rodents and rabbits. These reflex responses are lost in a graded manner. For example, vocalisation in response to pinching the tail or digit is lost before the reflex twitch or withdrawal disappears. The magnitude of these withdrawal responses falls gradually, until they are completely absent at moderate to deep planes of anaesthesia.

Endotracheal intubation and artificial ventilation

Endotracheal intubation is the insertion of a tube into the trachea. Intubation can only be carried out in anaesthetized animals. Intubation is necessary when respiration is to be maintained by artificial ventilation, but is also useful in spontaneously breathing animals since it ensures that the airway remains unobstructed and allows ventilation to be assisted if respiratory depression occurs.

The technique for endotracheal intubation varies in the different species, but is always easier if an appropriate laryngoscope is available. Blades suitable for larger species are available commercially and techniques for intubation are described in standard veterinary text books (e.g. Short, 1987; Hall and Clarke, 1991). Blades for small rodents need to be specially constructed, and those described by Costa *et al.* (1986) are simple to manufacture and easy to use. A guide to the sizes of endotracheal tube appropriate for each species is given in table 15.6.

In all species, the animal must be sufficiently deeply anaesthetised to allow the mouth to be opened and the tongue pulled forward without eliciting any chewing or swallowing responses. The tongue is extended and a laryngoscope (fig. 15.1a) is inserted. This allows the operator to see the epiglottis and vocal folds. In cats, pigs, rabbits and non-human primates, the larynx should

Table 15.6

Diameter and length of endotracheal tubes in different species

	Outer diameter (mm)	Inner diameter (mm)	Length (cm)
Mouse	1.0	0.5	3
Rat	1.8	1.0	13
Hamster	1.6	1.0	8
Guinea pig	2.0	1.5	10
Rabbit	2.0–3.5	1.8–3.3	15

be sprayed with local anaesthetic prior to intubation to minimise the risk of laryngospasm. The endotracheal tube should be lubricated with a local anaesthetic ointment prior to insertion into the trachea. For intubation of mice, rats, hamsters and guinea pigs, either a purpose-made laryngoscope can be constructed, or the anaesthetized animal should be placed in dorsal recumbency, the mouth opened and fixed with an eye speculum, or purpose-made mouth gag. The tongue should be pulled out of the mouth and fixed with a vessel clip and a cotton wool plug. A strong light should be directed towards the ventral part of the neck. This light passes through the tissue. Using fine forceps, the base of the tongue should be pressed upwards and the opening of the larynx will become visible. It is also possible to carry out this procedure using an otoscope with a diameter of 4 mm (fig. 15.1b). For this the animal should be placed in sternal recumbency. Using cotton wool swabs

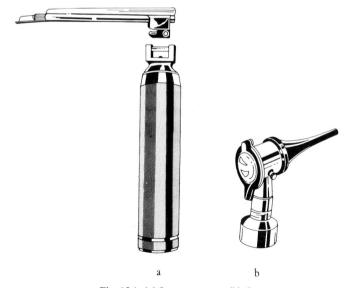

a   b

Fig. 15.1. (a) Laryngoscope; (b) Otoscope.

moistened with local anaesthetic, the mucous membranes of the mouth and pharynx are desensitized. The head is lifted backwards perpendicular to the table. The tongue is then pulled out of the mouth using a cotton wool plug. The otoscope is inserted into the mouth. The ventral side of the epiglottis becomes visible. A stylet is passed through the otoscope (0.8 mm) and the soft palate is pushed dorsally. The epiglottis will fall ventrally, revealing the vocal folds. The stylet is now pushed between the vocal folds and the otoscope is carefully removed. The endotracheal tube is passed over the stylet and, when it is in the trachea, the stylet is removed. With both methods, the tube must not be inserted too far in order to avoid ventilation of only one lung.

Rabbits can be intubated using a Wisconsin laryngoscope blade, although it is also possible to intubate rabbits without visualising the larynx. The rabbit must be placed in sternal recumbency. The head is raised and tilted backwards so that the mandible lies perpendicular to the table. The head is held in one hand with the thumb and index finger placed in the corners of the upper and lower jaw, thus holding the mouth open. The tube is inserted along the palate. As the tube reaches the pharynx the operator should listen for respiration sounds while passing the tube between the vocal cords. To check the proper position of the tube, a small mirror or a few hairs can be placed close to the end of the tube. The mirror will become misty and the hairs will be blown away when the animal exhales. Great care must be taken to avoid pushing the endotracheal tube against the larynx, as this delicate structure is easily damaged. The resulting oedema and haemorrhage can cause post-operative airway obstruction and death.

If intubation is difficult, or impossible, a tracheotomy may be carried out, provided that the animal is not required to recover from the procedure.

Most birds and reptiles are easy to intubate. After induction of anaesthesia, the mouth is opened and the entrance to the trachea can easily be seen at the base of the tongue.

Anaesthetic breathing systems

For the administration of oxygen and inhalational anaesthetics, different breathing systems are used. An essential requirement for any breathing system is the provision of sufficient oxygen and the adequate removal of carbon dioxide. The simplest technique is to deliver oxygen and anaesthetic gases by means of a close-fitting face mask. Using this system, the fresh gas flow rates from the anaesthetic machine should exceed three times the animal's minute volume. The minute volume is the quantity of gas inhaled in one minute and is calculated by multiplying the volume of one breath (the tidal volume, approximately 15 ml/kg of body weight) by the respiratory rate. Use of this simple system of gas delivery does not allow ventilation to be assisted, and the

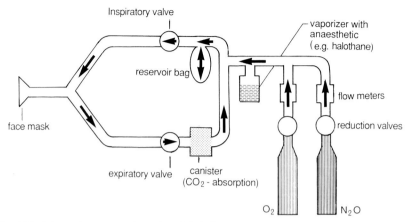

Fig. 15.2. Schematic presentation of an inhalation anaesthesia system (rebreathing system or anaesthetic circuit).

high fresh gas flows needed may be uneconomic when anaesthetising large animals. As an alternative, the animal can be connected via an endotracheal tube to a T-piece or Bain's circuit. Detailed descriptions of the use of these circuits are readily available (Short, 1987, Hall and Clarke, 1991). When anaesthetising larger animals ($> 7–10$ kg body weight), the relatively high gas flows needed when using a Bain's circuit or T-piece ($2.2 \times$ minute volume) may be uneconomic. In these circumstances a rebreathing system with a canister or carbon dioxide absorber (see fig. 15.2) may be used. Although these systems are economical to use, considerably more experience is necessary to maintain an adequate and stable depth of anaesthesia. Use of closed circuit anaesthesia is described in Short (1987), and Hall and Clarke (1991).

Artificial ventilation

When artificial ventilation is used, fresh gas is forcibly blown into the lungs using either manual pressure or a mechanical ventilator. Animals must be artificially ventilated during thoracotomy or when a muscle relaxant is used. It is also advisable to apply artificial ventilation during prolonged experiments ($> 1–1.5$ hours), in order to ensure adequate gas exchange. During artificial ventilation a positive airway pressure exists during inspiration. The expiratory phase is a passive phase caused by the elasticity of the lungs. The increase in intrathoracic pressure during inspiration reduces cardiac output and, to minimise this effect, a relatively short inspiratory phase is normally employed, occupying about 30% of the respiratory cycle.

Although every species has its own ventilatory requirements, as a general rule a tidal volume of 15 ml/kg must be administered to ensure adequate

Table 15.7

Artificial ventilation

Species	Frequency/ min	Tidal volume (ml)	Inspiration/ expiration time (%)	Pressure (cm H_2O)
Mouse	100–130	0.5–1	35/65	5–15
Rat	50–80	3–10	35/65	5–15
Guinea pig	30–50	8–20	35/65	5–15
Rabbit	30–50	40–60	35/65	5–15
Bird	6–12	depends on size		5–15

respiratory function. The respiratory rate required varies in different species, ranging from 10–20 breaths per minute in dogs, sheep and pigs, to 60–150 breaths per minute in rabbits and small rodents (table 15.7). Ventilators designed for use in man can usually deliver tidal volumes ranging from 50 to 1500 ml at rates of 8–60 breaths per minute. Human infant ventilators are capable of supplying smaller tidal volumes, but it is preferable to use a purpose-designed laboratory animal ventilator (e.g. the Harvard Rodent Ventilator) for small rodents. These ventilators should be capable of delivering tidal volumes as low as 0.2 ml at frequencies of up to 150 per minute.

During mechanical artificial ventilation, attention must be paid to the airway pressure to prevent overinflation and barotrauma. Inflation pressures should generally not exceed 10 cm of water in small animals. To attain good artificial ventilation, it is advisable to use a capnograph, to measure the carbon dioxide content in the expired gas, and to maintain this within the normal range of 4–5%. Unfortunately, many capnographs are incapable of recording accurately the expired carbon dioxide concentration from small (< 500 g) animals, because the volume of expired gas is too small.

Neuromuscular blocking agents

In order to facilitate artificial ventilation, but also in order to obtain relaxation of the skeletal muscles, neuromuscular blocking agents (muscle relaxants) are sometimes administered. When using these drugs, one should remember that the animal is completely immobilized and will not move in response to painful stimuli, even if consciousness has returned. Muscle relaxants should therefore only be used under strictly defined conditions, and only under the supervision of an experienced animal anaesthetist. When using muscle relaxants, the heart rate and blood pressure should be monitored continuously. An increase in either of these parameters in response to surgical stimuli should be assumed to indicate an inadequate depth of anaesthesia, and additional anaesthetic should be administered. Dose rates of neuromuscular blocking agents are listed in table 15.4.

Monitoring of vital functions

Throughout the period of anaesthesia, it is important to assess the adequacy of the animal's vital functions, and to ensure these are maintained within acceptable limits. The extent and complexity of this monitoring will depend upon the nature and duration of the experimental procedure. A basic assessment of the animal can be undertaken by simple observation, for example the colour of the mucous membranes, the pattern and rate of respiration and the heart rate and pulse can be assessed easily in most species. Repeated observation of these parameters is often difficult during an experimental procedure, and so it is often useful to employ electronic monitoring devices. Monitoring equipment also enables accurate assessment of parameters such as blood oxygen and carbon dioxide concentrations and body temperature, which cannot be obtained by simple observation. Electronic monitoring may include:

– electrocardiogram and heart rate;
– cardiac output;
– arterial, pulmonary artery and central venous pressure;
– capnogram (expiratory CO_2 concentration);
– arterial blood gas and acid base status (PaO_2, $PaCO_2$, pH, base excess, bicarbonate, buffer capacity);
– arterial oxygen saturation using a pulse oximeter;
– respiratory volume and frequency;
– airway pressure;
– body temperature;
– electroencephalogram (brain activity).

It is also advisable to monitor the proper function of the anaesthetic equipment, particularly during prolonged periods of anaesthesia — for example the concentration of inhalational agents and inspiratory oxygen concentration. When considering purchase of monitoring equipment, ensure that the device will function successfully in small animals. For example, many heart rate monitors are incapable of recording heart rates in excess of 250 beats per minute and the normal resting heart rate of rodents and rabbits will often exceed this rate.

During anaesthesia of small (< 10 kg) animals, special attention must be paid to the maintenance of the body temperature. Small animals cool rapidly when anaesthetised, and this is a significant cause of increased mortality. Heating blankets, heating lamps and other devices should be used to

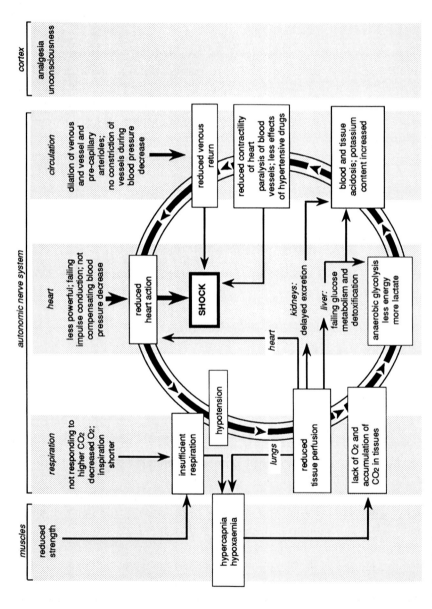

Fig. 15.3. Complications during anaesthesia may result in an autonomous process of disregulation of vital functions, leading to shock and death.

maintain body temperature. Body temperature should be monitored continuously, using an electronic thermometer, to ensure that both hypothermia and hyperthermia are avoided.

It may be necessary to provide intravenous fluid to replace the volume lost from the respiratory tract and by haemorrhage following surgery. Detailed descriptions of fluid therapy are given by Michell *et al.* (1989). As a basic guide, approximately 10–20 ml/kg/hour of Lactated Ringers solution should be infused intravenously. In small mammals, 10–15 ml/kg of normal (0.9%) saline can be administered subcutaneously or intraperitoneally, although this will be absorbed slowly and will be ineffective for the treatment of acute fluid deficits. All fluids should be warmed to body temperature before administration.

If the animal's eyes remain open during anaesthesia, ophthalmic ointment or artificial tears should be applied to prevent drying of the cornea or, alternatively, the eyelids should be taped closed.

Complications of anaesthesia

Most anaesthetic agents have several (unwanted) pharmacological side effects. Occasionally, serious complications may occur because of the depression of vital organ systems. Fig. 15.3 illustrates that anaesthetics can induce a sequence of self-reinforcing physiological reactions. In extreme situations this can result in a severe disruption of circulatory functions, leading to shock and death.

Respiratory depression and arrest

Depression of spontaneous ventilation can occur when the concentration of injectable or inhalational anaesthetic agents is too high. This will result in hypoxaemia and hypercapnia. Eventually ventilation will stop and cardiac arrest will occur. The mucous membranes turn purple-blue, because of the increased concentration of non-oxygenated haemoglobin in the blood (cyanosis). If inhalation anaesthetics are being administered, the vaporizer should be switched off and the anaesthetic circuit flushed with oxygen. If injectable anaesthetics are being administered by continuous infusion, the infusion pump should be switched off. If oxygen is being supplied, the fresh gas flow rate should be increased to approximately three times minute volume and ventilation assisted by manually depressing the reservoir bag or occluding the outflow of a T-piece or Bain's circuit in patients which are intubated. In small animals which are not intubated, oxygen should be administered by face-mask and ventilation assisted by manually compressing the chest. If

respiratory arrest occurs during parenteral anaesthesia, then artificial ventilation has to be continued until detoxification (metabolism or excretion) of
the anaesthetic has advanced to an acceptable level. Respiratory function can
be stimulated by administration of doxapram (5–10 mg/kg by any convenient
route).

Cardiac arrhythmias and cardiac arrest

Unless cardiac activity is being monitored with an electrocardiogram, arrhythmias are difficult to diagnose. Arrhythmias can cause serious disturbances in
circulatory function, and may require therapy. Detailed information on this
topic can be found in Short (1987). If cardiac arrest occurs, it can be treated
by external cardiac massage: the thorax should be compressed at a rate of
70–80 per minute and this should be coupled with the measures described
above for correcting respiratory failure. As an emergency measure, adrenaline
(0.1 ml/kg of 1 : 10,000) should be administered by intracardiac injection.

Cardiac failure and hypotension

Hypotension can arise because of vasodilation or depression of myocardial
contractility caused by the anaesthetic agent, or as a result of blood loss or se-
questration of blood into the tissues during surgical manipulations. Decreased
capillary refill, low arterial blood pressure, tachycardia, and pale colour of
the skin and mucous membranes are some of the signs of hypotension. Intravenous administration of fluids is usually required to correct this problem.
It is preferable to use whole blood to treat haemorrhage. Blood should be
collected from a donor animal of the same species in acid citrate dextrose (1
part ACD to 3.5 parts of blood). The incidence of adverse transfusion reactions is low following a single transfusion and, in any event, cross-matching is
rarely practicable. Blood should be replaced at a rate of 10% of the animal's
circulating volume every 30 minutes but, if rapid haemorrhage has occurred,
then replacement should also be as rapid as possible. If blood is not available,
plasma volume expanders such as Haemaccel (Hoechst) should be used or, if
these are unavailable, Lactated Ringer's solution or Normal saline should be
administered.

Regurgitation

During anaesthesia, dogs, cats, and primates may vomit, and this material
may be inhaled into the lungs. As mentioned earlier, fasting for 12–16 hours
reduces the risk of vomiting. Ruminants will regurgitate during anaesthesia,
and intubation with a cuffed endotracheal tube is essential in these species.

Withholding food for 16–24 hours in these species may be beneficial in reducing the tendency for gas accumulation in the rumen.

Long-term anaesthesia

In some experiments, particularly those concerned with monitoring physiological processes, a stable plane of anaesthesia lasting several hours may be required. This can be achieved either by the use of long-acting anaesthetics, by continuous infusion of short-acting drugs, or by use of volatile anaesthetics.

Post-operative care

Monitoring procedures may need to be continued in the immediate post-operative period to ensure that the animal is recovering satisfactorily. It is particularly important to maintain body temperature, and an incubator should be provided for small animals. This should be maintained at 25–35°C for adult animals, and 35–37°C for neonates. Large animals should be provided with heating pads or heating lamps. Body temperature should be monitored regularly to check the adequacy of the measures used. The bedding material provided should be comfortable and should also provide effective insulation. Sawdust and woodshavings are not suitable, as the animal may inhale particles of bedding and dust may adhere to the animal's eyes, mouth and nose. Purpose-made bedding material such as "Vetbed" is preferable for all species, alternatively towels or blankets should be used. The animal should be housed individually in quiet surroundings and should be observed frequently until normal activity has resumed. Endotracheal tubes should be removed as soon as the swallowing reflex has returned, but continued attention should be paid to respiratory function until recovery from anaesthesia is complete.

Post-operative pain relief is required after all surgical procedures. In order to provide an appropriate analgesic for an appropriate time period, it is important to attempt to assess the degree of pain which is present. Pain assessment in animals is difficult, and considerable experience of the normal behaviour of the species is necessary. Significant signs of pain may include abnormal behaviour, altered posture, reduction of food and water intake and weight loss (see chapter 14). Since small rodents are relatively inactive during the day, it may be necessary to observe animals during the dark phase of their photoperiod in order to make an accurate assessment of their well-being.

Post-operative pain can be alleviated by the administration of opiates (e.g. morphine), non-steroidal anti-inflammatory drugs (NSAID'S, e.g. flunixin), or local anaesthetics. The use of these agents has been reviewed by a number

Table 15.8

Doses of analgesics for post-operative pain relief (drugs listed in alphabetical order)

A. Mouse and rat

Drug	Mouse	Rat
Aspirin	120 mg/kg per os 4 hourly	100 mg/kg per os 4 hourly
Buprenorphine	0.05–0.1 mg/kg s.c. 12 hourly	0.01–0.05 mg/kg s.c., i.v. 8–12 hourly
Butorphanol	1–5 mg/kg s.c. 4 hourly	2 mg/kg s.c. 4 hourly
Codeine	60–90 mg/kg per os 20 mg/kg s.c. 4 hourly	60 mg/kg s.c. 4 hourly
Flunixin	2.5 mg/kg s.c., i.m. 12 hourly	2.5 mg/kg s.c., i.m. 12 hourly
Morphine	2.5 mg/kg s.c. 2–4 hourly	2.5 mg/kg s.c. 2–4 hourly
Nalbuphine	4–8 mg/kg i.m. 4 hourly	1–2 mg/kg i.m. 3 hourly
Paracetamol	300 mg/kg per os 4 hourly	100–300 mg/kg per os 4 hourly
Pentazocine	10 mg/kg s.c. 3–4 hourly	10 mg/kg s.c. 4 hourly
Phenacetin	200 mg/kg per os 4 hourly	100 mg/kg per os 4 hourly
Pethidine	10–20 mg/kg s.c. or i.m. 2–3 hourly	10–20 mg/kg s.c. or i.m. 2–3 hourly

B. Guinea pig, rabbit, dog and cat

Drug	Guinea pig	Rabbit	Dog	Cat
Aspirin	85 mg/kg per os 4 hourly	100 mg/kg per os 4 hourly	10 mg/kg per os 6 hourly	!
Buprenorphine	0.05 mg/kg s.c. 8–12 hourly	0.01–0.05 mg/kg s.c. or i.v. 8–12 hourly	0.01–0.02 mg/kg i.m., s.c., i.v. 8–12 hourly	0.005–0.01 mg/kg s.c. or i.v. 8–12 hourly
Butorphanol	–	0.1–0.5 mg/kg i.v. 4 hourly	0.4 mg/kg s.c. or i.m. 3–4 hourly	0.4 mg/kg s.c. 3–4 hourly
Codeine	–	–	0.25–0.5 mg/kg per os with paracetamol 6 hourly	–
Flunixin	–	1.1 mg/kg s.c., i.m. 12 hourly	1 mg/kg per os	1 mg/kg s.c., daily for up to 5 days
Ibuprofen	10 mg/kg i.m. 4 hourly	10 mg/kg i.v. 4 hourly	5–10 mg/kg per os 24–48 hourly	–
Morphine	2–5 mg/kg s.c. or i.m. 4 hourly	2–5 mg/kg s.c. or i.m. 2–4 hourly	0.5–5 mg/kg s.c. or i.m. 4 hourly	0.1 mg/kg s.c. 4 hourly
Nalbuphine	–	1–2 mg/kg i.v. 4–5 hourly	0.5–2.0 mg/kg s.c., i.m. 3–8 hourly	1.5–3.0 mg/kg i.v. 3 hourly

Table 15.8 (continued)

Drug	Guinea pig	Rabbit	Dog	Cat
Paracetamol	–	–	10–20 mg/kg per os plus codeine 6 hourly	!
Pentazocine	–	5 mg/kg i.v. 2–4 hourly	2 mg/kg i.m. 4 hourly	8 mg/kg i.p. 4–6 hourly
Pethidine	10–20 mg/kg s.c. or i.m. 2–3 hourly	10 mg/kg s.c. or i.m. 2–3 hourly	10 mg/kg i.m. 2–3 hourly	10 mg/kg s.c. or i.m. 2–3 hourly

C. Primates, pig, sheep and goats

Drug	Primates	Pig	Sheep and goats
Aspirin	20 mg/kg per os 6–8 hourly	–	–
Buprenorphine	0.01 mg/kg i.m. or i.v. 8–12 hourly	0.01–0.05 mg/kg i.m. 8–12 hourly	0.005–0.01 mg/kg i.m. 4–6 hourly
Flunixin	2.5 mg/kg i.m. daily	1 mg/kg s.c. daily	1 mg/kg s.c. daily
Morphine	1–2 mg/kg s.c. 4 hourly	up to 20 mg total dose i.m. 4 hourly	10 mg total dose i.m., s.c. 4 hourly
Pentazocine	2–5 mg/kg i.m. 4 hourly	2 mg/kg i.m. 4 hourly	–
Pethidine	2–4 mg/kg i.m. 3–4 hourly	2 mg/kg i.m. 4 hourly	200 mg i.m. total dose 4 hourly

Dose rates based on published data (reviewed by Flecknell, 1984 and Liles and Flecknell, 1992) and clinical experience at the Clinical Research Centre, Harrow and the Comparative Biology Centre.

of authors (Flecknell, 1984; Flecknell, 1991; Liles and Flecknell, 1992). In general, opioids are required to control post-operative pain and, of the drugs available, buprenorphine has a prolonged duration of action in most species (6–12 hours) and can be used safely to provide effective pain relief. NSAID's are generally less effective analgesics, but flunixin and carprofen appear to have a potency approaching that of some opioids (table 15.8). In many instances, effective pain relief can be provided by administering opioids during the first 24 hours post-operatively, followed by the use of a NSAID for a further 24 hours. Post-operative pain rarely seems to persist for longer than 72 hours.

Analgesics have side effects that may interfere with particular experimental protocols. Opiates can cause respiratory depression, hypotension and constipation, but these effects are rarely of clinical significance in animals. The effects of opiates can be reversed not only by naloxone but also by one of the mixed-type opioid drugs like buprenorphine, nalbuphine, or pentazocine.

NSAIDs reduce the synthesis of prostaglandins and can have negative effects on the wound-healing process, although this seems to be of little clinical significance. They can disturb blood coagulation, and some may affect renal function. Careful assessment of the pharmacology of the different analgesics available should enable an appropriate analgesic regimen to be developed. If systemic analgesics are contraindicated, surgical wounds may be infiltrated with bupivacaine, a long-acting local anaesthetic, to provide a short (4–6 h) period of analgesia.

In the post-experimental period, the animal must be observed several times a day. Attention must be paid to the surgical wound and the animal must be prevented from mutilating the affected body area, or from disturbing implanted instrumentation (catheters, transducers etc) by biting, licking or scratching. In carnivores and primates, neck collars are sometimes needed to prevent licking of the wound. In chronic experiments, it may be advisable to implant catheters and other instrumentation beneath the skin.

Euthanasia

The EC Directive (see chapter 2) states that an animal should not be kept alive after an experiment if pain and distress are likely to be experienced, and the keeping alive of the animal is not necessary in order to achieve the aims of the experiment. Laboratory animals are also killed in order to obtain organs or tissues for further experimentation, or to examine the morphological effects of the experiment.

There are some specific requirements to be considered when animals are euthanised. The most important is that the method must be humane. When organs or tissues are harvested for further experimentation, the method should have no influence on the studies which will be undertaken on these organs and tissues. Furthermore the method must be reliable and effective, economical, easy to perform, and must be safe for the laboratory personnel. Before attempting any method of euthanasia, it is essential that the personnel involved have undergone appropriate training. In addition to selecting a method of euthanasia that is humane, it is important that animals are handled carefully to minimise any distress. Vocalisations and the release of pheromones from frightened animals may cause anxiety and distress in other animals. For this reason, whenever practicable, animals should not be killed in the presence of others.

There are several methods by which animals can be killed and these can be classified into two broad groups: the pharmaco-chemical methods and the mechanical-physical methods (table 15.9).

Pharmaco-chemical methods

A drug or other chemical compound is administered that leads to the death of the animal. The most frequently used method is the administration of an over-dose of a general anaesthetic, leading to cardiac and respiratory arrest and the death of the animal. Intravenous or intraperitoneal injection of pentobarbitone (100–150 mg/kg) is frequently used because it is rapidly acting, easy to administer and relatively inexpensive. Barbiturates may cause pooling of blood in organs due to vasodilation, which may affect histological studies.

Euthanasia, using inhalational anaesthetics, can be carried out with ether, halothane, enflurane or isoflurane. Frequently, carbon dioxide is used as an inhalational agent for euthanasia. Exposure to 100% CO_2 can induce severe dyspnoea in several animal species and appears to cause distress in conscious animals. It is therefore preferable to use a combination of CO_2 and O_2 (6:4) and a humidifier. After the animal has lost consciousness, the concentration of CO_2 is raised to 100%. Animals must remain in 100% CO_2 for at least 10 minutes to ensure that they are dead. Neonatal animals are relatively resistant to the effects of CO_2, and exposure may need to be continued for 30–60 minutes, so other methods are preferable. Carbon dioxide and other inhalational agents can induce pulmonary oedema, and this may interfere with subsequent postmortem investigations.

Mechanical-physical methods

Because most pharmaco-chemical methods have the potential to interfere with certain experiments, mechanical-physical methods may be preferable e.g. for harvesting organs and tissues destined for biochemical or histological postmortem examination. Whenever possible, a sedative or anaesthetic drug should be administered before employing this method. The use of all mechanical-physical methods may be distressing to the personnel involved. This aspect should be taken into consideration when selecting a method for euthanising the animals. Physical methods include decapitation and dislocation of the cervical vertebrae. Decapitation can be performed by using scissors or a guillotine. Dislocation of the cervical vertebrae is carried out by stretching the animal and rotating the neck. The spinal cord is disrupted and nerve impulses to the vital organs such as the respiratory system and the heart are no longer transmitted. Dislocation of the cervical vertebrae is an acceptable method in mice, rats, hamsters, gerbils, puppies, kittens and small birds, but not in larger animals. If it is done quickly and expertly it is a painless method. To confirm death, this method can be followed by exsanguination or destruction of the brain.

Table 15.9
Methods of euthanasia

Drug/Method	Species	Site of action	Safety	Application	Induction rate
Ether	rodents, cats, pups, small birds	direct in-activation of cortex, subcortex, vital centres medulla oblongata	inflammable explosive	easy in perspex box	slow
Halothane	rodents, cats, pups, small birds	same as ether	chronic inhalation can be dangerous	easy to perform	quick
Carbon dioxide	rodents, cats, pups, small birds	same as ether, plus myocard depression	danger minimal	closed box	quite fast
Barbiturates	all animals	same as ether	safe	animal has to be immobilised for i.v. injection	fast induction
Cervical dislocation	laboratory animals weighing less than 200 grams	direct inactivation of brain	safe	experience and skill necessary	quite fast
Decapitation	rodents and young rabbits	direct inactivation of brain	chance of mechanical injury	easy with minimal skill	medium fast; unconscious after 13 seconds
Microwave	mice, rats and animals of equal weight	special equipment needed	no changes in tissues used for brain research	very effective if animal in correct position	only small animals
Freezing	small animals under 20 grams body weight	total inactivation of enzym activity	safe	effective liquid nitrogen	acceptable quick
T61	dogs, cats, laboratory animals, birds	anaesthesia, unconsciousness; muscle relaxation	safe in case animal can be handled easily	if not intravenously not always effective	fast induction; sometimes muscle twitching

For neonates and small animals weighing less then 20 grams, euthanasia can also be carried out by instantaneous freezing of the animals by immersing them in liquid nitrogen, although the efficacy of this procedure in producing rapid loss of consciousness has been questioned. An alternative technique is the application of microwaves to the central nervous system, which causes instantaneous death without any change in the biochemistry of the animal. If microwaves are employed, it is essential that only specially constructed apparatus is used.

Larger animals such as pigs, ruminants and horses, can be rendered unconscious by captive bolt pistols, and then killed immediately by exsanguination from a cut through the carotid arteries.

Literature

Association of Veterinary Teachers and Research Workers (1989) Guidelines for the recognition and assessment of pain in animals. University Federation for Animal Welfare, Potters Bar, Herts.

Costa D L, Lehmann J R, Harold W M and Drew R T. Transoral tracheal intubation of rodents using a fibreoptic laryngoscope. Lab Anim Science 1986; 36: 256–261.

Flecknell P A. The relief of pain in laboratory animals. Lab Anim 1984; 18: 147–160.

Flecknell P A. Laboratory animal anaesthesia. London: Academic Press: 1987.

Flecknell P A. Pain reduction and pain relief in laboratory animals. Scand J Lab Anim Sc 1991; 18: 147–155.

Flecknell P A and Mitchell M. Midazolam and fentanyl/fluanisone: assessment of anaesthetic effects in laboratory rodents and rabbits. Lab Anim 1984; 18: 143–146.

Flecknell P A, Liles J H and Williamson H A. The use of lignocaine-prilocaine local anaesthetic cream for pain-free venepuncture in laboratory animals. Lab Anim 1990; 24: 142–146.

Glen J B. Animal studies of the anaesthetic activity of ICI 35 868. Brit J Anaesth 1980; 52: 731–741.

Green C J, Knight J, Precious S and Wardley-Smith B. Alphaxalone–alphadolone anaesthesia in laboratory animals. Lab Anim 1978; 12: 85–89.

Hall L W and Clarke K W. Veterinary anaesthesia. London: Balliere-Tindall, 1991.

Kero P, Thomasson B, and Soppi A M. Spinal anaesthesia in the rabbit. Lab Anim 1981; 15: 347–348.

Liles J H and Flecknell P A. The use of non-steroidal anti-inflammatory drugs for the relief of pain in laboratory rodents and rabbits: a review. Lab Anim 1992; 26: 241–255.

Lovell D P. Variation in pentobarbitone sleeping time in mice: 1. Strain and sex differences. Lab Anim 1986; 20: 85–90.

Michell A R, Bywater R J, Clarke K W, Hall L W and Waterman A E. Veterinary fluid therapy, Oxford: Blackwell Scientific Publications, 1989.

Morton D B and Griffiths P H M. Guidelines on the recognition of pain, distress and discomfort in experimental animals and an hypothesis for assessment. Vet Rec 1985; 116: 431–436.

Nevalainen T, Phyhala L, Voipio H M and Virtanen R. Evaluation of the anaesthetic potency of medetomidine–ketamine combinations in rats, guinea pigs and rabbits. Acta Vet Scand 1989; 85: 139–143.

Remie R, Bertens A P M G, Van Dongen J J, Rensema J W and Van Wunnik G H J. Anaesthesia of the laboratory rat. In: Van Dongen J J, Remie R, Rensema J W and Van Wunnik G H J, eds. Manual of microsurgery on the laboratory rat, Part I. (Van Dongen, Remie, Rensema and Van Wunnik), Amsterdam: Elsevier, 1990 : 61–80.

Report of the AVMA panel on Euthanasia. J. Am. Vet. Med. Assoc. 1986; 188 (3): 252–268.

Short C E. Principles and practice of veterinary anaesthesia. Baltimore: Williams and Wilkins, 1987.

Whelan G and Flecknell P A. The assessment of depth of anaesthesia in animals and man. Lab Anim 1992; 26: 153–162.

16 Experimental procedures

Introduction

This chapter contains a brief description of some basic procedures, such as the administration of drugs and the collection of body fluids. Basic principles of surgery together with some surgical procedures will also be discussed. The description of technical procedures is designed to give a general background and is not intended to be used as a direct practical guide. The use of experimental techniques requires specific skills that can be obtained only by intensive and careful training under the supervision of an experienced laboratory animal scientist or animal technician. One should never use a technique that has not been fully explained and demonstrated by an experienced person. Also, practising on a dummy or a non-living or unconscious animal should always precede the use of techniques in conscious animals.

For a more detailed description of the procedures described in this chapter, see the list of recommended literature.

Administration of drugs or other substances

There are three methods for the administration of drugs to laboratory animals distinguishable by the route of administration. They are enteral, parenteral or via the skin.

Application on the skin or the mucous membranes

When using this method of application, the drug is applied in solution or ointment form on the (shaven) skin or directly on a mucous membrane. This method is not very accurate, due to the variability of skin penetration. The applied substance may cause discomfort to the animal, for example, when the drug is irritating the skin or the mucous membrane.

Fig. 16.1. Curved blunt cannula for oral dosing.

Enteral administration

In this method the substance is brought into the gastrointestinal tract via the mouth (orally) or through the anus using a suppository. The latter method is not very practical when working with small laboratory animals. The simplest procedure of administration is through the food or drinking water. This is not possible, however, with substances which are unpalatable or which irritate the gastric wall. When administered via the drinking water, the substances must be soluble and chemically stable. This method causes difficulties when it comes to measuring accurate individual doses.

It is possible, and also more accurate, to administer substances by means of a stomach tube (external diameter for mice: 0.8 mm; for rats: 1–2 mm; for guinea pigs: 1.5–2 mm; for rabbits/cats: 3–5 mm; for dogs: 5–7 mm). A curved needle with a blunt end is recommended for this purpose when dealing with small laboratory animals (fig. 16.1). The animal needs to be held firmly by the scruff whilst passing the tube along the palate into the oesophagus; the mouth can be kept open with the use of an eyelid dilator (fig. 16.2a), for larger animals e.g. dogs or pigs a surgical gag may be required (fig. 16.2b). In cats, primates and horses a catheter passed through the nose is preferable. This method, however, does require experience as it is important to prevent the tube from entering the trachea. If this does happen, the animal will cough and it is possible to feel the tube touching the cartilage rings of the trachea. Also air can be sucked or blown into the tube, which is not possible when the tube has rightly passed into the oesophagus.

The presence of condensation on a mouth glass held in front of the tube will also be an indication that the tube has passed into the trachea.

Parenteral administration

Parenteral administration refers to any method of administration other than those mentioned above, mainly, therefore, via an injection.

Injection methods.   The most frequently used injection methods are:

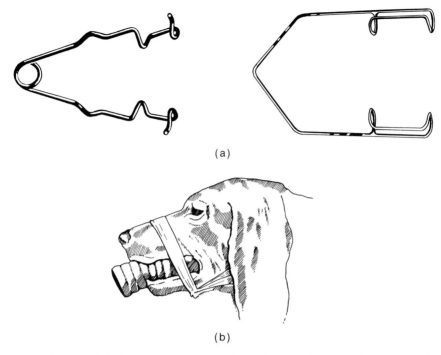

(a)

(b)

Fig. 16.2 (a) An eyelid dilator for dogs or cats can be used as a gag for small laboratory animals.
(b) Mouth gag for larger animals.

- intracutaneous (i.c.) or intradermal (i.d.): into the skin;
- subcutaneous (s.c.): under the skin; resorption of the substance is slow;
- intramuscular (i.m.): into the muscles; the muscles of the posterior thigh or back are the most commonly used; resorption is quicker but this method is as a rule more painful;
- intraperitoneal (i.p.): into the peritoneal cavity; resorption is relatively fast through the peritoneum;
- intravenous (i.v.): into the vein, this is the fastest and the most accurate method.

In table 16.1, specifications are given for several injection techniques in mammals. Table 16.2 shows injection sites in birds, reptiles and amphibians.

When applying injection techniques, there are several points that deserve special attention:

– Use clean, sharp and sterile needles.

– Use appropriate needle size. A thin needle causes less pain and prevents the fluid from flowing back. (The required thickness of the needle (gauge) will depend upon the viscosity of the fluid. When using very thin needles, there is a risk of cracking.)

Table 16.1

Techniques: some specifications per species

	Mouse 20–25 g	Hamster[3] 25–30 g	Rat 250 g	Guinea pig 350 g	Rabbit 2,5 kg
Oral	blunt cannula; firm restraint; vertical posture, pass tube along palate into oesophagus				tube and mouthgag
Max.vol.[1]	0.5	0.5–1.0	1.0	1.0	7.5
Diameter (mm)	1.0	1.0	2.0	2.0	5.0
Intracutaneous	skin of the back				
Max. volume	0.1 ml per injection site for all species				
Needle[2]	26 G				
Subcutaneous	scruff of the neck	scruff of the neck	scruff of the neck	skin over-lying neck	skin over-lying neck/back
Max. volume	0.5–1.0	0.5–1.0	1.0–5.0	1.0–2.0	1.5–5.0
Needle	26 G	26 G	24 G	24 G	21 G
Intramuscular (i.m.) muscles of the posterior thigh					
Max. volume	0.05	0.05	0.1	0.1	0.2
Needle	26 G	26 G	25 G	25 G	25 G
Intraperitoneal	lateral to the midline next to the umbilicus				
Max. volume	1.0	1.0	5.0	10.0	20.0
Needle	25 G	25 G	24 G	24 G	21 G
Intravenous	lateral tail vein	sublingual vein (diffiult)	tail vein; hindlimb vein; jugular vein	frontlimb-, hindlimb vein	marginal ear vein
Max. volume	0.2	0.3	0.5	0.5	1–5
Needle	25 G	27 G	23–25 G	26–27 G	23–21 G

[1] Maximum volume in ml; [2] needle size in G (Gauge):

27 G = 0.40 mm	23 G = 0.60 mm
26 G = 0.45 mm	22 G = 0.70 mm
25 G = 0.50 mm	20 G = 0.90 mm
24 G = 0.55 mm	19 G = 1.00 mm

– Never inject more fluid than the recommended maximum volume (table 16.1).

– Avoid air bubbles in the injection fluid (embolism).

– The injection fluid must be brought to room or body temperature prior to use. Injection of cold fluids is painful!

– Care must be taken when giving intraperitoneal injections, as there is a risk of damaging internal organs. To avoid the urinary bladder the injection should be given slightly off the midline. The needle should neither be inserted horizontally (between the skin and the abdominal wall) nor vertically (risk of causing damage to the kidney). The injection should be placed into the lower

Cat 4 kg	Dog 20 kg	Pig 50 kg	Primate 10 kg	Sheep 60 kg	Horse 500 kg
nasal tube 10.0	tube and gag 20.0	tube and gag 100	nasal tube 30	tube and gag 100	nasal tube 100
skin over-lying neck or dorsal chest 2.0 23 G	skin over-lying neck or dorsal chest 10.0 21 G	skin over-lying neck 19 G	skin over-lying neck 24 G	skin over-lying neck or dorsal chest 19 G	skin over-lying dorsal chest 19 G
muscles of the posterior thigh or back or chest 0.2 25 G	0.2 21–23 G	20 G	25 G	20 G	20 G
n/a [4]	n/a	midline between umbilicus and pelvic rim	n/a	n/a	n/a
frontlimb-, hindlimb vein 2–5 21–24 G	frontlimb-, hindlimb vein 10–15 21–24 G	ear vein; jugular vein 16–24 G	frontlimb-, hindlimb vein 21–25 G	jugular vein vein 16–19 G	jugular vein vein 16–19 G

[3] Syrian hamster; [4] not applicable.

Table 16.2

Sites of injection in birds, reptiles and amphibians

	Birds	Snakes	Tortoises	Frogs
Subcutaneous	neck	–	limb	–
Intramuscular	pectoral muscle; hind limb muscles	dorsal muscles	hind limb muscles	–
Intraperitoneal	halfway sternum-cloaca	2/3 heart-cloaca	between tail and limbs	midline
Intravenous	hind limb veins; wing vein	intracardial	ventral abdominal vein; jugular vein (anaesthetized)	–
Dorsal lymph sac	–	–	–	+

left quadrant of the abdomen. There is low risk of causing damage to the intestines (mainly due to their mobility).

– To reduce the risk of damage it is important to use a short needle.

– Some injection fluids can cause tissue irritation (for example, if the pH is too high or too low), and should therefore be administered after having been diluted with saline. These substances should, by preference, be given intravenously, as they quickly become diluted in the blood. When using the intraperitoneal route, dilution also occurs, but there is a risk of peritonitis and/or invagination of the intestines.

– Administration of large amounts of fluid should be carried out intravenously (in large animals) but can also be given intraperitoneally or orally, depending upon the experiment. Always inject slowly, especially when administering large volumes intravenously, to avoid pain and shock.

From the site of injection, drugs or other substances will be transported by the blood circulation to the target tissues. The rate of this process will depend upon the route of administration; it will be most rapid using intravenous injections and much slower when using oral administration.

Special injection techniques.   If a compound has to act directly on the brain, the blood-brain barrier can be circumvented by injecting directly into the cerebrospinal fluid. The site for this injection is the lumbosacral area (between the last lumbar vertebra and the sacrum) or the cerebello-medullary cistern (between the skull and the first cervical vertebra). It is also possible to inject compounds directly into the brain (intercranially).

For the exact administration of drugs into specific sites of the brain, a stereotactic apparatus is necessary. The head of the anaesthetized animal is fixed in such a way that the required sites of the brain can be precisely indicated, using species specific coordinates (see page 316).

Compounds can also be administered directly into other specific locations of the body, for example, into a joint or into the trachea.

Collection of body fluids

Collection of blood

Blood samples can be obtained from various sites of the body, using a variety of methods: from the veins, from the arteries, or by puncturing the orbital vessels or cardiac puncture. When repeated blood sampling is required, the implantation of indwelling cannulae should be specifically considered. The choice of the method will depend upon several factors, such as the purpose of blood collection (arterial, venous or a mixture of the two), the duration and frequency of sampling and whether or not it is a terminal experiment. It is important to choose the method of blood collection whilst designing the experiment, because in some species (for example, the hamster), collection of blood is only possible in the anaesthetized animal.

Vein puncture.   For blood collection, veins are selected which lie close to the skin and which can easily be distended by pressure. The most commonly used vessels are the veins of the neck (the jugular vein), the thigh (the femoral vein), the cephalic vein on the dorsal side of the fore limb and the saphenous vein on the medial or lateral side of the hind limb (table 16.3). With regard to rabbits, the marginal ear vein is the most commonly chosen blood vessel.

When collecting blood, the hair covering the chosen area should be clipped or shaved, then swabbed with a suitable antiseptic. Having distended the vein, using pressure, the needle should then puncture the skin and be advanced into the vein. The blood can either be allowed to drip from the needle directly into sample tubes, or a syringe or vacuum tube can be used. Before removing the needle the pressure on the vessel should be released. Haemostasis is achieved by applying gentle manual pressure.

Puncture of the orbital blood vessels.   In small rodents the veins are both small and often difficult to reach. Therefore blood sampling from the orbital blood vessels is sometimes used as an alternative. For this procedure the anaesthetized animal is firmly held by the skin at the nape of the neck. This causes distention of the jugular vein. A fine glass tube or a Pasteur's pipette is then placed at the inner canthus of the eye and gently advanced alongside the globe into the vessels. The tube ruptures the vessels and blood can be withdrawn by capillary action. Contamination with tissue fluids and porphyrins from the Harderian gland can occur. It is not possible to take sterile blood samples using this method. Also complications, such as haemorrhage, inflammation and blindness, may occur especially when the same eye is used repeatedly. Moreover, this technique may be aesthetically unpleasant for the operator to perform. For these reasons this method is not considered acceptable in some countries.

Cardiac puncture.   In this method, blood is collected directly from the ventricle of the heart of the anaesthetized animal. Puncturing the atrium can be dangerous, due to the risk of leakage into the pericardium, resulting in cardiac arrest and death. When the animal has to survive the procedure, these risks have to be taken into account.

Blood collection from arteries.   In order to obtain oxygenated blood, arteries can be punctured or cannulated. For this purpose, the femoral artery (thigh)

Table 16.3

Collection of blood: site and maximum volumes

	Mouse	Hamster	Rat	Guinea pig	Rabbit	Cat	Dog	Primate	Pig	Sheep	Horse
Jugular vein	+	+	+	+	+	+	+	+	+	+	+
Vein forelimbs						+	+	+		+	
Vein hindlimbs						+	+	+		+	
Femoral vein	+	+	+	+	+	+	+	+			
Ear vein				+	+				+		
Tail vein	+		+								
Orbital puncture	+	+	+	+					+		
Cardiac puncture	+	+	+	+	+	+	+	+	+	+	+
Tailtip	+		+								
Max. vol. (ml)	0.3	0.3	2.0	5.0	15	20	100–500[1]	20–200[1]	200–500[1]	200–600[1]	500–7000[1]

[1] Depends on body weight (see text)

or the carotids (neck) are frequently used. In rabbits, the central ear artery is most suitable.

Collection from the tail.   In small rodents, like mouse and rat, small volumes of blood, e.g. for a blood smear, may be obtained by snipping off the tip of the tail. In the rat this method can only be considered acceptable when performed under general anaesthesia. Afterwards, the wound should be cauterized. In situations where anaesthesia is contra-indicated, puncturing of the tail vein can be useful. The tail must first be warmed in order to dilate the vessels. The animal should be placed into a restraining device, after which a "butterfly" needle (23 G–19 G) is introduced into the lateral tail vein and blood can then be dripped directly into a sample tube. If a vein is punctured percutaneously (through the skin), contamination with tissue fluids may occur, which can influence the outcome of the experiments. If the experiment requires sterile blood, then surgical exposure of the vein under anaesthesia may be necessary.

Collection site in other species.   In birds, blood samples can be obtained by cardiac puncture or by a small incision in the comb. The wing vein, the limb vein or the jugular vein can also be used. In tortoises and snakes, cardiac puncture or puncture of the jugular vein can be performed under anaesthesia.

Maximum volumes.   The total volume of blood in a living animal is rather constant and is about 8% of its body weight. If the sample volume exceeds 10% of the total blood volume, hypovolaemia and cardiovascular failure ("shock") may occur. As a general rule, a maximum of approximately 8 ml/kg bwt can be removed (table 16.3).

Implantation of indwelling cannulae.   For blood collection, the same size needles can be used as for intravenous administration of drugs. In large animals, trocars (large hollow needles containing a sharp metal wire) can be used. Sometimes repeated blood sampling is required. In larger animals (the size of the rabbit or larger), it is possible to perform vein punctures daily. In small rodents, an indwelling cannula can be implanted via the jugular vein into the cranial vena cava or via the femoral vein into the caudal vena cava. The catheter should be looped under the skin of the neck or the back, respectively, exteriorized at the top of the head and secured there with screws and acrylic glue. The catheter's dead space is usually filled with polyvinylpyrolidone, in saline with heparin (PVP-solution).

Exsanguination.   To obtain the maximum amount of blood, decapitation can be performed using a guillotine or scissors, or by puncturing the aorta under anaesthesia. In this way about 30 ml/kg bwt or up to 50% of the total blood volume can be obtained. In mice, exsanguination is also possible by removing the eyeball under anaesthesia and collecting blood from the eye artery.

Collection of faeces and urine

Metabolic cages (fig. 16.3).   Metabolic cages must be used for the quantitative collection of excreta, such as urine and faeces. The animals are housed

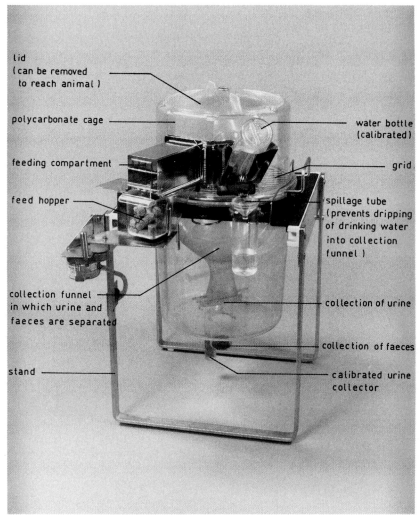

Fig. 16.3. Metabolic cage for small rodents facilitating the separate collection of urine and faeces.

on a grid above a funnel in which the urine and/or faeces are collected and separated.

Mice and rats often urinate and/or defecate purely as a result of being picked up, which may provide the opportunity for collecting small samples of urine and faeces.

Catheterization.   In several species, it is possible to collect urine by urethral catheterization. A catheter is introduced into the urethra and aseptically advanced up into the bladder. In male animals this procedure is relatively simple due to the fact that the urethra terminates in the penis; however, it is necessary to use sedation in some species e.g. the cat.

In the majority of female mammals the urethra opens into the vagina and is not visible. In the mouse, the rat, the hamster and the guinea pig, however, the urethra and the vaginal orifice are completely separate. The urethral orifice is located ventrally from the vaginal orifice. If catheterization has to be performed in female animals, very detailed knowledge of the anatomy is required, together with well developed technical skills.

The outer diameter of the catheter used will depend upon the species (for example, for a guinea pig: 0.5 mm, for a dog: 3 mm).

Collection of other body fluids

Other body fluids which are sometimes collected are cerebrospinal fluid (liquor), bile, lymph or ascites fluid.

Liquor.   The collection of liquor can be achieved at two different places: by puncturing the cerebello-medullary cistern between the skull and the first cervical vertebra (atlas) or from the lumbosacral space between the last lumbar vertebra and the sacrum. The dura mater should be punctured between the vertebrae with a cannula containing a mandrin. The mandrin should then be removed and cerebrospinal fluid can be collected using suction. The procedure is generally carried out under sedation or local anaesthesia.

Bile.   For the collection of bile in the rat, the abdomen of the anaesthetized animal is opened and a cannula is introduced into the bile duct (ductus choledochus). The bile duct runs from the portal area of the liver to the duodenum. This procedure is generally part of a terminal experiment, as no bile passes to the intestines after cannulation and therefore digestion of food will be impaired. For chronic experiments, a loop can be made in the bile duct.

Lymph.   For the collection of lymph the thoracic duct, which lies ventral to the spine between the vertebrae and the aorta, can be cannulated.

Ascites fluid.   The implantation of hybridomas into the peritoneal cavity of mice and rats makes it possible to obtain monoclonal antibodies. The animals will produce peritoneal fluid (ascites), into which the monoclonal antibodies are secreted. The ascites can then be collected and the monoclonal antibodies purified. The amount of ascites should not exceed 20% of the bodyweight. The collection of ascites through puncturing should preferably be performed under general anaesthesia. It is not advisable to puncture more than once, as haemorrhages or peritonitis can result. It should be mentioned that this technique may cause severe discomfort to the animal. *In vitro* techniques must be used whenever possible.

Surgical procedures

Introduction

Surgical procedures may be carried out on laboratory animals for various reasons, e.g. for the teaching of technical skills, the testing of surgical techniques or materials, or for obtaining a (patho)physiological model (such as a renal arterystenosis for the induction of a hypertensive model, or a partial hepatectomy for the induction of a regeneration model).

In recent years, a distinction is often made between macro- and micro-surgery. The term microsurgery refers to surgery which is performed under an operation microscope. This development has facilitated organ transplantations even within small rodents e.g. the rat.

The performance of surgical procedures requires specific skills which can only be gained by training under experienced supervision in a well-equipped laboratory. Specific knowledge with reference to anaesthesiology and anatomy is a prerequisite.

Hygiene and asepsis

Every surgical procedure brings with it the risk of infection. Attention must be paid to asepsis (prevention of contamination through working under sterile conditions) and also, where necessary, to antisepsis (prevention of infections by using disinfectants, for example). The operating room, the animal, the surgeon and the instruments are all possible sources of contamination. Although an operation will never be performed under entirely sterile conditions, it is possible to minimize risks by taking adequate precautions. Work should be carried out in clean rooms. After having removed the hair, the incision area should be prepared with antiseptics such as 70% ethyl alcohol and/or iodine solution. Sterile drapes and instruments should be used along with sterile clothing i.e. gowns, gloves, face masks, caps etc. In practice, these precautions are usually not fully applied when using small rodents, although it has never been substantiated that these animals can resist surgically induced infection better than other animals. This implies that, for small rodents, it is also advisable to work under aseptic conditions and, if necessary, in combination with antibiotic prophylaxis.

Instruments (fig. 16.4)

A great variety of surgical instruments is available. A basic set of instruments would consist of: a scalpel, straight or curved anatomical forceps, straight or curved surgical forceps, ring-handled preparation scissors (sharp/sharp and

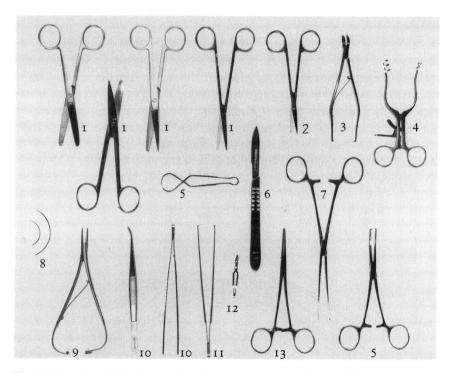

Fig. 16.4. Overview of a basic set of surgical instruments. *1* = ring handled scissors, (straight and curved, blunt/blunt, blunt/sharp, sharp/sharp). *2* = preparation scissors. *3* = skin clamp applicator. *4* = wound holder. *5* = towel clip. *6* = scalpel, holder and blade. *7* = serrated tip forceps (Pean). *8* = needles. *9* = needle holder. *10* = anatomical forceps (curved and straight). *11* = surgical forceps. *12* = bulldog haemostatic clamp. *13* = rat-toothed tip forceps (Kocher).

sharp/blunt), towel clips, artery forceps, a needle holder, needles, skin clamps and a skin clamp applicator or suture material. Some procedures will require specific instruments in addition to those mentioned, for example, a wound holder.

Haemorrhages

Specific knowledge of the anatomy of the blood vessels is a prerequisite for successful surgery. Some bleeding during surgery is inevitable, but severe loss of blood can be prevented by blunt dissection or by avoiding sanguinary tissues. For example, less bleeding will occur when using the linea alba instead of an incision through the abdominal muscles when performing abdominal surgery. When employing blunt dissection, the closed scissors are brought into the tissues and then opened, thereby tearing the tissue from the blood vessels. Haemostasis can be aided by electrocautery, or by ligating the blood vessel with thread, or with clamps (liga-clamps).

Suturing

The closing of the incision at the end of a surgical procedure generally requires the restoration of the original anatomical situation. The various tissue layers which were separated have to be sutured. For example, in the case of an incision into the abdominal wall, the peritoneum, the abdominal muscles, the subcutaneous tissue and the skin must be sutured (fig. 16.5). Sometimes two layers are sutured simultaneously e.g. the peritoneum with the abdominal muscles and the skin with the subcutaneous tissue. It is vital that no subcutaneous cavity develops, in which germs can multiply, thus causing inflammations.

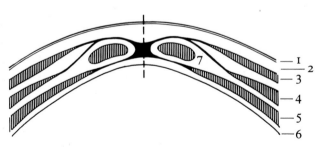

Fig. 16.5. Section through the skin and the abdominal wall. The incision should preferably be made along the midline (linea alba). *1* = skin, *2* = subcutis, *3* = m. obliquus abdominis ext., *4* = m. obliquus abdominis int., *5* = m. transversus abdominis, *6* = peritoneum, *7* = m. rectus abdominis.

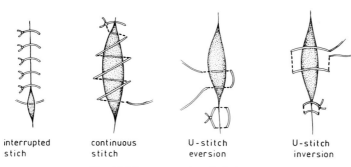

| interrupted stich | continuous stitch | U-stitch eversion | U-stitch inversion |

Fig. 16.6 Some examples of stitches.

The most basic stitches are shown in fig. 16.6: the interrupted stitch and the continuous stitch. The continuous stitch can be executed quicker than the interrupted stitch but, if the suture breaks, the wound can unravel completely and therefore this method is not recommended for larger wounds. A variant of the interrupted stitch is the U-stitch, which allows both inversion and eversion of the wound edges. Inverted stitches are used when closing the urinary bladder and the uterus; the mucosal layer is not pierced (risk of leakage), only the muscle layer and the serosa. Everted stitches are used for the skin, as they minimize the risk of contamination of the wound. Stitches should not be applied too tightly, since this causes local tissue damage and necrosis. A certain degree of swelling of the wound can be expected to occur under normal conditions.

Suture material can be either absorbable or non-absorbable. Absorbable material can be made from catgut, vicryl or dexon, which vary in absorption rate. Non-absorbable material can be cotton, silk, mersilene, nylon or stainless steel.

Absorbable material is not as strong as non-absorbable material, and is more expensive.

Non-absorbable suture material, however, has the disadvantage that it can cause fistulas when remaining within the body. Threads can be made by one fibre (monofil) or plaited by several fibres (polyfil). Suture material is available in various diameters, from 5 to 12-0 USP (= U.S. Pharmacopea, where thread diameters are described, 5 being the thickest and 12-0 the thinnest). The chosen diameter will depend upon the tissue and the tension.

Needles with eyes have to be threaded manually and the needle eye can cause tissue damage. A system which causes less damage to the tissue is where the needle is bonded to the thread (atraumatic).

Needles can be obtained in a variety of curved or straight shapes and sizes. Their tips are, as a rule, either round or triangular. The latter, hav-

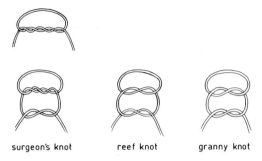

surgeon's knot   reef knot   granny knot

Fig. 16.7. Some examples of knots.

ing cutting edges, are generally used for piercing through tough tissue such as skin. Round-tipped needles are used for soft tissue, such as the intestines.

Having placed the stitches, the suture has to be knotted (fig. 16.7). One such possibility is a surgeon's knot, in which the first half hitch contains an extra twist to prevent slipping, for example, for tissues under tension. A reef knot can also be used, for example, for skin. A granny knot should not be used, because it comes undone easily. Skin wounds can be closed using metal clamps, using application forceps.

Wound treatment

The wound requires daily inspection. A drain which has been placed into the wound, can be removed after 2–3 days. Draining the wound may be necessary if the wound has been contaminated, or when a quantity of exudate is expected.

A wound which is closed properly and heals normally, requires no special treatment. Post-operative infections should be treated with antibiotics.

It is advisable to allow an infected wound to heal per secundam by forming scabs, whilst treating them with saline and mild disinfectants (Hibitane®, Betadin®).

Post-operative care

If the animal has lost much blood and/or fluids during an operation, then fluid therapy may be necessary. Small laboratory animals should be treated after an operation with saline given subcutaneously to prevent dehydration.

Hypothermia must be prevented. This can be achieved by the use of heating aids, such as aluminium foil or cotton wool placed over the body, or with lamps and heating pads.

The wound should be inspected daily. If the animal is trying to remove the stitches, dressings or an Elizabethan collar should be applied. Sutures or skin clamps should be removed after 7–10 days.

Post-operative analgesia.   See chapter 15.

Invasive techniques

Ectomies.   One of the purposes of surgical procedures is the creation of a specific animal model. An important technique used to achieve this is the ectomy. Ectomy (ectomein: to cut out) means the removal of organs or parts of organs. The reason for carrying out this procedure may be the study of the effect of the removal of certain hormones. The most frequently used ectomies in laboratory animals involve the endocrine and the immune system.

The endocrine system:
- hypophysectomy (hypophysis): the central regulation of the endocrine system is removed;
- (para)thyroidectomy ((para)thyroid glands): these glands are located in the neck region lateroventral to the larynx); it is difficult to remove these separately;
- pancreatectomy (pancreas);
- adrenalectomy (adrenals);
- gonadectomy (gonads).

The immune system:
- thymectomy (thymus; located centrally in the thoracic cavity): not used very often anymore, since the development of genetically thymus-deficient animals, the so-called "nude mouse" or "nude rat";
- lymphadenectomy (lymph nodes);
- splenectomy (spleen).

Other ectomies:
- hepatectomy (liver): generally one lobe is removed, a so-called partial hepatectomy. To reach the liver, located in the cranial part or the abdominal cavity, a laparotomy is necessary;
- nephrectomy (kidney);
- hysterectomy (uterus);
- removal of parts of the brain.

Fistulas.   Fistulas are artificial orifices within the body (stomata), which open into certain parts of the gastrointestinal tract, the gall bladder or the urinary bladder. Fistulas to the gastrointestinal tract can be used in studies of the digestion of nutrients, together with studies of secretory products from the gastrointestinal tract.

Transplantations.   Formerly, the most frequently performed transplantation was (partial) skin transplantation for genetic quality monitoring of inbred strains. At present, other methods for controlling the genetic integrity of inbred strains are increasingly being used (chapter 7). Transplantation of lungs, heart, liver, kidney and pancreas can also be performed in laboratory animals. Due to the development of microsurgery, these techniques can be carried out in animals as small as the rat. The purpose of these procedures is to study reject reactions, and to test medications which can prevent the rejection.

Implantations.   Implantation means the introduction of tissue from one individual into another. The implantation of tumour material is common, especially in the "nude mouse", into which human tumour material is often brought. This technique is carried out frequently under the skin, but can also be performed in other areas, for example, under the capsule of the kidney or liver, or in the cheek pouch of the hamster.

Shunts.   Shunts are connections between blood vessels, which are generally made between arteries and veins e.g. the arterio-venous shunt between the carotid artery and the jugular vein. Shunts between veins can, however, also be made, such as a portocaval shunt between the portal vein and the caudal vena cava. Blood coming from the intestines will not reach the liver, but will pass directly to the caudal vena cava.

Stereotactical procedures

In brain research, stereotactical techniques are commonly employed for the application of unipolar or bipolar needle electrodes into several areas of the brain. Through these electrodes, potentials can be diverted or current pulses can be administered. The same techniques can be used to introduce thin cannulae into the brain, through which small amounts of drugs can be administered which will either stimulate or inhibit the function of some areas of the brain.

   For the application of instruments into special areas of the brain, a stereotactic atlas and a stereotactic apparatus are needed. These use a three-dimensional classification of the brain, derived from the bony skull. There are three distinguishable planes:

   – a horizontal plane which passes through the centre of the bony outer ear and the rim of the orbit (in the mouse, rat and guinea pig this is the maxillar rim between the incisors);

– a frontal plane which passes through the centre of the bony outer ear and runs perpendicular to the horizontal plane;

– a sagittal plane which passes through the median of the skull and runs perpendicular to the horizontal plane.

Using the stereotactic apparatus and the coordinates from the atlas, electrodes or cannulas can be implanted into specific defined areas of the brain.

Perfusions

Perfusion refers to the act of flushing the body or an organ with fluids. The blood is removed from the body and/or the organ and replaced with perfusion fluid. The animal will not survive such an experiment unless just one organ is perfused (e.g. isolated, perfused kidney). The arteries and the veins of the organ (in the liver also the portal vein) are freed from the surrounding tissue in the anaesthetized animal. A cannula is introduced into the artery and fixed using a ligature. After cutting through the veins and the arteries, the organ is removed from the body and the cannula is connected to the perfusion fluid. The organ can now be studied extracorporally for a while, or cells can be isolated for an *in vitro* cell culture.

Imaging techniques

Radiological studies are frequently performed upon laboratory animals. This requires knowledge regarding adequate anaesthesia and cannulation techniques. When contrast fluid has been introduced through the cannulae, the blood flow through the organ can be studied.

Scanning techniques are used for the study of organ transplants and for tumour growth. For this technique, special radioactively labelled substances are injected which attach themselves to the transplanted tissue or tumour material. The volume of the transplantant or tumour can be estimated by a scanner. In a CT-scan (computer tomography) the absorption of photons is used. With NMR (nuclear magnetic resonance) a superior tissue differentiation can be achieved. NMR is a technique whereby differences in magnetic quality of compounds within different tissues become visible and result in an image of the tissue. The signal is derived from protons of the compounds present in the body.

Literature

Anderson R M, Romfh R F. Technique in the use of surgical tools. New York: Appleton-Century-Crofts, 1980.

Boer J de, Archibald J, Dowe H G, eds. An introduction to experimental surgery. Amsterdam: Excerpta Medica, 1975.

Dongen J J van, Remie R, Rensema J W, Wunnik G H J van. Manual of microsurgery of the laboratory rat. Amsterdam: Elsevier, 1990.

First report of the BVA/FRAME/RSPCA/UFAW Joint Working Group on Refinement. Removal of blood from laboratory animals and birds. Laboratory Animals 27, 1–22, 1993.

Tuffery A A, ed. Laboratory animals: an introduction for new experimenters. Chichester: Wiley, 1987.

Waynforth H B. Experimental and surgical technique in the rat. London: Academic Press, 1980.

17 Alternatives to animal experimentation

Introduction

The concept of alternative methods has already been discussed in chapter 1. To summarize, every method or procedure that results in the replacement of an animal experiment, or the reduction of the number of animals required, or the refinement of procedures so that animal suffering is reduced, is considered to be an alternative method. This definition corresponds to the "Three Rs" of Russell and Burch.

Although widespread acceptance of this concept of alternative methods is relatively recent, several methods are already in existence which have resulted in the replacement, reduction or refinement of animal use.

The introduction of anaesthetics was very significant for the refinement of animal experiments. Ether was the first anaesthetic to be administered to a human patient, in 1846. Soon afterwards the same substance was also used in animal experiments. In Great Britain, the use of anaesthetics was made compulsory for painful experiments in 1876, on the introduction of the Cruelty to Animals Act.

Tissue culture is another alternative approach which has a long history. In 1885, Wilhelm Roux succeeded in keeping cells from a chicken embryo alive in a warm saline solution. Growth of cells *in vitro* (literally: in glass), was described for the first time in 1907 by Ross Harrison. The cell culture technique expanded rapidly after the introduction of antibiotics. The addition of antibiotics to the culture medium opened up the possibility of culturing cells under relatively simple conditions. Recent developments in this field are specifically related to the standardization of cell culturing techniques. Synthetic culture fluids are of a major interest, as they can replace serum factors such as hormones, which can vary considerably with regard to both quality and quantity.

The impetus for the development of alternative methods may to a large extent be ethical, but other factors also play a role. The use of laboratory animals is expensive, and the performance of animal experiments is time-consuming and often difficult to standardize. Alternative methods which allow the replacement of the whole animal are usually less complex and the experimental conditions are easier to standardize. However, it should be pointed out that the simplicity of an alternative may be its strength, especially when mechanisms at the organ/tissue/cell level are under investigation; but can also be its weakness, due to the fact that the response in a simplified system may differ from the response of the organism as a whole. This can be a drawback, just as species differences limit the application to man of data obtained in animal experiments.

When considering the impact of alternative methods on the reduction of animal usage, it is important to make a distinction between fundamental or innovative research and applied research.

Generally speaking, the introduction of an alternative method is easier in fundamental or innovative research than in applied research. The effect on the use of animals, however, can be restricted because of the unique nature of many experimental procedures within fundamental research.

A great deal of applied research, such as safety testing, requires strict confirmation to standard operating procedures and regulatory guidelines. The introduction of alternative methods in this field needs the approval of national regulatory agencies, such as the US Food and Drug Administration (FDA) as well as international organizations such as the World Health Organization (WHO) and the Organization for Economic Coordination and Development (OECD).

To gain such approval, extensive validation studies have to be carried out. For this reason, the introduction of alternative methods within applied research is very laborious and time-consuming, but the impact it can have could be substantial, especially if the guidelines and regulations of the various countries were uniform. Unfortunately, this is rarely the case, and products are still often tested according to different national test requirements.

The optimalization and harmonization of the requirements of animal test procedures, and the mutual recognition of test results, would not only reduce the number of animals used, but would also speed up the introduction of alternative methods.

This chapter aims to give a short review of some categories of alternative methods, each with its own advantages and limitations.

The British organisation, FRAME (Fund for the Replacement of Animals in Medical Experiments), has classified alternative methods according to the technique or methodology applied. Although mainly restricted to replacement and reduction, in this chapter the classification laid down by FRAME will be followed to a large extent. The following items will be dealt with:

– *in vitro* techniques;
– the use of lower organisms;
– immunological techniques;
– quantitative structure–activities relationship analysis;
– mathematical modelling of physiological processes;
– human models;
– other alternative methods.

In addition, attention will be given to the storage, exchange and use of experimental data, to the use of alternative methods in education, and to the effects of alternative methods on animal use statistics.

In vitro techniques

Tissue cultures are, at present, the most important category of alternative methods to animal experimentation.

The term "tissue culture" encompasses a broad collection of techniques which are used to keep cells, tissues, organs or parts of organs alive outside the body in a nutrient culture medium, for at least 24 hours. An environment is created for the living cell, which resembles, as far as possible, the normal physiological conditions found *in vivo*.

Tissue cultures can be divided into two main categories: organotypic cultures and cell cultures. *Organotypic cultures* consist of parts of a tissue or organ, or sometimes an intact (e.g. embryonic) organ, which has been placed into culture medium. The aim of organotypic culture is to maintain the structural and functional relationships between the cells and tissues of the organ in question.

However, the compact three-dimensional structure of organotypic cultures obstructs nutrients from reaching all the cells. This means that organotypic cultures usually have only a limited life-span. When employing this technique, fresh material from animals or humans is required for each experiment.

Cell cultures can be distinguished from organotypic cultures, due to the fact that the connection between the individual cells is broken down chemically or mechanically. When dispersed cells are placed in culture medium, this is known as a primary cell culture. If the cells are cultured for more than one generation, they are called secondary or tertiary cell cultures. Depending upon the type of cell and the technique used, cells can be kept as a monolayer or as a cell suspension. The life time of primary cell cultures is limited. In some cases, the cells can be transformed into *continuous* cell cultures; this means that they retain the potential to divide "for ever" if treated appropri-

Table 17.1

Poliomyelitis vaccine production: the impact of changes in methodology on the number of monkeys used in The Netherlands

Year	Technique	Number of monkeys per year
1965	– use of imported monkeys	
	– dissociation of cells by *in vivo* trypsinization of kidneys	4570
	– culturing of cells in monolayers	
1970	– replacement of monolayers by culturing on Sephadex micro carriers	1590
1975	– replacement of imported monkeys by captive bred monkeys	463
1980	– replacement of primary cell cultures by tertiary cultures	
	– replacement of *in vivo* trypsinization by *in vitro* trypsinization	47
Near future	– use of cell lines instead of cell cultures	0

ately. The culturing of cells usually results in the loss of morphological and biochemical properties, resulting in a progressive divergence from features of the original cell type.

Cell cultures have a wide application, for example in pharmacology for receptor binding studies. They are also frequently used in vaccine production; for example, in the Netherlands the poliomyelitis vaccine is produced from kidney cells of the monkey (*Macaca fascicularis*). The effect of technical improvements of the *in vitro* production of this vaccine on the number of monkeys required in the Netherlands is shown in table 17.1.

Use of lower species

There are some situations where the use of lower organisms, such as bacteria, moulds, insects, molluscs or yeasts, can reduce the required number of vertebrate animals. One example of this is the use of bacteria in the Ames Test, to screen new compounds for mutagenic properties, which are believed to be one of the causes of carcinogenesis. The test is used as an indicator of the potential carcinogenic properties of a compound. Frequently, compounds which have a positive result in the Ames Test, will not be tested any further (*in vivo*). However, there is growing evidence that the predictive value of the Ames Test is rather limited. The Ames Test is often considered to be complementary to the existing animal tests. The introduction of the Ames Test has not contributed greatly to the reduction in animal use, but has resulted in a marked increase in the number of chemicals screened for potential carcinogenicity.

Another example of the use of lower organisms as an alternative method is the Limulus Amoebocyte Lysate test (LAL), which is used for pyrogenicity testing. Until recently, rabbits were used exclusively for this test, which is requested for all materials that will be administered parenterally. If there is a certain increase of body temperature after the intravenous administration of the test material, it is considered to be pyrogenic. In the LAL test, the amoebocyte lysate is extracted from blood cells of *Limulus polyphemus* (the horseshoe crab). This lysate is converted into a gel by endotoxin, which is the most important pyrogenic compound.

The LAL test greatly reduced the number of rabbits used for this purpose, despite the fact that, for a number of products, the LAL test cannot be applied for technical reasons.

It should be realized that ethical objections which are voiced against the use of vertebrates, may be equally applicable to some classes of invertebrates. For example, it is known that the nervous system of many cephalopod molluscs is extremely well developed and is comparable in several aspects with the nervous systems of lower vertebrates.

Immunological techniques

Immunological techniques form the basis for a number of *in vitro* methods. Their application is especially useful in diagnostic testing, vaccine quality control and fundamental immunological research. Well-known techniques in this area include the *enzyme linked immunosorbent assay* (ELISA), the *haemagglutination test* and the *radioimmuno assay* (RIA). These *in vitro* assays are very sensitive, but in some cases they lack specificity i.e. in the ability to distinguish between related antigens or antibodies, so an animal test is still necessary.

In 1975, Köhler and Milstein made a special contribution to the improvement of the specificity of antibodies. They succeeded in producing hybridoma cells by fusing antibody-producing lymphocytes and a certain type of lymphoid cell-derived cancer cells, namely, myeloma cells. After selection and cloning, each hybridoma cell clone is able to produce an antigen-specific antibody (a monoclonal antibody).

Until recently, many animals, particularly mice, were used for the production of monoclonal antibodies. These animals were injected intraperitoneally with hybridoma cells. After ten to fourteen days, the ascites fluid containing the monoclonal antibodies could be collected. This technique causes substantial suffering to the animals, due to the fact that the ascites fluid increases pressure on the organs in the abdomen and in the thoracic cavity (fig. 17.1).

Fig. 17.1. *In vivo* production of monoclonal antibodies by means of ascites in the mouse.

This *in vivo* production can now be replaced by *in vitro* techniques, for example by culturing hybridoma cells *in vitro* in fermentation and/or dialysing systems (fig. 17.2). By improving and making optimal use of the existing

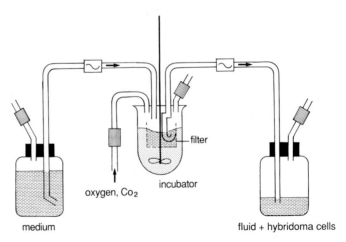

Fig. 17.2. *In vitro* production of monoclonal antibodies in a continuous perfusion system. Hybridoma cells are in the incubator (centre). The monoclonal antibodies, together with the culture medium, are sucked away and collected in the right-hand vessel. The culture medium is added from the left-hand vessel.

systems, *in vitro* monoclonal antibody production is now gradually replacing the *in vivo* production in mice.

Quantitative structure–activity relationship analysis

It is well known that a relationship exists between molecular structure, the physical–chemical properties and the biological activities of compounds. Using this knowledge, it is possible to predict the biological activities of many types of new compounds, for example their toxicity, or to improve the effectiveness of drugs by introducing minor changes into their molecular structures. This method can also be used to select and prioritize when analyzing a series of related compounds. An initial screening can be made, ensuring that only a small number of drugs, selected from a much larger number of potential candidate compounds, are tested on animals.

For the development of new drugs, profound and detailed knowledge is vital, for example knowledge of the three-dimensional structure of the receptor or about the biological processes that are involved in its effects. Specific groups of atoms, the placing of groups within the molecule, electron charges, etc., may all contribute to the biological activity of the drug and therefore must be understood and taken into account.

Biological activity can only be defined by (animal) research and human experience when working with known substances, although *in vitro* studies are making an increasing contribution. The computer can then be used to design new compounds with the required structures.

In the past, chemists used three-dimensional models to gain insight into the shape and dimensions of molecules, and for searching for relationships between molecules. New developments in computer graphics now provide the opportunity to visualize molecules on the computer screen. It is also possible to rotate the molecules on the screen, thereby visualizing changes in conditions and electron charges. The molecules can also be manipulated, enabling energy changes within the molecule to become visible, for example to investigate how a substance interacts with a receptor.

The structures of two or more substances can be visualized and compared, so that similarities and differences become clear. Three-dimensional graphics can show whether the compound fits with the receptor. This technique can help to discover compounds with specific activities and to screen out compounds, which are not likely to be effective.

This phase in drug discovery must always be followed by *in vitro* tests and animal experiments. However the number of compounds which needs to be tested on animals can be reduced by a preliminary selection on the basis of desired biological activity.

Mathematical modelling of physiological processes

Many of the processes which take place in living organisms can be expressed as mathematical equations, so mathematical models of many physiological, biochemical, pathological and toxicological events can be developed. In most cases, these models are produced and used on computers, so they are known as computer models or computer simulations.

Computer simulations are often based upon empirical data; i.e. the mechanism of the process is not yet fully understood, but the computer can provide a simulation comparable with what is known from real experiments.

A wide variety exists in the complexity of computer models, ranging from the dynamics of subcellular processes, which can be described as linear functions, to the simulation of a complete organism, in which the simulation consists of a series of multi-dimensional functions.

Simple models have the advantage that they can give a clear insight into the relationship between different parameters. However, the simpler the model, the more likely it is to be incomplete and therefore to give an inaccurate view of the real situation. Complex models come closer to reality, but the system may become too complex to understand and to provide a useful insight into the process under investigation.

For the development of models, a detailed knowledge of the *in vivo* process being researched is also required. This knowledge can only be gained by means of animal experiments and human experience. If a "complete" model is to be built, all processes that exist *in vivo* must be described in advance.

When the point is reached at which it is possible to construct a sufficiently complete model, there would be no justification for carrying out further research on animals. However, since most computer models can only provide an approximation of reality, a (limited) number of animal experiments remain necessary for this purpose, for example in order to complete and verify the data which has been collected from the predictive model. It is also possible that the computer model will produce new hypotheses, and that more animals will then have to be used to investigate these hypotheses. This means that the number of animals used can even increase as a result of mathematical modelling.

Human models

Most of the results that have been obtained through experimenting on animals will be applied to man. This implies that the human being would be a better model for research and testing. However, there are not only ethical, but also legal and practical objections against the use of human models. Nevertheless, there are some occasions when humans can justifiably be used as test subjects. One such example is in drug development. National and international authorities require tests on safety and effectiveness to be performed, before any newly developed drug can be registered. Initially, the new drug is tested upon animals, which reduces the risk to humans in the subsequent clinical trial phase. As in the case of animals, human "guinea pigs" can only be used in compliance with strict regulations. The risk involved must not outweigh the desired effect hopefully to be achieved through the treatment. When performing such a clinical test on healthy people, only a minimal risk can be tolerated. There must not be any irreversible side effects from the treatment. Patients and healthy volunteers must be fully informed prior to the commencement of the experiment, and approval from a medical ethical committee must be attained.

When using human volunteers, the problem of inter-species extrapolation is bypassed. Extrapolating data from animal experiments to man can cause problems due to the differences between man and animals, with respect to anatomy, physiology, biokinetics, and pharmacological and toxicological responses. It is also possible that some effects which may occur in humans, for example dizziness, changes in mood, etc., are either not noticeable in the animal, or may occur at such a low frequency as not to be detected. By using human volunteers, these problems are to a great extent removed; the results only have to be extrapolated within the same species.

Other alternative methods

Many compounds which enter an organism will undergo biotransformation. Absorption, distribution and excretion also play a major role in determining the concentration of a potential drug or toxicant at target sites. Insight into these processes will facilitate and improve the extrapolation of the results from animal tests and their application to man.

Until recently, invasive methods were generally used, when studying the biokinetics, but new non-invasive techniques are now available. One such example is nuclear magnetic resonance (NMR), also known as magnetic resonance imaging (MRI). This technique is based upon the fact that the nuclei of atoms such as carbon, hydrogen and phosphorus, return to their original energy level after being brought into imbalance from strong magnetic forces. Biokinetic processes can be observed in detail using this technique.

In some cases, for example with demonstrations for teaching purposes, the use of laboratory animals can be replaced by using organs obtained from the slaughterhouse. Another example of this is the use of bovine eyes from the slaughterhouse for the *in vitro* eye irritation test, in place of the Draize test, one of the routine toxicity tests, which is performed on rabbits. Some parameters of the rabbit eye irritation test can be simulated very well using isolated eyes of calves (or chickens) from the slaughterhouse. Total replacement of the eye irritation test on rabbits will only be possible if the other aspects of the test (e.g. inflammation and recovery from damage) can also be replaced. In order to achieve this, the non-animal test will need to be extended by using the chorio-allantois membrane (CAM) of embryonated chicken eggs and cell culture systems.

The number of animals required for standard tests can also be reduced as the quality of the animals improves. This can be illustrated by the following example. Potency testing is an important part of the quality control of inactivated vaccines. These tests are obligatory for every new batch of vaccine, and many animals are therefore used in these tests. The WHO and the European Pharmacopoeia have formulated guidelines for these tests. One of the requirements, which directly effects the number of animals used, is related to the statistical reliability of the potency test. In the past, approximately 20 animals per vaccine dose had to be used in each potency test in order to fulfil the statistical standards laid down by the regulators. By improving the quality of the animals used, and thereby increasing standardization, the number of animals needed for potency testing can be decreased. By means of a computer simulation test, the effects of smaller numbers of animals on the 95% confidence interval in potency tests has been calculated. This has shown that, when high quality animals are used, the number of animals can be reduced from 20 to 12 per vaccine dose, while still maintaining the reliability of the test.

Storage, exchange and use of research data

In many cases, the decision whether or not to perform an animal experiment is based upon the results of previous animal experiments, as the hypothesis to be tested is deduced from earlier results. This implies that, as in other branches of science, easy access to research data is a prerequisite for progress. Thus, for the scientist, as well as for the animal, it is very important that all relevant data are kept up to date and are readily available.

Scientific journals are the most important source of information, as these cover the latest results of research. Journals are a *primary* source of information. Information from congresses, etc. also belongs to this primary information category. *Secondary* source information is obtained from other publications, such as books, review articles, reports, etc. Reference manuals, citation indexes and data books also belong to this category.

Apart from these two categories, there is also the "grey" literature, which consists of reports that are not formally published (lectures, symposium reports, invited papers, etc.). Publications which are "in preparation" also belong to this group.

Generally speaking, the accessibility of data from the primary and secondary sources is satisfactory. Most scientists working in the field of innovative scientific research have access to computerized databases or CD-ROM for literature retrieval. Information can also be exchanged at congresses and other scientific meetings. Also databases covering all aspects of animal experimentation and alternatives are being developed. In this context PREX should be mentioned. This is an on-line information service of the Utrecht University with databases on various fields of laboratory animal science. These databases are available by computer network or modem connections.

With routine protocol testing, for example toxicity testing, the results are reported only to those who initiated the experiment and the regulatory authorities for which the tests were conducted. The results are not usually published in the open, peer-reviewed literature.

In animal experiments, data are obtained from both control animals (no treatment applied) and from test animals. The control animals are used as a "yardstick", as they supply reference values for physiological, immunological, morphological and other data. This data can be extremely valuable, but can only be retrieved with an adequate accessibility to scientific publications. Such access to data would ensure that no additional and unnecessary animal experiments need to be carried out. The availability of this data would improve the design of experiments and contribute to a reduction in animal use .

Animals that have been subjected to treatment (injection of drugs, surgery, behaviourial manipulation, etc.) can either respond to the treatment, showing a positive result, or show no measurable effect, when compared with the control animals. In the latter situation, the results are indicated as "negative" results. Publications in the field of innovative research almost exclusively present results of animal experiments in which something positive and significant has been found. Thus, a large part of the results obtained from animal experiments are not being published at all. As mentioned above, this is also the case for a large part of the toxicity testing. There is a risk that these tests will be repeated by other investigators, and that animals will be used unnecessarily. Databases containing comprehensive information, including negative results, together with data from toxicity testing, can effectively contribute to a reduction in the use of laboratory animals.

Alternative methods in education

Animal experiments for educational purposes can often be replaced by alternative methods. The process of learning and the development of skills are the ultimate goals of animal experiments in education, rather than the verification of scientific hypotheses. Animal experiments in education are, therefore, very often a repetition of an earlier experiment. For that very reason, these experiments can be replaced relatively easily. The animal here is the learning tool. The way in which the animal experiment should be simulated depends upon the learning goals of the experiment. The teaching of facts, for example in anatomy, requires other learning tools than teaching insight into dynamic processes, for example blood pressure regulation. Alternative methods which have been developed for research can also be employed in education; for example the reduction of pain through anaesthesia; the use of computer modelling; the substitution of vertebrates by lower species; the use of *in vitro* systems; the use of human models; the use of waste material from slaughterhouses. In addition, some specific alternatives are available for use in education, for example physical/chemical or three-dimensional models; preserved preparations; integration in research; audiovisual material; education by computer. Audiovisual material is the most widely applied alternative method used for educational purposes, both for the teaching of facts and for the development of ethical values. New computer technology has permitted the introduction of interactive learning programmes (fig. 17.3). Interactive video programmes and computer simulations are being designed as an aid for the student in understanding complex concepts. The student is able to engage in dialogue with the interactive programme, has to make decisions (for example on the administration of drugs or anaesthetics), and has to answer questions. The limitations of computer simulations for research purposes do not apply to education, as the model does not necessarily have to be complete. In education, the goal is to teach the basic principles of science, and this can be achieved by a properly-designed teaching programme based upon well-known facts.

The effect of alternative methods on the use of laboratory animals

Since the beginning of the 1980s, the use of animals in experiments has been declining in most European countries. This can be put down to the synergistic effects of several factors: to improved legislation on the control and registration of animal use, to increased efficiency, to the improved quality of laboratory animals, to economic factors, and to the greater emphasis placed on the ethical aspects of animal use. The use of alternative methods is only

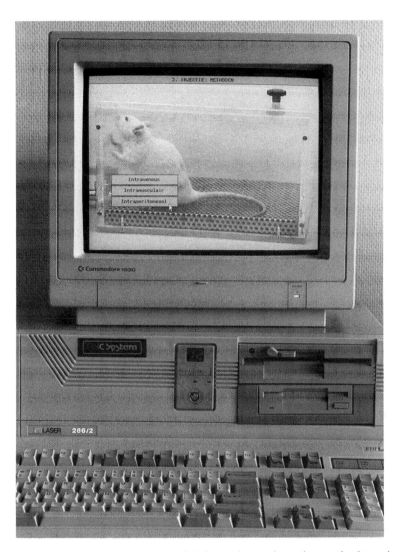

Fig. 17.3. Audiovisual materials are frequently being used as an alternative to animal experiments in education. Here a computer programme, simulating the effects of anaesthetics is combined with interactive video technology. Students can perform fictitious experiments and see the effect on the animal.

one factor, and one which has yet had only limited impact. However, the use of animals in education may present an exception. In The Netherlands, a reduction of about 50% has been achieved, mainly because of the introduction of alternative methods.

The limited effect of alternative methods upon the use of animals for research and testing can be ascribed to the incompleteness of these systems, compared with the use of intact organisms. Physiological processes, such as absorption, biotransformation and excretion, can only be imitated to a certain degree in tissue cultures, and computer simulations are a simplification of reality.

For these reasons, the possibility of extrapolating the results obtained from these systems, and applying them to humans, is limited. When extrapolating information from laboratory animals to human beings, species-specific differences must be taken into account. However, when computer simulations, lower species or *in vitro* systems are used, the distance between the model and man is even greater. This means that an animal experiment must sometimes still be performed, in order to confirm the results obtained in the alternative tests. There are only a few alternative methods which can totally replace the animal experiment. In practice, the introduction of alternative methods is still impeded by insufficient validation.

Validation is the process whereby the relevance and reproducibility of a new method is established. It usually requires a comprehensive comparison of the alternative method with the animal experiment. This is preferably carried out by collaboration between several independent laboratories. Validation is of particular importance in regulatory testing, as the results of these studies form the major basis upon which the authorities decide whether or not an alternative method is acceptable.

The future of alternative methods

It is anticipated that, in the near future, the search for alternative methods will become increasingly important, as there is a growing consensus amongst scientists that the use of animals must be reduced to the absolute minimum and replaced whenever possible. In several countries, a centre for the study and validation of alternatives has been established now (see list at the end of this chapter).

As stated above, the impact of alternative methods on animal use is limited at present and there is still a long way to go. Although more funds will probably be made available for the development and validation of alternative methods, it will not be possible for these techniques to replace animal use totally in the foreseeable future. It is, therefore, also important that the search for methods of refining animal experiments should continue, thus reducing the suffering of the animals which still have to be used.

Centres for alternatives to animal experimentation

Germany: Zentralstelle zur Erfassung und Bewertung von Ergänzungs- und Ersatzmethoden zum Tierversuch (ZEBET) Bundesgesundheidsamt. P.O. Box 33-00-13, 1000 Berlin 33, Germany

Great Britain: Fund for the Replacement of Animals in Medical Experiments (FRAME). Eastgate House, 34 Stoney Street, Nottingham NG1 1NB, Great Britain

Italy: European Centre for the Validation of Alternative Methods (ECVAM). Joint Research Centre, Ispra Site, T.P., 020 21020 Ispra, Italy

Netherlands: National Centre for Alternatives to Animal Experiments (NCAD). Utrecht University, Yalelaan 17, De Uithof, 3584 CL Utrecht, The Netherlands

Switzerland: Schweizerisches Institut für Alternativen zu Tierversuchen (SIAT). ETH-Zürich, Turnerstrasse 1, 8006 Zürich, Switzerland

U.S.A.: The Johns Hopkins Center for Alternatives to Animal Testing (CAAT). Johns Hopkins School of Public Health, 615N Wolfe Street, Room 1604, Baltimore, MD 21205-2179, U.S.A.

Literature

ATLA (Alternatives to Laboratory Animals), is an international, peer-reviewed journal devoted to all aspects of the development, validation and use of alternatives to laboratory animals. Nottingham: FRAME, 1983 onwards.

Balls M, Bridges J, Southee J, eds. Animals and alternatives in toxicology. Basingstoke: Macmillan Press, 1991.

Carson E R. The role of mathematical models. ATLA 1986; 13(4): 295–299.

Hendriksen C F M. Laboratory animals in vaccine production and control. Replacement, Reduction and Refinement. Dordrecht: Kluwer Academic Publishers, 1988.

Köeter H B W M and Hendriksen C F M, eds. Animals in biomedical research: replacement, reduction, and refinement: present possibilities and future prospects. Amsterdam: Elsevier Science Publishers BV, 1991.

Langley G, ed. Animal experimentation, the consensus changes. London: MacMillan Press, 1989.

Marsh N and Haywood S, eds. Animal experimentation: improvements and alternatives, Supplement to ATLA. Nottingham: FRAME, 1985.

McGiffin H and Brownley N. Animals in education: the use of animals in high school biology classes and science fairs. Washington: The Institute of Animal Problems, 1980.

OTA Report: Alternatives to animal use in research, testing and education. Washington: US Congress, Office of Technology Assessment, 1986.

Reduction of animal usage in the development and control of biological products. Proceedings of a Symposium organized by the IABS, London, April 1985. Basel: Karger, 1986.

Russell W M S and Burch R L. The principles of humane experimental technique. London: Methuen, 1959.

Smith D H: Alternatives to animal experiments. London: Scolar Press, 1978.

18 Ethical aspects of animal experimentation

Introduction

Since the publication of Peter Singer's book *"Animal Liberation"* in 1975, there has been a continuous flow of books and essays concerning ethical aspects of animal experimentation. Singer's main point is that the difference in the treatment of sentient non-human (higher) vertebrates compared with the treatment of (certain groups of) human beings, is something that cannot be consistently argued for. Accepting the proposition that animals can be used for experiments which are not admissible in human beings is, according to Singer, a matter of unjustifiable discrimination. He labelled this type of discrimination "speciesism" as an analogy to racism and sexism, which also discriminate on morally irrelevant grounds. Singer's views have met substantial opposition from traditional ethicists who argue that direct obligations can only exist towards persons capable of being aware of the duties and obligations involved, and who are therefore capable of reciprocation. All human beings are considered to be potentially similar and thus should be treated in the same way. In contrast, animals are not morally conscious beings and do not, therefore, need to be considered on a level of equality in our moral deliberations.

This kind of criticism has stimulated Tom Regan to write his book *"The Case for Animal Rights"* (1984). He defends the position that we have a direct obligation towards higher vertebrates not to harm their well-being, in the same way that we are under an obligation towards the mentally retarded, the elderly, and children. They all have a value of their own which, to Regan, is the primary moral argument for the equal treatment of both human beings and (higher) non-human vertebrates.

In this chapter we have abstained from discussing the merits or shortcomings of moral defences or moral rejections of animal research, but instead have focused upon the problems and procedures caused as a result of the pre-

t of the morally restricted use of animals in scientific research.
1er working with live animals needs to evaluate his experiments
1s. How such an evaluation may be achieved, and the possible
may be encountered during the process, are discussed in this

The moral relevance of animals

Animals are often viewed as merely a means to the solution of a problem. Animals are not regarded as ends in themselves. In scientific publications, animals are generally assigned to sections dealing with "Materials and Methods", and in the research laboratory animals are no more than experimental objects: they are considered as live instruments, their only value being their capacity to maximize the reliability and validity of scientific experiments.

In the field of ethics, the approach whereby the value of animals is dependent upon human objectives has been labelled *anthropocentric*. The animal here appears to be reduced to its instrumental value. In the course of the last decade, however, the anthropocentric approach has met with an increasing amount of criticism. In literature specialized in professional ethics, a fundamental discussion has arisen concerning the moral status of animals in relation to the moral status of human beings. According to the prevailing public opinion in western civilization, only human beings are considered to be morally relevant, the argument being that only human beings are capable of self-consciousness, of being responsible for their actions, of justifying their decisions and of making promises. Counter-argument here would be that, although these characteristics may be typical for moral actors, ethics has to concern itself with a wider domain of subjects. This wider domain includes subjects which may not be moral actors, but which are nevertheless considered to be equally in need of our moral concern. An example here would be people who possess the characteristics at issue to a lesser degree, for example, the mentally retarded, who is of course nevertheless regarded as morally relevant. When it comes to experimenting on human beings, it is precisely because of their vulnerability that those groups of people, who may not be (fully) capable of asserting themselves, are supposed to receive special forms of protection not provided to those fully equipped to reach an independent, conscious decision to participate as experimental subjects in scientific research. Therefore, experiments carried out on patients and elderly people, who may find themselves in positions of dependency similar to those of the mentally retarded, also meet with heavier criticism and scrutiny than would normally be the case.

Any serious consideration of the moral position of animals requires a detailed analysis of which similarities and differences between animals and human beings are considered to be morally relevant ones. For example, when adopting the thesis that animals are morally irrelevant because they lack the characteristics typical of the moral actor, it is also necessary to justify the moral distinction in the treatment of a class of people which lacks, in a similar way, the key characteristics associated with moral actorship. This theoretical distinction does have consequences for the welfare and health of the animals.

The problem of the moral status of animals can also be illustrated by referring to the declaration of human rights. Some of the most fundamental human rights apply to every human being, irrespective of differences in race, sex, culture, etc. In other words, as far as these fundamental human rights are concerned it is not possible to provide a moral justification for the unequal treatment of men and women, or of coloured and white people. These are differences which are morally irrelevant with respect to the basic rights of humanity.

Similarly, in the debate concerning the moral status of animals, the question is central as to whether the external differences between humans and animals does incorporate the morally relevant aspects which may be used to justify unequal treatment. A question closely related to this is whether or not there are certain general rights which may apply to both humans and animals, and which may serve as grounds for saying that, with respect to these particular rights, equal treatment is justifiable in principle. The "in principle" clause here implies that equal treatment is justified in the absence of a more fundamental ethical requirement, which may overrule these shared rights. Rights are usually conferred on entities which are said to possess intrinsic value (German: Eigenwert). The acknowledgement of the intrinsic value of animals is viewed by many as a logically necessary prelude to the discussion of the "rights" of animals. To others, the acceptance of the "intrinsic value" of animals raises no problems, whereas they may object to the idea of extending "rights" to animals. They make the assumption that, for the sake of animal welfare, the acceptance of such rights is not necessary; they consider it to be sufficient that we accept to have certain duties to the animals.

The *biocentric* approach emphasizes that all living creatures possess intrinsic value. In the *zoocentric* approach the intrinsic value of animals in particular is acknowledged. It implies that animals should not be used exclusively as a means, and that they ought to be protected for their own good. When justifying this idea, reference is made to the fact that what we are concerned with here are organisms with a considerable degree of autonomy. They are subjects with species-specific interests, to whom it matters whether these interests are accommodated or not. These species-specific interests are particularly susceptible to damage caused by human beings. The intrinsic value of animals is, like all values, "conferred" by man. In contrast to instrumental value, intrinsic value, however, is not derived from human interests and objectives. Many people prefer, therefore, to speak of the "acknowledgement" of the intrinsic value of animals to emphasize its special character. It is said that the intrinsic value of animals is a necessary antecedent to our valuation of animals, and it would be a fallacy to reverse matters by representing the intrinsic value as its consequence.

The acknowledgement of the intrinsic value of animals implies that we have direct moral obligations towards animals, as opposed to the traditional indirect obligations (e.g. because the animal happens to be the property of another person, or because other people might be offended by cruel behaviour with respect to animals). This acknowledgement that animals have a value of their own is being incorporated into the value systems of an increasing number of people. This process is being reflected by reforms of, and amendments to, various animal protection laws.

Acknowledgement of the intrinsic value of animals has consequences for the researcher which have, as yet, not been exhaustively reflected upon. A few of these consequences are listed below:

– The scientific quality of an experiment is a necessary condition to be satisfied prior to any ethical evaluation taking place: i.e. experimental procedures, which are found to be methodologically unsound, are to be viewed as ethically unacceptable;
– When alternative methods are available, which do not require the use of animals, performance of the animal experiment should not be allowed, even if the alternative method is more expensive;
– If there is no alternative available, and there is a conflict between human and animal interests, due weight must be given to all interests under consideration. It must be understood that violation of the intrinsic value of animals cannot be justified; It may, however, be tolerable if the consequences of not performing the experiment are graver than the adverse effects imposed on the animals;
– In cases where the experimental use of animals is considered to be tolerable, it is essential that the animals involved are allowed to pursue their species-specific behaviour as far as possible *before*, *during*, and *after* the performance of the experiment.
– Researchers engaged in animal experiments have the moral obligation to search for alternative methods in order to reach their scientific aims.

Acknowledgement of the intrinsic value of animals is interpreted by some ethicists as a *principle of moral justice*. This means that animal protection must not be dependent upon human compassion or sympathy, but should be regarded as a direct moral obligation to treat animals respectfully due to their intrinsic value. Justice in relation to animals is often misunderstood as a demand for animals to be treated like people. Although some animals have similar characteristics and requirements as human beings, they are also in many ways very different. Justice would dictate that they receive similar treatment to humans in similar circumstances (as animals are capable of feeling pain and suffering in the same or a similar way to ourselves), but that they also receive different treatment in different circumstances.

For a long time, the presumption has been that animals are receiving greater justice the more they are treated like human beings. That is, however, not true as animals do not "want" a life style worthy of men, but one worthy of their own species. Every animal is, after its kind, a perfect being in itself and not, as is often assumed, merely an intermediate form of life between unicellular organisms and human beings. To judge animals in terms of their man-like qualities, and to ascribe to them inherent values appropriate to man, would merely constitute a new form of anthropocentric thinking.

Advocates of "animal rights" would make the same point by saying that animals "have a right to be treated as such". Their position would protect animals against exclusively utilitarian deliberations based on the animals' usefulness to human aims, in the same way that the conferral of rights on human beings provides individuals with a safeguard against considerations based upon what is commonly called the "general interest". This would imply that certain actions may be considered inadmissible, irrespective of the importance of the expected benefits for human beings.

Acknowledgement of the intrinsic value of animals may also lead to acceptance of the idea that humans and animals should be viewed as equals, at least in some relevant moral aspects. A consequence of taking this position is that questions may be raised concerning medical ethics which require experiments on human subjects to be preceded by animal experiments. It may also be argued that criteria applied to animal experiments should, to a certain extent, be similar to the criteria applied to experiments performed on human subjects; for example the scientific merit of the experiment, the selection of subjects, and a cost-benefit analysis. It should, however, be recognized that in animal experiments "informed consent" of course cannot be obtained from the experimental subject. An "animal counsel" might be appointed in order to ensure that the animals' best interests are taken fully into consideration.

Moral problems in ethical dialogue

The acceptance of the intrinsic value of animals as a point of departure implies that researchers will have to make allowances for the animals' interests.

Should a conflict of interests arise between human beings and animals, the moral actors (those who are capable of making a moral decision) are the ones who are responsible for an ethically justifiable deliberation. When faced with the question as to whether or not a decision is ethically justified, two aspects should be examined in detail. First, the procedures followed to arrive at the judgement (who should be involved in the decision-making process), and secondly, the content of the judgement (i.e. the validity of the arguments used). This section focuses upon the first aspect; the content of the judgement will be looked into in the next section.

The starting point in normative ethics (in contrast to descriptive ethics) is the individual person, the moral actor, who is capable of making a free choice between alternative courses of action. The choice should be based upon a rational consideration of all the relevant facts, values, and normative principles, and this should be done with an attitude of impartiality and disinterestedness. What this implies is that it is not sufficient to say "this is my choice"; on the contrary, the assumption is that any other moral actor in the same or similar circumstances would arrive at the very same judgement. This is why normative ethics are sometimes said to show a tendency towards universalization (i.e. general applicability), when pronouncing prescriptive statements.

If ethical deliberation and choice are considered valid not only for the individual himself but also for anyone else in the same circumstances, it would follow that out of respect for the autonomy of other persons, arguments used in a decision-making process should be submitted to the scrutiny of other moral actors. It is in this context that we usually speak of a person having to "justify" or "account for" his actions. This ethical accountability does not entail a duty to answer to higher placed persons, authorities, or institutions, which would be the case if the accountability at issue was a legal or public one arising out of one's position in the social structure (positional duty). Ethical accountability is based on the acceptance of the fundamental equality of all other moral actors irrespective of their social position. As far as ethical issues are concerned, any moral actor should have the fundamental freedom to participate in discussions and decision-making. The ethicist should also not be allowed to take up a privileged position in the decision-making process on the grounds of having attained a certain expertise with respect to substantial ethical argumentation.

Although the concept of the ethically autonomous person is an important starting point, it is also obvious that its definition and place in normative ethics implies a strong social element. Herefore, on one hand, deciding an ethical issue may be an extremely personal and individual process in which one's conscience, philosophy of life, and moral qualities ("virtues") play an important role. On the other hand, however, its tendency towards universalization will turn normative ethics into a social process in which the rational components of individual deliberations are called into question in a dialogue. It follows, therefore, that the establishment of a dialogue concerning ethical questions will constitute an essential element of normative ethics.

Since research involving animal experiments raises ethical questions, researchers cannot afford to dispense with this kind of dialogue. In so far as researchers have not been trained to apply ethical reasoning to their own research, participation in this dialogue will require a process of readjustment. The objective bias of scientific research can easily lead to the rejection or evasion of ethical problems. In the natural sciences, this bias is apparent in the tendency which exists to reduce animated nature to a material "object", apparent in an emphasis on the non-moral, instrumental value of animals, and in a view of ethics which more often than not is emotivistic. The latter term indicates a view in which scientific statements are represented as objective, rational and universal, whereas moral statements are represented as their opposites: subjective, irrational, and contingent. In other words, moral statements are suggested to be no more than the expression of someone's emotions. When taking this view of ethics, science and ethics are bound to be conceived of as two separate enterprises diametrically opposed to, and therefore hard to combine with, each other. Where ethics are, however, based upon reasoning, the idea of consensus is considered as a realistic possibility and that therefore a dialogue backed up by arguments may very well be expedient. What needs to be understood is that the exclusion of ethics on the part of researchers may result in a "moralizing" attitude on the part of the public, leading to an undifferentiated rejection of animal experiments and an indisposition to listen to arguments. What may then develop instead of a dialogue is a process of antagonism in which considerations of strategy will replace those of ethics.

Negotiations based on strategy may be accompanied by the use of rhetoric language, or fallacious reasoning, aimed at getting the most out of a bartering process. The conclusion of this process will be a compromise leaving both parties dissatisfied, as their differences of opinion will remain unaltered. The party who has had to yield will persevere in its desire to achieve its frustrated aims. Should it actually have the power to enforce its aims, it would certainly do so. If, on the other hand, both parties wish to solve their conflict, it will for all practical purposes become a necessity to adopt measures other than strategic ones, and to enter into a discussion concerning the content of the conflict, the presuppositions of their differing points of view, and the merits of their diverging opinions. This is a procedure which requires both parties to try to reach a consensus about what is to be considered morally right and wrong, without resorting to instigations and threats.

One way of arriving at an ethical dialogue between researchers on the one hand and parties outside the field of scientific research on the other, is to establish an ethics committee such as the "Animal Experimentation Committees" (AECs) or the "Animal Care and Use Committees" (ACUCs). Members of such committees need to have some experience in conducting an ethical dialogue. It is of the utmost importance that local committees exchange suggestions with respect to procedures to be followed and ethical criteria to be applied, in order to be able to learn from each other and to achieve some form of consistency. It goes without saying, due to the nature of an ethical dialogue, that its results should be accessible to the public.

A model for ethical reasoning

Ethical dialogue is primarily concerned with arguments. If a dialogue is to be conducted regarding the admissibility of an animal experiment, an attempt should be made to keep to the kind of arguments that are pertinent to the subject. This has to do with the nature of the question giving rise to the dialogue. It also provides a method of solving conflicts when the debating parties differ in their opinions.

The dialogue at issue here is the question as to whether a proposed animal experiment is admissible or inadmissible from an ethical point of view. This question involves more than the mere approval or disapproval of a random piece of conduct. It involves an assessment of carefully planned actions which are always performed intentionally. A person acting intentionally has reasons for his actions. These reasons may be represented as something "behind" a researcher pushing him on as it were, or as something "in front of" him which he is aiming for. In the former case, the researcher's reasons may be called his "motives"; in the latter case, they may be called his "objectives". In a dialogue, these reasons should be made explicit, and should be discussed as to whether or not they are important enough to justify performing the proposed animal experiment. This type of deliberation is what is meant by using arguments pertinent to the subject.

Take, for example, the case where researchers on the one hand, and members of an ethics committee on the other, have a disagreement with regard to a proposed animal experiment. The researchers are inclined to consider it justified, whereas some committee-members have serious objections. In the last section we have discussed that strategic negotiations aimed at enforcing and imposing a particular opinion on others is not satisfactory from an ethical point of view. What is missing in such cases is a genuine attempt to elucidate and possibly to solve a substantial disagreement. When researchers and a committee become involved in a struggle for supremacy, the basis for ethical dialogue will be undermined in the process.

Why should the reasons submitted by researchers, whether or not they are sufficient to justify performance of a proposed animal experiment, be the object of an inquiry, and why should any attempts be made to resolve disagreements by means of arguments? These questions can be answered by the fact that there is an intention to arrive at an accountable collective decision. The decision at issue, i.e. "admissible" or "inadmissible", is a moral judgment regarding the propriety of actions. The term often used in this context is "normative direction for conduct". Being able to account for such a decision implies the ability to state reasons in support of it, reasons which are sufficient to justify the decision. There may be good reasons for deciding in favour of admissibility, but there may also be grave reasons for deciding against it, for example, the experiment in question will cause the laboratory animals to suffer severe discomfort and/or the experiment's scientific value is only of minor or moderate importance. In a dialogue, such points of criticism should not be simply discarded. The reasons in favour of the experiment should be specified and shown to be greater than the reasons for deciding against the experiment, or — more strongly — why the reasons in favour invalidate the reasons against. To summarize, the purpose of a dialogue is to arrive at justifiable normative directions for conduct. Arguments that ultimately carry weight are the ones providing good reasons, i.e. reasons which are sufficient to justify normative directions for conduct.

Ethical reasoning may also be the object of assessment with respect to its quality. Good reasoning should be valid, and arguments supporting such reasoning and conclusions should be both tenable and relevant. Validity has a bearing upon relationships of logical entailment between arguments and conclusion. Prominent ethicists disagree on the question of how strict a logically valid entailment should be, but it is beyond dispute that valid reasoning should be consistent and provide sufficient reasons for making its conclusion acceptable. Tenable arguments are those which correspond with the issue, i.e. they correspond with the facts of the case and the norms and values subscribed to. Those arguments are called relevant which have something to add to the authority of a judgment that a certain piece of conduct is morally right.

In order to arrive at good reasons for normative directions for conduct, it is advisable to take the following points into consideration:
- Has it been established that the proposed animal experiment satisfies required standards of scientific quality?
- Are the animals involved in the experiment expected to suffer any adverse effects? Assessment of adverse effects should account for their severity, duration and frequency.
- Are there any possibilities for replacement, reduction or refinement of the animal experiment?

- What degree of importance should be attached to the animal experiment? Is the experiment of primary or only of marginal importance; and of actual or only of potential importance?
- Will the adverse effects suffered by the animals be compensated for by the importance of the animal experiment?

The first question on the list needs to be examined in more detail i.e. the process of deliberation in which one interest is balanced against another. First of all, it is necessary clearly to articulate which intuitive moral judgments there are with respect to the proposed experiment at issue. Subsequently, it will be necessary to search for those ethical principles which we are committed to and which we think may be pertinent to the case we are concerned with. Finally, it is necessary we may try to establish a correlation between these ethical principles on the one hand, and intuitive moral judgments on the other, in order to derive from this correlation good reasons for a conclusive decision. The procedure described can be illustrated by means of the following example as to whether an acute toxicity test is ethically admissible or not. The substance to be tested is an insecticide. It is estimated that the test will cause the animals involved to suffer considerable discomfort. The test has been requested by a private concern, since the insecticide has to meet certain legal requirements if the company in question is to be allowed to sell it on the market. The test would need to be conducted on rats.

It is necessary to articulate clearly which intuitive moral judgments we have concerning this particular case, for instance, that it is right to test a substance with respect to its toxicity prior to its being used by consumers. These intuitions present themselves as self-evident and almost as unquestionable; often they are rooted in upbringing and experience, and they deserve serious consideration with regards to ethical reasoning. However, intuitive moral judgments alone form insufficient ground for a justified decision. They may be misplaced or distorted, as a result of the fact that we may only perceive what we wish to perceive, and intuitive moral judgments may also be incompatible. Along with the intuition that testing a substance for toxicity is the right thing to do, we may, for example, also have an intuition that it is wrong to cause rats to suffer. In such case, intuitive judgments are not sufficient when determining which decision should be taken.

It may be necessary, then, critically to examine our intuitive moral judgments. In a dialogue conducted by a committee, these intuitive moral judgments and lines of reasoning can be examined for compatibility with those of others. It is also possible to try to find ethical principles that are pertinent to the case at issue. Examples here would be the principle that we ought to promote other people's health, the principle that we ought to protect animals from suffering or that we ought to respect their autonomy, the principle of non-maleficence, the principle of beneficence, or the principle of justice.

These ethical principles may be used critically to examine intuitive moral judgments, by means of establishing a correlation between them. This process of reasoning proceeds in three successive stages. First of all, intuitive moral judgments may be critically assessed, both by viewing them from the perspective of certain ethical principles and by confronting them with morally relevant facts. For example, the intuition that it is wrong to make rats suffer may be critically assessed as to whether or not it should be considered misplaced. If it is possible to produce good reasons for protecting rats from suffering pain, then the intuition does not seem to be misplaced.

Conversely, in the second stage, ethical principles may be critically examined in the light of intuitive moral judgments and whatever information is relevant to the problem. Ethical principles should not be isolated from the intuitions and experience from which they originate. One subject for discussion may surround, for example, whether the principle of justice should be taken to imply that animals and human beings ought to be treated equally, or whether it should be understood as implying no more than that rats ought to be taken into consideration in so far as that they have the ability to experience suffering consciously. In the latter case, a generalized requirement to treat animals and humans equally would not represent a correct interpretation of the principle of justice.

In the third stage, the process of establishing a correlation between ethical principles and intuitive moral judgments may continue until a reflective equilibrium has been reached. Intuitive moral judgments are critically assessed and ethical principles are reciprocally examined until a certain degree of correspondence has been reached between acceptable intuitive moral judgments on the one hand, and accepted ethical principles on the other. When that stage is reached, intuitive moral judgments and judgments examined for their compatibility with certain ethical principles are said to be consistent. In the example used above, the reflective equilibrium under concern may be approached in this way. The validity of the intuitive moral judgment would acknowledge that it is wrong to cause rats to suffer. It would, however, also be acknowledged that it would be unacceptable to consider this judgment so important as to prevent us from alleviating potential human suffering. Therefore, we would acknowledge the validity of the principle that we ought to promote other people's health, but not to the extent that obligations derived from this principle should always override the obligation to protect rats from suffering. Is the conclusion, therefore, that we are obliged to allow the toxicity test to be performed? This would depend upon how important the result of the test is expected to be for promoting people's health. Refrained from performing the test may only delay official approval of the insecticide by a few months, i.e. until other information would become available by which an approval is possible as well. In that event, the intuitive moral judgment may be that, until that time, it would be better to carry on without the insecticide. Acceptable intuitive moral judgments, together with authoritative ethical principles, might then constitute sufficient reasons to reach a negative decision: meaning that under the circumstances, the toxicity test is to be viewed as ethically inadmissible. In reality, the situation presenting itself is generally much more complex. The insecticide might, for example, be considerably superior to similar products, or its being brought onto the market might be of eminent importance to the economic survival of the company producing it. If so, the ethical principle of beneficence may also be at issue, which may give rise to a reconsideration of the intuitive moral judgment which was initially acknowledged.

Pitfalls in ethical argumentation

The previous section illustrated a possible line of reasoning which may be useful to follow when trying to find good reasons for a particular ethical decision. Sound reasoning is an important piece of equipment in such an approach. In this section, some of the pitfalls and fallacies which may frustrate a constructive ethical dialogue will be discussed.

One of the major pitfalls constituting an impediment to constructive ethical discourse may be in the form of an irritated response when positions believed to be sacrosanct come into question ("why engage in animal experiments?"). Viewed from the perspective of ethical discourse, a response of evasion ("there aren't any alternatives") or of escapism ("lay-people with a lack of scientific expertise in a committee are only going to cause problems") are inappropriate. History has shown several examples of research methods, which were presumed to be unassailable by a small subculture of experts engaged in their practise, which will no longer be tolerated in most civilized countries.

Another pitfall in ethical argumentation is related to an inability to allow for lines of reasoning beyond the scope of one's own conceptual framework. Every social group has its own particular set of moral precepts, which is also the case for a group of researchers. These norms and values, taken to be self-evident by the members of a particular social group, will not be doubted until an alternative presents itself, or until outsiders (members of their families, anti-vivisectionists, or their students) draw attention to and call into question the underlying moment of choice with respect to their conduct. If participants in an ethical dialogue show an indisposition to have their own preferences or presuppositions genuinely called into question, controversies will develop which will prevent a constructive ethical dialogue.

It is vitally important to establish a correct balance between the research method proposed and any alternative methods which may deserve consideration. Here the pitfall would be to overlook the fact that a choice between two alternative methods accounts for four aspects to be balanced against each other, i.e. the arguments for and against both methods. Often, arguments in favour of one alternative are balanced against arguments disfavouring the other, e.g. "*advantage* of an animal experiment is the possibility to examine the entire physiological system; *disadvantage* of a cell culture is that in the course of time characteristic functions of cells will disappear". A particular position has, in effect, been taken disregarding the fact that there are still two other aspects which need to be brought into question: "*disadvantage* of an animal experiment is that the animals involved may suffer adverse effects; *advantage* of a cell culture is its speed, its reproducibility, and the large number of tests which can be performed within a short space of time".

Situations of choice may give rise to quandaries. To find oneself in such situation is to acknowledge the existence of good arguments both for and against alternative experimental procedures, while neither the arguments for nor the arguments against have the cogency to invalidate the other. For instance, a situation may arise in which one procedure will involve the use of twenty rats, while the other is expected to achieve similar results of equal validity with the use of "no more" than five chimpanzees. In this example, the differences of number and emotional distance to the animals are at issue, which are aspects which are difficult to relate to each other. The quandary faced here is, in point of fact, a choice between two evils. A quandary which often occurs is the question whether the researcher uses a few animals several times (e.g. 2, 10 or 20 times) or whether he will use more animals only once. The quantitative reduction of the number of animals must be weighed up as an alternative against the reduction in suffering of the individual animal. When taking the perspective of the individual animal, the reduction in suffering has to take preference over the quantitative decrease. In the previous section, we have seen that quandaries may be solved by resorting to principles of a more fundamental nature. The pitfall with respect to the type of choices between alternatives is that they are conceived of as subjects of dispute. This often results with the parties to the alleged dispute becoming engaged in a trench warfare, instead of attempting to elucidate the structure and background of the quandary and turning it into the subject of discussion.

It would be very helpful to an ethical dialogue to be able to have a reliable assessment of the severity of discomfort to be expected for the animals involved, and of the relevancy attached to the objectives expected to result from an animal experiment. Here the pitfall presents itself in the form of an unqualified acceptance of arguments assigned by an authority, particularly when the authority in question happens to be the expert who is himself engaged in the animal research. This does not mean that it is wrong to respect the expertise of competent and accomplished men and women; it does mean, however, that to accept an argument without qualification on the sole ground that it has been advanced by someone with authority will reduce any further discussion to a superfluous exercise. It is precisely this discussion about presupposed norms and values which constitutes the foundation of ethics. To categorize adverse effects of research procedures on the basis of a pre-established index of severity may result in a subsequent neglect of the real problems under consideration, which will again jeopardize a serious ethical discussion.

When attempting to arrive at a process of deliberation, whereby the balance to be achieved will be based on related variables, the choice often made is for costs and benefits to be balanced out against each other. The pitfall here is one of "reduction"; instead of deliberating on ethical grounds, attention is focused exclusively on economic aspects. Costs incurred, for example, by the acquisition, housing and care of laboratory animals may be balanced out against expenditures expected to be saved on health care facilities as a result of introducing, for example, a new therapy into the system. Although this is an important and necessary deliberation within the framework of effective health care management, it is not an ethical one. It may turn into an ethical deliberation, but only when the motives (values) behind these economic efforts are brought into question ("why should any efforts be directed at achieving a minimum in expenditures on laboratory animals and a maximum in savings on medical techniques?"). By asking questions such as these, the economic discussion is abandoned and the ethical discussion is entered into. One conceivable answer to this question might refer to the axioms of utilitarianism requiring the minimization of suffering and the maximization of happiness of the greatest number (of morally relevant beings: subjects capable of suffering or of having interests).

An important category of pitfalls, which frequently recurs in ethical reasoning, is constituted by what are commonly referred to as fallacies. Fallacies are specious arguments: persuasive on the surface, but incorrect on closer inspection. Their most powerful, and at the same time most alarming, feature is that they often (irrelevantly) capitalize on human sentiment. Consequently, they may defeat any attempt of conducting a dialogue based on rational arguments. Classical fallacies are the spurious counter-arguments derived from the art of rhetoric. The common denominator of these arguments is that they do not respond to arguments advanced by the opponent, but that they elaborately expound on another (irrelevant) aspect. Examples here would be:
– *appeal to the public*: "If AIDS research centres are not granted exemption from restrictions on import trade in chimpanzees, this country will not produce the solution to the AIDS epidemic." In addition to making the questionable assumption that chimpanzees are indeed necessary to AIDS

research, this argument implicitly addresses national sentiment in order to persuade the audience.

- *argumentum ad hominem (personal attack)*: "Is this man being paid by some animal welfare organization?" Argument suggesting that the speaker in question is to be regarded as suspect, in order to be at liberty to dispense with the effort to refute whatever has been proposed by him.
- *unwarranted appeal to compassion*: "Such a poor little puppy ...." Argument designed to emphasize natural feelings of sympathy that young animals in particular tend to evoke, in order to evade substantial discussion of the moral principles and facts at issue.
- *argument from authority*: "The (British) Home Office Guidance on the operation of the Animals (Scientific Procedures) Act 1986 (or the (US) Animal Welfare Act) requires ...." Or alternatively, the authority of a personality such as Albert Schweitzer may be used as a means of intimidating opposing partners in a dispute. What should count, and therefore should be discussed, are the arguments used by these authorities instead of their names.
- *appeal to involvement*: "In your family too, there may be someone suffering from a heart condition ...." Argument persuading the audience to form their opinion on the basis of their potentially personal involvement rather than a rational assessment of the moral problem under review.

A second group of fallacies is not specious in the sense that they distract from relevant arguments by irrelevantly focusing on human sentiment, but rather in the sense that they draw logically false inferences between premises. These inferences may in themselves be relevant enough, but the result is that the conclusions reached are of a somewhat dubious nature. Examples of this group are:

- *argument from ignorance*: "Animals do not feel pain, because it has never been verified that they do feel pain." The lack of verification of one thing does not lead to the conclusion that the reverse must be true.
- *circular argument (begging the question)*: "Animal research will always be necessary. After all, testing drugs on animals will warrant their safety for human consumption. In those cases where animal research turns out to be inconclusive, or even to yield false prognoses, we should actually increase the number of animal tests." The matter in dispute is assumed to be true. Logically false presupposition is that there are no alternatives at all to the one in question.
- *argument from correspondence*: "With animal research it will be the same as with the first steam engine; after a while no one is going to have a problem with it anymore." Logically false assumption here is that analogies will show a correspondence in every aspect, whereas they may only show correspondence in some (minor) aspects.

- *unwarranted generalization*: "Animal experiments do not always lend themselves to reliable extrapolation to human beings; therefore it is better not to engage in animal research at all." What has been observed to be true in some cases is inferred to be true in all cases.
- *a priori reasoning (accident)*: "Benefits to people are a good thing. Gene therapy may be a benefit to many people. Therefore gene therapy is a good thing." What may very well be true as a vague, general rule, is inferred to be true in a particular and very specific case.
- *post hoc ergo propter hoc (after this, therefore on account of this)*: "If animal research had not been tolerated in the past, science would never have progressed." Sequence is confused with consequence. The inference is logically false, since it cannot possibly be falsified, as is the case with all historical arguments.
- *naturalistic (is/ought) fallacy*: "The natural order of things is such that plants, animals, and humans can only survive at the expense of other forms of life. The use of animals for the benefit of humanity thus fits into the natural order of things." From the way things are it is inferred that this is the way they ought to be: values are inferred from facts. The argument is typically conservative in that it rejects out of hand any possibility of change in the future.
- *on not being consequent*: "Being against animal experimentation and still accepting medicines for your sick child is not consequent." Although not consequent it might very well be consistent ("consequent" referring to acts, as opposed to "consistent" referring to principles). The opponent suggests that you are betraying your own ethical principles. In other words that you are not "strong" enough to participate in a serious discussion, which is of course an "argumentum ad hominum". The point is, however, that the principle of equal treatment under equal conditions is misused because it has been overlooked that different conditions allow for (or even require) a different treatment. The difference in this example is that the direct moral obligation towards your own child overrules (not erases!) the general moral principle to care for animals.
- *equivocation*: "Researchers have the obligation to minimize adverse effects of their research procedures on the animals involved." Ambiguous terms and concepts are used to conceal a lack of consensus. "Adverse effects" is open to different interpretations made by researchers on the one hand, and representatives of animal welfare organizations or activist groups on the other. For example, to the latter, laboratory confinement will in itself constitute an unacceptable hardship, while to the former confinement presents no problem so long as legally required standards on this point are satisfied. What exactly is implied here by the obligation to "minimize"? Will it still apply when its discharge may become economically inexpedient?

Conclusions

When performing research involving animals, it is important for researchers to be well aware of the fact that animal experimentation has become a fundamental part of scientific procedures in the study of living nature. From the perspective of animal experimentation, the instrumental value of animals is central to the success of the experiment. With the acknowledgement that at least all vertebrates should be considered to possess a value of their own (Eigenwert), animal experimentation is no longer regarded as self-evidently justified from an ethical point of view. In addition to having at least to make an attempt at reduction, refinement, and replacement of animal experiments, researchers will also have to embark upon the question of whether the methods used will be compensated for by the results of their research. Solving this question will require an ability to engage in ethical reasoning and to examine ethical arguments for their compatibility to those of others. This "ethical dialogue" should be conducted by ethics committees. Such ethical reasoning may be required to meet certain standards, both with respect to form and to content, in order for researchers to be able to maintain that there are "good reasons" in the ethical sense to pursue their lines of research. Awareness of fallacies (logical pitfalls in ethical argumentation) is an important element in the process of finding good reasons. By promoting, as far as possible, the public nature of ethical deliberation, a collective process of learning may develop, resulting in the interests of humans and animals being balanced against each other with increasing care. Public accessibility provides, at the same time, a safeguard for society against neglect of the acknowledgement that animals possess a value of their own. To the researcher engaged in animal experimentation, it may be a comfort to know that a positive judgement by an ethics committee to perform an animal experiment is supported by people who lack any direct interest in the research in question.

Literature

Clark S R L. The moral status of animals. Oxford: Clarendon Press, 1977

Linzey A. Christianity and the rights of animals. London: SPCK, Holy Trinity Church, 1987

Regan T. The case for animal rights. London: Routledge, 1984.

Rollin B E. Animal rights and human morality. New York: Prometheus Books, 1981

Schweitzer A. Civilization and ethics. 3rd ed. London: Adam & Charles Black, 1955

Singer P. Animal liberation. A new ethics for our treatment of animals. New York: Avon Books, 1975.

Smith J A, Boyd K M, eds. Lives in the balance: The ethics of using animals in biomedical research. Oxford: Oxford University Press, 1991.

Annex

Council Directive of 24 November 1986
on the approximation of laws, regulations and administrative provisions of
the Member States regarding the protection of animals used for
experimental and other scientific purposes

(86/609/EEC)

THE COUNCIL OF THE EUROPEAN COMMUNITIES,

Having regard to the Treaty establishing the European Economic Community, and in particular Article 100 thereof,

Having regard to the proposal from the Commission [1],

Having regard to the opinion of the European Parliament [2],

Having regard to the opinion of the Economic and Social Committee [3],

Whereas there exist between the national laws at present in force for the protection of animals used for certain experimental purposes disparities which may affect the functioning of the common market;

Whereas, in order to eliminate these disparities, the laws of the Member States should be harmonized; whereas such harmonization should ensure that the number of animals used for experimental or other scientific purposes is reduced to a minimum, that such animals are adequately cared for, that no pain, suffering, distress or lasting harm are inflicted unnecessarily and ensure that, where unavoidable, these shall be kept to the minimum;

Whereas, in particular, unnecessary duplication of experiments should be avoided,

---

[1] OJ No C 351, 31.12.1985, p. 16.
[2] OJ No C 255, 13.10.1986, p. 250.
[3] OJ No C 207, 18.8.1986, p. 3.

HAS ADOPTED THIS DIRECTIVE:

Article 1

The aim of this Directive is to ensure that where animals are used for experimental or other scientific purposes the provisions laid down by law, regulation or administrative provisions in the Member States for their protection are approximated so as to avoid affecting the establishment and functioning of the common market, in particular by distorsions of competition or barriers to trade.

Article 2

For the purposes of this Directive the following definitions shall apply:

(a) *'animal'* unless otherwise qualified, means any live non-human vertebrate, including free-living larval and/or reproducing larval forms, but excluding foetal or embryonic forms;

(b) *'experimental animals'* means animals used or to be used in experiments;

(c) *'bred animals'* means animals specially bred for use in experiments in facilities approved by, or registered with, the authority;

(d) *'experiment'* means any use of animal for experimental or other scientific purposes which may cause it pain, suffering, distress or lasting harm, including any course of action intended, or liable, to result in the birth of an animal in any such condition, but excluding the least painful methods accepted in modern practice (i.e. 'humane' methods) of killing or marking an animal; an experiment starts when an animal is first prepared for use and ends when no further observations are to be made for that experiment; the elimination of pain, suffering, distress or lasting harm by the successful use of anaesthesia or analgesia or other methods does not place the use of an animal outside the scope of this definition. Non experimental, agricultural or clinical veterinary practices are excluded.

(e) *'authority'* means the authority of authorities designated by each Member State as being responsible for supervising the experiments within the meaning of this Directive;

(f) *'competent person'* means any person who is considered by a Member State to be competent to perform the relevant function described in this Directive;

(g) *'establishment'* means any installation, building, group of buildings or other premises and may include a place which is not wholly enclosed or covered and mobile facilities;

(h) *'breeding establishment'* means any establishment where animals are bred with a view to their use in experiments;

(i) *'supplying establishment'* means any establishment, other than a breeding establishment, from which animals are supplied with a view to their use in experiments;

(j) *'user establishment'* means any establishment where animals are used for experiments;

(k) *'properly anaesthetized'* means deprived of sensation by methods of anaesthesia (whether local or general) as effective as those used in good veterinary practice;

(l) *'humane method of killing'* means the killing of an animal with a minimum of physical and mental suffering, depending on the species.

Article 3

This Directive applies to the use of animals in experiments which are undertaken for one of the following purposes:

(a) the development, manufacture, quality, effectiveness and safety testing of drugs, foodstuffs and other substances or products:

   (i) for the avoidance, prevention, diagnosis or treatment of disease, ill-health or other abnormality of their effects in man, animals or plants;

   (ii) for the assessment, detection, regulation or modification of physiological conditions in man, animals or plants;

(b) the protection of the natural environment in the interests of the health or welfare of man or animal.

Article 4

Each Member State shall ensure that experiments using animals considered as endangered under Appendix I of the Convention on International Trade in Endangered Species of Fauna and Flora and Annex C.I. of Regulation (EEC) No 3626/82[1] are prohibited unless they are in conformity with the above Regulation and the objects of the experiment are:

— research aimed at preservation of the species in question, or

— essential biomedical purposes where the species in question exceptionally proves to be the only one suitable for those purposes.

Article 5

Member States shall ensure that, as far as the general care and accommodation of animals is concerned:

(a) all experimental animals shall be provided with housing, an environment, at least some freedom of movement, food, water and care which are appropriate to their health and well-being;

(b) any restriction on the extent to which an experimental animal can satisfy its physiological and ethological needs shall be limited to the absolute minimum;

(c) the environmental conditions in which experimental animals are bred, kept or used must be checked daily;

(d) the well-being and state of health of experimental animals shall be observed by a competent person to prevent pain or avoidable suffering, distress or lasting harm;

(e) arrangements are made to ensure that any defect or suffering discovered is eliminated as quickly as possible.

For the implementation of the provisions of paragraphs (a) and (b), Member States shall pay regard to the guidelines set out in Annex II.

---

[1] OJ No L 384, 31.12.1982, p. 1.

Article 6

1.   Each Member State shall designate the authority of authorities responsible for verifying that the provisions of this Directive are properly carried out.

2.   In the framework of the implementation of this Directive, Member States shall adopt the necessary measures in order that the designated authority mentioned in paragraph 1 above may have the advice of experts competent for the matters in question.

Article 7

1.   Experiments shall be performed solely by competent authorized persons, or under the direct responsibility of such a person, or if the experimental or other scientific project is authorized in accordance with the provisions of national legislation.

2.   An experiment shall not be performed if another scientifically satisfactory method of obtaining the result sought, not entailing the use of an animal, is reasonably and practicably available.

3.   When an experiment has to be performed, the choice of species shall be carefully considered and, where necessary, explained to the authority. In a choice between experiments, those which use the minimum number of animals, involve animals with the lowest degree of neurophysiological sensitivity, cause the least pain, suffering, distress or lasting harm and which are most likely to provide satisfactory results shall be selected.

Experiments on animals taken from the wild may not be carried out unless experiments on other animals would not suffice for the aims of the experiment.

4.   All experiments shall be designed to avoid distress and unnecessary pain and suffering to the experimental animals. They shall be subject to the provisions laid down in Article 8. The measures set out in Article 9 shall be taken in all cases.

Article 8

1.   All experiments shall be carried out under general or local anaesthesia.

2.   Paragraph 1 above does not apply when:

(a)   anaesthesia is judged to be more traumatic to the animal than the experiment itself;

(b)   anaesthesia is incompatible with the object of the experiment. In such cases appropriate legislative and/or administrative measures shall be taken to ensure that no such experiment is carried out unnecessarily.

Anaesthesia should be used in the case of serious injuries which may cause severe pain.

3.   If anaesthesia is not possible, analgesics or other appropriate methods should be used in order to ensure as far as possible that pain, suffering, distress or harm are limited and that in any event the animal is not subject to severe pain, distress or suffering.

4.   Provided such action is compatible with the object of the experiment, an anaesthetized animal, which suffers considerable pain once anaesthesia has worn off, shall be treated in good time with pain-relieving means or, if this is not possible, shall be immediately killed by a humane method.

Article 9

1.   At the end of any experiment, it shall be decided whether the animal shall be kept alive or killed by a human method, subject to the condition that it shall not be kept alive if, even though it has been restored to normal health in all other respects, it is likely to remain in lasting pain or distress.

2.   The decisions referred to in paragraph 1 shall be taken by a competent person, preferably a veterinarian.

3.   Where, at the end of an experiment:

(a)   an animal is to be kept alive, it shall receive the care appropriate to its state of health, be placed under the supervision of a veterinarian or other competent person and shall be kept under conditions conforming to the requirements of Article 5. The conditions laid down in this subparagraph may, however, be waived where, in the opinion of a veterinarian, the animal would not suffer as a consequence of such exemption;

(b)   an animal is not to be kept alive or cannot benefit from the provisions of Article 5 concerning its well-being, it shall be killed by a humane method as soon as possible.

Article 10

Member States shall ensure that any re-use of animals in experiments shall be compatible with the provisions of this Directive.

In particular, an animal shall not be used more than once in experiments entailing severe pain, distress or equivalent suffering.

Article 11

Notwithstanding the other provisions of this Directive, where it is necessary for the legitimate purposes of the experiment, the authority may allow the animal concerned to be set free, provided that it is satisfied that the maximum possible care has been taken to safeguard the animal's well-being, as long as its state of health allows this to be done and there is no danger for public health and the environment.

Article 12

1.   Member States shall establish procedures whereby experiments themselves or the details of persons conducting such experiments shall be notified in advance to the authority.

2.   Where it is planned to subject an animal to an experiment in which it will, or may, experience severe pain which is likely to be prolonged, that experiment must be specifically declared and justified to, or specifically authorized by, the authority. The authority shall take appropriate judicial or administrative action if it is not satisfied that the experiment is of sufficient importance for meeting the essential needs of man or animal.

Article 13

1.   On the basis of requests for authorization and notifications received, and on the basis of the reports made, the authority in each Member State shall collect, and as far as possible

periodically make publicly available, the statistical information on the use of animals in experiments in respect of:

(a)   the number and kinds of animals used in experiments;

(b)   the number of animals, in selected categories, used in the experiments referred to in Article 3;

(c)   the number of animals, in selected categories, used in experiments required by legislation.

2.   Member States shall take all necessary steps to ensure that the confidentiality of commercially sensitive information communicated pursuant to this Directive is protected.

Article 14

Persons who carry out experiments or take part in them and persons who take care of animals used for experiments, including duties of a supervisory nature, shall have appropriate education and training.

In particular, persons carrying out or supervising the conduct of experiments shall have received instruction in a scientific discipline relevant to the experimental work being undertaken and be capable of handling and taking care of laboratory animals; they shall also have satisfied the authority that they have attained a level of training sufficient for carrying out their tasks.

Article 15

Breeding and supplying establishments shall be approved by or registered with, the authority and comply with the requirements of Articles 5 and 14 unless an exemption is granted under Article 19 (4) or Article 21. A supplying establishment shall obtain animals only from a breeding or other supplying establishment unless the animal has been lawfully imported and is not a feral or stray animal. General or special exemption from this last provision may be granted to a supplying establishment under arrangements determined by the authority.

Article 16

The approval or the registration provided for in Article 15 shall specify the competent person responsible for the establishment entrusted with the task of administering, or arranging for the administration of, appropriate care to the animals bred or kept in the establishment and of ensuring compliance with the requirements of Articles 5 and 14.

ticle 17

1.   Breeding and supplying establishments shall record the number and the species of animals sold or supplied, the dates on which they are sold or supplied, the name and address of the recipient and the number and species of animals dying while in the breeding or supplying establishment in question.

2.   Each authority shall prescribe the records which are to be kept and made available to it by the person responsible for the establishments mentioned in paragraph 1; such records shall be kept for a minimum of three years from the date of the last entry and shall undergo periodic inspection by officers of the authority.

Article 18

1.   Each dog, cat or non-human primate in any breeding, supplying or user establishment shall, before it is weaned, be provided with an individual identification mark in the least painful manner possible except in the cases referred to in paragraph 3.

2.   Where an unmarked dog, cat or non-human primate is taken into an establishment for the first time after it has been weaned it shall be marked as soon as possible.

3.   Where a dog, cat or non-human primate is transferred from one establishment as referred to in paragraph 1 to another before it is weaned, and it is not practicable to mark it beforehand, a full documentary record, specifying in particular its mother, must be maintained by the receiving establishment until it can be so marked.

4.   Particulars of the identity and origin of each dog, cat or non-human primate shall be entered in the records of each establishment.

Article 19

1.   User establishments shall be registered with, or approved by, the authority. Arrangements shall be made for user establishments to have installations and equipment suited to the species of animals used and the performance of the experiments conducted there; their design, construction and method of functioning shall be such as to ensure that the experiments are performed as effectively as possible, with the object of obtaining consistent results with the minimum number of animals and the minimum degree of pain, suffering, distress or lasting harm.

2.   In each user establishment:

(a)   the person or persons who are administratively responsible for the care of the animals and the functioning of the equipment shall be identified;

(b)   sufficient trained staff shall be provided;

(c)   adequate arrangements shall be made for the provision of veterinary advice and treatment;

(d)   a veterinarian or other competent person should be charged with advisory duties in relation to the well-being of the animals.

3.   Experiments may, where authorized by the authority, be conducted outside user establishments.

4.   In user establishments, only animals from breeding or supplying establishments shall be used unless a general or special exemption has been obtained under arrangements determined by the authority. Bred animals shall be used whenever possible. Stray animals of domestic species shall not be used in experiments. A general exemption made under the conditions of this paragraph may not extend to stray dogs and cats.

5.   User establishments shall keep records of all animals used and produce them whenever required to do so by the authority. In particular, these records shall show the number and species of all animals acquired, from whom they were acquired and the date of their arrival. Such records shall be kept for a minimum of three years and shall be submitted to the authority which asks for them. User establishments shall be subject to periodic inspection by representatives of the authority.

Article 20

When user establishments breed animals for use in experiments on their own premises, only one registration or approval is needed for the purposes of Article 15 and 19. However, the establishments shall comply with the relevant provisions of this Directive concerning breeding and user establishments.

Article 21

Animals belonging to the species listed in Annex I which are to be used in experiments shall be bred animals unless a general or special exemption has been obtained under arrangements determined by the authority.

Article 22

1.   In order to avoid unnecessary duplication of experiments for the purposes of satisfying national or Community health and safety legislation, Member States shall as far as possible recognize the validity of data generated by experiments carried out in the territory of another Member State unless further testing is necessary in order to protect public health and safety.

2.   To that end, Member States shall, where practicable and without prejudice to the requirements of existing Community Directives, furnish information to the Commission on their legislation and administrative practice relating to animal experiments, including requirements to be satisfied prior to the marketing of products; they shall also supply factual information on experiments carried out in their territory and on authorizations or any other administrative particulars pertaining to these experiments.

3.   The Commission shall establish a permanent consultative committee within which the Member States would be represented, which will assist the Commission in organizing the exchange of appropriate information, while respecting the requirements of confidentiality, and which will also assist the Commission in the other questions raised by the application of this Directive.

Article 23

1.   The Commission and Member States should encourage research into the development and validation of alternative techniques which could provide the same level of information as that obtained in experiments using animals but which involve fewer animals or which entail less painful procedures, and shall take such other steps as they consider appropriate to encourage research in this field. The Commission and Member States shall monitor trends in experimental methods.

2.   The Commission shall report before the end of 1987 on the possibility of modifying tests and guidelines laid down in existing Community legislation taking into account the objectives referred to in paragraph 1.

Article 24

This Directive shall not restrict the right of the Member States to apply or adopt stricter measures for the protection of animals used in experiments or for the control and restriction of the use of animals for experiments. In particular, Member States may require a prior authorization for experiments or programmes of work notified in accordance with the provisions of Article 12(1).

Article 25

1.   Member States shall take the measures necessary to comply with this Directive by 24 November 1989. They shall forthwith inform the Commission thereof.

2.   Member States shall communicate to the Commission the provisions of national law which they adopt in the field covered by this Directive.

Article 26

At regular intervals not exceeding three years, and for the first time five years following notification of this Directive, Member States shall inform the Commission of the measures taken in this area and provide a suitable summary of the information collected under the provisions of Article 13. The Commission shall prepare a report for the Council and the European Parliament.

Article 27

This Directive is addressed to the Member States.

Done at Brussels, 24 November 1986.

For the Council
The President
W. WALDEGRAVE

Index

Aδ-fibres, 258
AALAS, 5
abnormal behaviour, 77
absolute barrier, 156
acclimatization, 225
acepromazine, 270, 272, 280
ACTH, 92
active coping, 89, 94
ACUC, 342
acute stress response, 94
ad libitum feeding, 122
adaptation, 76, 80, 95, 96, 105, 168
adaptive response, 259
adjunctive behaviour, 87, 88
administration of drugs, 299
adrenalectomy, 26, 315
adrenaline, 91, 290
adrenocorticotropic hormone, 92
AEC, 342
African clawed toad, 68
agar plate, 181
agonistic behaviour, 87
alanine-transaminase, 145
alarm phase, 92
alcuronium, 277
aldehyde, 159
allergy, 251
alopecia, 184
alphadolone, 270, 272, 280
alphaxalone, 270, 272, 280
alternatives to animal experiments, 12, 319–
    332
ambivalent behaviour, 88
Ambystoma mexicanum, 68
Ames test, 200, 322
ammonia, 144
amoebocyte lysate, 323
amphibians
    African clawed toad, 68

anaesthetic dose rates, 276
axolotl, 68
handling, 69
housing, 68
identification, 69
injection sites, 303
nutrition, 69
physiology, 68
reproduction, 69
use, 68
amygdala, 93
anaerobic bacteria, 153
anaesthesia, 12, 267–295, 356
anaesthesia complications, 289
anaesthesia monitoring, 287
anaesthetic chamber, 278
anaesthetic dose rates
    amphibians, 276
    birds, 276
    cat, 272
    dog, 272
    ferret, 272
    fish, 276
    gerbil, 271
    goat, 273
    guinea pig, 271
    mouse, 270
    pig, 273
    primates, 273
    rabbit, 271
    rat, 270
    reptiles, 276
    sheep, 273
    Syrian hamster, 270
anaesthetic potency, 278
anaesthetic techniques
    artificial ventilation, 285, 286
    assessment depth, 281
    general anaesthesia, 268

anaesthetic techniques (*continued*)
  inhalation anaesthesia, 275
  intubation, 282–285
  local anaesthesia, 269
  monitoring, 287
  premedication, 274
analgesia, 267–295
analogy postulate, 255
analysis of variance, 218
analytical error, 223, 224
anamnesis, 173
anaphylactic shock, 31
anatomical forceps, 311
animal diets, 110, 113
animal experiment, 1
animal facility, 13
animal model, 1, 189–196, 204
animal rights, 339
animal suffering, 255
animal technician, 7
animal use
  amphibians, 68
  cat, 51
  chicken, 59
  dog, 47
  dove, 61
  drug research, 4
  fish, 71
  gerbil, 33
  guinea pig, 36
  Japanese quail, 63
  monkeys, 44
  mouse, 18
  Netherlands, 4
  pig, 53
  purposes, 4
  rabbit, 40
  rat, 26
  reptiles, 66
  species, 4
  Syrian hamster, 30
  toxicity testings, 4
  UK, 4
  vaccine testings, 4
animal welfare, 278
animal welfare officer, 7
Animal Care and Use Committee, 342
Animal Experimentation Committee, 342
Animal Welfare Act, 9
anogenital distance, 18
anorexic activity, 123
antagonists, 277

Antechinus, 94
anthropomorphism, 97, 336
antibiotics, 31, 37, 164
anticholinergics, 270, 272, 274
antimicrobial substance, 160
antisepsis, 310
anxiety, 256
anxiolytics, 264
apathy, 261
appendix caeci, 41
appetitive behaviour, 257
aquarium conditions, 72
arginine, 111
armadillo, 127
arterio-venous shunt, 316
artery forceps, 312
artificial insemination, 43, 54
artificial tears, 289
artificial ventilation, 282, 285, 286
ascites fluid, 310, 323
ascorbic acid, 112
asepsis, 310
asparagine, 111
aspartate-transaminase, 145
aspirin, 292, 293
associations
  AALAS, 5
  FELASA, 5, 7
  ICLAS, 5
atherosclerosis, 33, 35, 40
atipamezole, 277, 280
atracurium, 277
atraumatic needle, 313
atropine, 91, 106, 270, 272, 274
atropine-esterase, 41
audiogenic seizure, 28
authenticity, 137
authority, 11, 354
autochthonous flora, 152, 153
autoclaving, 114, 160
autolysis, 175
autonomic nervous system, 91
autopsy, 175
autoradiograph, 138
axolotl, 68
azaperon, 272

Bacillus piliformis, 169, 181
backcross, 132
background pathology, 169–171
background strain, 134
balanced anaesthesia, 269

barbiturates, 279, 294, 296
barotrauma, 286
barrier system, 151, 155
beagle, 48
behaviour
    adjunctive, 88
    agonistic, 87
    ambivalent, 88
    cat, 51
    clinical examination, 174
    conditioning, 79
    conflict, 87, 88
    coping, 89, 93, 94
    dog, 48
    exploratory, 81
    F_1-hybrids, 131
    fight/flight, 89, 91
    guinea pig, 37
    homeostasis, 76
    learning, 78, 79
    pain, 262
    pig, 53
    redirected, 88
    sensitive period, 81
    social, 81
    stereotypes, 88, 89
    tree shrew, 84
    well-being, 96
behavioural pathology, 87
Bentham, Jeremy, 3
benzodiazapine, 280
Bernard, Claude, 2, 3
between-experiment variation, 101–103, 107
bias, 226, 227
biguanide, 159
bile duct, 309
bioassay, 190
biocentric approach, 337
biochemical markers, 138
biological products, 146
biotin, 112
biotransformation, 154
birds
    anaesthetic dose rates, 276
    artificial ventilation, 286
    blood parameters, 60
    blood sampling, 307
    cloaca, 58
    diaphragm, 58
    environmental requirements, 60
    erythrocytes, 58
    gizzard, 58, 59

    granivorous, 59
    injection site, 303
    metabolic rate, 58
    nutrition, 59
    physiological parameters, 60
    preening glands, 58
    proventriculus, 59
    respiration, 58
    thrombocytes, 58
block design, 232, 233
blocking, 226
blood coagulation, 295
blood parameters
    birds, 60
    cat, 49
    dog, 49
    gerbil, 35
    goat, 49
    guinea pig, 35
    mouse, 19
    pig, 49
    primates, 45
    rabbit, 35
    rat, 19
    sheep, 49
    Syrian hamster, 19
blood sampling, 171, 304, 305, 306, 307
blood volume, 19, 35, 45, 49, 60
body surface
    gerbil, 35
    guinea pig, 35
    mouse, 19
    rabbit, 35
    rat, 19
    Syrian hamster, 19
body temperature
    birds, 60
    cat, 49
    dog, 49
    gerbil, 35
    goat, 49
    guinea pig, 35
    mouse, 19
    pig, 49
    primates, 45
    rabbit, 35
    rat, 19
    sheep, 49
    Syrian hamster, 19
body weight
    birds, 60
    cat, 49

body weight (*continued*)
    dog, 49
    gerbil, 35
    goat, 49
    guinea pig, 35
    mouse, 19
    pig, 49
    primates, 45
    rabbit, 35
    rat, 19
    sheep, 49
    Syrian hamster, 19
bold conjecture, 198, 202, 203
Bouin's fixative, 177, 182
Brachydanio rerio, 71
breathing system, 284
breeding age
    birds, 60
    cat, 49
    dog, 49
    gerbil, 35
    goat, 49
    guinea pig, 35
    mouse, 19
    pig, 49
    primates, 45
    rabbit, 35
    rat, 19
    sheep, 49
    Syrian hamster, 19
Bruce-effect, 22
bulldog haemostatic clamp, 311
bupivacaine, 269, 295
buprenorphine, 292, 293
butorphanol, 292

C-fibres, 258, 259
cadmium, 115, 116
caecotrophy, 41
caecum, 37, 41, 153
Caesarean section, 151
cage floor size
    birds, 60
    cat, 49
    dog, 49
    gerbil, 35
    goat, 49
    guinea pig, 35
    mouse, 19
    pig, 49
    primates, 45
    rabbit, 35

rat, 19
sheep, 49
Syrian hamster, 19
cage height
    birds, 60
    cat, 49
    dog, 49
    gerbil, 35
    goat, 49
    guinea pig, 35
    mouse, 19
    pig, 49
    primates, 45
    rabbit, 35
    rat, 19
    sheep, 49
    Syrian hamster, 19
calcium, 111, 115
Calhoun, 82
Callithrix, 44
caloric intake, 121
cancer bioassay, 124
cancer research, 5
Canis familiaris, 47
canister, 285
cannibalism, 32, 59
Cannon, 91
cannula, 300
capnogram, 287
capnograph, 286
Capra hircus, 55
captive bolt pistol, 297
Carassius auratus, 72
carbohydrates, 112, 119, 121
carbon dioxide, 294, 296
carbon dioxide absorber, 285
carcinogens, 251
cardiac arrest, 289, 290, 305
cardiac arrhythmias, 290
cardiac output, 287
cardiac puncture, 305, 306, 307
cardiovascular depression, 279
carotids, 307
carprofen, 293
carry-over effect, 235
cat (*Felis catus*)
    anaesthetic dose rates, 272
    behaviour, 51
    blood sampling, 306
    blood volume, 49
    body temperature, 49
    body weight, 49

cat (*continued*)
  breeding, 49
  cage floor size, 49
  cage height, 49
  delivery, 52
  duration of life, 49
  duration of pregnancy, 49
  environmental temperature, 49
  glucose, 49
  haematocrit, 49
  haemoglobin, 49
  handling, 52
  heart rate, 49
  housing, 51
  injection sites, 303
  injection techniques, 303
  leucocytes, 49
  litter size, 49
  MAC-values, 279
  muscle relaxants, 277
  number of chromosomes, 49
  nutrition, 52
  oestrous cycle, 49, 52
  oral administration, 303
  origin, 51
  post-operative pain relief, 292, 293
  postcopulatory ovulation, 52
  relative humidity, 49
  respiration rate, 49
  sexual maturity, 49
  techniques, 52
  use, 51
  ventilation, 49
  water intake, 49
  weaning age, 49
  weight at birth, 49
  weight at weaning, 49
catalogues of inbred strain, 195
catecholamines, 91, 263
catgut, 313
catheter, 309
catheterization, 269, 309
caudal vena cava, 307
Cavia porcellus, 36
Caviidae, 18
cell culture, 321
cellulose, 122
central animal institute, 247
centralization of animal experiments, 247, 248
centres for alternatives, 333
cephalic vein (forelimbs), 305, 306

cerebello-medullary cistern, 304
cerebrospinal fluid, 269
cervical dislocation, 294
cestodes, 183
cheek pouches, 31
chemically defined diet, 113
chicken (*Gallus domesticus*)
  anaesthetic dose rate, 276
  blood parameters, 60
  blood sampling, 307
  cannibalism, 59
  environmental requirements, 60
  gizzard, 61
  handling, 61
  housing, 59
  identification, 61
  nutrition, 61
  origin, 59
  physiological parameters, 60
  reproduction, 61
  techniques, 61
  use, 59
chimpanzee, 44, 45
Chinese hamster, 30, 32
chloralhydrate, 276
chloralose, 270, 272
chlorhexidin, 160
chloride, 111
chloropromazin, 106
choice of animal model, 204
cholecalciferol, 111
choline, 112
chorio-allantois membrane (CAM), 328
chromium, 111
chromosomes ($2n$)
  cat, 49
  coprophagy
  dog, 49
  gerbil, 35
  germ-free animals, 112
  guinea pig, 35, 37
  hamster, 31
  mouse, 19, 21
  pig, 49
  primates, 45
  rabbit, 35, 41
  rat, 19
  sheep, 49
  Syrian hamster, 19
chronic pain, 260, 261
chronic stress, 87, 88, 94
ciliates, 182

classical barrier system, 157
cleaning, 159
clinical examination, 174
cloaca, 58
closed formula diet, 113
coagulation plug, 22
coccidia, 182
codeine, 292
coefficient of inbreeding, 128
coefficient of variation, 217, 219
cognitive map, 82
coisogenic strain, 131
collection of
— blood 304, 306
— body fluids, 304–310
— faeces, 308
— urine, 308, 309
colonization resistance, 150, 152, 153
colostrum, 54, 57
Columba livia, 58, 61
commercial diets, 116
comparability of results, 107
competence, 7, 11, 12, 356
competent person, 354
complement fixation test, 161
completely randomized design, 230
complications of anaesthesia, 289–291
computer graphics, 325
computer simulation, 326, 330
computer tomography, 317
concealment of pain behaviour, 262
conditioning, 79
conflict behaviour, 87, 88
congenic strain, 132
consanguinity, 128
conservation-withdrawal response, 89
constipation, 293, 295
contamination, 144
continuous stitch, 313
control animals, 227
control diet, 120
control group, 210, 227
controllability, 86, 87, 92, 94, 256
Convention for the Protection of Vertebrate
    Animals, 10
conventional animals, 145, 150, 155
conventionalization, 163
coping, 89, 93, 256, 257
copper, 111
coprophagy
    germ-free animals, 112
    guinea pig, 37

hamster, 31
mouse, 21
rabbit, 41
corneal reflexes, 281
Corpus Hippocraticum, 2
corticosteroids, 31, 38,145, 263
corticosterone, 87, 92, 95
corticotropin-releasing hormone, 92
Corynebacterium pseudotuberculosis, 182
Coturnix coturnix, 63
Council Directive, 10, 353
Council of Europe, 10
cranial vena cava, 307
CRF animals, 150, 151, 156
Cricetidae, 18
Crisetulus griseus, 30
cross-over design, 233, 234
crude fibre, 38, 42
Cruelty to Animals Act, 2, 9, 14, 319
cryopreservation, 141
culture media, 181
cyanocobalamine, 111
cyanosis, 289
cynomolgus, 44, 45
cystine, 111
cytostatics, 251

d-tubocurarine, 277
Darwin, Charles, 3
Dasypus novemcinctus, 127
databases, 329
DDT, 115, 116
decapitation, 295, 296, 307
decontamination, 159
deductive philosophy, 198
defensive phase, 259
deficiency, 114
digestible energy, 111
degrees of freedom, 220–222
dehydration, 72
Demodex spp., 186
denaturation, 139
depth of anaesthesia, 281
dermatophyte, 183
Descartes, René, 2
descriptive ethics, 340
descriptive research, 197
design of animal experiments, 209–239
determining sample size
    for microbiological screening, 162
    mathematical equations, 215–219
    resource equation method, 220–223

diabetes, 190
diagnosis, 160, 172
diagnostic techniques, 175, 178
dialogue, 341
diastema, 18
diazepam, 270, 272, 280
diets
    chemically defined, 113
    closed formula, 113
    commercial, 116
    composition, 114
    control, 120
    energy density, 120
    meal, 118
    natural ingredients, 113
    open formula, 113
    pellet, 118
    purified, 114
    semi-moist, 118
    standardization, 117
    zinc concentration, 116
diphenyl-hydramin, 106
diphtheria, 37
Directive for the Protection of Vertebrate
    Animals, 10
discomfort, 193, 255, 256
disease history, 173
disinfection, 156, 159, 160
dislocation of the cervical vertebrae, 296
displacement behaviour, 87
dissociative anaesthetics, 280
distress, 256, 257
DL-α-tocopheryl, 111
DNA markers, 138
documentation and information, 328
dog (*Canis familiaris*)
    aggression, 48
    anaesthetic dose rates, 272
    blood sampling, 306
    blood volume, 49
    body temperature, 49
    body weight, 49
    breeding, 49
    cage floor size, 49
    cage height, 49
    duration of life, 49
    duration of pregnancy, 49
    echoscopy, 50
    environmental temperature, 49
    glucose, 49
    haematocrit, 49
    haemoglobin, 49
    handling, 50
    heart rate, 49
    housing, 48
    injection sites, 303
    injection techniques, 303
    leucocytes, 49
    litter size, 49
    MAC-values, 279
    muscle relaxants, 277
    number of chromosomes, 49
    nutrition, 49
    oestrous cycle, 49, 50
    oral administration, 303
    origin, 47
    post-operative pain relief, 292, 293
    relative humidity, 49
    respiration rate, 49
    sexual maturity, 49
    socialization period, 48
    techniques, 50
    umbilical cord, 50
    use, 47
    ventilation, 49
    weaning age, 49
    weight at birth, 49
    weight at weaning, 49
dog distemper, 30
domestication, 75, 77
donor strain, 134
dorsal lymph sac, 276, 303
double cervix, 41
dove (*Streptopelia risoria*)
    anaesthetic dose rate, 276
    blood sampling, 307
    handling, 63
    housing, 62
    identification, 63
    nutrition, 62
    origin, 61
    reproduction, 62
    techniques, 63
    use, 61
doxapram, 290
Draize test, 328
dramatype, 103
drinking nipple, 21, 32
drinking water, 21, 149
droperidol, 280
ductus choledochus, 309
Dunkin-Hartley line, 37
duplication of experiments, 360
dura mater, 269

dysbacteriosis, 31
dystocia, 39

ear mange, 184, 185
ear mite, 185
ear pinch reflex, 282
ear vein, 306
EC Directive, 11, 75, 295
echoscopy, 50
ectomy, 315
ectoparasite, 175, 184
ectromelia virus, 158, 179
education and training, 7, 11, 330, 358
Eigenwert, 351
Eimeria stiedei, 182
elective media, 181
electrocardiogram, 287, 290
electrocautery, 312
electroencephalogram, 287
electrophoresis, 138, 139
embolism, 302
embryo-banking, 141
emotional expression, 85, 261
Encephalitozoon cuniculi, 182
β-endorphin, 92, 93
endotoxaemia, 31
endotracheal intubation, 282
endotracheal tube, 283–285
energy density, 110, 119, 120
energy requirement, 105, 118–120
energy value, 112
enflurane, 278, 296
enkephalins, 258
enteral administration, 300
environmental conditions, 225
environmental temperature
    birds, 60
    cat, 49
    dog, 49
    gerbil, 35
    goat, 49
    guinea pig, 35
    mouse, 19
    pig, 49
    primates, 45
    rabbit, 35
    rat, 19
    sheep, 49
    Syrian hamster, 19
enzyme-linked immunosorbent assay, 161
ephedrin, 106
epidural anaesthesia, 269

epilepsy, 33
epinephrine, 269
error, 220, 223
Escherichia coli, 153
estimation number of animals, 215
ether, 270, 272, 278, 294, 296, 319
ethical aspects of animal experimentation
    animal rights, 339
    anthropocentric approach, 336
    argumentation, 346–350
    biocentric approach, 337
    dialogue, 339–342
    fallacies, 348–350
    human rights, 337
    instrumental value, 338
    intrinsic value, 337, 338
    normative ethics, 340
    principles of moral justice, 338
    speciesism, 335
    zoocentric approach, 337
ethics, 336
ethics committee, 14, 342
ethological needs, 76
etiology, 171
etomidate, 270
etorphine, 280
euthanasia
    legislation, 13, 357
    mechanical–physical, 296
    pharmaco-chemical, 295
everted stitch, 313
excitation stage, 281
exhaustion phase, 92
experimental data, 212
experimental designs
    completely randomized, 230
    cross-over, 233
    factorial, 236–237
    Latin square, 234–236
    publication, 206
    randomized block, 231, 232
    split-plot, 237
experimental techniques
    artificial ventilation, 285, 286
    cat, 52
    catherization, 309
    chicken, 61
    collection body fluids, 304–310
    collection of faeces, 308
    dog, 50
    ectomy, 315
    endotracheal intubation, 282–285

experimental techniques (*continued*)
  enteral administration, 300
  euthanasia, 294–296
  exsanguination, 307
  goat, 57
  guinea pig, 39
  indwelling cannula, 307
  injection methods, 300–304
  mouse, 23
  perfusion, 317
  pig, 55
  pigeon, 63
  rabbit, 43
  rat, 28
  stereotactical procedure, 316
  surgical procedures, 310–317
  suturing, 312–314
experimental unit, 213, 214
exploratory behaviour, 81
exploring, 82
exsanguination, 296, 297, 307
extra-orbital lacrimal gland, 27
extrapolation
  animal model, 192
  homology, 192
  philosophical aspects, 200, 201
  qualitative, 193
  quantitative, 193
  standardization, 107
eye speculum, 283
eyelid dilator, 301

F_1 hybrids, 104, 130, 136
face mask, 285
factorial design, 221, 236–237
faeces, 308
fallacies, 348–350
false extrapolation, 194
false negative result, 210, 212
false positive result, 210, 211
fat, 111, 112, 119, 121
fear, 256
feather pecking, 80, 88
feeding regime, 122
FELASA, 5, 7
Felis catus, 51
femoral artery, 305
femoral vein, 305, 306, 307
fentanyl, 270, 272, 280
fermentation, 56
ferret, 272
fibre, 111, 119, 121

fight/flight response, 89, 91
filariasis, 33
filter top, 157
fish
  anaesthetic dose rate, 276
  aquarium conditions, 72
  dehydration, 72
  goldfish, 72
  guppy, 71
  handling, 73
  identification, 73
  nutrition, 72
  physiology, 71
  reproduction, 73
  trout, 71
  use, 71
  zebra fish, 71
fistula, 313, 315
flagellates, 182
fleas, 184
flotation method, 182, 184
fluanisone, 270, 272, 280
flunixin, 292, 293
fluoride, 111
folic acid, 111
food intake, 119
Food and Drug Administration (FDA), 246
footpad inflammation, 38
formalin, 176, 177
fossa perinealis, 37, 41
fostering
  goat, 57
  hysterectomy, 151
  pig, 54
  rabbit, 43
  sheep, 57
FRAME, 320
freezing, 294, 297
frogs, 276, 303
FSH, 92
fungi, 183

Galen, 2
gallamine, 277
Gallus domesticus, 58
Gallus gallus, 59
gamma-irradiation, 159
gas scavenging, 278
gauge, 301, 302
Gaussian distribution, 212
general anaesthesia, 268
General Adaptation Syndrome (GAS), 92

genetic
— analysis, 133
— contamination, 137, 140
— distance, 141
— drift, 141
— heterogeneity, 135
— models, 167
— profile, 140
— quality control, 137
— standardization, 127–141
— uniformity, 127–135
— variation, 135
genetically defined strains, 128
genotype, 103
gerbil (*Meriones linguiculatus*)
    atherosclerosis, 33, 35
    birth weight, 34
    blood volume, 35
    body surface, 34
    body temperature, 34
    body weight, 34
    brain infarcts, 33
    breeding, 36
    breeding age, 34
    cage floor size, 34
    cage height, 34
    cholesterol metabolism, 33
    duration of oestrus, 34
    duration of pregnancy, 34
    environmental temperature, 34
    epilepsy, 33
    filariasis, 33
    glucose, 35
    haematocrit, 35
    haemoglobin, 35
    handling, 36
    heart rate, 34
    housing, 35
    leucocytes, 35
    life span, 34
    litter size, 34
    monogamous pairing, 36
    number of chromosomes, 34
    nutrition, 35
    obesity, 33, 35
    oestrous cycle, 34
    oestrus detection, 36
    origin, 33
    overpopulation, 35
    relative humidity, 34
    respiration rate, 34
    sebaceous gland, 35

    sexual maturity, 34
    urine, 33
    use, 33
    ventilation, 34
    water intake, 34, 35
    weaning age, 34
germ-free (GF) animals, 112, 150
gerontology, 155
gizzard, 58, 59, 61
GLP (good laboratory practice), 246
glucose, 19, 35, 45,49, 60
glutamic acid, 111
glutaraldehyde, 177
glycine, 111
glycopyrrolate, 270, 272, 274
GMP (good manufacturing pratice), 146
gnotobiotic animals
    definition, 151, 161
    isolator, 156
    nutrition, 114
    use, 154
goat (*Capra hircus*)
    abomasum, 55
    behaviour, 55
    blood volume, 49
    body temperature, 49
    body weight, 49
    breeding, 49
    cage floor size, 49
    cage height, 49
    colostrum, 57
    duration of life, 49
    duration of pregnancy, 49
    environmental temperature, 49, 56
    fermentation, 56
    fostering, 57
    haematocrit, 49
    haemoglobin, 49
    handling, 57
    heart rate, 49
    housing, 56
    identification, 58
    leucocytes, 49
    litter size, 49
    nutrition, 56
    oestrous cycle, 49, 56
    oestrus synchronization, 56
    omasum, 55
    relative humidity, 49
    respiration rate, 49
    reticulum, 55
    rumen, 55

goat (*continued*)
    rumen gas, 56
    rumination, 56
    sexual maturity, 49
    techniques, 57
    ventilation, 49, 56
    weaning age, 49
    weight at birth, 49
    weight at weaning, 49
goldfish, 72
gonadectomy, 315
good laboratory practice (GLP), 246
good manufacturing practise (GMP), 146
Gram staining, 181
granivorous, 59
growth hormone, 92
guafenesin, 277
guinea pig (*Cavia porcellus*)
    abortion, 38
    anaesthetic dose rates, 271, 273
    antibiotics, 37, 164
    artificial ventilation, 286
    birth weight, 34
    blood sampling, 306
    blood volume, 35
    body surface, 34
    body temperature, 34
    body weight, 34
    breeding, 39
    breeding age, 34
    brucellosis, 37
    caecum, 37
    cage floor size, 34
    cage height, 34
    coprophagy, 37
    corticosteroids, 38
    crude fibre, 38
    delivery, 39
    diphtheria, 37
    Dunkin-Hartley line, 37
    duration of oestrus, 34
    duration of pregnancy, 34
    dystocia, 39
    endotracheal tube, 283
    environmental temperature, 34, 38
    footpad inflammation, 38
    fossa perinealis, 37
    glucose, 35, 49
    haematocrit, 35
    haemoglobin, 35
    hair-biting, 38
    handling, 39
    heart rate, 34
    histamine, 38
    housing, 38
    identification, 39
    immunological research, 37
    injection sites, 302
    injection techniques, 302
    Kurloff's bodies, 37
    leptospirosis, 37
    leucocytes, 35
    life span, 34
    litter size, 34
    lordosis, 39
    MAC-values, 279
    microorganisms, 144
    muscle relaxants, 277
    number of chromosomes, 34
    nutrient allowances, 111
    nutrition, 38
    obesity, 39
    oestrous cycle, 34, 39
    oral administration, 302
    origin, 36
    otology, 37
    post-operative pain relief, 292, 293
    postpartum mating, 39
    relative humidity, 34, 38
    respiration rate, 34
    sebaceous glands, 37
    sexual maturity, 34
    sleeping periods, 37
    techniques, 39
    tuberculosis, 37
    use, 36
    vaginal membrane, 37,39
    vaginitis, 38
    ventilation, 34
    vitamin C, 38
    water intake, 34
    weaning age, 34
guppy, 71
Gustafsson isolator, 156

habituation, 79
haematocrit, 19, 35, 45, 49, 60
haemoglobin, 19, 35, 45, 49, 60
haemopericardium, 171
haemorrage
    blood sampling, 305
    collection of ascites, 310
    prevention, 312
    surgery, 289

haemostasis, 312
haemothorax, 171
hair-biting, 38
halogen, 159
halothane, 268, 270, 272, 275, 276, 294, 296
hamster, *see* Syriam hamster
handling
    amphibians, 69, 70
    cat, 52
    chicken, 61
    dog, 50
    dove, 63
    fish, 73
    gerbil, 36
    goat, 57
    guinea pig, 39
    Japanese quail, 65
    mouse, 23
    pig, 55
    pigeon, 63
    primates, 47
    rabbit, 43
    rat, 28
    sheep, 57
    Syrian hamster, 33
Hanta virus, 146, 148
Harderian gland, 26, 305
harem system, 23
Harvey, 2
Haverhill, 145
hazards, 251, 252
Health Research Extension Act, 9
heart rate
    birds, 60
    cat, 49
    dog, 49
    gerbil, 35
    goat, 49
    guinea pig, 35
    mouse, 19
    pig, 49
    primates, 45
    rabbit, 35
    rat, 19
    sheep, 49
    Syrian hamster, 19
heat loss, 27
heating lamp, 291
heating pad, 291, 314
helminths, 183
hemagglutination inhibition test, 161
hemorraghic fever associated viruses, 157

HEPA filters, 23, 149
hepatectomy, 315
hepatitis, 144, 252
herbivorous, 37
hibernation, 30, 31
hip glands, 31
hippocampus, 82, 93, 95
histamine, 31, 38, 280
histidine, 111
histology, 179
history of animal use, 2
Histricomorpha, 18
HIV, 252
hoarding, 32
homeostasis, 76, 80, 94, 168
homology, 192
homozygosity, 128
horse, 303, 306
horseshoe crab, 323
housing
    amphibians, 68
    cat, 51
    chicken, 59
    dog, 48
    dove, 62
    gerbil, 35
    goat, 56
    guinea pig, 38
    Japanese quail, 64
    mouse, 20
    pig, 53, 54
    pigeon, 62
    primates, 46
    rabbit, 41
    rat, 27
    reptiles, 66
    sheep, 56
    standardization, 106
    Syrian hamster, 31
human models, 326
human rights, 337
Hume, David, 198, 200
hybridoma, 310
hybridoma cells, 323, 324
hydronephrosis, 170
hygiene, 310
hypercapnia, 288, 289
hypertension, 190
hyperthermia, 27, 289
hypnorm, 270, 272, 280
hypnosis, 268, 279
hypocerebellism, 169

hypophysectomy, 315
hypotension, 270, 288, 290, 293
hypothalamus–pituitary system, 91
hypothermia
    hibernation, 30
    monitoring anaesthesia, 289
    post-operative care, 314
hypothesis, 198, 199, 202, 210
hypovolaemia, 307
hypoxaemia, 288, 289
hypoxic (toxic) stage, 281
hysterectomy, 150, 151, 153, 315

ibuprofen, 292
ICLAS, 5
identification
    amphibians, 71
    chicken, 61
    dog, 50
    dove, 63
    fish, 73
    goat, 58
    guinea pig, 39
    legislation, 359
    mouse, 23
    pig, 55
    pigeon, 63
    rabbit, 43
    rat, 28
    sheep, 58
    Syrian hamster, 33
imaging techniques, 317
immobilization, 268
immuno-electron microscopy, 161
immunofluorescence test, 161
immunosuppression, 87, 95
impact of legislation, 14
implantation, 316
imprinting, 81
in vitro techniques, 321
inbred strain, 104, 128–130
inbreeding coefficient, 135
inbreeding depression, 130
incubation period, 60
indicators of discomfort, 257
indicators of well-being, 98
individual variability, 223
induced animal model, 191
induced pathology, 167
induction chamber, 274, 275
induction of general anaesthesia, 274
induction stage, 281

inductive inference, 200
inductive reasoning, 198
inductive–hypothetico–deductive philosophy, 198
indwelling cannula, 307
infant ventilators, 286
inhalational anaesthetics, 275
injectable anaesthetics, 279
injection techniques, 300–304
inositol, 112
insertion, 134
inspection, 358
inspectorate, 14
Institutional Animal Care and Use Committee, 10
Institutional Animal Committees, 9
instrumental value, 338
insulin, 92
intangible variance, 104
interactive video technology, 300, 331
intercranial, 304
intercross, 132
intercurrent disease, 169
inter-individual variation, 101, 102, 105, 223, 228, 233
internal fungi, 183
internal milieu, 76, 81
interrupted stitch, 313
intracutaneous injection, 301, 302
intradermal injection, 301
intra-individual variation, 102, 223, 224, 238
intramuscular injection, 301–303
intraperitoneal injection, 301–303
intravenous injection, 301–303
intrinsic error, 224
intrinsic value, 337, 338
intrinsic variability, 223
intubation, 282
intuitive moral judgment, 344, 345
invagination of the intestines, 304
invasive techniques, 315
inverted stitch, 313
iodine, 111
iron, 111
iron deficiency, 55
isocaloric diet, 122
isoflurane, 268, 270, 272, 275, 276, 296
isogenic strain, 129, 225
isohistogenicity, 137
isolator, 151, 155–157
isoleucine, 111

Japanese quail (*Coturnix coturnix*)
  anaesthetic dose rate, 276
  blood parameters, 60
  blood sampling, 307
  environmental requirements, 60
  environmental temperature, 64
  handling, 65
  housing, 64
  nutrition, 65
  origin, 63
  physiological parameters, 60
  relative humidity, 65
  reproduction, 65
  use, 63
  ventilation, 65
jugular vein, 305, 306, 307

ketamine, 270, 272, 276, 280
key question, 194
key substrate, 194
kidney cortex, 26
Kilham Rat Virus, 169
kinidin-sulphate, 106
Koch, Robert, 3
Kuhn, Thomas, 199
Kurloff's bodies, 37

laboratory animal science, 1
laboratory animal specialist, 7
lactate dehydrogenase virus, 145
lactobacilli, 153
Lagomorpha, 17, 41
LAL test, 323
Laminar Air Flow (LAF), 157
laryngoscope, 282, 283
laryngospasm, 283
latent infections, 104, 144
Latin square designs, 234–236
learned helplessness, 257
learning, 78–81, 93
legal requirements, 244
legislation, 9–16, 353–361
Leptospira spp., 182
leucine, 111
leucocytes, 19, 35, 45, 49, 60
LH, 92
lice, 184
lidocaine, 269
life span
  birds, 60
  cat, 49
  dog, 49

  gerbil, 35
  goat, 49
  guinea pig, 35
  mouse, 19
  pig, 49
  primates, 45
  rabbit, 35
  rat, 19
  sheep, 49
  Syrian hamster, 19
liga-clamps, 312
ligature, 317
lignin, 115
limb vein, 307
limitations of legislation, 14
Limulus Amoebocyte Lysate (LAL) test, 323
Limulus polyphemus, 323
linkage analysis, 133
liquid nitrogen, 297
liquor, 309
litter size
  cat, 49
  dog, 49
  gerbil, 35
  goat, 49
  guinea pig, 35
  mouse, 19
  pig, 49
  primates, 45
  rabbit, 35
  rat, 19
  sheep, 49
  Syrian hamster, 19
lizards, 276
local anaesthesia, 269
local anaesthetics, 291
local infiltration, 269
local nerve block, 269
locomotory activity, 261
log book, 243
long-term anaesthesia, 291
long-term experiments, 163
longevity, 110
lordosis, 32, 39
Lorz, 77
lumbosacral area, 304
lymph, 310
lymphadenectomy, 315
lymphadenitis, 182
lysine, 111

MAC-value, 278

Macaca fascicularis, 44, 322
Macaca mulatta, 44
Magendie, 2
magnesium, 111
magnetic resonance imaging (MRI), 327
major histocompatibility complex, 137
management of animal experiments, 241–252
manganese, 111
Mareks disease virus, 192
marginal ear vein, 305
marmoset, 44–46
marsupials, 94
materials and methods, 206
mathematical modelling, 326
mating systems, mouse, 22
maximum injection volume, 302, 306, 307
maze, 82
Mead, 220, 221, 222
meal, 118
meal feeding, 123
mean, 212
measurement error, 224
Medawar, Peter, 7
medetomidine, 270, 272, 280
median survival time, 155
menadione, 111
Meriones unguiculatus, 33
Merkwelt, 83
Mesocricetus auratus, 30
metabolic weight, 119, 193
metabolism cage, 21, 308
methionine, 111
methodology, 197
methohexitone, 270, 272, 279
methotrime, 280
methoxyflurane, 270, 272, 275
metomidate, 270, 276
Mexican salamander, 68
microagglutination test, 161
microclimate, 105
microbiological
— contamination, 147–149
— examination, 178–184
— quality, 104, 143
— quality control, 160
— standardization, 143–165
microsatellites, 139
Microsporum spp., 145, 183
microsurgery, 310
microwaves, 294, 297
midazolam, 270
minerals, 111

minimal alveolar concentration, 278
minimal inbreeding, 136
minimum treatment effect, 216
minute volume, 284
miscegenation, 137
mites, 184
modified barrier system, 157
monitoring anaesthesia, 287
monitoring equipment, 287
monkeys
    anaesthetic dose rates, 273
    anatomy, 46
    behaviour, 46
    blood sampling, 306
    chimpanzee, 44
    cynomolgus monkey, 44
    handling, 47
    housing, 46
    injection techniques, 303
    MAC-values, 279
    marmoset, 44
    nutrition, 46
    oral administration, 303
    orang-utan, 46
    origin, 44
    physiology, 46
    post-operative pain relief, 293
    Prosimiae, 44
    reproduction, 47
    rhesus monkey, 44
    Simiae, 44
    spider monkey, 46
    squirrel monkey, 44
    tupaia, 46
    use, 44
    vitamin D, 47
monoclonal antibodies, 310, 323, 324
monogamous pairing, 36
monolayer, 321
monozygotic animals, 127
moral actor, 340
moral relevance of animals, 336
morbidity, 169, 172
morphine, 31, 291, 292, 293
mortality, 169, 172
mosaic population, 136
mouse (*Mus musculus*)
    aggressive behaviour, 20
    anaesthetic dose rates, 270
    anogenital distance, 18
    artificial ventilation, 286
    bedding material, 20

mouse (*continued*)
    blood sampling, 306
    blood volume, 19
    body temperature, 19
    body weight, 19
    breeding age, 19
    Bruce-effect, 22
    cage floor size, 19
    cage height, 19
    coagulation plug, 22
    coprophagy, 21
    dental formula, 18
    diastema, 18
    drinking water, 21
    duration of pregnancy, 19
    endotracheal tube, 283
    environmental temperature, 19
    glucose, 19
    haematocrit, 19
    haemoglobin, 19
    handling and simple techniques, 23
    harem system, 23
    heart rate, 19
    housing, 20
    identification, 23
    inguinal canal, 18
    injection sites, 302
    injection techniques, 302
    leucocytes, 19
    life span, 19
    MAC-values, 279
    mating systems, 22
    microorganisms, 144
    muscle relaxants, 277
    number of chromosomes, 19
    nutrient allowances, 111
    nutrition, 21
    oestrous cycle, 19, 22
    oral administration, 302
    overcrowding, 20
    pheromones, 22
    placenta haemochorialis, 22
    polygamous breeding, 23
    post-operative pain relief, 292
    postpartum mating, 23
    relative humidity, 19
    respiration rate, 19
    sexual maturity, 19
    transport, 23
    urethra, 18
    use, 18
    vaginal smear, 22
    vaginal swabs, 22
    ventilation, 19
    water intake, 19
    weaning age, 19
    weight at birth, 19
    weight at weaning, 19
    Whitten-effect, 22
mouse hepatitis virus, 145, 169
mousepox virus, 143, 164, 171
mouth gag, 283, 301
mouth glass, 300
MS-222, 276
Muridae, 18
Mus musculus, 18
muscle relaxants, 277, 285, 286
muscle relaxation, 280, 281
muscular dystrophy, 190
mutualism, 152, 153
Mycoplasma spp., 143, 144, 161, 179, 181
mycoses, 183
Myomorpha, 18
myxomatosis, 164

nalbuphine, 292
naloxone, 89, 277, 280
natural habitat, 77
natural-ingredient diets, 113, 119
neck collar, 295
necrosis, 172
needle holder, 312
needle size, 302
negative models, 192
negative pressure, 157
negative results, 329
nematodes, 183
nephrectomy, 315
nephritis, 146
neuroendocrine feedback mechanisms, 93
neuroendocrine system, 91
neuroleptanalgesics, 280
neuromuscular blocking agent, 286
nicotinic acid, 111
ninebanded armadillo, 127
nitrosodimethylamine, 115
nitrous oxide, 278
nociception, 260, 267
nociceptive signals, 258
nocturnal animals, 17
nomenclature, 129
non-selective media, 181
non-steroidal anti-inflammatory drugs
    (NSAIDs), 291

noradrenaline, 91
norepinephrine, 269
normal distribution, 212, 213, 217
normative ethics, 340
noxious stimulus, 259, 267
NSAID, 291
nuclear magnetic resonance (NMR), 317, 327
nucleated thrombocytes, 58
nude, 315
null hypothesis, 210, 211
number of blocks, 220
number of chromosomes, *see* chromosomes
    (2*n*)
number of treatments, 220
nutrient availability, 112
nutrient requirements, 109, 110
nutrition
    amphibians, 68, 69
    cat, 52
    chicken, 61
    dog, 49, 50
    dove, 62
    fish, 72, 73
    general aspects, 109–125
    gerbil, 35
    goat, 56
    guinea pig, 38
    Japanese quail, 65
    mouse, 21
    pig, 54
    pigeon, 62
    primates, 46, 47
    rabbit, 42
    rat, 28
    reptiles, 66
    sheep, 56
    Syrian hamster, 32

obesity, 33, 35, 39
oestrogen, 92
oestrous cycle
    cat, 49
    dog, 49
    gerbil, 35
    goat, 49
    guinea pig, 35
    mouse, 19
    pig, 49
    primates, 45
    rabbit, 35
    rat, 19
    sheep, 49

Syrian hamster, 19
oestrus detection, 36
oestrus synchronization
    goat, 56
    rat, 28
    sheep, 56
olfactory signals, 261
one-sided test, 212, 217, 218
ontogeny, 77, 80
open-formula diet, 113
operant conditioning, 79, 80, 85, 87
ophthalmic ointment, 289
opiate blockade, 258
opiate receptor, 259
opiates, 259, 291, 293
opportunistic pathogens, 153
oral administration, 300, 302, 303
orang-utan, 46
orbital puncture, 305, 306
organization of animal experiments, 241–252
organotypic culture, 321
origin
    cat, 51
    chicken, 59
    dog, 47
    gerbil, 33
    guinea pig, 36
    pig, 53
    primates, 44
    rabbit, 40
    Syrian hamster, 30
orphan animal models, 192
Oryctolagus cuniculus, 40
otology, 37
otoscope, 283
outbred animals, 104
outbred stock, 135, 136
outcrossing, 137
overcrowding, 20, 27
overinflation, 286
overpopulation, 35
Ovis aries, 55
oximeter, 287
oxytocin, 92
oxyurids, 183

P-substance, 259
p-value, 211, 212
pain, 255, 257–260
— behaviour, 259, 260
— expression, 262
— pathway, 259

pain (*continued*)
— relief, 268, 291
— signals, 259, 262
pain and distress
    adaptive response, 259
    analogy postulate, 255
    anxiety, 256
    apathy, 261
    chronic pain, 260, 261
    concealment of pain behaviour, 262
    defensive phase, 259
    distress, 256
    fear, 256
    indicators of discomfort, 257
    learned helplessness, 257
    locomotory activity, 261
    nociception, 260
    nociceptive signals, 258
    olfactory signals, 261
    P-substance, 259
    pain, 257–260
    pain behaviour, 259, 260
    pain signals, 259, 262
    perceptive phase, 259
    primary pain, 258, 260
    recognition, 255-265
    recuperative phase, 259
    secondary pain, 258, 259
    signs of pain, 260
    social facilitation, 263
    stereotypes, 257
    suffering, 256
    vocal signals, 261
pair feeding, 123
paired sera, 178
palatability, 113, 119
palpebral reflex, 282
Pan troglodytes, 44
pancreatectomy, 315
pancuronium, 277
pantothenic acid, 112
papilloma virus, 192
paracetamol, 292, 293
paradigm shift philosophy, 199
parallel randomized design, 230
parasites, 144, 161
parasympathetic nervous system, 91
parenteral administration, 300
parvo virus, 179
passive coping style, 89, 94
Pasteurelle pneumotropica, 144
pathogen group, 157

pathogenesis, 168
pathology, 168
PCR, 139
pedal reflex, 282
pellets, 118
pentachlorophenol, 106
pentazocine, 292, 293
pentobarbitone, 31, 106, 268, 270, 276, 279, 296
peracetic acid, 156, 160
perceptive phase, 259
perfusion, 317
peritoneum, 312
peritonitis, 304, 310
pethidine, 292, 293
phenacetin, 292
phenol, 159
phenotype, 103
phenylalanine, 111
pheromones
    mouse, 22
    rabbit, 41
    Syrian hamster, 31
phosphorus, 111
phylogeny, 77
physiological response, 90
physiological stress response, 93
phytate, 112
pig (*Sus scrofa*)
    abnormal behaviour, 53
    anaesthetic dose rates, 273
    artificial insemination, 54
    blood sampling, 306
    blood volume, 49
    body temperature, 49
    body weight, 49
    breeding, 49
    cage floor size, 49
    cage height, 49
    colostrum, 54
    delivery, 54
    duration of life, 49
    duration of pregnancy, 49
    environmental temperature, 49, 54
    establish new groups, 54
    fostering, 54
    glucose, 49
    haematocrit, 49
    haemoglobin, 49
    handling, 55
    heart rate, 49
    housing, 53

pig (*continued*)
    injection sites, 303
    injection techniques, 303
    iron deficiency, 55
    leucocytes, 49
    litter size, 49
    MAC-values, 279
    muscle relaxants, 277
    number of chromosomes, 49
    nutrition, 54
    oestrous cycle, 49, 54
    oral administration, 303
    origin, 53
    post-operative pain relief, 293
    relative humidity, 49, 54
    respiration rate, 49
    sexual maturity, 49
    standing-reflex, 54
    techniques, 55
    transport, 55
    use, 53
    ventilation, 49
    water intake, 49
    weaning age, 49
    weight at birth, 49
    weight at weaning, 49
pigeon (*Columba livia*)
    anaesthetic dose rate, 276
    blood parameters, 60
    blood sampling, 307
    environmental requirements, 60
    handling, 63
    housing, 62
    identification, 63
    nutrition, 62
    origin, 61
    physiological parameters, 60
    reproduction, 62
    techniques, 63
    use, 61
pinworms, 183
pitfall in ethical argumentation, 346
placebo, 216, 227
placenta haemochorialis, 22
placental barrier, 151
planning experiments, 243, 249
pneumonia, 144
Poecilia reticulata, 71
poliomyelitis vaccine production, 322
polygamous breeding, 23
polymerase chain reaction (PCR), 139
Popper, Karl, 198, 199, 201, 202

porphyrins, 26, 305
portocaval shunt, 316
post-copulatory ovulation, 42, 52
post-operative care, 291, 314
post-operative pain relief, 292, 293
postmortem examination, 175–178
postpartum mating, 23, 39
postpartum oestrus, 28, 32
potassium, 111
potency testing, 328
power, 203, 213, 215–219, 223, 228
pre-anaesthetic fasting, 274
pre-experimental treatment, 231
precision, 225, 226, 238
predator, 258
predictability, 86, 87, 89, 92, 256
predictive value of a test, 203
preening glands, 58
preference test, 97
pregnancy
    cat, 49
    dog, 49
    gerbil, 35
    goat, 49
    guinea pig, 35
    mouse, 19
    pig, 49
    primates, 45
    rabbit, 35
    rat, 19
    sheep, 49
    Syrian hamster, 19
premedication, 270, 272, 274
PREX, 329
prilocaine, 269
primary cell culture, 321
primary milieu, 103
primary pain, 258, 260
primates
    anaesthetic dose rates, 273
    anatomy, 46
    behaviour, 46
    blood sampling, 306
    chimpanzee, 44
    cynomolgus monkey, 44
    handling, 47
    housing, 46
    injection techniques, 303
    MAC-values, 279
    marmoset, 44
    nutrition, 46
    oral administration, 303

primates (*continued*)
  orang-utan, 46
  origin, 44
  physiology, 46
  post-operative pain relief, 293
  Prosimiae, 44
  reproduction, 47
  rhesus monkey, 44
  Simiae, 44
  spider monkey, 46
  squirrel monkey, 44
  tupaia, 46
  use, 44
  vitamin D, 47
primers, 139
principle of moral justice, 338
probability, 210, 211, 215, 216
probe, 138
procaine, 269
process of deduction, 199
progenitor strain, 133
project plans, 243
prolactin, 92
proline, 111
propanidid, 276
prophylaxis, 311
propofol, 268, 270, 272, 280
Prosimiae, 44
prostaglandins, 295
protein, 111, 112, 115, 119, 121
protozoa, 182
pruritus, 184
Pseudomonas aeruginosa, 149
pseudopregnancy, 43
Psoroptes cuniculi, 185, 186
Public Health Service, 9
publication of results, 205
purified diets, 114, 115
putrefaction, 175
pyridoxine, 111
pyrogenicity test, 40, 323

quail, *see* Japanese quail
qualitative extrapolation, 192
quality control, 143
quality barrier, 150
quantitative extrapolation, 192
quantitative traits, 134
quarantine, 155

rabbit (*Oryctolagus cuniculus*)
  anaesthetic dose rates, 271

antibiotics, 164
appendix caeci, 41
artificial insemination, 43
artificial ventilation, 286
atherosclerosis, 40
atropine-esterase, 41
birth weight, 34
blood sampling, 306
blood volume, 35
body surface, 34
body temperature, 34
body weight, 34
breeding, 43
breeding age, 34
caecotrophy, 41
caecum, 41
cage floor size, 34
cage height, 34
coprophagy, 41
crude fibre, 42
double cervix, 41
duration of oestrus, 34
duration of pregnancy, 34
endotracheal tube, 283
environmental temperature, 34, 42
fossa perinealis, 41
fostering, 43
glucose, 35
group housing, 41
haematocrit, 35
haemoglobin, 35
handling, 43
heart rate, 34
housing, 41
identification, 43
injection sites, 302
injection techniques, 302
leucocytes, 35
life span, 34
litter size, 34
MAC-values, 279
microorganisms, 144
muscle relaxants, 277
number of chromosomes, 34
nutrient allowances, 111
nutrition, 42
oestrous cycle, 34, 42
oral administration, 302
origin, 40
pheromones, 41
post-copulatory ovulation, 42
post-operative pain relief, 292

rabbit (*continued*)
  pseudopregnancy, 43
  pyrogenicity test, 40
  relative humidity, 34
  respiration rate, 34
  sacculus rotundus, 41
  sebaceous glands, 41
  sexual maturity, 34
  techniques, 43
  tonsilla ileocaecalis, 41
  transport, 44
  urine, 41
  use, 40
  ventilation, 34
  water intake, 34
  weaning age, 34
radiation, 114
radioactive isotopes, 251
random bred, 135, 136
randomization, 227, 228, 230
randomized block designs, 231–233
rat (*Rattus norvegicus*)
  adrenal glands, 26
  adrenalectomy, 26
  aggressive behaviour, 27
  anaesthetic dose rates, 270
  artificial ventilation, 286
  audiogenic seizures, 28
  blood sampling, 306
  blood volume, 19
  body surface, 19
  body temperature, 19
  body weight, 19
  breeding, 28
  breeding age, 19
  cage floor size, 19
  cage height, 19
  duration of oestrus, 19
  duration of pregnancy, 19
  endotracheal tube, 283
  environmental temperature, 19
  extra-orbital lacrimal gland, 27
  gall bladder, 27
  glucose, 19
  grooming, 26
  haematocrit, 19
  haemoglobin, 19
  handling, 28
  Harderian gland, 26
  heart rate, 19
  heat loss, 27
  hyperthermia, 27
  identification, 30
  injection sites, 302
  injection techniques, 302
  kidney cortex, 26
  leucocytes, 19
  life span, 19
  litter size, 19
  MAC-values, 279
  microorganisms, 144
  muscle relaxants, 277
  number of chromosomes, 19
  nutrient allowances, 111
  nutrition, 28
  oestrous cycle, 19, 28
  oral administration, 302
  overcrowding, 27
  porphyrins, 26
  post-operative pain relief, 292
  postpartum oestrus, 28
  relative humidity, 19
  respiration rate, 19
  retinal atrophy, 28
  ringtail, 28
  sexual maturity, 19
  synchronization of oestrus, 28
  techniques, 28
  ultrasonic sounds, 28
  use, 26
  vaginal plug, 28
  ventilation, 19
  water intake, 19
  weaning age, 19
  weight at birth, 19
  weight at weaning, 19
rat-bite fever, 145
Rattus norvegicus, 26
re-use of animals, 357
rebreathing system, 285
recipient female, 141
recipient strain, 132
reciprocal crosses, 137
recognition of pain and distress, 255–265
recombinant congenic strains, 133
recombinant inbred strains, 133
recovery, 275
recuperation, 261
recuperative phase, 259
rederivation, 150, 151, 153
redirected behaviour, 87, 88
reduction, 6, 102
refinement, 6, 319
Regan, Tom, 335

regional anaesthesia, 269
registration, 13
regulatory agencies, 320
regurgitation, 290
relative humidity
    birds, 60
    cat, 49
    dog, 49
    gerbil, 35
    goat, 49
    guinea pig, 35
    mouse, 19
    pig, 49
    primates, 45
    rabbit, 35
    rat, 19
    sheep, 49
    Syrian hamster, 19
Reo3 virus, 144
repeated measures designs, 237
replacement, 6, 319
reproducibility of animal experiments, 101, 203, 204, 245
reproduction
    amphibians, 69
    cat, 52
    chicken, 61
    dog, 50
    dove, 62
    fish, 73
    gerbil, 36
    goat, 56, 57
    guinea pig, 39
    Japanese quail, 65
    mouse, 22
    pig, 54,55
    pigeon, 62
    primates, 47
    rabbit, 42, 43
    rat, 28
    reptiles, 66
    sheep, 56, 57
    Syrian hamster, 32
reptiles
    anaesthetic dose rates, 276
    anatomy, 66
    blood sampling, 307
    housing, 66
    identification, 67
    injection sites, 303
    lizard, 65, 276
    nutrition, 66

    physiology, 66
    reproduction, 66
    sexing, 67
    snake, 65, 276
    use, 66
research protocol, 204
resistance phase, 92
resource equation method, 215, 220
respiration rate
    birds, 60
    cat, 49
    dog, 49
    gerbil, 35
    goat, 49
    guinea pig, 35
    mouse, 19
    pig, 49
    primates, 45
    rabbit, 35
    rat, 19
    sheep, 49
    Syrian hamster, 19
respiratory depression, 279, 289, 293
restricted feeding, 123
restriction enzyme, 138
retinal atrophy, 28
retinol, 111
retrovirus, 134
reversed classical barrier, 157
rhesus monkey, 44, 45
riboflavin, 111, 115
righting reflex, 282
ringtail, 28
ringworm, 146
Rodentia, 18
rodents, 17
rotation scheme, 136
rumen gas, 56
rumination, 56
Russel and Burch, 6

sacculus rotundus, 41
safety in the animal house, 250–252
safety procedures, 252
safety testing, 146
Saimiri, 44
salicylate, 106
salivary secretions, 274
salivation, 278
Salmo trutta, 71
Salmonella, 143, 149
sample size, 162, 215–223

saphenous vein (hindlimbs), 305, 306
sarcodines, 182
scalpel, 311
scentmarks, 84
Schaedler flora, 153
SCID, 155
scientific philosophy, 200
screening, 161
sebaceous gland
    gerbil, 35,
    guinea pig, 37
    rabbit, 41
    Syrian hamster, 31
secondary milieu, 103
secondary pain, 258, 259, 261
sedation, 268
sedatives, 270–272, 274, 280
sedimentation, 182, 184
selection of animal models, 194–196
selective media, 181
selenium, 111, 115, 116
self-injection, 252
Selye, 92
semi-moist diet, 118
Sendai virus, 144, 145, 164, 169, 179
sensitive period, 81
serological examination, 161, 164, 179–182
serum neutralization test, 161
sexual maturity
    birds, 60
    cat, 49
    dog, 49
    gerbil, 35
    goat, 49
    guinea pig, 35
    mouse, 19
    pig, 49
    primates, 45
    rabbit, 35
    rat, 19
    sheep, 49
    Syrian hamster, 19
sham operation, 227
sheep (*Ovis aries*)
    abomasum, 55
    anaesthetic dose rates, 273
    behaviour, 55
    blood sampling, 306
    blood volume, 49
    body temperature, 49
    body weight, 49
    breeding, 49

cage floor size, 49
cage height, 49
colostrum, 57
duration of life, 49
duration of pregnancy, 49
environmental temperature, 49, 56
fermentation, 56
fostering, 57
glucose, 49
haematocrit, 49
haemoglobin, 49
handling, 57
heart rate, 49
housing, 56
identification, 58
injection sites, 303
injection techniques, 303
leucocytes, 49
litter size, 49
MAC-values, 279
muscle relaxants, 277
nutrition, 56
oestrous cycle, 49, 56
oestrus synchronization, 56
omasum, 55
oral administration, 303
post-operative pain relief, 293
relative humidity, 49
respiration rate, 49
reticulum, 55
rumen, 55
rumen gas, 56
rumination, 56
sexual maturity, 49
techniques, 57
ventilation, 49, 56
weaning age, 49
weight at birth, 49
weight at weaning, 49
shock, 289, 307
shunt, 316
sign stimuli, 79
significance level, 210, 211, 216, 228
signs of pain, 260, 291
Simiae, 44
Singer, Peter, 335
sites of injection, 303
size of an experiment, 215–223
skin
— application, 299
— biopsy, 269
— clamp applicator, 312

skin (*continued*)
— clamps, 312
— grafting, 137
— penetration, 299
snakes, 276, 303, 307
social facilitation, 263
social structure, 94
socialization period, 48
sodium, 111
solitary housing, 85
solubilising agent, 280
SOP (standard operating procedure), 246
sources of contamination, 147–149
soya bean protein, 112
species-specific behaviour, 78
speciesism, 335
specified pathogen free (SPF), 146, 154
SPF animals
    barrier system, 157
    definition, 154
    in experiments, 163, 225
    life span, 155
    nutrition, 112, 114
    screening, 162
    susceptibility, 149
SPF barrier, 156
spider monkey, 46
spinal anaesthesia, 269
splenectomy, 315
splenomegaly, 176
split-pot designs, 237
spontaneous animal models, 191
spontaneous pathology, 167
squirrel monkey, 44
staining techniques, 183
standard deviation, 102, 212, 213, 216, 217, 218
standard operating procedures (SOP), 252
standardization
    and animal experimentation, 101–108, 245
    and well-being, 98
    genetic, 127–141
    microbiological, 143–165
standardized variable (*z*), 213
standing-reflex, 54
Staphylococcus aureus, 149
statistical analysis, 213, 229
statistical power, 102, 216
steady state, 268
stereotactic apparatus, 304
stereotactic atlas, 316
stereotactical procedures, 316

stereotypes, 88, 89, 257
sterilization, 156, 159
steroids anaesthetics, 280
stimulus, 80
stimulus conditioning, 87
stitches, 313
strain symbol, 129
stratification, 226
stray animals, 13
Streptobacillus moniliformis, 143, 145
Streptococcus fecalis, 153
Streptopelia risoria, 58, 61
stress, 75–98
stress-related diseases, 96
stress-related pathology, 94
stressor, 90–93, 96
Student's *t*-test, 219, 221
substrain designation, 129
subcutaneous injection, 301–303
suffering, 255, 256
sulphur, 111
supply of animals, 13, 195
supplying establishment, 358
surface anaesthesia, 269
surgical forceps, 311
surgical gag, 300
surgical instruments, 311
surgical procedures, 310–317
surgical stage, 281
survival rate, 141
Sus scrofa, 53
suture material, 312, 313
suturing, 312
swallowing reflex, 282
sympathetic nervous system, 91
Syrian hamster (*Mesocricetus auratus*)
    adrenal glands, 31
    aggressive behaviour, 31
    aggressive behaviour, 32
    anaesthetic dose rates, 270
    anaphylactic shock, 31
    antibiotics, 31
    artificial ventilation, 286
    blood sampling, 306
    blood volume, 19
    body surface, 19
    body temperature, 19
    body weight, 19
    breeding, 32
    breeding age, 19
    cage floor size, 19
    cage height, 19

Syrian hamster (*continued*)
  cannibalism, 32
  cheek pouches, 31
  coprophagy, 31
  corticosteroids, 31
  dog distemper, 30
  drinking nipple, 32
  duration of oestrus, 19
  duration of pregnancy, 19
  dysbacteriosis, 31
  endotoxaemia, 31
  endotracheal tube, 283
  environmental temperature, 19
  glucose, 19
  haematocrit, 19
  haemoglobin, 19
  handling, 33
  heart rate, 19
  hibernating, 30
  hibernation, 31
  hip glands, 31
  histamine, 31
  hoarding, 32
  housing, 31
  hypothermia, 30
  identification, 33
  influenza, 30
  injection sites, 302
  injection techniques, 302
  leptospirosis, 30
  leucocytes, 19
  life span, 19
  litter size, 19
  lordosis, 32
  MAC-value, 279
  mating, 32
  morphine, 31
  muscle relaxants, 277
  number of chromosomes, 19
  nutrient allowances, 111
  nutrition, 32
  oestrous cycle, 19, 32
  oral administration, 302
  origin, 30
  pentobarbitone, 31
  pheromones, 31
  postpartum oestrus, 32
  relative humidity, 19
  respiration rate, 19
  sebaceous glands, 31
  sexual maturity, 19
  stomach, 31
  techniques, 33
  territory, 31
  urine, 31
  use, 30
  vaginal excretion, 32
  ventilation, 19
  water intake, 19
  weaning age, 19
  weight at birth, 19
  weight at weaning, 19
systematic error, 102, 227
systemic haemodynamic response, 270

T61, 294
tachycardia, 270, 290
tail pinch reflex, 282
tail vein, 306, 307
tailtip, 306
tapeworms, 183
Taq-polymerase, 139
techniques, *see* experimental techniques
territory, 82
tertiary milieu, 103
test group, 210, 216
testing of hypotheses, 210–213
testosterone, 92
therapy, 186
thiamin, 111
thiopentone, 270, 272, 279
thoracic duct, 310
thoracotomy, 285
thymectomy, 315
thyroidectomy, 315
thyrotropin, 92
thyroxine, 92
tidal volume, 284, 286
tiletamine, 280
tissue culture, 319, 321
Tolman, 83
tonsilla ileocaecalis, 41
tortoises, 276, 303, 307
towel clip, 311
toxicity, 114
toxicity tests, 4, 104, 127, 194
Toxoplasma gondii, 182
trace elements, 111
tracheotomy, 284
training, 7
tranquillisers, 274, 280
transformation of data, 213
transgenic animals, 134, 191
transplantation, 316

transport
   mouse, 23
   pig, 5
   rabbit, 44
   Syrian hamster, 33
transportation (stress), 105
treatment combinations, 221
treatment effect, 102, 103
tree shrews, 84, 94
Treponema pallidum, 148
Trexler isolator, 156
tribromoethanol, 281
Trichophyton spp., 145, 183
Trixacarus caviae, 186
trocar, 307
trout, 71
true treatment effect, 219
Tryon-effect, 131
tumour development, 124
Tupaia glis, 46, 84
two-sided test, 212, 217, 218
type I error, 211, 216, 217, 219
type II error, 212, 216, 217
tyrosine, 111
Tyzzer's disease, 169

U-stitch (eversion), 313
U-stitch (inversion), 313
ultrasonic sounds, 28, 83
Umwelt, 83, 84
uniformity, 137, 225
urethane, 270, 272, 276
urethra, 309
urethral orifice, 309
urine
   collection, 308, 309
   gerbil, 33
   rabbit, 41
   Syrian hamster, 31
user establishment, 13, 359

vaccination, 164
vaccine testings, 4
vaccines, 154
vaginal
— excretion, 32
— membrane, 37, 39
— orifice, 309
— plug, 28
— smears, 22
— swabs, 22
vaginitis, 38

validation of alternative techniques, 332, 360
validity, 203, 204
valine, 111
variation, 101–103, 107, 225
variation coefficient, 219
vasoconstriction, 269
vasodilation, 270, 290
vasopressin, 92, 93
vecuronium, 277
vein puncture, 305
ventilation
   birds, 60
   cat, 49
   dog, 49
   gerbil, 35
   goat, 49
   guinea pig, 35
   mouse, 19
   pig, 49
   primates, 45
   rabbit, 35
   rat, 19
   sheep, 49
   Syrian hamster, 19
vertical transmission of microorganisms, 151
Vesalius, 2
viability, 130
Victoria Street Society, 2
vigour, 130
virus isolation, 179
viruses, 144, 161, 179
vitamin B, 112
vitamin C, 38
vitamin D, 47
vitamin K, 112, 114
vitamins, 111
vitrification, 141
vivisection, 2
vocal signals, 261
vomiting, 290
Von Uexküll, 83

wash-out period, 235
water intake
   cat, 49
   gerbil, 35
   guinea pig, 35
   mouse, 19
   pig, 49
   primates, 45
   rabbit, 35
   rat, 19

water intake (*continued*)
  Syrian hamster, 19
weaning age
  cat, 49
  dog, 49
  gerbil, 35
  goat, 49
  guinea pig, 35
  mouse, 19
  pig, 49
  primates, 45
  rabbit, 35
  rat, 19
  sheep, 49
  Syrian hamster, 19
weight at birth
  cat, 49
  dog, 49
  gerbil, 35
  goat, 49
  guinea pig, 35
  mouse, 19
  pig, 49
  primates, 45
  rabbit, 35
  rat, 19
  sheep, 49
  Syrian hamster, 19
weight at weaning
  cat, 49
  dog, 49
  gerbil, 35
  goat, 49
  guinea pig, 35
  mouse, 19
  pig, 49
  primates, 45
  rabbit, 35

  rat, 19
  sheep, 49
  Syrian hamster, 19
weight of egg, 60
Weiss, 86, 256
well-being
  abnormal behaviour, 87, 88
  concept, 76, 77
  controllability, 86
  coping, 89
  homeostasis, 76
  legislation, 11
  predictability, 86
  preference test, 97
Whitten-effect, 22
wild caught animals, 251
wing vein, 307
wire mesh floors, 20
Wirkwelt, 83
within-experiment variation, 102, 103, 107
wound holder, 312
wound treatment, 314
wound-healing, 295

Xenopus laevis, 68
xylazine, 270, 272, 280

z-value, 213, 217
zebra fish, 71
Ziehl-Neelsen staining reaction, 181
zinc, 111, 112, 115, 116
zolezepam, 280
zoocentric approach, 337
zoonoses
  biological material, 148
  definition, 145
  examples, 145
  safety aspects, 251